23981

Creating a Successful Christian Marriage

Creating a Successful Christian Marriage

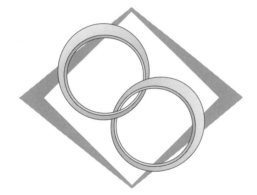

Fourth Edition

Cleveland McDonald
& Philip M. McDonald

Baker Books
A Division of Baker Book House Co
Grand Rapids, Michigan 49516

Published by Baker Books
a division of Baker Book House Company
P.O. Box 6287, Grand Rapids, Michigan 49516-6287

Second printing, October 1996

Printed in the United States of America

For information about academic books, resources for Christian leaders, and all new releases available from Baker Book House, visit our web site:
http://www.bakerbooks.com

Unless otherwise indicated, Scripture references are taken from the King James Version.

Library of Congress Cataloging-in-Publication Data

McDonald, Cleveland.
    Creating a successful Christian marriage / Cleveland
McDonald and Philip M. McDonald.—4th ed.
        p.   c.m.
    Includes bibliographical references and index.
    ISBN 0-8010-6310-8
    1. Marriage—Religious aspects—Christianity. I.
McDonald, Philip M. II. Title.
    BV832.M2   1994
    248.4—dc20   93-29180

To
my wife, **Helen Marie**
whose love, encouragement, and
secretarial ability made the first edition,
and now this volume, possible

and to
Philip, Becky, and their four children—
Matthew, Mark, Nathan, and Danielle—
whose contributions made this volume
more worthwhile

and to
William and Becky, who faithfully waited
as "single adults" for God's best until he brought
them together in his will

Contents

Preface to the Fourth Edition

The challenge to revise a textbook that has been so well received has resulted in an expanded edition. In preparation for rewriting, we sent a questionnaire to sixty Christian institutions, asking them to rank subjects that should be included in a Christian text. More than forty instructors replied, and they included several hundred responses from their students. We cannot list all these individuals, but we thank them for their cooperation.

The replies from professors and students were tabulated separately. It was amazing how closely they agreed on what subjects should be included or omitted. They were not interested in such subjects as abortion, homosexuality, or date rape. Consequently, these areas are not treated at length.

However, they did indicate a desire for chapters in several areas not treated at length in the first edition, and so new chapters on "The Single-Parent Family" and "Communication" have been written. There was a desire for a chapter on "Intimacy." Parts of the previous chapter on "Adjustment in Marriage" have been included in the new chapter. Much interest was expressed in divorce and remarriage. Some of the original chapter on "Problems in the Christian Family" has been incorporated into a new chapter on "The Blended Family."

A unique feature of the text is a new chapter written by Philip McDonald on "International Living." As America becomes involved in a world economy, more young families will be living abroad in government, business, and missionary service. This chapter will help prepare them for their roles.

Philip, who has four preteen children, has also written an entirely new chapter on "Parenting."

Each of the remaining chapters has been revised, and some have been completely rewritten. The chapter title and paragraph headings may be the same, but every paragraph has been carefully considered and many rewritten. More than 90 percent of the sources cited are new, and have appeared since the first edition was published. The deciding criterion for changing or omitting was always, "What will be most beneficial to a young person preparing for marriage?"

The new edition has been organized into seven sections, each of which treats one aspect of the family. Some of the chapters have been moved to reflect this new arrangement.

This text, like the first, is written from the functional viewpoint rather than the institutional. It is specifically designed to equip young people to make an intelligent choice of a mate, and to learn what to anticipate in marital interaction. Biblical principles from the original edition have been reiterated to encourage growth in Christian maturity and conduct.

Sociological jargon has been avoided and some inclusive language used. Suggested readings for each chapter have been added to help the student who desires more information on the subject of that chapter. The "Personality Inventories" that students found so helpful are retained.

An instructor's manual including a test bank has been compiled. The additional items for discussion will enable professors to broaden the students' knowledge.

Several professors who answered the questionnaire asked that the text remain "thoroughly biblical." We have attempted to keep and to strengthen this emphasis. However, we carefully point out that in several areas there is not agreement among Bible scholars on certain subjects. This is particularly true in reference to interpretations concerning the roles of men and women. After presenting opposing viewpoints, we have professed to what we believe in upholding the traditional family and its values.

The need for instruction in biblical principles of family living is greater than ever. The problems facing Christian young people and the Christian home have multiplied since the printing of the first edition. They seem to increase with each passing year. This volume is sent forth with the prayer that it will bring glory and honor to our Lord Jesus Christ. May he be pleased to use it in the formation and encouragement of Christian homes here and abroad.

Preface to the First Edition

Solomon said, "Of making many books there is no end; and much study is a weariness of the flesh." Although there are many books published today covering various phases of Christian courtship and marriage, and many Christian high schools, colleges, seminaries, and Bible institutes offer courses in this area, there is no textbook written specifically for such courses.

The author has studied the subject at the University of Pittsburgh and Ohio State University and has been teaching a course in Marriage and the Family for nineteen years in a Christian liberal arts college. He believes this volume will help fill this void in Christian literature that has existed so many years.

Those teaching in the field know there are two different ways of approaching a course on the family—the functional and the institutional. The functional course is primarily designed as a preparation-for-marriage course which attempts to give students some instruction in the process of mate selection, and of the interaction which takes place in marriage and family life. The institutional course treats the family from a sociological perspective and is concerned with the relationship of the family to other institutions of society.

This text is definitely written for the functional course in a Christian institution. Hopefully, it will enable students to make a wise choice of a mate and the adjustments needed to live happily together. Most any young person can learn to drive an automobile, but the insurance companies have discovered that a course in driver's education makes a better and safer driver. Similarly, any fellow or girl can date and get married, but it can be a much more enjoyable experience if they know something about the interaction that takes place. As one married student said to the writer, "I wish I had taken this course five years ago, for our marriage could have been so much happier if I had known these things when we began our married life."

There is a real need for more and better premarital counseling. Part of the problem has been the lack of a single volume covering the many areas which the pastor wishes to treat in his limited time with an engaged couple. The pastor can now recommend the purchase and reading of this volume by the young couple prior to counseling sessions. He may even require the completion of the personality inventories to discover significant differences which can form the basis for some of the counseling sessions. A premarital counseling program based on the text should prepare the couple to enter marriage with a realistic view of what is involved in family living.

Another purpose in writing this book is to provide a comprehensive volume that will be a source of information to many pastors, Christian Education directors, and youth leaders who have not had the privilege of systematically studying these subjects in a classroom setting. Hopefully, these counselors will be better prepared to deal with questions concerning dating, courtship, and marriage after reading this volume.

The sociological basis used in organizing the text is modern role theory. This theory is very compatible with the Bible, for Jesus said, "As ye would that men should do to you, do ye also to them likewise" (Luke 6:31). Certainly young people must be aware of their own roles if they are going to interact with others. Many of the difficulties of courtship and marriage adjustment arise because the roles of male and female are no longer clearly defined in American culture. Also, very little education is given the youth of our society to help them successfully play the roles of lover, spouse, or parent. Someone has stated, "The only course in marriage and family living most young people ever get is the one they receive in their parental home." Unfortunately, many Christian young people do not receive very much help from their parents. On the other hand, much of the so-called sex education in public schools presents a negative view of family roles and values. Consequently, much of the learning in marriage and family living is through trial and error in an "on the job" setting, a factor which

helps to account for the high rate of marriage failure. This text emphasizes the necessity for individuals to know their spiritual, psychological, and emotional needs in order to fulfill role expectations, and to meet the various needs of those with whom they interact.

Another aim of this volume is to alert the young person to subtle cultural pressures that bear upon him. For example, Christian young people are not immune to the romantic love complex foisted on our culture by Hollywood and television. An attempt is made in these pages to counteract this by stressing the importance in courtship of seeking psychological compatibility rather than physical compatibility, since the major part of marital interaction is psychological rather than physical. It may be idealistic to think that most young people will choose their mates on the basis of psychological rather than physical compatibility, but even if only a few follow this suggestion their marriages will be happier. The author hopes no couple having studied this text will face each other after the honeymoon year is over and say, "Why did we ever marry each other?"

Another cultural influence of which Christian young people are often unaware is the pressure for social status conformity—the "keep up with the Joneses" syndrome of American life. This "status seeking," as Vance Packard terms it, is intertwined with the materialism that is seriously affecting Christian homes and churches today. Inasmuch as conflict over financial problems is a major cause of unhappiness in many homes, two chapters of this text are devoted to money management. If young people learn their roles as Christian stewards well, many of the financial situations that cause unhappiness can be avoided.

The author realizes that the first attempt to write a full-length textbook has its shortcomings, and he welcomes criticism and suggestions that will help to make any future edition more useful to its readers.

Acknowledgments

We are indebted to many people for their assistance in writing this book. My thanks to Dr. Clifford Johnson, now retired from his position as academic dean at Cedarville College, whose encouragement gave the initial impetus to write the first edition. Dr. James Jeremiah, president of Cedarville College at that time, arranged for a leave of absence during the winter quarter of 1971 to provide time to begin the actual writing.

Cornelius Zylstra, editor of Baker Book House, gave much needed encouragement and answered numerous questions in planning and publishing the original volume. Jim Weaver, presently editor for academic books, has been most helpful in facilitating the publication of this revised and enlarged edition. Without his support, the volume would never have materialized.

We are grateful to the librarians of the following colleges who permitted us to research and write in their libraries: Calvin College (Grand Rapids), Cedarville College (Cedarville, Ohio), Florida Southern College (Lakeland), Grand Rapids Baptist College, Southeastern Bible College (Lakeland, Florida), South Florida Community College (Avon Park), and Warner Southern College (Lake Wales, Florida).

A special word of thanks is due Mr. and Mrs. Ole Tilma, who so graciously gave us the use of their "missionary apartment" in May, 1992 in order to be close to the Grand Rapids libraries. We are also grateful to Dr. Irene Alyn, who in the summer of 1992 provided the use of her home near Cedarville College library. These dear friends saved thousands of miles of commuting that would have been necessary had we remained in Florida for that period.

A long list could be made of dear friends in various churches who prayed for us. Their part in the successful completion of the book has been recorded by the Lord of heaven and will be rewarded at the judgment seat of Christ.

I am especially thankful that my son, Philip, has agreed to become the co-author. He has excellent educational qualifications, and has had missionary service in Africa and Asia. These experiences have prepared him to write about family living in a global economy.

We are greatly indebted to Linda Triemstra of Gold Leaf Editorial Services, who gave us invaluable assistance and encouragement in preparing the manuscript for the final printing.

Last but not least, I am grateful for Helen Marie, my loving wife and typist, who became adept at reading my handwriting. She never grew weary of typing and proofreading seemingly endless revisions. Her critical judgment and suggestions for changes resulted in a more readable volume. Her love and commitment have enabled me to experience a happy and successful Christian marriage. Our prayer is that thousands of students who study this book will also have this joyous experience.

Cleveland McDonald

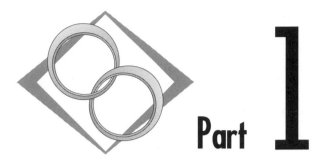

Part **1**

The Formation of the Family

Culture and the Secular Family

For I am the Lord, I change not . . .

—Malachi 3:6

Change Is Inevitable

John and Mary stood before the pastor and exchanged their vows. Later, they impatiently awaited the end of the reception so they could start on their honeymoon. Two years later, Cheri was born. Four years later John and Mary stood before a judge who "dissolved" their marriage. Mary received custody of Cheri and joined the ranks of millions of single parents. John was given visitation rights and became liable for child support, which he seldom paid. Mary had to find employment, but her income was not enough to live on and she was eventually forced to go on welfare.

In the meantime, John met and married Gretchen. They had a son, Jason, Cheri's half-brother. Mary married Steve, who had custody of his son. Mary gave birth to another daughter, Jody. Now Cheri had a half-brother, a half-sister, a stepbrother, a stepfather, and a new set of grandparents. Unfortunately, Mary and Steve's marriage ended in divorce. When Mary fell in love with Wayne, she decided to let him just move in (cohabit) with her and the girls. Cheri and Jody had to adjust to this new situation. Imagine the difficulties Cheri had in keeping track of her relatives.

This story is typical of the changes that have taken place in family structures the last few years. No-fault divorces, single parents, inadequate child support, welfare mothers, cohabitation, and confused children are all part of the family scene in American culture. More changes may have taken place in marriage and family living in the last three decades than occurred in the previous three centuries (Henslin 1985, 34). Changes have come so rapidly that society has not been able to adjust to them. As a result, new social problems have arisen (Hales 1988, 21).

The so-called new morality has led to a breakdown in traditional Judeo-Christian morality, resulting in a tremendous increase in sexually transmitted diseases (STD), illegitimate births, and abortions (Edelman 1987, 52). No-fault divorces create millions of single-parent families that have inherent difficulties (Gay 1988, 61–70). Mothers entered the workforce by the millions and latchkey kids became a national concern (Coleman 1986, 2). Homosexuality came out of

> *More changes may have taken place in marriage and family living in the last three decades than occurred in the previous three centuries.*

the closet with serious social implications for the populace as a whole. The term *AIDS* (Acquired Immune Deficiency Syndrome) is now familiar to everyone (Reiss 1990, 107). Cohabitation is practiced by more than two million couples (Hales 1988, 44). Lawsuits as a result of the failure of such relationships added "palimony" to our cultural vocabulary (Coleman 1985, 197).

Family violence, date rape, pornography, sexual harassment, drug and alcohol addiction, and alternative family lifestyles are some of the other problems resulting from the breakdown of traditional morality. These changes affect all families, Christian as well as non-Christian. As one writer states, "In America, our society's well-being is widely believed to be closely related to family stability. Erosion of family bonds is generally regarded as a threat to the nation's social fabric. People sense that their fates are linked with the future of marriage and the family as social institutions" (Garrett 1982, 205).

The family does not exist in a vacuum. It is interrelated with four other basic institutions of society: religious, economic, governmental, and educational institutions. Changes in one area dramatically affect the others (Korman and Leslie 1985, 5).

Change Is Progressive

Prior to the nineteenth century, America was a rural nation with a patriarchal form of family life. The father was the source of power and authority. The wife and children were subservient to him and had few legal rights of their own (Lamanna and Riedmann 1988, 228–29). The wife's role was clearly defined in that she cared for the home and children, and also helped with the farm work when necessary. The girls helped the mother and learned their roles. The boys were taught to farm and were expected to contribute their labor until they reached the legal age of maturity and began families of their own.

The patriarchal family was part of an extended kin group. Aged parents were cared for by one of the sons or daughters who also inherited the farm. Since there was little geographical mobility, young people tended to marry individuals in the same area; siblings, aunts, uncles, and cousins lived within a short distance of each other. They attended the same school and church and were available to help one another in time of need. Family reunions as we know them were unnecessary because the kin group met frequently at church and social gatherings.

The patriarchal family was a productive family. It produced its own food and had a surplus to sell. Children were an economic asset as they provided labor to produce what the family needed (DeVault and Strong 1989, 26).

Industrialization and Change

The Industrial Revolution of the nineteenth century changed not only the economy of America, but also the family. As factories multiplied, the need for workers increased. These workers came from rural areas to the cities and the urbanization of the nation began. During the last 150 years, the number of farms has decreased annually; now less than 2 percent of the population is engaged in farming (Statistical Abstract of the United States 1991, 643).

Workers left their villages and towns where religious and primary-group controls were strong. In cities and suburbs, secular and weak secondary-group controls predominated. As a result, many modifications in family structure, values, and behavior took place (Skolnick 1987, 131).

In the city crowded living conditions replace the spaciousness of the country. Families housed in small homes and apartments with little rooms often have little or no privacy. A tour of the countryside in the East or Midwest, where many of the large, old farmhouses still stand, graphically illustrates the change. Many of these homes have five or more bedrooms to accommodate the large number of children plus a hired man or two. The growth of suburban areas around the cities since World War II is an attempt to regain some of the space and privacy of rural areas.

Children, once an economic asset because of the labor they provided on the farm, are, in the city, an economic liability. With the benefit of improved methods of contraception, couples have fewer children. Today, children who are born into a rapidly changing society are exposed to new ideas and more frequently rebel against the "old-fashioned" ideas of their parents (Mace and Mace 1985, 224). This leads to family conflict and often to violence. Youthful rebellion results in other social problems such as premarital sex, abortions, drug and alcohol addiction, and juvenile delinquency (Bynum and Thompson 1989, 23–24).

On the farm the family worshiped, worked, and prayed together, but in the city life is fragmented to the extent that each member goes his or her own way. The church has ceased to be the center of religious and recreational activity. Instead of attending a covered-dish dinner at the church, Dad has his bowling game, Mom her PTA meeting, sister her Campfire Girls powwow, and brother his Boy Scouts meeting. City churches now develop activities to meet the needs of various interests and age groups: women's missionary societies, men's prayer breakfasts, Boys' Brigade, Pioneer Girls, Awana Clubs, and athletic teams. Rarely, in today's society, does the family function as a unit.

Opportunities where the family can work together are also few. Occasionally, there are small businesses such as service stations or "mom and pop" restaurants where each member can share in its operation. More often, however, the father performs specialized work that fails to provide any opportunity for family togetherness as the farm once did (Garland and Garland 1986, 77). In addition to the loss of family togetherness, children have also tended to lose the value and habit of work they assimilated on the farm.

In the twentieth century, craft and labor unions gained increased wages and benefits for workers. This contributed to a higher standard of living and an increasingly materialistic philosophy of life. Though this philosophy has

> *The patriarchal family was a productive family. It produced its own food and had a surplus to sell.*

spread to the rural areas today, its major impact has been on the city dweller.

Unionization of workers also shortened the work week, which left more time available for recreation. An entire new industry has been created to cater to the recreational needs of the populace. The emphasis on entertainment and athletics has distorted American values so the superstars earn more for a few performances than the president of the United States earns in four years.

In many families the budget, of time as well as money, suffers from trying to meet all the recreational desires of its members. Equipment for sports, boating, or camping is expensive. The average family finds it difficult to satisfy everyone and disagreements and conflicts often cause marital problems.

The philosophy of materialism puts greater emphasis on material possessions than on spiritual values and ideals. It is perhaps epitomized by the phrase *American dream,* a slogan that seems to assume that every family is entitled to a home in the suburbs, one or more new cars, a camping trailer, and a large pleasure boat. The fact that both parents have to work, or that father must work a second job while children are raised by babysitters, does not seem too high a sacrifice as long as the American dream is realized. Skolnick (1987, 164) writes, "Of all the changes in family life that have occurred in the twentieth century, this [the two-worker family] may be the most profound. It is producing pressures for changes in marital roles, the division of labor in the family, and child care, and it is creating new perceptions of self in both men and women."

> *The philosophy of materialism puts greater emphasis on material possessions than on spiritual values and ideals.*

This materialism is encouraged by high-pressure advertising. The family is urged through television, radio, and the print media to buy the latest-model cars, appliances, and other necessities of life, even if the present models are still functioning adequately. After the urge to buy is generated, an "easy-credit" system removes any remaining obstacle, such as common sense or the realities of the family budget, to the purchase.

Tim LaHaye (1982, 148) states, "Everyone is vulnerable to the temptations of materialism in some form. . . . The Bible admonishes, 'Love not the world, neither the things that are in the world. If any man love the world, the love of the Father is not in him' (1 John 2:15). Your problem may be food, cars, clothes, or a hundred other items, but be sure of this: You are vulnerable to some enticing area of materialism.

That is why TV advertisers will pay up to $275,000 per minute for prime-time commercials." One of the greatest challenges facing Christian families today is finding the balance between material and spiritual values.

Urbanization and Role Changes

In the rural family, authority was based on the hierarchical system whereby the father exercised power over the other members of the family (Mace and Mace 1985, 242–43). The wife and children responded with unquestioned obedience. The needs and desires of the individual members were subordinated to the welfare of the family. Since there were no other means of support and divorce was taboo, the wife stayed with the husband, even if she was unhappy or suffering abuse. Unhappy or mistreated children had to endure their situations until they were able to marry (daughters) or leave home to find employment (sons).

This situation changed when the family moved to town. Women received more education and began to work outside the home. These new opportunities made them less willing to remain in incompatible unions. A woman could now work and care for her children. As the number of divorces increased, divorce became more acceptable. In the city the primary group pressure of, "What will the relatives and neighbors think?" weakened because people were separated from the kin group and often did not even know their neighbors! The authoritarianism of the father was gradually replaced by democratic individualism, where the importance of each member of the family in determining his or her future and that of the family was recognized.

To maintain the standard of living dictated by an increasingly materialistic society, it often became necessary for the wife and mother to seek employment to augment the family income. This trend has continued so that today more than 50 percent of all married women are employed outside the home. Often these working mothers have young children, making the problem of proper day care for the children a national concern. Many want the government to provide day-care centers nationwide. Christian homes and churches face these same issues and must make decisions balancing economic necessities with faith and God's Word.

Geographic Mobility and the Family

It is seldom recognized how immigration during the Industrial Revolution affected the American family. The first wave of immigrants from northern Europe moved westward and settled in the Midwest. In the latter part of the nineteenth and the first part of the twentieth century, immigrants from southern Europe arrived in great numbers (Korman and Leslie 1985, 185–83). They settled mainly in the cities and supplied the workforce for factories. Families of immigrants usually lived close to one another, and whenever possible perpetuated the culture of their homeland. Vestiges of these communities with their own language, churches, and newspapers still exist in our great cities. They brought with them the customs, traditions, and values of family life in their homeland and preserved these as much as possible. However, as their children attended schools and colleges and were influenced by the popular culture, they often intermarried with "outsiders." As a result, subsequent generations became more assimilated into the larger culture (Korman and Leslie 1985, 298).

The most recent immigration wave brought two large groups into the country: Southeast Asians, who have settled mostly on the West Coast, and Latin Americans, who settled mostly in the southwestern states. Many Cubans, Jamaicans, and others from the Caribbean area have settled in Florida (Korman and Leslie 1985, 281–98). Hispanics are one of the fastest-growing segments of the population.

Internal migration has also occurred. During the Great Depression, many families moved in search of employment. Again, the move was largely rural to urban. World War II accelerated the trend. Approximately 20 percent of American families move each year, resulting in a "generation without roots." Children have little opportunity to really know their relatives, or to establish lasting friendships with neighbors or peer groups. In rural society, if one parent was missing, there were other members of a close-knit kin group with whom the child could identify. Now, many boys are reared by widowed or divorced mothers and have no male role models with whom the growing boys can identify.

> *Approximately 20 percent of American families move each year, resulting in a "generation without roots."*

The Maces (1985, 240) make the salient point that "there is an important *religious* issue involved here . . . the concept of God as the loving heavenly Father is central to theological teaching. What is this concept going to mean to a generation of young people, many of whom have never experienced a loving earthly father?" Constant moving also makes for insecurity in the child's personality, and may account for many of the maladjusted children receiving treatment in mental health clinics.

Parents also suffer from this mobility. Whenever a couple moves into a new situation, they are usually cut off from relatives and friends. Until they are able to make new friends, they are forced to depend upon each other for the fulfillment of all of their emotional needs. This adds an additional stress to the marital relationship, particularly if the wife is at home all day with the children. The family that has to change residence frequently will have to work harder to make the marriage a success. This includes Christian businessmen, pastors, missionaries, Christian education directors, and others whose employment requires mobility for promotion, or to fulfill the will of God for their lives.

Secularism and the Family

One of the changes that has taken place in American culture is the increasing gulf between Judeo-Christian principles and the secularism of society. Webster defines secularism as "a system of doctrines and practices that rejects any form of religious faith and worship." The term *secular humanists* has been used to identify those who would remove religious influence from the institutions of American society.

> *The term* secular humanists *has been used to identify those who would remove religious influence from the institutions of American society.*

Hitchcock (1982, 10) says of the humanists, "In their self-definition God does not exist, and it is a destructive illusion to believe in him. They promote a way of life that systematically excludes God and all religion in the traditional sense. Man, for better or for worse, is on his own in the universe. 'Secular' . . . comes from the Latin 'seeculism' which means 'time' or 'age.' . . . To call someone secular means that he is completely time-bound, totally a child of his age, a creature of history, with no vision of eternity."

One of the foremost opponents of secular humanism, Tim LaHaye (1982, 32), describes it as "an anti-Christian system of thought that influences every decision and most of a person's actions. It is anti-God, anti-moral, anti-self restraint, and anti-American. Amazingly, humanism often masquerades as humanitarianism. In reality, there is nothing humanitarian about it, because its beliefs make it anti-human." He also states (1982, 32–33), "humanism has to be labeled family enemy number one. . . . Unconditional war has been declared; anti-moral humanism and historic Christianity are in a struggle for survival, with the traditional family at stake."

The debate concerning secular humanism continues. Webber (1982, 31) argues for "Christian humanism [, which] may be contrasted to humanism in the following four convictions: confidence in God in Christ; a supernatural world-view; the power of Christ acting through the church; and incarnational humanitarianism."

Paul Kurtz (1983, vii), the foremost spokesman for secular humanists has written *In Defense of Secular Humanism.* His thesis is that it is possible to lead a morally good life and to contribute to society but not believe in God. He believes that humanism is basic to the progress of modern science. It is a totally naturalistic philosophy. He continues by stating (5) that the secular humanist shares some concerns with the Moral Majority (Jerry Falwell's group), such as concern about the breakdown in family life, excessive promiscuity, pornography, and drugs, but he is critical of the Bible. He attributes the "breakdowns in modern society, if there have been breakdowns . . . primarily to technology, not to secular humanism."

Francis Schaeffer (1983, 14–15), one of the foremost Christian apologists of the twentieth century, finds the conflict between humanism and the Christian world view based on their concepts of "final reality." For the Christian, final reality "is the infinite-personal God who is truly there. . . . To this God things are not neutral. Therefore, there are absolutes; there is right and wrong in the world." For the humanist, "final reality is thought of as purely material—or as mere energy, eventually—which has existed eternally in some form, and which has its present configuration by pure chance. . . . In this view final reality yields no value system, no basis for law, and no concept of man as unique and important."

It is apparent from Schaeffer's viewpoint that the conflict is between a Judeo-Christian view of a God with absolute values of right and wrong and a humanistic system "with only personal, arbitrary, relative values." Thus, it appears that this conflict is the present form of the age-old struggle between God and Satan, right and wrong, darkness versus light, sin against righteousness. It began somewhere in the dateless past (Isa. 14) and will culminate in the end of the ages with the destruction of Satan (Rev. 20) (Duncan 1979, 23).

This current phase of the conflict corresponds with the rise of religious liberalism in the churches. As the churches abandoned their belief in God and the supernatural, it became easy for the naturalistic philosophy of humanism to grow and finally become the most predominant social force in American culture (Duncan 1979, 23–27). Schaeffer (1983, 14–15) makes an important point when he writes, "About eighty years ago in the United States we began to move from a Judeo-Christian consensus, or ethos, toward a humanist consensus." He indicates that the movement has matured in the last forty years. He believes the Judeo-Christian ethic has been supplanted by humanism.

The results of secularism with its relativistic value system are many. Monogamous marriage as instituted by God is rejected, and divorce is accepted. Remarriage is no longer frowned upon and a form of serial polygamy now exists. A person may have only one wife or husband at a time, but if they divorce, they can have several one after the other.

This secular view of man and society, with its denial of biblical moral authority, makes possible such changes as the sexual revolution of the "new morality," the "situation ethics" of Joseph Fletcher, and the hedonistic philosophy of Hugh Hefner. The demands of the radical element of the women's liberation movement for the legalization of abortion and the elimination of marriage can occur only in a secular society.

The believer in Bible prophecy is not surprised to see these trends in our culture. The apostle Paul wrote in 2 Timothy 3:1–5, "This know also, that in the last days perilous times shall come. For men shall be lovers of their own selves, covetous, boasters, proud, blasphemers, disobedient to parents, unthankful, unholy, without natural affection, truce breakers, false accusers, incontinent, fierce, despisers of those that are good, traitors, heady, highminded, lovers of pleasures more than lovers of God; having a form of godliness, but denying the power thereof: from such turn away."

> *It appears that the conflict between humanism and Christianity is the present form of the age-old struggle between God and Satan, right and wrong, darkness versus light, sin against righteousness.*

Technological Change

Industrialization and urbanization were accompanied by changes in technology that affected family life. The invention of the automobile and the development of mass production made for widespread ownership of automobiles. One of the first changes occurred in the area of dating. Prior to this it was fairly easy for parents to chaperone young people when the were dating. The car enabled young people to choose their own friends and "to spend their evenings outside of parental approval, often in the backseat of parked cars" (Henslin 1985, 211). It also led to drive-in restaurants and theaters. It made possible the rise of suburban communities.

The invention and widespread use of television also has had a dramatic impact on American family life. At first television was hailed as a means of reuniting families as they would watch programs together. Programs were censored and many family-oriented programs were televised. However, as time passed,

27

censorship relaxed until programs destructive to family life and values predominate.

The invention and use of television has had a dramatic effect on American family life.

Programming for television is influenced by secular humanism. Franky Schaeffer (1982, 26–27) reports on a survey of two hundred journalists and broadcasters: "The results of this survey are startling and confirm, even beyond one's worst suspicions, the religious commitment of the media to secular humanism." Tim LaHaye (1982, 106) asks, "In the past few years, why has television programming descended from filth, smut, and innuendo to depravity? Because the humanists who control the industry are out to destroy (they call it 'alter') the moral fiber of our country, without which the traditional family cannot exist."

As indicated, this type of programming has serious implications for the family. David Mains (1985, 35) comments that he is "awed by this ingenious takeover of such a powerful media tool for molding people's thinking. . . . People are being influenced by these mind changers." He relates that the average person spends forty-two hours a week in front of a television set. If a Christian views only half this much, it amounts to twenty-one hours a week. He concludes, "overexposure to secular input is *dangerous*" (italics added). If the Christian family desires to accomplish the goal of being an example to lost neighbors, and to rear children who will love and serve the Lord, then television viewing must be controlled. If this is not possible, then the set must go. Some programs such as news, sporting events, travelogues, and nature studies have value, but even here, the humanist slant of the news and the evolutionary content of the nature programs must be explained to children.

Duvall and Miller (1985, 196–97) state, "the television set is an ever-present, inexpensive and effective babysitter for busy parents, and a focus of fascination for pre-schoolers." The problem is that children are exposed then to sex, profanity, and violence. A study by the National Institute of Mental Health concludes that there is "consistent associations between heavy television viewing of violent programs and aggressive behavior in preschool children." The study reported that "there is an average of five violent acts per hour of prime-time and eighteen acts per hour on children's weekend programs." A Task Force Report of the American Psychological Association in 1992 concluded that "by age 13, the average child will have witnessed 8,700 murders and more than 160,000 other assorted violent acts on television" (*Good Housekeeping*, July 1992, 188).

It is incumbent upon parents to resist using the television set as a babysitter and to choose wisely the programs their children view. There are excellent programs such as *Sesame Street* that are both entertaining and educational.

It is estimated that the average high-school graduate "will have been exposed to three hundred fifty thousand commercials, and vicariously participated in eighteen thousand killings" (LaHaye 1982, 1040). This violence on the television screen is now being carried out in homes, schools, and streets. The abuse of family members is a national disgrace. The violence in some city schools requires the presence of police to keep peace in the hallways. Crime and violence make it unsafe to walk city streets. This desensitization to violence is a result of violence viewed by these young people on the television screen (Butler and Gutknecht 1985, 240).

Fortunately, "both Christians and non-Christians are responding to television violence by demanding less violent TV programming. The National Coalition on Television Violence . . . the Coalition for Better Television . . . draw Christian people together to oppose and boycott sponsors, if necessary, to halt the tide of violence. Christian people need to seize leadership in this matter and restrict the watching of television violence in their own homes" (LaHaye 1982, 106).

The widespread use of videocassette recorders has added a new dimension to television viewing. Videocassettes from both Christian and non-Christian sources are available. In this case also, the choice of programs determines the educative value of the instrument.

The computer is another technological invention that is changing the manner in which American families operate. "The computer . . . is now changing centuries-old ways of doing things and may possibly bring about the greatest social revolution in the whole history of mankind. . . ." (Spencer 1986, 3). When they first came on the scene, it was predicted that eventually every family would have a computer in the home. Not every household has a personal computer, but the majority have an embedded computer that is part of an appliance such as a television set or a camera that performs some specialized function. All late-model automobiles now incorporate one or more such computers (Graham 1989, 10).

A small percentage of households do have personal computers. These are used mainly for recordkeeping, but some are used to keep recipes or daily and weekly schedules (Butler and Gutknecht 1985, 257). They have become indispensable for home businesses. Video games are also widely played on home computers (Dertouzos and Moses 1980, 4).

Another popular use for home computers is word processing. An individual can now work at home and transmit his finished product via phone lines to another state or fax them anywhere in the world. The computer "may be used in the home or in the office, or it may dissolve the distinction between the two, putting us back into a world of cottage industries where people work at or near their homes with their families and friends—and their homes can be anywhere in the world, thanks to satellite communications" (Bradbeer, DeBono, and Laurie 1982, 21).

Some companies are already allowing employees to work out of their homes as it saves overhead expenses for the firm. For example, Blue Cross/Blue Shield of Washington, D.C., has home workers file insurance claims into the company's computers; workers are paid by the number of claims they

process. This permits the women to be with their small children. "According to Electronic Services Unlimited, as many as ten thousand employees in the United States are similarly earning their living staying at home" (Butler and Gutknecht 1985, 260). By 1989 the number of "telecommuters" had increased to five million (*Newsweek,* 24 April 1989).

Computers are being used by schools and introduced to children at the primary level. Almost any subject can be enhanced by the use of the computer. Math and word processing together represent the large majority of computer educational programs. They, of course, only scratch the surface of the world of knowledge and skills that are part of any child's school experience (Butler and Gutknecht 1985, 255). Today's children are being prepared to take their place in the information age that is now upon us.

> *The computer is another technological invention that is changing the manner in which American families operate.*

Computers can also be used in the home to enable adults to continue their education. There are college courses available on television, but the individual may not be home at the time a course is given. "The educational computer program in the home could presumably be run at any available time, and the computer system might even remind the student to continue a course if he had been avoiding it for awhile" (Dertouzos and Moses 1980, 8).

Other uses of the home computer are for transmission of information (electronic mail), control of basic appliances in the home (heating and air conditioning), the electronic transfer of funds, and establishing an electronic home library (Dertouzos and Moses 1980, 13). It is apparent computers will play an increasing role in the life of the American family.

Social Policy and Change

Many changes in the American family have taken place because of governmental actions. Various terms are used in reference to the relationship of these actions and the family: social policy, family policy, or public policy are all used. Moen and Schorr (Steinmetz and Sussman 1987, 795) define family policy as "a widely agreed on set of objectives for families, toward the realization of which the state (and other major social institutions) deliberately shape programs and policies." The total number of governmental agencies that affect the family is enormous. "A government's social policy helps set the rules of the game—the stakes, the risks, the payoffs, the tradeoffs, and the strategies for making a living, raising a family . . ." (Finsterbusch and McKenna 1990, 208).

Laws, regulations, and restrictions affect the individual in the family from birth to death. However, no one public policy is concerned primarily with the interests of the family.

> # Laws, regulations, and restrictions affect the individual in the family from birth to death.

Such a policy is impossible due to the pluralistic nature of American society. Conservatives and liberals differ as to what constitutes a "normal" family. Each of these groups attempts to influence governmental decisions affecting any aspect of family living.

Conservatives are concerned about laws attempting to change the structure or functioning of the traditional family. They argue against laws making divorce easier. They disapprove of Aid for Families with Dependent Children (AFDC) regulations permitting unmarried women to continue bearing children. They work to change a Supreme Court decision (*Roe v. Wade*) that legalizes abortion. They oppose laws permitting minors to secure abortions without the consent of their parents. They resist a welfare system that creates an "underclass" locked into a permanent state of poverty and hopelessness. In effect, they are opposed to any governmental action that tends to weaken the nuclear family, and they support most any measure that strengthens the family.

Many governmental policies do strengthen the family. Unemployment insurance is a blessing to multitudes of families in time of economic stress. Social Security and Medicare make life more livable for millions of senior citizens. Medicaid and Aid for the Aged help less fortunate seniors. Aid for Families with Dependent Children has enabled many mothers to rear their children. (It is the abuse of the program that conservatives oppose.) Since family policy affects all families, Christians must be concerned and active in support of groups and legislation. Clinton (Regier 1982, 258) issues this challenge, "If we believe any good can come through government programs, we citizens must also act based on social research and biblical values and take responsibility to see that all channels of influence and integration are pursued. Family action councils, lobbyists, and personal involvement are necessary, working together."

Change and the Christian Family

It is difficult to differentiate between a nominal Christian family and a non-Christian one. The non-Christian or secular family leaves God out of its life. They do not attend church and humanistic values guide their behavior. Their economic life is dominated by materialism. Weddings are handled by a justice of the peace. When death strikes, the body is cremated. They do not have a need for God at any time.

The nominal Christian home is not too different from a secular home. When asked how his family differed from the unsaved family next door, one young man wrote:

My parents are both professing Christians, but the only difference between them and the next door neighbors is that my parents do attend church regularly on Sunday morning. They do not feel any obligation to be present at the evening service nor on Wednesday night unless it is a very special occasion. I do not know if they have private devotions, but we have never had worship together as a family. Several times we have started saying grace before meals, yet it has never become established as a regular practice. One more thing. My folks don't swear, drink, or smoke, and the neighbors do.

This young man did not find his home much different from the secular home next door.

Two young women responded to the same question in a more positive manner:

The relationship between my father and mother is such that my father is head of the house and God is the head of his life. Because he is guided by the Lord, the decisions he makes are usually right. My mother is submissive to my father and even though he is the head, he loves and takes care of his family well and uses his authority with love and guidance from the Lord.

Our home life is different from that of a family of non-Christians because we have a basic trust and personal relationship with Christ. Because of this our language is different, our habits are different also. More than this there is a stronger bond between our family which helps us meet and defeat trials and temptations which come along. Christ is the head of our household and has His protecting hand on all of our family. I personally feel that if more families had a Christian basis, there would be less homes splitting up and more homes truly happy.

The responses of these young women indicate they have come from homes that are truly Christian, whose secular neighbors are able to see evidence of Christianity as it applies to family life.

A truly Christian home has identifying features. It is one where the Lord Jesus Christ is loved by all members and is overtly demonstrated to each other. This bond of love manifests itself in various ways: harmonious relationships, family worship, regular church attendance, active witness to friends and neighbors, service to the Lord in the local church and in the community.

The Christian home is the first line of defense against the encroaching tide of secular humanism. Churches and Christian schools are only as strong as the families in them. Satan is a crafty foe who knows where to attack, and he is doing everything in his power to destroy the Christian home. However, "greater is he that is in you than he that is in the world." Believers have the inspired Word of God and the indwelling power of the Holy Spirit to enable them to build a Christian home that glorifies the heavenly Father. The Maces (1985, 278) suggest that "an acid test of any Christian life is and must be, how the person concerned manages his or her interpersonal relationships—in marriage first, then in the family group. . . ." The succeeding chapters are designed to help meet the great challenge of creating strong Christian homes that will withstand the pressures of a secular society.

> *The Christian home is the first line of defense against the encroaching tide of secular humanism.*

Study Questions

1. In what ways has the "new morality" affected the American family?
2. Why should the average person be concerned about changes in the family?

3. What changes take place in the family when the wife enters the workplace?
4. How does geographic mobility affect the family?
5. Define secular humanism. How does it differ from humanitarianism? From the humanities?
6. What impact has television viewing had on the American family? How does it contribute to the violence in American culture?
7. What are the advantages of a home computer? The disadvantages?
8. Why should a Christian be concerned about governmental family policies?
9. Discuss the manner in which two governmental family policies affect your family.
10. Define and contrast the secular home and the Christian home. Which term describes your home?

Suggested Readings

Butler, E. W., and D. B. Gutknecht, eds. 1985. *Family, self, and society.* 2d ed. New York: Univ. Press of America. A valued selection of articles dealing with "emerging issues, alternatives, and interventions" in family life.

Cherlin, A. J., ed. 1988. *The changing American family and public policy.* Washington, D.C.: The Urban Institute Press. The Urban Institute is interested in providing information to government-policy decisionmakers to enable them to pass legislation that will help to alleviate social ills. Six sections in this volume concern families and how public policy relates to them. Section 1 has an adequate treatment of changes in the American family.

Coleman, W. L. 1983. *Making TV work for your family.* Minneapolis: Bethany House. A booklet designed to involve children in decisions concerning use of the television set.

Geisler, N. L. 1983. *Is man the measure? An evaluation of contemporary humanism.* Grand Rapids: Baker. One of America's leading apologists demonstrates the dangers of secular humanism in American culture.

Graham, N. 1989. *The mind tool: Computers and their impact on society.* St. Paul: West. A textbook that describes the various uses of the computer in education, health care, business, and finance.

Hitchcock, J. 1982. *What is secular humanism?* Ann Arbor: Servant. Hitchcock gives a short but adequate historical background of secular humanism, emphasizing the American experience. He also critiques areas such as the mass media and the churches.

Liebert, R. M., and J. Sprafkin, eds. 1988. *The early window: The effects of television on children and youth.* 3d ed. Elmsford, N.Y.: Pergamon. Written "for those concerned with television and its role in the future of society." Presents scientific evidence concerning many facets of television viewing and its negative influence on children and youth.

Lull, J. 1990. *World families watch television.* Newbury Park, Calif.: Sage. A collection of articles on television viewing in various countries. The article on the U.S. states that in 1987 the average American family watched television for seven hours a day.

Slocum, R. E. 1986. *Ordinary Christians in a high-tech world.* Waco: Word. Written by a Presbyterian layman, a physical scientist, who is concerned about the effects of modern technology on the church and family.

Woodbridge, J. D., ed. 1985. *Renewing your mind in a secular world.* Chicago: Moody. "What do Christians need to know about renewing their minds?" The articles discuss the rise of secular humanism and the biblical resources available to help the believer renew his mind.

2

Culture and the Christian Family

> Therefore shall a man leave his father and his mother, and shall cleave
> unto his wife; and they shall be one flesh.
>
> —Genesis 2:24

The Crisis in Christian Families

The house shook. The doors swayed and creaked. The windows shattered. In Frostproof, Florida, November 1990, Pauline Bennett awoke to find her house being swallowed by the earth. The limestone layer beneath the foundation caved in, causing the house to sink beneath the surface. The foundation had failed. Mrs. Bennett was able to get out of the house, but her belongings met a watery grave.

Collapsing foundations are typical in many marriages today. Couples start out to build a house that is supposed to last a lifetime, but something happens—the foundation gives way and a marriage is destroyed. Even Christian couples who think they are building their homes on a biblical foundation become disappointed and divorce. The reason is often "incompatibility."

It is no longer just young families buckling under the stress of the child-rearing years. An increasing number of empty-nesters and senior citizens are also using the courts to solve their problems. Even highly visible Christian leaders are divorcing their wives, marrying other women, and continuing on "in the Christian ministry as if nothing ever happened" (Swindoll 1980, 15).

The Gangels (1987, 16) observe that "surely men and women dedicated to Jesus Christ and to each other can stem the tide or, at least, stand as pockets of resistance in a society seemingly hellbent on destroying the family." They relate that the same problems—delinquency, drug use, abortion, unwed mothers, unfaithfulness, separation, and divorce—that "contribute to family breakdown in the society at large, seem to have found their way into the Christian community as well." Consequently, our churches face such problems as remarriage, single parent families, and blended or reconstituted families.

The Necessity for Bible Knowledge

What is happening to our Christian families? The causes are multiple, but certainly one of the major reasons is a failure to understand the true biblical basis for Christian marriage. For a marriage to withstand the pressures of a secular society, a couple must know and practice what God, the creator of marriage, has to say about it. Young people who take the time and effort to discern what the Bible has to say about marriage will not "lightly nor unadvisedly" enter into holy matrimony. When they do, they will have a purpose and determination to create a homelife that will give them all the joy and blessing that God intended. No other human relationship can give such happiness or satisfaction. On the other hand, no other relationship can bring such misery, pain, and unhappiness as a marriage in which love has turned to hatred.

> *For a marriage to withstand the pressures of a secular society, a couple must know and practice what God, the creator of marriage, has to say about it.*

In order to lay a foundation on which to build a marriage that will last a lifetime, it is necessary to study God's Word to learn what he says about marriage and the home. In doing the study, one finds that various passages treating the subject are interpreted differently by men and women of equal scholarship. Just as godly teachers dif-

fer on such topics as salvation (Calvinism versus Arminianism), or prophecy (pretribulation rapture versus midtribulation rapture), so in the field of marriage and the family there are different interpretations. This arises because, as Protestants, no individual speaks *ex cathedra;* each person is free to determine what he or she believes a particular verse teaches.

Another reason for diversity in interpretations is indicated by Anderson and Guernsey (1985, 25): "What does the Bible teach concerning the family and roles within the family? Whatever assumptions one brings to the Bible will determine one's interpretations of the text." Within the evangelical community, there is a diversity of beliefs ranging from the most conservative groups to those that reach to the borders of liberalism. Considering these factors, it is easy to understand why scholars can study the same Scripture and reach very different interpretations.

This also applies to writers who are interested in formulating a theology of marriage and the family. Moore (1987, 11) writes, "What we need is a theology that argues for the centrality of love as the focus of human living. Short of such theology, there is little hope that order can be restored either to our lives or our thinking."

The Balswicks (1989, 19–33) describe attempts to build a theology based on the concept of covenant and proceed to present their view of such a theology. Anderson and Guernsey (1985, 26) entitle their volume *On Being Family: A Social Theology of the Family,* in which they also use "God's covenant love" as the foundation on which to build the structure of the family. Because their basic assumptions derive from their backgrounds, these authors reject the view "that traditional marriage" is biblical (Moore 1987, 39–40; Balswick and Balswick 1989, 79; Anderson and Guernsey 1985, 24). It is important to remember that although these people present a different interpretation, they continue to hold to the authority of Scripture as the Word of God and believe in the importance of good families for the health of the church and community. A large body of social science knowledge is helpful in understanding the behaviors that occur in family relationships, but it cannot take the place of biblical teaching about the family.

John MacArthur, Jr., (1983, 10) writes, "It may disturb you to be brought face to face with God's design for the family. But His guarantee is that if you will bow to its power and promise, no matter how it violates the world's thinking, you will come into the blazing sunlight of full joy in those most intimate and essential relationships." Swindoll (1980, 16–17), after relating how Christians are failing marriage, states, "We need to blow the dust off God's original blueprint for marriage and the home. Our great need is to hear what He has to say to His people about His design. After all, marriage is His invention. . . . As the Master Architect, the Lord is the most qualified authority, so we seek His counsel first and foremost."

Steve Clinton of the International Leadership Council states (Regier 1988, 253), "The basis of the American traditional family life is found in the teachings of the Bible." It is apparent these godly Christian leaders are truly convinced that the key to a secure and fulfilling Christian marriage is a knowledge and practice of what God has to say about this wonderful relationship.

The Divine Origin of Marriage

Humanists believe in the evolution of the family as a social invention, but they do not know when it began. Christians have no doubts about the origin of the family; they have an inspired record of the first marriage and family.

The first mention of marriage is found in Genesis 1:26–31, "And God said, Let us make man in our image, after our likeness; and let them have dominion over the fish of the sea, and over the fowl of the air, and over the cattle, and over all the earth, and over every creeping thing that creepeth upon the earth."

The creation of man was preceded by a council of Father, Son, and Holy Spirit. Verse 26 reads, "Let us make man in our image." The "image" is not physical but refers to the spiritual nature and personhood of God. As persons we have the ability to relate to God and to each other. The Penners (1981, 36–37) write, "The meaning of God's image is that we are created to be in relationship."

The newly created couple are given the blessing of God and two mandates—to rule over the creation and to be fruitful and multiply. The latter command indicates the establishment of marriage. The result was that God looked at what he had created and saw that not only was it good (as were the previous acts of creation), but that it was very good. Hoekema (1986, 15) writes, "Man, therefore, as he came from the hands of the Creator, was not corrupt, depraved, or sinful: he was in a state of integrity, innocence and holiness. Whatever in human beings today is evil or perverted was not part of man's original creation. At the time of his creation, man was very good."

> **Christians have no doubts about the origin of the family; they have an inspired record of the first marriage and family.**

The text states, "male and female he created them." It was here that God endowed the couple with their sexuality. Humans are male and female biologically with the proper anatomical organs for reproduction. They also are endowed with separate sexual natures that cause them to respond to each other and to situations in different ways. In American culture, they are each socialized as male and female, and this socialization adds a third dimension to male-female relationships.

The Balswicks (1989, 177) make this succinct statement: "God created us as sexual beings and pronounced this creation very good! Acceptance of one's sexuality begins with the ability to acknowledge and be thankful for it as part of God's design and intention. Our sexuality is good in God's sight!"

The Penners (1986, 1) elaborate on this theme: "Our sexuality is much broader than mere sexual intercourse. It refers to the whole person. . . . It includes all the characteristics and feelings that make us male and female." God made us as we are and we must accept our sexuality as his gift to us.

A popular cliché says a man never really is able to understand a woman and vice versa. However, the social sciences have accumulated much knowledge about each sex. It is incumbent upon young people in their preparation for marriage to learn as much as they can about these differences. This information can help to develop better interpersonal relationships and make the tasks of adjusting to each other much easier.

Eve Created as Adam's Companion

In chapter 2 of Genesis, in the more extended account of the creation of Eve, we encounter something that is "not good." In this inspired record of the beginning of the human family, God saw Adam "alone" and decided to make a helper "fit" or "suitable" or "face to face" to him. Swindoll (1980, 19) explains, "Literally, 'corresponding to' him. She would provide those missing pieces from the puzzle of his life. . . . In God's original design, the plan was to have each partner distinct and unique, needing each other and therefore finding fulfillment with each other."

> *Eve was not created to be merely a helpmate, as is often suggested, but as a companion who would fulfill the social needs of Adam.*

Eve was not created to be merely a helpmate, as is often suggested, but as a companion who would fulfill the social needs of Adam. He had, and all his descendants have, a need for communication and fellowship with other human beings. This desire is most perfectly met in the marriage relationship. Wheat (1977, 20) comments, "and the Lord God said, It is not good that the man should be alone. . . . In those few words God taught us that for the man there is no substitute, no alternative plan, no better companion than his wife."

The Gangels (1987, 20) stress the importance of companionship in these words, "The strategic role of fellowship in marriage provides the bull's eye on the family target. Everything else is secondary. Everything else takes a lower place of esteem, because if companionship isn't working, the family isn't working."

This need for companionship extends beyond marriage. The social nature cries out for fellowship with other human beings. Such interaction is necessary for the development of personality, as the social psychologists have demonstrated. Hoekema (1986, 77–78) expresses this view as follows: "Men and women cannot attain to true humanity in isolation. . . . It is only through contacts with others that we come to know who we are and what our strengths and weaknesses are . . . that we can fully develop our potentialities." He also indicates that men need fellowship with other men, and women need the companionship of other women.

Some churches teach that Eve was created merely to bear children. The command to "be fruitful and multiply, and replenish the earth" (Gen. 1:28) came after the creation, indicating that creation was a secondary purpose of marriage rather than its primary one. Children are a heritage of the Lord and are included in the plans of most couples when they marry. It is a misunderstanding of the Scriptures and of the sexual nature of man to insist that the only legitimate reason for the sexual union of husband and wife is to beget children. God endowed men and women with complementary sexual drives, and these are gratified in the sexual relationship in which a couple most fully express their love for one another.

In this regard, Hurley (1981, 32) states, "God shaped a woman from the flesh of Adam. . . . The loving companionship of the two would issue, in due course, in the birth of children, and mankind would become a community serving God through their love and service of Him and of one another."

Jewett (1975, 49) observes, "The procreative function . . . is only one among many aspects of a complex, creative, dynamic, all-pervasive human fellowship . . . which expresses itself in and through a variety of specific relationships to the benefit of both the individual and society as a whole." Companionship and fellowship constitute the core of the marriage relationship as instituted by God. Children bring great happiness to a home, but the fellowship of husband and wife may last for decades after the nest is empty. Thus, the relationship, not the children, is central.

Saint Augustine remarked that God did not take a bone from Adam's head from which to create Eve that she might be above him, nor a bone from his foot that she might be beneath him, but from his side that she might be beside him. Another has said that she was taken out of his side to be equal with him, under his arm to be protected, and near his heart to be loved. This was a blissful state with Adam and Eve caring for the garden as God had instructed them.

After the creation of Eve, Genesis states that the Lord "brought her to the man." Someone has pointed out that God the Father had the privilege of giving away the first bride. Swindoll (1980, 20) observes, "I am especially impressed with the fact that God *personally* brought that particular person to Adam. What a thought." He points out that each person's mate is prepared by God himself. Each spouse has a different personality and many other differences but God designed these to "add variety and color" to the marriage.

Mason (1985, 24–29) elaborates upon this first meeting of Adam and Eve. He immediately recognized her as his companion, as his completion, for he called her "woman, for she was taken out of man." After six thousand years of fallen humanity, women are still praised by men for their beauty and grace. How inconceivable must have been the beauty and grace of Eve, the flower of the female race.

> *How inconceivable must have been the beauty and grace of Eve, the flower of the female race.*

The reaction of Adam to this lovely woman can only be imagined. In today's terms, he probably exclaimed, "Wow!" Mason reflects that there is something of this awe, this wonder seen in marriage today. A man and woman in holy matrimony are given the opportunity to see each other as they have never seen or will ever see any person. He comments (1985, 27) that "we long to stand in awe of one another. . . . We long for our whole body to tingle with the thrill of knowing that this one fascinating being . . . has been created especially for us and given to us unreservedly for our help, comfort and joy."

Mason emphasizes the necessity for couples to return to their first encounter and remember that it was their difference as male and female that drew them together in the will of God. He states, "marriage, as simply as it can be defined, is the contemplation of the love of God in and through the form of another human being" (1985, 30).

The Most Important Verses

Genesis 2:24–25 are the two most important verses concerning marriage in the Bible. It is a Holy Spirit-inspired commentary on the creation added by Moses, the human author of Genesis. Miles (1983, 22) concludes, "this passage is the heart, the touchstone, of God's intended purpose for a husband and a wife in their marriage relationship." They are so significant that the Holy Spirit records them three times in the New Testament. In Matthew 19:5 and Mark 10:7, Jesus repeated these words to affirm the permanence of the marriage tie

37

when answering the Pharisees' question concerning divorce. In Ephesians 5:31 Paul quotes these verses again in his great treatise on how husbands are to love their wives. Such a repetition emphasizes the importance of the truths contained in these verses.

Trobisch (1987, 129) indicates that Genesis 2:24 lists the three elements necessary for a truly biblical marriage: there must be a "leaving," a "cleaving," and a fusion into "one flesh." Unless all three of these take place, there is no true marriage between the people involved. Consequently, two young people who engage in premarital sex are not married. Even though physically there is a "one-flesh" union, there is no "leaving" and no "cleaving." They are guilty of what the Bible calls fornication, the sin of a sexual union between two unmarried persons.

> *Genesis 2:24 lists the three elements necessary for a truly biblical marriage: there must be a "leaving," a "cleaving," and a fusion into "one flesh."*

The Wheats (1981, 21) make the interesting observation that God first separated Eve from Adam, but in this verse they are asked to come together again. They then list three commands. "First, when we marry, we should stop being dependent on our parents or our in-laws. . . . Second, the man is the one responsible for holding the marriage together by "cleaving" to his wife. Cleaving in this sense means to be welded inseparably. . . . Third, we are commanded to be joined together in sexual union, to be 'one flesh.'" Other Bible scholars use other terms to describe the realities of verses 24 and 25. Swindoll (1980, 21–35) finds the verses representing "severance," "permanence," "unity," and "intimacy." He relates that in his marriage counseling, he found one or more of these principles violated in most cases.

The Principle of Leaving

"Leaving" or "severance" requires the young couple to establish a new home separate from their parents—sometimes the farther away the better. They are a new family and need to learn to live independently. This does not mean they are to sever all ties with the parents; that would be foolish. It does imply that they are to look to each other and to God for wisdom in decision making. Parental input may be sought on occasion, but the issue under consideration must be decided by the couple.

In like manner, the couple must find their source of emotional support in each other. Love and respect for parents are still a part of the command "to honor they father and mother." However, there is a new love for one another that needs to be nourished and matured into a conjugal love if it is to last a lifetime.

Conversely, parents must relinquish control of the newlyweds. Swindoll (1981, 29) indicates that during a wedding ceremony, he asks the parents to have a part in which they publicly release "their parental authority and entrust their offspring to the new home beginning that day." Another suggested this declaration should be taken a step further and that parents should write out vows publicly stating they relinquish control of the bride and groom. The failure of parents to make this separation creates great difficulty and heartache for many couples.

The public act of "leaving" informs society that two young people are beginning a new home. Most cultures of the world have some form of wedding ceremony legitimizing the new union. Marriage of a couple not only concerns themselves but affects the group at large. Legal or cultural requirements must be met. In America, the children may become a burden to taxpayers when a divorce occurs. All communities, primitive or advanced, exercise some control over inheritances. Thus, a public "leaving" has many consequences.

Why does it say that only the husband is to "leave father and mother"? One suggested answer is that when Moses wrote Genesis, it was already the custom for the bride to leave her home to go with her husband. When the servant of Abraham found Rebekah as a bride for Isaac, he took her to Isaac's home (Gen. 24:1–66).

When one reads of cultures where either spouse goes to live in the family of the other and the problems associated with such a lifestyle, the value of "leaving" is evident. Establishing a nuclear family separate from the parents gives the newlyweds opportunities to develop a healthy and happy relationship, one that would be impossible in a multifamily setting.

However, in a highly mobile society in a large country such as the United States, the young family can become too isolated from the families of orientation. In times of illness or accidents, the parental families are too distant to help. When the young wife faces childbirth, she desires her mother to be with her, but oftentimes the distance and expense are too great.

This imposes great hardship on the young couple in an urban setting where secondary social relationships prevail. In such situations it is difficult to find someone to assist the new mother and baby. In view of this, some states have established laws, and the federal government has debated laws, that require employers to grant a leave of absence to employees for a period of time to care for ill family members. The Family and Medical Leave Act was passed by Congress and signed by President Bill Clinton in 1993. The act provides up to twelve weeks of unpaid leave.

The Cleaving Principle

Today the discussion of "cleaving" would take place before the "leaving." However, at the time when Moses wrote, arranged marriages were the practice. The parents arranged a marriage for two young people, they began their marriage, and then the "cleaving" began. American young people find it strange that a couple can come together with little or no prior knowledge of each other and learn to love one another in a romantic sense. We read that when Rebekah was brought to Isaac, "she became his wife and he loved her" (Gen. 24:67).

Whereas the leaving is a public act, the cleaving is a private one. It is an act of commitment. The word *cleave* means to join together, to glue together, to weld together. Morris (1981, 98) observes that the same word is used in Job 19:20, "My bone cleaveth to my skin and to my flesh. . . ." The New Testament uses the word *join*. Jesus replied to the Pharisees, "Wherefore what God has joined together, let not man separate" (Matt. 19:6). The individuals who take the oath of marriage are joined by God into an indissoluble union.

The text does not use the word *love*, a word so frequently used in American culture. The marital union requires a commitment far more lasting than the romantic love on which most marriages are based. This love is a physical love, a love from afar that desires physical union. Once that is achieved, the romantic love ceases unless it is nurtured and helped to grow into a mature love that also emphasizes care and companionship. Cleaving requires an act of the will to devote one's entire life to the spouse for a lifetime of sharing.

> *Cleaving requires an act of the will to devote one's entire life to the spouse for a lifetime of sharing.*

The word *commitment* might be substituted for love in this sense. A man and woman commit their entire future to each other with a determination that with God's help they will conquer whatever life offers. It is the commitment of the traditional marriage vows that they take each "for better, for worse, for richer, for poorer, and in sickness and in health . . . till death do us part." By the divorce rate today, one can conclude that many couples are changing the latter phrase to "till divorce do us part."

Swindoll (1980, 32) states that he and his wife, Cynthia, used to take the permanence of their commitment for granted. To avoid this, they now "periodically, through the year (especially on New Year's Day, our anniversary, and each other's birthday) affirm our commitment, eyeball to eyeball, stating our love and devotion to each other. . . . We do not consider separation an option, no matter how hot the disagreement. . . ."

> *God not only endowed Adam and Eve with their sexuality as male and female, but also gave them a sexual nature that desired fulfillment with each other.*

In the New Testament, where the husband is exhorted to love his wife, the Greek term is *agape*. This is the kind of love that God has for lost sinners. It is a sacrificial love. It receives satisfaction by giving rather than by receiving. It is beautifully described by Paul in 1 Corinthians 13. This is the kind of love exhibited in the commitment known as "cleaving." One writer (Murphey 1984, 30) states that "agape cradles meaning and purpose to life, giving to married living a strong, deep force of loyalty, honesty, honor, and steadfastness. It affords deep spiritual companionship of unique mystery and strength, for agape love is the foundation of marriage."

This *agape* love is given by the Holy Spirit— "the fruit of the Spirit is love" (Gal. 5:22). Adam and Eve did not have this power of the Holy Spirit, but believers today are exhorted to "be filled with the Spirit" (Eph. 5:17). As the Holy Spirit fills the hearts, then spouses can love each other with the love that longs to give rather than receive. This kind of love is the great need in Christian marriages today. It is the love that newlyweds should strive for in their relationship.

The One-Flesh Principle

The "leaving" and the "cleaving" result in two becoming one flesh. In Genesis 1:28 God had commanded his newly created couple to "be fruitful and multiply." This required the sexual union of Adam and Eve. God not only endowed them with their sexuality as male and female, but also gave them a sexual nature that desired fulfillment with each other. In their uniting they became "one flesh."

One result of the "one-flesh" union is the conception and birth of children. Carmody and Tully (1984, 52) comment, "Fitted together sexually, the partners are one flesh literally. And from this literal integration come children, a new sort of single flesh. The pink flesh of Baby Jones is an individual, a unified whole, that represents the union of Mother and Father Jones." For those couples fortunate enough to conceive children, this pleasure is exceeded only by the satisfaction received from the frequent expression of their mutual love in the "one-flesh" relationship.

The act of intercourse joins the body, soul, and spirit into one. Swindoll (1980, 32) comments, "The whole idea of mutual acceptance, giving, listening, forgiving, belonging, and direction was implied. It is two individuals willingly blending into each other's lives, desiring to share with and thereby complete the other."

In Hebrew the word that represents this blending of selves that occurs in sexual intercourse is translated as "know." Genesis 4:1 reads, "And Adam knew Eve his wife; and she conceived, and bore Cain, and said, I have gotten a man from the Lord." According to Alcorn (1985, 178) this Hebrew word for "know," *yadah*, "speaks of an intimacy wherein two parties see each other as they truly are. The concept is . . . a personal, intimate, and experiential knowledge of another."

In reference to this truth, it is important to recognize that the husband and wife are the only creatures that mate face to face. Trobisch (1987, 45), in his discussion of the word *know*, observes that it means "to know someone by name." In Genesis 4:1, "Adam knew Eve, *his* wife." You can never know what *the* woman or *a* woman is like; you can only know *your* wife. That means that you cannot know a woman except in marriage, in the atmosphere of faithfulness, where the sex act is one of the expressions of love."

In premarital sex it is impossible to really "know" the person with whom sex takes place. The loss of virginity should take place within the confines of marriage, on the wedding night, so that the couple can truly learn to "know" each other in the scriptural sense. Hazelip (1985, 88) indicates, "In physical intimacy we communicate something of ourselves to another person that no words can express—we truly 'know' our partner. . . . Only when one experiences the total joy of physical intimacy in this atmosphere of trust will he or she understand that true sexual fulfillment can never be found outside of marriage."

Thus, the phrase "they shall be one flesh" is evidence that sex is God-given and becomes sinful only when it is misused and perverted. God intends for husband and wife to express their love through the sexual relationship. This is expressly stated in 1 Corinthians 7:3–5: "Let the husband render unto the wife due benevolence; and likewise also the wife unto the husband. The wife hath not power of her own body, but the husband; and likewise also the husband hath not power of his own body, but the wife. Defraud ye not one the other, except it be with consent for a time, that ye may give yourselves to fasting and prayer; and come together again, that Satan tempt you not for your incontinency." Husbands or wives can receive legitimate sexual satisfaction only from each other, and the exhortation here is to be careful to meet each other's needs unless there is mutual consent to abstain in order to achieve some spiritual goal.

The "one-flesh" principle also indicates the monogamous nature of marriage. It is true that in other Old Testament passages there is evidence of concubinage, but such was not the case in the beginning. The highest, purest, and happiest form of marriage has always been that which God instituted—the union of one man and one woman for life. When a Christian couple take vows to live with each other "till death do us part," they affirm the truth of Genesis 2:24.

> *The highest, purest, and happiest form of marriage has always been that which God instituted—the union of one man and one woman for life.*

The Leadership Principle

Genesis 2:25 states, "the man and his wife were both naked, and they felt no shame." They lived and labored in the garden unhampered by any kind of covering. They enjoyed the beauty of each other's bodies (and how beautiful they must have been in their sinless state). They relished their oneness in this new relationship. It is difficult to comprehend the bliss of a companionship that knew no disharmony or disquietude. Everything they did was in perfect accord. Nothing was hidden from the other.

Swindoll (1980, 33–34), in his exposition of this text, writes, "The Hebrew term translated 'naked' suggests the idea 'laid bare.' . . . When the verse adds that Adam and Eve 'were not ashamed . . .' the idea is reciprocal—they weren't ashamed 'before or with one another.' . . . The picture is they had no hidden areas, no hang-ups, no embarrassments, no fears. There was total transparency. . . ."

Unfortunately for them and for believers today, the fall into sin changed this wonderful situation. When Adam and Eve sinned, they knew they were naked and attempted to cover themselves with fig leaves. Graciously God offered the first blood sacrifice and covered them with skins of animals.

As a result of sin, it is difficult for husbands and wives to be figuratively naked and open with one another. Physical nakedness in the bedroom is accepted, but to lay bare the thoughts and intents of the soul is difficult for most people. Yet the marriage relationship gives the opportunity for two individuals to "know" one another, to be transparent, to be vulnerable to each other.

> ## Sin had entered the human race and now leadership was necessary. God chose to invest the husband with the leadership role.

David and Vera Mace (1985, 45) make the statement that "marriage . . . is a terrifying closeness, because it means that married people surrender their right to a completely private life of their own. . . . Marriage means the invasion of our privacy, the giving up of our pretenses. But the sense of belonging to one another brings rich and satisfying compensations. To achieve this intimacy should be a high priority in every marriage relationship."

The Bible does not indicate how long the blissful union of Adam and Eve lasted before Eve succumbed to the temptation of Satan. Adam also disobeyed God and judgments were pronounced that changed the relationship of husband and wife. The curse God placed upon Eve was threefold: she was to experience pain in childbirth, her desire was to be to her husband, and he was to rule over her. Hoekema (1986, 136) explains that "'desire' here probably means the wife's longing for sexual fellowship with her husband. . . . The word translated 'will rule' (mashal) is also used to describe the governing authority of a monarch. Because of the fall into sin, the harmonious relationship between husband and wife has become distorted."

The original relationship in which Eve shared an egalitarian position of face to face or side by side to Adam was changed. Sin had entered the human race and now leadership was necessary. God chose to invest the husband with the leadership role. Because of sin, this leadership principle is needed wherever people meet in groups, or chaos is the result.

God also pronounced judgment upon Adam. Before the fall, childbirth and labor were painless, but now both Adam and Eve are to endure the pain resulting from their sin. Families today face the same painful experiences in childbearing and struggling to provide for their existence.

Mosaic Law and the Family

Additional evidence from the Old Testament for the divine origin of marriage is found in the law given by Moses to the children of Israel. God had a plan and a purpose in his choice of Israel, and stable family life was a necessity for their fulfillment. After giving the "great commandment" (Deut. 6:4–5), faithful Israelites are exhorted to teach all the commandments "diligently unto their children."

Three of the Ten Commandments have direct reference to the family. The fifth, "Honor thy father and thy mother; that thy days may be long upon the land which the Lord thy God giveth thee" (Exod. 20:12), was accompanied by severe sanctions on those who disobeyed (Exod. 21:17; Deut. 21:18–20). Dale (n.d., 133) in his treatise, *The Ten Commandments*, explains the necessity of such sanctions: "If parental authority came to be generally disregarded, the whole structure of society would be dissolved. The discharge of filial duty was the condition of the permanence of national existence."

As sexual sins are disruptive to family life, two of the commandments are prohibitions against such sins: the seventh, "Thou shalt not commit adultery," and part of the tenth, "Thou shalt not covet thy neighbor's wife" (Exod. 20:14–17). Kahn (1964, 86) observes, "The moral context of sex was marriage, *holy* matrimony. . . . the purpose of the commandment against adultery and all other irresponsible sexual behavior was to preserve and protect that context, to outlaw all attitudes and all behavior which would degrade, threaten, or destroy marriage, the home, the family. It was a simple direct code: purity before marriage, fidelity after it, for both men and women."

Song of Solomon

There are several appealing love stories in the Old Testament: Isaac and Rebekah, Jacob and Rachel, Ruth and Boaz. None compares with the love of Solomon for his bride, the Shulamite maiden. Although Solomon had hundreds of wives and concubines, he had a special love for her that he recorded for us.

In affirming the fact that God intends for the marriage relationship to be a most pleasurable experience, the Penners (1981, 45) write, "The Bible endorses the concept of sexual pleasure and assumes a healthy passion. Read the Song of Solomon: it contains some of the most beautiful and erotic poetry ever written. . . . The Song of Solomon is loaded with erotic messages of two lovers enjoying each other's bodies fully." The book is a series of "love poems" describing true love between a bride and groom. Phipps (1975, 44–45) uses the meanings of two Hebrew words to prove this view. His conclusion is, "The Song of Songs is about intimate love. . . . That the Song focuses on the betrothed or married couple is made explicit by the term *kallah*, which means 'spouse' and is used frequently in reference to the female partner (4:8 to 5:1, cp. Gen. 11:31, 38:11)."

The Song describes the bliss of love in terms that are offensive to some readers. In reference to this, Phipps (1975, 65) comments that "only those who come to the Song with the preconceived idea that the portrayal of lovemaking is smutty, find the book repugnant. To render a New Testament proverb negatively: 'To the impure, all things are impure.'" The inclusion of the Song of Solomon in the canon of sacred Scriptures (under the guidance of the Holy Spirit) is God's seal of approval upon its contents. "It glorifies a bond that is sweeter than honey, and stronger than a lion. The affirmation that 'love is as strong as death' (Chap. 8:6) is excelled only by the New Testament proclamation that love is stronger than death" (Phipps 1975, 65).

> *The inclusion of the Song of Solomon in the canon of sacred Scriptures (under the guidance of the Holy Spirit) is God's seal of approval upon its contents.*

The book is difficult to understand since the love poems are not in chronological order. However, the reader who follows an outline such as found in the New International Version or the New Scofield Reference Bible will be highly rewarded.

Christ and Marriage

Jesus did not give a discourse on marriage. There is the Sermon on the Mount and Olivet Discourse, but nothing corresponding to these in reference to the family. It is necessary to look at his life and teachings to determine his attitude.

Jesus lived a life of celibacy. This was part of his self-denial, for he could have taken a wife and remained sinless. He had instituted marriage in the garden and "marriage is honorable in all" (Heb. 13:4), so nothing prohibited him from taking a wife. However, he did tell the disciples in Matthew 19:12 that there were those "who made themselves eunuchs for the kingdom of heaven's sake." In order to carry out the ministry that the will of God demanded, he chose to live a single life. He was free to move about preaching and healing without the care of a family. He also was able to live a life of poverty so that he could identify with the poorest of the poor in their needs (Heb. 2:17–18).

The Lord Jesus performed his first miracle at the wedding in Cana of Galilee. He used the marriage ceremony as illustrations of truth in the parable of the marriage feast in Matthew 22:1–14, and the story of the ten virgins in Matthew 25:1–13. In Matthew 5:27–32, "Jesus strongly approved of monogamy, and condemned even the thought of adultery" (Garrett 1982, 40).

> ## The culture surrounding the believer may deny or belittle the biblical basis of marriage, but the truths of the Scriptures have stood the test of time.

In Matthew 19:1–12 (Mark 10:1–12; Luke 16:18) Jesus amplifies what he had stated in the Sermon on the Mount (Matt. 5:27–28, 32) concerning adultery and divorce. He also reaffirmed the Genesis account of the institution of marriage by quoting Genesis 2:24–25 and adding the prohibition, "What, therefore God hath joined together, let not man put asunder" (Matt. 19:6). He also taught that marriage is for this life alone: "For when they shall rise from the dead, they neither marry, nor are given in marriage, but are as the angels of heaven" (Mark 12:25).

Christ's attitude toward women is seen in his reception of the gifts of certain women who "ministered to him of their substance" (Luke 8:3). When he encountered fallen women such as the woman at the well (John 4) and the woman taken in adultery (John 8), he treated them with dignity, love, and forgiveness. While enduring the suffering of the cross, he was concerned about the future needs of his mother and asked the apostle John to care for her.

It is possible that the Lord Jesus had the families of Mary and Joseph, and of Mary, Martha, and Lazarus in mind when he chose to compare the relationship of the believer to God as son to father. In his humanity, he had experienced the love of Joseph as an earthly father. In his deity, he enjoyed a relationship with God as his heavenly Father. So in the Sermon on the Mount in Matthew 6, he instructs his followers to pray to "our Father, who art in heaven." He then makes eleven other references to the Father in the same chapter. In John 14:1–6 he informs the disciples that the Father's house is their final destination. The truth of the family of God is one of the most precious to instructed believers.

The Apostle Paul and Marriage

There is a question as to whether the apostle Paul ever married, but it is clear from his epistles that he commended marriage. In several passages he gives explicit directions to husbands, wives, and children (Eph. 5; Col. 3; and 1 Cor. 7, 11). Paul thought so highly of the marriage relationship that he compares the union of husband and wife to that of the believer and Christ. His teachings on the roles of husbands and wives are explained in the chapter on roles in Christian marriage. His clear presentation of the sexual relationship in marriage (1 Cor. 7) is examined in the chapter on intimacy in marriage.

The culture surrounding the believer may deny or belittle the biblical basis of marriage, but the truths of the Scriptures have stood the test of time. Whenever two Christian young people take their stand on the principles of God's Word and diligently apply them in their daily living, they find fulfillment and satisfaction that the world cannot experience.

First John 4:4 states, "Ye are of God, little children, and have overcome them: because greater is he that is in you, than he that is in the world." In the light of such a promise, the Christian couple is assured of victory in spite of the pressures of the secular humanist society that surrounds them.

Study Questions

1. What reasons can you give for the break-up of Christian marriages?
2. Why do godly men and women interpret the same biblical texts differently?
3. Discuss the phrase "made in the image of God."
4. What implications for the roles of men and women are contained in the phrase "helpmeet fit for him"?
5. How did the fall of man change family relationships?
6. Which is your favorite Old Testament love story? Why?
7. Which verses in the Song of Solomon support the thesis that it is a collection of lyrics illustrating the passion of married love?
8. Give several reasons why you think Jesus chose to remain unmarried.
9. List several ways in which the love between husband and wife correspond to the love of Christ for his bride, the church.
10. Discuss the relationship of biblical principles to success in Christian marriage.

Suggested Readings

Alcorn, R. 1985. *Christians in the wake of the sexual revolution*. Portland, Ore.: Multnomah. Written to give Christians a moral foundation for right thinking about sex. A good chapter on "Sex: God's gift to humanity."

Anderson, R. S., and D. B. Guernsey. 1985. *On being family: A social theology of the family*. Grand Rapids: Eerdmans. The subtitle is a contradiction in terms since "theology" literally means the study of God. The authors discuss the family from the respective views of their backgrounds as sociologist and theologian. They use the covenant theory as a basis for their expositions.

Gangel, K., and E. Gangel. 1987. *Building a Christian family*. Chicago: Moody. This book stresses the necessity of a good biblical foundation for the home. Companionship is listed as the first priority in a marriage.

Hoekema, A. A. 1986. *Created in God's image*. Grand Rapids: Eerdmans. A scholarly treatise on the doctrine of man. Hoekema necessarily treats of the creation of man in Genesis 1 and 2.

Kang, C. H., and E. R. Nelson. 1979. *The discovery of Genesis*. St. Louis: Concordia. A most interesting study that demonstrates how "the truths of Genesis were found hidden in the Chinese languages." The characters are dissected and corroborate the Genesis account of creation.

Leonard, J. H., Jr., and R. P. Olson. 1990. *Ministry with families in flux: The church and changing patterns of life*. Louisville: Westminster/John Knox. Although the writers reject the biblical family as the norm, they do offer suggestions as to how the church can minister to alternate family lifestyles.

Linzer, N. 1984. *The Jewish family*. New York: Human Sciences. The author, a professor in a Jewish university, indicates that three models of family life are found among Jews today: authoritarian, egalitarian, and mediating. The mediating family combines features of the other two. The book also has an interesting chapter on Holocaust-survivor families.

Money, R. 1984. *Building stronger families*. Wheaton: Victor. The writer takes six qualities that characterize strong families and supplies scriptural support for each one. Strong families express appreciation, communicate well, spend time together, have a commitment to family, have strong religious values, and have ability to deal with crisis in a positive manner.

Swindoll, C. R. 1980. *Strike the original match*. Portland, Ore.: Multnomah. A collection of sermons designed to encourage and enrich marriages. It has an excellent treatment of Genesis 2:24–25.

Trobisch, W. 1987. *The complete works of Walter Trobisch*. Downer's Grove, Ill.: InterVarsity. A reprint of the collected works of a Swiss missionary who taught Christian concepts of the family to African congregations. He and his writings were well received in both Europe and America. He was one of the first to use the "leaving, cleaving, one-flesh" principles.

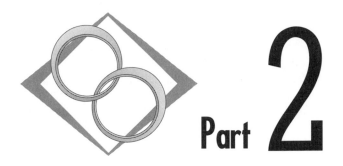

Part 2

Factors in Successful Marriage

Cultural Influences

That ye might walk worthy of the Lord unto all pleasing . . .

—Colossians 1:10

The guests at a wedding reception usually admire first the beauty and then the taste of the bridal cake. Pictures are taken as the bride and groom make the first cut. No one would be foolish enough to say that such a beautiful creation just "happened." They know that the necessary ingredients are blended in the correct proportions and then baked. After this, the cake is artfully decorated by skillful hands before the final product is ready for display. Yet many times the couple who cuts the wedding cake has not given as much thought to what is required to create a lovely marriage as the baker has given to producing the cake. Certain prerequisites are necessary if a couple expects to achieve success in their marriage. The spiritual, physical, and emotional elements of each partner must be blended together so that the "two become one" in Christ (Mason 1985, 71).

Four Criteria of Success

Successful marriage in our culture is usually gauged by the amount of happiness that the relationship brings to the individual partners. Marriage for any reason other than to bring happiness is frowned upon by most Americans. If a great amount of happiness ensues, then the marriage is termed successful. On the other hand, if unhappiness results from the union, then the marriage is judged a failure, and at least one partner will usually seek a divorce.

Happiness, according to *Webster's Dictionary,* is a difficult term to define since it refers to a subjective emotional state, "a feeling of great pleasure, contentment." An event or an experience that brings pleasure to one partner may be interpreted differently by the other; hence, happiness at best is a relative term. However we define it in marriage, there are those pleasant experiences, cumulative in nature, that evoke a positive emotional response called happiness, so that we term the relationship a happy one. When unpleasant experiences evoking a negative emotional response accumulate, then unhappiness results and the relationship is a failure. This is true not only in marital unions, but in any other human relationship, such as those of student-teacher, employee-employer, or pastor-parishioner.

> *Marriage for any reason other than to bring happiness is frowned upon by most Americans.*

In earlier days, marriage did not demand as much emotional satisfaction from the partners, as there were other criteria by which to judge the success of the relationship (Leonard 1990, 4). The wife was concerned about the ability of the husband to provide for the family, and if he succeeded well in this role, his failure to provide personal happiness was overlooked. The husband wanted a wife who would be a good housekeeper and a good mother to rear his children. If she succeeded in these areas, the marriage was still deemed a success. Changes in the family (see chap. 1) have altered these basic roles of husband and wife. The wife can now be a breadwinner and the husband can hire a babysitter or housekeeper.

These changes, plus the cultural emphasis on romantic love, mean that if happiness is lost, the marriage is a failure and the couple will divorce. Swindoll (1980, 30) writes, "'Till death do us part' is, unfortunately, a mere verbal formality. . . . The whole concept of establishing a permanent bond between husband and wife is quickly becoming a foreign thought." Such easy abrogation of marriage

vows is contrary to the Bible, yet Christian young people are succumbing to this secular mentality. It is natural that they should expect happiness from marriage and want to experience it, but it does not follow that because they encounter periods of strain and unhappiness, they are morally free to break the relationship. Most marriages face these unpleasant periods, and it is then that the resources of God's Word, prayer, and godly counseling should be utilized.

Any problem in a Christian marriage can be solved if the couple will sincerely seek the help of God. Yates (1986, 26) asserts, "With God's help you can rebuild your marriage. But it will take time, honesty, and the help of caring Christian friends. God is not looking for the perfect marriage; he is much more concerned about the person who knows he or she has failed but is seeking His help. He can bring about true progress in such situations." Many times the difficulties arise because the couple has not really considered what it takes to make a successful marriage, and does not realize that a real effort must be made to blend these ingredients into a harmonious relationship. When a Christian marriage does fail, it is usually because one or both partners are so backslidden they do not respond to the Holy Spirit's workings.

In addition to happiness and a permanent union, a third criterion of success in a Christian marriage may be how well the couple performs the will of God for their relationship. This again is a subjective measurement that each couple must make. From God's view marriage is not successful simply because a couple enjoys a measure of happiness. God judges how well they complete the life plan he reveals to them. Ephesians 2:10 reads, "For we are his workmanship, created in Christ Jesus unto good works, which God hath before ordained [planned] that we should walk in them." This does not mean that all are to engage in full-time Christian service, but to find the plan of God and to do the will of God should be the supreme desire of every couple who follow Christ. He is to be head of the home, and at his judgment seat an accounting will be made by every husband and wife in relation to his will.

In recent years a fourth criterion for successful marriage has been suggested. Marriage is seen as the vehicle by which each spouse enables and encourages the other to grow and develop to his or her fullest potential. Besson (1985, iv) purposes "to help couples find their own uniqueness and to encourage them to grow together, each at his or her own pace, yet *always* growing. . . . They will share love, joy, commitment, intimacy and the ultimate result will be a happy marriage. . . . Their lives will become entwined as do the roots of two great trees growing side by side."

However, as a couple seek the plan of God for their lives, they often discover that his plan includes growth and stimulation in other areas, such as the intellectual. For some this may mean more formal education in a college or a university. For others, it may mean attending evening classes of a local Bible institute. The growth of community colleges and adult education classes provide many opportunities for learning in a wide diversity of subjects at very little cost. Correspondence courses and educational television classes are available for those who cannot leave home. Public libraries have a wealth of information available for those who like to read. The local newspaper and a weekly news magazine may help to keep a couple informed on current events.

A Christian couple active in a local church and in the community has many opportunities for social development. Sometimes one partner is more outgoing or has more leadership qualities than the other. In this situation the less favored person can grow through the emotional support given to the more active spouse. The latter must guard against becoming so involved that he or she neglects to provide adequate opportunities to participate in social events with the mate.

Christian marriage, when rightly perceived, offers the greatest potential for growth and fulfillment. A husband who loves his wife as Christ loves the church will encourage that wife to become all that the will of God desires for her. As the couple submits to the lordship of Christ in their lives, they can experience the richness of his grace in every area of their relationship.

> **A husband who loves his wife as Christ loves the church will encourage that wife to become all that the will of God desires for her.**

Necessity of the New Birth

Certain requirements must be met if the couple is to have a successful Christian marriage. The first of these is that both individuals must be born again. They must experience the new birth described in John 3:5, 7: "Jesus answered and said unto him [Nicodemus], Verily, verily, I say unto thee, except a man be born again, he cannot see the kingdom of God. . . . Marvel not that I said unto you, 'Ye must be born again.'" Collins (1982, 28) explains, "the new birth comes when we yield ourselves completely to Christ and trust Him to forgive our sins and guide our actions. The new birth is an inner spiritual transformation which comes when Christ enters our lives. We don't earn this new status by our efforts or by good works; it is a gift from God (Eph. 2:8–9)."

Both partners may be religious and attend church regularly and theirs may be called a Christian marriage, but it cannot be that in reality if they are not born again. This type of relationship will be more successful than that of a nonchurch-going couple, but they will miss the joy and blessing that comes only from knowing the Lord Jesus Christ as personal Savior.

Personal relationship to Christ is merely the beginning for the couple who desires the most happiness in marriage. Both should also be consecrated to God. This means each individual surrenders himself to God and sincerely

51

seeks to do the will of God in the marriage relationship. A disparity in the degree of submission to God can cause great unhappiness. Consider the case of Joe and Jane:

> Joe (twenty-five) and Jane (twenty-four) met in the local church in the youth meeting. They both came from nominal Christian homes, had been baptized as teenagers, and regularly attended church. However, Jane seemed more inclined toward spiritual things than did Joe. He had agreed they would have a Christian home, but a few months after the marriage, he became lax in attending church services and did not wish to lead in family devotions. At the same time, Jane was faithful in hearing the Word preached, received it with faith, and grew in grace and knowledge of the Lord Jesus. The spiritual gulf widened between them until it affected other areas of the relationship.

It is easy to see that although both were saved, the unhappiness in this home occurred because Jane did not wait for a mate who had the same degree of consecration that marked her life. The experience of Joe and Jane also illustrates the necessity of each spouse striving to maintain a personal relationship with the Lord Jesus through daily prayer and Bible study.

Importance of Personality Compatibility

Good basic character and personality certainly are necessary. All saved and consecrated young people do not have the same characteristics. It is important to remember that personalities can be changed, but it does take a great amount of self-effort to effect any desired change. By the time a person reaches marriage age, the personality and its patterns are nearly fixed.

This fact is corroborated by the types of personalities that Field (1986, 26–28), a marriage and family therapist, encountered in his practice. He discovered, as did other therapists, that persons in marriages fit seven different personality categories such as active-passive or helper-helpee. He asks and answers the question, "Does a marriage personality ever change? Not usually. Just as the personality of a child is developed between six months and

six years of age, the basic marriage personality is formed during the mutual accommodation stage (premarital through two years postmarital). . . . The basic personality . . . will usually not change dramatically, but the degree of marital health may fluctuate."

> # By the time a person reaches marriage age, the personality and its patterns are nearly fixed.

Any woman who marries a man with the idea that she will change undesirable traits after the ceremony is inviting disaster. If a person is not honest and trustworthy, the words of the marriage ritual will not change him. If a young woman is self-centered and vain during courtship, she will carry these traits into marriage. If a person is loose with the truth while dating, the same behavior can be expected later. The individual who is not concerned about his dress or is slovenly in his speech will probably remain the same person unless some miracle happens. The woman who is shy and afraid of her own voice will not become the life of the party simply because she marries. The young man who is careless in handling his money, or who exhibits instability by failure to hold a steady job, can be expected to behave the same way after the ceremony. It is important that a young person seek a mate with sound character and a complementary personality for the greatest fulfillment in marriage.

Since marriage does place such great demands upon the personalities involved, it is incumbent upon each Christian young person to have a well developed personality. Personality inventories are found at the end of several chapters to encourage the reader to assess the level of his or her development. Areas of weakness discovered through the use of these inventories can be strengthened through diligent effort and the wise use of spiritual resources.

The daily use of the Bible for personal development is stressed by Achtenmeier (1976, 25): "The Christian life is lived by conducting a daily and running dialogue with the Word of God, through which is mediated to us the power and working of Jesus Christ. We read the Word, or hear it preached, then apply it and find it so. Then we return and understand it better through that experience."

Influences of the Cultural Background

A common cultural background is another requirement for a successful Christian marriage. The challenge to partners in marriage is to harmonize the individual personalities so that the majority of emotional responses from their interaction are pleasurable. The honeymoon period (usually the first year) is a time when many of the adjustments are made. It is axiomatic that the fewer the differences in backgrounds, the fewer the adjustments in marriage. Conversely, the greater the differences, the more numerous the adjustments that will need to be made. Other things being equal, the differences to be resolved will be fewer and the marriage happier when backgrounds are nearly homogeneous.

Many elements constitute the cultural background. The area in which a person lives is usually indicative of his or her social class. Americans like to believe that the society is classless, but stratification studies, as well as common observation of social practices, demonstrate that there are many class levels. Each of these can be identified by similarities in dress, speech, lifestyle, and value patterns. When an individual marries up or down in the class system, it requires many changes to adjust to the new social level. The general rule is that the greater the distance that divides the individuals on the social scale, the more difficult the adjustments. Eshelman (1991, 288) observes, "Status endogamy [marriage within the group] in our own society and around the world, is a desirable social norm, particularly for higher-status parents in regard to their children. . . . Conditions supporting class endogamy are essential to preserve family lineage and status.

. . . Most marriages are class endogamous." Popular literature likes to dwell on the rich upper-class man marrying the poor woman. In real life this seldom occurs, and when it does the failure rate is very high.

> *Other things being equal, the differences to be resolved will be fewer and the marriage happier when backgrounds are nearly homogeneous.*

Most Christians are found in the middle or working class, and our churches and Christian schools and colleges often reflect such stratification. A young man and woman who meet at a Christian college are generally of the same socioeconomic level. However, there are exceptions: Christian young people from upper-middle-class homes often attend a Christian college, and with more opportunities of higher education open to lower-income groups, there is an increasing number of Christian young people from this group who enroll in Christian colleges. If young people are aware of these class differences and values, and have a knowledge of their pervasive influence on human behavior, they can marry across class lines and make the necessary compromises to achieve happiness. Meier (1988, 11) gives this advice, "To those who are not married yet, I would say, consider marrying someone with a background similar to your own. Research shows that marriages that skip more than one social class in a nine-class system usually do not last."

Necessity for Similar Education

The educational level of the couple should be similar, for any great disparity can create problems. A woman with a high-school education and a man with a college degree have different experiences, and there will be many parts of his life that she may not enter into because she has not attended college. It is rare for a woman with a college education to marry a man who has had only a high-school education. Lamanna and Riedmann (1988, 189) comment, "while partners may come from different economic backgrounds, for example, they have usually met in another homagamous group: college. College-educated women and men tend to marry each other; so do non-college-educated people."

> ## "College-educated women and men tend to marry each other; so do non-college-educated people."

When a woman marries a man with less education and happiness results, it is usually because the wife is careful to encourage her husband and not flaunt her educational superiority. One college student described such a relationship when he wrote about his parents' difference in education, "My father is a mechanic who graduated from high school. My mother not only has her bachelor's degree but also a master's degree in education. She is a principal of an elementary school. My parents get along very well. Father runs the garage and mother does the bookkeeping for him. A stranger observing their interaction would never know my mother has a master's degree."

One problem encountered on college and university campuses today is the intellectual gulf that occurs when couples marry at the end of the freshman or sophomore year, with the wife dropping out to help support the husband in his studies. Quite often this aid includes not only the bachelor's degree, but also a master's degree and a doctor's degree. Unless the young wife continues to read and keep informed in her husband's field, it is not too long before she is unable to communicate with him in his area of specialization. Propinquity puts him in contact with attractive single women who are in his classes and who speak his language. All to often triangular affairs develop, and the wife who worked to put her husband through college and graduate school is divorced when her husband desires to marry the woman with the college education. A mate who manifests an interest and understanding of the demands and pressures the other partner faces each day will strengthen the marital relationship.

Religion and the Choice of a Marriage Partner

Similarity of religious home life can contribute much to the happiness of a marriage. Eshelman (1991, 292) points out, "Religion is probably second only to race in the segregation of males and females into categories that are granted approval or disapproval with respect to marriage." Preferably, young persons should look for a mate within their own denomination. It is true that saved young people from different denominations have many common beliefs, but they also have some real denominational distinctives. A couple may agree on the new birth but hold widely varying views regarding such doctrines as baptism, church government, eternal security, or others. These difficulties are avoided if marriage is within the denomination. Again, marriage may take place across denominational lines, but individuals will have to work harder to make it a success.

Family Size and Compatibility of Marriage Partners

Ordinarily, a young person does not think of the size of the family from which he or his spouse came as having any connection with success or failure in marriage. Yet the number of siblings in a family has a definite effect upon the personality development of each child. The individual reared in a home where there are brothers and sisters has a different experience than the only child. He has had to learn to share his possessions and affections of his parents with his siblings. This should give him an advantage over the only child in interacting on a favorable basis with other people. However, an only child is often stereotyped as selfish and egotistical, which is not always true, as many are generous and humble in attitude.

The union of two young persons who have been reared as an only child in their respective families will necessitate some real adjustments. If they have lived in college dormitories, many of the rough edges of their personalities will have been rubbed off by the close personal interaction of dorm life. When an only child marries a person reared in a large family, the intermeshing of their personalities will be more difficult to achieve. Ideally, all children will have siblings to help prepare them for marriage, but this is not always possible. Much thought should be given to this aspect when choosing a mate.

Age at Time of Marriage

The age at which young people marry also has a bearing on the success of the marriage. The median age at first marriage for both men and women has been steadily rising. Unfortunately, many teens marry when they do not have maturity to handle responsibilities. Larson (Pocs 1989, 63) indicates that "the divorce rate for teenage marriages is three to four times higher than for later marriages. . . . Even among those which survive, couples married as teenagers report more tension and higher rates of marital dissatisfaction than those who marry later. . . ."

Dating at earlier ages, the stress of saving sex for marriage, increased affluence, and willingness of upper- and middle-class parents to subsidize early marriages are factors that contribute to the increase in teenage marriages. Yet, maturity is an important factor in a successful marriage.

Since the median age of first marriages for men is over two years older than the median age for women, it is apparent that men like to marry women younger than themselves. Eshelman (1991, 281) writes, "several explanations may include the husband's slower physiological maturity than that of his wife, the traditional responsibility of the husband to be the major breadwinner, which requires more time for preparation, the slight excess of males through the early twenties, or the mating gradient. . . ." This last term refers to the tendency of higher-status men to seek out lower-status women, and these women in turn seek out higher-status men. He also reflects that this same principle is operable when upper-class males can date freshman women, but male freshmen are mainly limited to dating freshman women. When they become seniors, the situation is reversed—the man can date a woman from any class, but the female is limited to junior-senior males.

> *Ideally, all children will have siblings to help prepare them for marriage, but this is not always possible.*

The important fact to remember is that young people need time to mature sufficiently to care for the heavy responsibilities of marriage. It has been said, "Our birthdays tell us how long we have been on the road, but they do not tell us how far we have come." There is no direct correlation between age and maturity. Some thirty-year-olds are immature, and some twenty-year-olds are mature. However, other things being equal, the fact remains that it takes time to mature. If a young couple is mature, if they have compatible personalities, and if they face marriage realistically, then age, class, or cultural differences between the bride and groom is not as important as a determinant to success in marriage.

Ethnic Background

The question of nationality as a background factor is not as important today as it was a couple of generations ago. For a native-born American to marry a first-generation Italian or German meant a meeting of two cultures. In some instances such a situation still prevails today: Puerto Rican citizens settling in our large cities, Cuban refugees arriving in Florida, Mexicans moving to the southwestern United States, and Asians settling on the West Coast. These immigrants all bring their native culture with them. Young men in military service overseas often marry nationals of the country where they serve and bring their brides home. Greater adjustments will be necessary in any case in which a native-born individual marries a person from another culture.

> *Greater adjustments will be necessary in any case in which a native-born individual marries a person from another culture.*

Racial Background

A similar situation exists in reference to interracial marriage. The white and African-American communities each constitute a subculture within our society.

Strong cultural influences oppose this type of union, and Christian young people contemplating such a marriage should give serious thought to all the factors involved. Several of the issues the couple must consider are mentioned by Kelly (1969, 270–73). These include the motivation for such a marriage, the reactions of family and friends to the union, the possibility of differences in social, ethical, educational, and religious values, the question of the permanence of the marriage, and finally, the opportunity for the couple's children to "have a normal and emotionally healthy childhood." He further states, "Life should be easier for the coming generation in interracial marriage. But this progress is slow and uneven. Prejudice dies hard and those of minority groupings still feel many harsh reminders of discrimination and injustice."

Most churches still exhibit and practice racial discrimination. The couple in an interracial marriage is not fully accepted by either culture, which means that they must find more of their satisfactions within the family unit. Thereby the relationship experiences more stress than does the homogeneous marriage. The children in such a family perhaps pay the greatest price because neighborhood children can be very cruel in their attitudes and actions toward those of mixed blood (Cretser and Leon 1984, 24). The problems of identification for the children is also a real one. The story of Paul illustrates this difficulty:

> Paul was the son of an interracial marriage. The family lived in a large Eastern city where such marriages were tolerated. The parents were born-again Christians and Paul was saved at an early age. After graduation from high school, he enrolled in a small Christian college. He was nominally accepted by the men, but women refused to date him. After being rebuffed several times, he went to the dean of students and cried bitterly, "Who am I?"

In spite of liberalized civil rights and fair-housing laws, there has been little increase in African-American-white marriages. Porterfield (Cretser and Leon 1984, 19) reports: "In 1960 there were 51,409 black-white marriages in existence; in 1970 . . . 64,789 . . . and by 1977 . . . 125,000." The indication is that even though there is less objection by society to these types of marriages, they will not greatly accelerate in number in the near future. The chances for success of such marriages is greater today, but such marriages still require the maximum effort by the spouses to make the marriages successful.

Communication

Successful marriages are always characterized by successful communication within the relationships. Hazelip (1985, 18) reports on one study of more than five hundred professionals who listed "communicating and listening" as the primary characteristic of happy families. Listening is important in communicating, but usually this is not a problem in courtship. People in love will give attention to what the other person is saying. There are so many new things to learn about each other that listening comes naturally.

In a restaurant it is easy to tell married couples from dating couples. A wife may be looking around to see what other women are wearing or ordering or the husband may appear distracted and not paying attention to his wife. A dating couple is usually attentive to each other and oblivious to their surroundings. Unfortunately, many times this ability to communicate is lost as the young couple progresses through the life cycles of their marriage.

Nevertheless, the importance of young people establishing frank and open communication early in the dating relationship cannot be overemphasized. If a person is unable to talk about certain subjects to the dating partner after the relationship becomes serious, it is evident that a problem exists. If it cannot be resolved, then the person ought to break the relationship and look for another partner with whom he can freely communicate. Some people are by nature or by socialization more reticent than others in the initial stages of a courtship, but as it progresses they ought to be able to express their feelings freely on a wide variety of subjects.

It is necessary for the couple contemplating marriage to discuss and come to agreement on several matters before the wedding. They need a clear understanding as to their role concepts, and what each expects of the other after the ceremony. The use and control of money can be determined in order to avoid the conflicts experienced by so many couples in this area. The number, spacing, and discipline of children merits serious discussion. Young people must also discuss their views concerning the use of leisure time. Married couples today have much more free time, and they need to know how they are going to spend it.

The relationship of the couple to the parental families needs to be explored. If there are problems, they must be worked through until the couple is united as to how the relationship can be handled. Any unhappiness by either of the in-laws with the impending marriage can have an adverse effect on the young people themselves. Although many young people may not think so, they do marry into their respective families and cannot easily cut themselves off from the parental families.

Another important area for discussion and agreement concerns the values and goals in the life of the partners. Hazelip (1985, 115) emphasizes this by stating, "Unless the bride and groom agree on where their marriage starts from and is going, they will miss the one thing that can make marriage happy. . . . When the builder begins to erect a house, he has a very clear idea of what the building is meant to look like when it is finished. Just as a builder has plans and diagrams, marriage needs its common value and goals."

> *An important area for discussion and agreement concerns the values and goals in the life of the partners.*

Reference is made in the beginning of this chapter to the necessity of harmony in spiritual matters. If there are serious disagreements or conflicts in the spiritual realm, the couple must resolve these. If they cannot, they face the possibility of missing much of the blessing that comes in Christian marriage to a couple united in their spiritual views.

Values and goals in life are often linked together because the goals usually reflect the values held by the person. For example, if a person greatly values money and high social status, he will undoubtedly not become a teacher or a Christian worker. His values will more likely direct him toward a career in business or medicine since our society provides greater monetary rewards to those filling these roles.

Young people reared in Christian homes have widely different value systems and goals in life. Therefore, two young people who are building a serious dating relationship need to discuss their values and goals to see if they are compatible. If the man values money highly and plans a career in business, and the woman does not value money but is more interested in full-time Christian work, there is little to be gained in continuing the relationship. It will be better for both to seek a partner with more compatible values and goals.

> *Spiritual goals help the family to keep priorities straight in all areas of life.*

During courtship it is always wise for the couple to set goals for their future marriage. Wright (1979, 44) reflects, "Individual goals and marital goals lend direction to a marriage relationship. Far too many couples drift through their marriage with little direction. In fact, surveying thousands of couples in the past few years, I have found only approximately four percent discussed, developed and implemented goals for their marriage."

Spiritual, material, and financial goals should be discussed prior to marriage. Spiritual goals help the family to keep priorities straight in all areas of life. Just as organizations today are committed to strategic planning for the future, a healthy family likewise needs to set objectives for the future according to the will of God and to strive to achieve them with the help of the Holy Spirit.

Compatibility

Dating partners will find it most helpful to discover each other's background, values, and goals in life and examine their psychological compatibility before they become emotionally involved with each other. Whenever the physical predominates in the relationship, it becomes difficult to make clear judgments on the basis of reason.

Compatibility is the ability of spouses to relate to each other in a manner that gives emotional satisfaction. As a couple live together, they quickly learn which actions please or dissatisfy each other. The Lasswells (1987, 220–21) take the view that "learning to live together harmoniously with another person for a lifetime, sharing in all facets of life—finances, emotions, sex, children, illness, criteria assessing success and failure—is perhaps the most challenging task we ever face."

A harmonious relationship is facilitated by learning about each other before marriage. This is one reason why couples who have the longest relationships before marriage tend to have the highest happiness rating when asked to judge their marriage. They have had more time for self-revelation so less occurs after the wedding. They have had time to make adjustments to each other's personalities, aided by the idealization provided by romantic love.

When God created Eve for Adam, he made her a "help fit for Adam"—that is, she was compatible with Adam. It is difficult for young persons today to find a compatible mate or one who fits their personalities. With so many potential partners they must date many different individuals in order to find one who is most compatible with them. Young people need to realize there are no perfect prospective mates, but if they will attempt to choose a compatible mate carefully, in the will of God, then work to make the many adjustments and compromises that are needed, they can have a successful Christian marriage with God's help and blessing.

The Cohesive Nature of Love

The final ingredient is love, which, like leaven, "leaveneth the whole lump." If most of the previously mentioned requirements are present in a relationship, then it will not be difficult for love to take root and grow. A necessary part of love, discussed in chapter 6, is physical attraction, but it is only a part and not the whole. One of the great problems in American courtship and marriage is that the media so often present a view that equates physical attraction as constituting the sum and substance of love. Often a man and woman meet, are physically drawn to one another by very natural God-given desires, and conclude they are "in love" and therefore should get married. They give little or no thought to the factors that contribute to compatibility in marriage, and they fail to realize that it is possible to be sexually attracted to many persons who would not make good partners in a marriage to last for a lifetime.

Love as a physical attraction is sufficient to begin a marriage, but not to sustain it. Other elements such as caring and companionship must predominate if the relationship is to endure. In a successful marriage, the romantic element will remain strong but will be superseded by the other components as the marriage matures.

> *Love as a physical attraction is sufficient to begin a marriage, but not to sustain it.*

The successful Christian marriage begins with the right choice of a mate according to God's will. The love in such a relationship grows and matures into a bond "stronger than death" (Song of Sol. 8:6). A relationship marked by this kind of love does not "just happen." The love of courtship is like a tender seedling that must be cultivated, watered, and cared for. With such care it blooms and produces the beauty incipient in the seedling. Likewise, romantic love matures and brings forth the beauty and fragrance of a family symbolic of the heavenly family.

Study Questions

1. Why is deriving emotional satisfaction from a marriage more important today than it was in a rural society?
2. What should a Christian couple do when they face stress in their marriage?
3. What criteria to gauge the success of a Christian marriage would you add to those listed in the text?
4. What spiritual requirements are necessary for success in marriage?
5. List elements that help to constitute the cultural background in American society. Why are these important?
6. What is meant by the "mating gradient"? How does it affect the dating of college students?
7. Discuss the intellectual gulf and how it may influence a marriage relationship.
8. Discuss the relationship between age at marriage and success in marriage.
9. What are some of your values? How are they influencing your goals in life?
10. Why is romantic love by itself a poor foundation on which to build a marriage?

Suggested Readings

Chapman, A., and S. Chapman. 1989. *Married lovers, married friends.* Minneapolis: Bethany House. Written by two well-known musical entertainers who have a ministry to families. In this volume they share lessons they have learned that encourage couples to be friends as well as lovers.

Chartier, J., and M. Chartier. 1986. *Caring together: Faith, hope, love in your family.* Philadelphia: Westminster. The principles of faith, hope, and love are the framework of this volume. The authors exhort believers to live these principles within the home so that a genuine spirituality results. This spirituality will affect our relationships "with God, person, neighbor, and world."

Dobson, J. 1980. *Emotions, can you trust them?* Ventura, Calif.: Regal. A small volume by an eminent psychologist discussing the effects of emotions in the Christian life. He writes about guilt, anger, romantic love, and inner feelings and impressions. Dobson stresses commitment as the major component of romantic love.

Field, D. 1986. *Marriage personalities.* Eugene, Ore.: Harvest House. A unique treatment of the marriage relationship as viewed by a Christian marriage therapist. He describes seven different marriage personalities and gives insight how each type may be helped.

Hazelip, H. 1985. *Happiness in the home.* Grand Rapids: Baker. This book discusses the elements that the author feels constitute a successful marriage. He amplifies such areas as "Christian values, satisfying intimacy, caring cooperation in parenting tasks."

Huggett, J. 1981. *Two into one: Relating in Christian marriage.* Downer's Grove, Ill.: InterVarsity. The writer states, "Our main concern is for newly-weds, and those preparing to be married, whose expectations of married life submitted to God are high, who are determined to create the best marriage ever." Those anticipating marriage will profit much from reading this short volume.

Meier, P., and R. Meier. 1981. *Family foundations: How to have a happy home.* Grand Rapids: Baker. Two experienced marriage therapists discuss seven elements they consider crucial for a healthy home. A good chapter on "Genuine Love" will enable young people to more clearly understand the biblical concept of *agape* love.

Montgomery, D., and E. L. Shostrom. 1986. *God in your personality.* Nashville: Abingdon. Written by two psychologists with decades of experience who set forth a theory of personality formation. It utilizes the ministry of the Holy Spirit and the reality of Christ's love to encourage growth in the believer throughout life.

Wright, H. N. 1979. *The pillars of marriage.* Ventura, Calif.: Regal. The author lists and develops eight areas that he considers basic to a successful marriage. An important feature is the self-help exercises following each section.

Christian Role Concepts

Submitting yourselves one to the other . . . in the fear of God.

—Ephesians 5:21

Definition of Roles

Henry picked up the phone. A familiar voice was on the line: "Honey, I have a report due at nine tomorrow morning, and I'm having difficulty getting it together. So my secretary and I will be working late tonight. Will you pick up Junior from the day-care center when you get off work? Oh yes, we're just about out of diapers and milk so will you please stop at the supermarket? While you're there, pick up a frozen pizza to microwave for Sally and you. She'll be home before you but she has her own key. I didn't have time to throw the laundry in the machine this morning, so if you'll do that for me, I'll appreciate it. Keep Junior awake as long as possible so he'll sleep through the night, but Sally has to be in by eight. I love you— I'll try to be home by nine."

A fictional phone call? Yes, but a similar call probably occurs many times a day across the United States. It aptly illustrates the myriad of role changes that have taken place in the country in the last thirty or forty years.

The term *role* refers to the behavior expected from a person who occupies a given position or *status*. A man who is a husband (status) is expected to perform the duties (roles) that the particular society assigns to that position. A woman who is a wife (status) also is expected to fulfill her obligations (roles) that society expects from her (Korman and Leslie 1985, 197).

The idea of roles has been developed by symbolic interaction theory (DeVault and Strong 1989, 68). However, the idea of roles originally was borrowed from the field of drama. Just as the actors must know their parts in order to play them, so the person with a given status must know what behavior society expects if he or she is going to succeed.

The child begins learning these roles in the home. Garrett (1982, 60) observes, "From the time the delivery doctor makes a hasty examination and announces, 'It's a girl' or 'It's a boy,' each baby is treated differently according to his or her sex. . . ." This difference is perpetuated by first names, and by dressing boys in blue and girls in pink. Children's knowledge of gender roles is increased as they have contacts with other socializing agencies such as play groups, church, school, peer groups, and others. Each young person approaching marriage has received a different socialization from that of every other person. Thus, each person has a different concept of the roles he or she is to play as husband or wife.

> *The term* role *refers to the behavior expected from a person who occupies a given position or* status.

Young people must study their background and look within the self to determine how they feel about roles that society expects them to play. Having done this, the task is to find a prospective spouse with corresponding or matching role concepts. The happiest marital interaction takes place between individuals who are well matched in this area, for they avoid much of the conflict caused by improper matching of role concepts.

The couple with complementary role concepts have fewer role differences to work out. It is this working out of role differences that causes much of the unhappiness in marriages. One of the main values of our system of dating and courtship is that it makes it possible for a young person to find a mate whose role concepts match the individual's rather than clashes with it.

Confusion of Roles in American Society

The rapidly changing expectations of the roles of men and women in American culture have resulted in much confusion and misunderstanding. This is illustrated by an experience Eshleman relates (1991, 19). He asked a group of students to "define and list characteristics of masculinity." They had great difficulty in determining what the characteristics were. He indicated that in the past there was agreement in that "the male, husband, and father was the head of the family, its main economic support, and its representative in the community." The movement away from the traditional role of the man to a more egalitarian role caused the confusion in the students' minds.

In a similar manner, the role of women has also changed. Kephart (1981, 353–54) elaborates, *"One of the chief differences relates to marital roles.* Today's young wife will probably be as well educated as her husband." He states that she will work outside the home and will help her husband make the decisions in the home. She will expect her husband to help with housework and care of the children. It is easy to see how conflict can arise when a man who expects his wife to follow the traditional role in the home marries a woman with an egalitarian role concept. Kephart (1981, 384–85) gives a case history of a couple with just such conflicting role concepts. Their marriage ended in divorce, which is often the result of such conflicts.

The Secular Women's Liberation Movement

There has been a women's liberation movement in this country for over a century. Women were active in the abolition movement prior to the Civil War. Their biggest accomplishment was the passage in 1920 of the Nineteenth Amendment, which gave women the right to vote. The movement faded into the background until large numbers of women entered the workforce in World War II, preparing the way for a renewal of the feminist movement and the publication in 1963 of a book that would ignite the interest of a new generation, Betty Friedan's *The Feminine Mystique.*

DeVault and Strong (1989, 47) emphasize the importance of this book by stating that it "became a national sensation when it attacked the traditionalist assumption that women found their greatest fulfillment in being mothers and housewives. It tapped into the fundamental discontent that many women were experiencing in suburbia." Feminists challenged the traditional roles and taught that fulfillment was found in employment outside the home. Contemporary women have a different view of male-female roles because of the feminist movement.

Friedan became one of the leaders of the feminist movement and was instrumental in founding the National Organization of Women (NOW) in 1966. The group began a concerted drive for full economic, political, sexual, and civil rights for women. These efforts led to an attempt to pass an Equal Rights Amendment to the Constitution, an amendment strongly opposed by conservative groups because of the ill effects on women's rights if it passed. The Amendment failed to be ratified by the required thirty-eight states by the deadline set by Congress.

Subsequently, the movement became divided over its goals and fractured into rival groups, ranging from radicals who called for the abolition of marriage and family to moderates who were willing to work within the system. Nevertheless, the publicity and discussion of the issues raised by the women's liberation movement had profound effects on American culture. Courses in women's studies were instituted at colleges and universities. Women gained entrance into traditional male occupations and were given opportunities to advance in the areas of supervision and management. More women were elected and appointed to public office. The appointment of Sandra Day O'Connor and Ruth Bader Ginsburg to the United States Supreme Court was possible because of changes in attitudes toward women.

Negative changes have taken place also, such as the widespread use of abortion, the rise in the divorce rate, the increase in the number of single-parent families, the large number of illegitimate births, and the significant number of cohabiting couples. These changes necessarily influenced the role of the man in society. On the job a man must accept women as equals, and at times as superiors. When women work outside the home, a predominantly male role, then the husband must participate in the typical feminine role by helping with child care and housework. If the wife contributes to the family income, then she tends to have a larger voice in its distribution. Sometimes she will earn more than her husband—will he be able to accept it? How will he react when she must leave for business trips and he is left with total care of the children? Zimbelman (1985, 58) comments, "He does not have any models that he can look to—he is truly a pioneer."

> *When women work outside the home, a predominantly male role, then the husband must participate in the typical feminine role by helping with child care and housework.*

The Evangelical Women's Movement

Christians are influenced by the society at large. Some Christian women responded to the women's liberation movement by finding new interpretations of the biblical passages concerning the roles of the husband and wife. *All We're Meant to Be* by Hardesty and Scanzoni (1974) was one of the first books to receive wide attention. It was a call for Christian women to break down the barriers within the church that kept women from full equality with men. "No longer pampered and protected by men, we women must take responsibility for our own lives. We must shoulder our share of the cultural mandate God has given us for the development of our own talents and preservation of the earth. The easy way out is closed" (Hardesty and Scanzoni 1974, 208).

One of the key verses used by the evangelical women's movement to substantiate its position is Galatians 3:28: "There is neither Jew nor Greek, there is neither bond nor free, there is neither male nor female; for ye are all one in Christ Jesus." They interpret this verse to mean that since the redemptive work of Christ removes the effects of the fall, then any distinctions between male and female resulting from the fall are removed as well. The egalitarian male-female relationship enjoyed before the fall has been restored in Christ. The idea of male dominance-female submission has been replaced by a relationship of true equality. DeJong (1979, 137) summarizes the position: "The central message appears to be that all those distinctions between people that were previously a source of alienation and separation have been superseded by their union in Christ." This applies not only to the marriage relationship, but to all areas of life such as in the church, government, and employment.

> # The feminists fail to distinguish between believers' standing or position before God and their daily conduct or deportment in the world.

There are two difficulties with this interpretation. First, it cannot refer to the present because there are still these natural distinctions around us. There are Jews and Greeks, there still are slaves and freemen in some parts of the world, and it is most evident that there are still males and females. Thus, it is absurd to argue that the verse applies to the present situation.

In the second place, it violates the primary rule of biblical interpretation: that the passage must always be interpreted in view of its immediate context. Verses 26 and 27 read, "For ye are all the sons of God by faith in Christ Jesus. For as many of you as have been baptized into Christ have put on Christ." Here Paul is teaching the unity of believers in reference to their standing before God. In commenting on this verse, MacArthur (1982, 18) makes the point that "men and women are equal *in the sight of God* [italics added] according to Galatians 3:28. . . . There is no second-class spiritual citizenship. Before God, there is only oneness; a man is not spiritually superior to a woman in any way."

The feminists fail to distinguish between believers' standing or position before God and their daily conduct or deportment in the world. These two lines of truth run throughout the Bible. For example, in writing to the Corinthians Paul states that they are "sanctified" and are "saints" (1:2), but in 1:11 he writes there are "contentions among [them]." He goes on to describe them as "carnal; for whereas there is among you envying, and strife, and divisions . . ." (3:3). In 5:1 he rebukes the believers for permitting fornication in the church. Are these the actions of "sanctified ones" or "saints"? How can we reconcile these opposites?

It can be done only by recognizing that when a sinner is saved, God gives him a new position in grace. He is then challenged to live daily a life of holiness by which he strives to make his actual walk conform to his standing in grace. In this case, the Corinthian believers were not living a life conforming to their position; thus, Paul admonishes them to change their behavior.

Like the secular feminist movement, there are several evangelical groups with differing interpretations. Diehl (Hagen 1990, 36–40), lists two main groups of evangelicals who differ from the traditional interpretation of roles: the "moderate hierarchalists or liberated traditionalists," who give a cultural interpretation to the roles, and the "biblical or evangelical feminists" who emphasize "the principles of equality and mutual submission." He also lists two other groups who are not evangelical since they deny the infallibility of the Bible: the "mainstream or reformist feminists" and the "radical or revolutionary feminists."

Those who hold to the traditional interpretation of roles and those in evangelical circles who differ both believe in the inspired Word of God. Good and godly men and women will arrive at differing interpretations of the same passage. Van Leeuwen (1990, 24), in a section called "No Easy Answers," recognizes the difficulties in interpretation when she writes, "It is true that Christians who share an equally high view of scriptural authority often differ about the finer details of this 'Biblical drama,' especially those parts that speak of men and women in their relationship to God and each other." She relates that we should not be surprised at this because we are all sinners, which makes "it impossible for us to read the Bible entirely as it should be read." She states that we must be willing to "see through a glass darkly" on some issues, and "strive to be charitable toward those with whom we disagree." However, given the differences concerning role concepts, it is easy to understand the confusion among Christian young people concerning roles.

It is important to study God's Word and to heed what he says concerning the proper roles for husband and wife. The Bible does not change to accommodate the desires of a degenerating culture. Young people who find their role concepts in the Scriptures and who seek a mate who also accepts these scriptural roles will have a solid basis for interaction in Christian marriage.

The task of determining what the Bible teaches concerning the roles of men and women is difficult because of attitudes prevalent in evangelical circles today. Collins (1982, 144) illustrates this when he comments, "Individuals who sincerely want the best for women, as well as for men, are reluctant to advocate distinct male and female roles lest they be labeled 'rigid,' 'insensitive,' or worst of all, 'chauvinistic.'" He continues by indicating that many sensitive Christians avoid the biblical teaching on roles for fear of being criticized. He believes that God gave distinct, "although overlapping," roles to men and women, and that many committed Christians do not teach these truths for fear of losing "contact with nonbelievers" if they advocate "unpopular biblical standards." It is with these issues in mind that the following interpretation of the husband-wife roles is given.

> *Many sensitive Christians avoid the biblical teaching on roles for fear of being criticized.*

Scriptural Roles for the Wife

Several passages in the New Testament discuss the roles of the husband and wife. They are Ephesians 5:18–33, Colossians 3:18–21, and 1 Peter 3:1–7. It is the interpretation of these verses that creates confusion. For centuries there was common agreement as to the meaning of individual words. Today, however, godly men and women cannot agree on what words such as "submission" and "headship" mean.

In commenting on Ephesians 5:22–24, Swindoll (1980, 41) states, "it doesn't take a Greek scholar to see that Paul gives a command, 'Wives, be subject to your own husbands. . . .' and then a comparison . . . 'as to the Lord.' For wives the basic role is one of submission, and the analogy is 'as to the Lord.'" There was a time one could make this statement without fear of contradiction. For years "submission" meant "submission."

Those who disagree with this interpretation argue that wives in the culture of that day were to submit to their husbands just as slaves in that culture submitted to their masters: out of love for God and their freedom in Christ. As slavery was abolished, so God's order has changed for women in today's culture.

In refuting this cultural argument as an interpretation, Sell (1982, 159) makes the point, "But egalitarians have trouble treating all the husband-wife passages in this way. Sometimes Paul gives reasons for submitting that are not bound up in culture. He says that the husband is the head of the wife as Christ is the head of the Church." He relates that when Paul compares the husband's headship to that of Christ, he gives "substantial reasons" for a special role of the husband in the home. Paul does not give "any such reasons for slaves to submit to their masters." He concludes that Paul gives theological reasons for the headship of the husband, but he does not give any such reason for slavery. Another reason the cultural comparison to slavery breaks down is pointed out by Hagen (1990, 41): "Others argue that the patriarchy issue is not exactly parallel to the slavery issue, because slavery was not instituted by divine revelation whereas patriarchy was." The author also says that the issue will continue to be debated in the evangelical church for a long time.

> **When Paul compares the husband's headship to that of Christ, he gives substantial reasons for the special role of the husband in the home.**

A third reason why the cultural interpretation of Ephesians 5 cannot be correct is a fallacy in the argument concerning slavery. This interpretation argues that since slavery has been abolished, so submission and headship have likewise been abolished. The Chris-

tensens (1977, 123) refute the argument: "In Ephesians he is telling people who *are* married or who *are* slaves, how they should conduct themselves. If we say, 'We do not believe in slavery today,' the parallel is not, 'We do not believe in the husband's headship.' The parallel is, 'We do not believe in marriage.' To draw a comparison between slavery and marriage in this context does not make a case against headship in marriage, but against marriage itself." No one is willing to argue that marriage as an institution should be abolished.

In the passage in Ephesians 5:18, Paul exhorts the believer to "be filled with the Spirit." Many writers begin their discussion of roles with verse 22, "Wives, submit yourselves unto your own husbands," but this submission is possible only as the wife knows the power of a life yielded to and filled with the blessed Holy Spirit. Before a husband can love his wife as God intends, he too must be filled with the Spirit of God.

It is necessary to note that these verses are introductory not only to the proper relationships between husband and wife, but also to those between parents and children, and to those between servants and masters. Christians must be filled with the Holy Spirit before they can properly play a role in any of the three most important areas of human relationships. The family that endeavors to establish the best Christian home can do so only as they are empowered by the Holy Spirit. He is pleased to exalt the Lord Jesus in the life of the believer, and he is pleased to exalt Christ in the home where two believers have become "one flesh."

The exhortation in Ephesians 5:22, "Wives, submit yourselves unto your own husbands, as unto the Lord," is a definite command for the wife to submit herself to the lordship of Christ in her daily life. She is to follow the example of the church who as the bride of Christ submits to his leadership. Achtenmeier (1976, 85) comments, "wives are to act toward their husbands as the church should act toward Christ—in faithfulness, in love, in service, in honor, in devotion—because what the wife does to her husband, she is in fact doing to Christ." She also indicates that if a wife "is unfaithful, nagging, complacent, or hostile" toward her husband, then "she so treats her Lord." When the wife is in the proper relationship to her Lord, she will also be in the right relationship with her husband.

The wife has a legitimate concern for equality in voting rights, in employment, and in the right of "equal pay for equal work." She does not have a right (as the radical feminists claim) to demand the abolition of marriage, or the right to assume leadership over the husband in the home. She is under divine obligation to submit first to the Lord as she yields her body to the control of the Holy Spirit, and he will enable her to submit to a Spirit-filled, loving husband.

In discussing this idea of submission, Mollenkott (1977, 126), one of the early evangelical feminist writers, makes an interesting observation: "In an *ideal* male-female Christian relationship, this would work out beautifully because the father or husband would already be following the example of Christ in a self-given concern for the women in his life. But for years Christians have been following a carnal dominance-submission pattern." The writer is correct in the first part of her statement, but is mistaken when she writes, "But for years Christians have been following a carnal dominance-submission pattern." She implies *all* Christians have followed a "carnal dominance-submission pattern," when in reality multitudes of Christian husbands and wives have followed the *ideal* set down in Scripture of a harmonious loving leadership-submission pattern. The fact that there have been those who failed to reach the ideal is not sufficient reason to seek a new interpretation of the passages setting forth what God has ordained as the ideal pattern.

MacArthur (1982, 13–14) observes, "A disobedient or fleshly believer will have discord in his family just as he will have discord in his own heart, because there is discord between himself and God. Being a Christian is definitely the starting point, but being controlled by the Spirit makes the *ideal* [italics added] a reality."

Christians fail to reach many of the ideal patterns of behavior that the Scriptures present. For example, most believers do not live up to the exhortation to "love thy neighbor as thyself." Yet they still make the attempt with the help of the Holy Spirit to demonstrate that kind of love. The fact that many fail to make the attempt is no reason to seek a new interpretation of the words to justify our failures.

Two other passages concerning the role of the wife are Colossians 3:18, "Wives, submit yourselves to your own husbands, as is fit in the Lord," and 1 Peter 3:1, "Likewise, ye wives, be in subjection to your own husbands." These verses reinforce the teachings that the wife is to be submissive to her husband. The Gangels (1979, 43) comment, "In the third chapter of I Peter, the Apostle is speaking to women whose husbands are unsaved, and the word rendered 'subjection' in the Authorized Version is precisely the same word that is used in the previous chapter for slaves and citizens of secular government."

In Colossians 3, the admonition for the husband and wife is preceded by an exhortation in verse 16 to "let the Word of Christ dwell in you richly." In Ephesians 5:22, the advice to the husband and wife is preceded by the command to "be filled with the Spirit." The necessity to be filled with the Word of God and the Holy Spirit cannot be overemphasized in this day of confusion concerning Christian role concepts.

> *Christians must be filled with the Holy Spirit before they can properly play a role in any of the three most important areas of human relationships.*

For example, in American culture, a Christian woman may be reared in a Christian home with a domineering mother. It is only natural for her to acquire the attitudes of her mother, and she may rebel at being submissive to her husband. She may find it difficult to allow him to take the leadership in the home. The resources referred to in Ephesians 5:18 and Colossians 3:16, the power of the living Word of God and indwelling Holy Spirit, will enable such a woman to submit to her husband. It is not the natural thing to do, but the Holy Spirit is given to the Christian wife to enable her to obey God and her husband in a supernatural manner. The world cannot understand such submission, for the "natural man receiveth not the things of the Spirit of God: for they are foolishness unto him, neither can he know them, because they are spiritually discerned" (1 Cor. 2:14).

> ## *Where mutual love exists as God intends it, a wife does not find it hard to accept her husband as the head of the home.*

There is also the possibility of a Christian woman marrying a Christian man who does not understand his role, or who may change after marriage into a worldly, carnal husband. A wife in such a situation must turn to the resources of the Word and Holy Spirit for victory in her daily life of submission.

The couple who can communicate will experience little difficulty. MacArthur (1983, 18) reflects that "the partners' spiritual natures are the same, their positions before God are equal, but in order for the family to function in harmony, the woman, with no loss of dignity, takes the place of submission to the headship of her husband." He teaches that the tenderness and gentleness of the wife are to complement the strength of the husband. To him, "the issue is not superiority or inferiority. Mutual submission in marriage blends without contradiction

with the concepts of headship and authority. As she submits to follow, so he submits to lead her. Both authority and submission are still preserved." The Christian wife is able to say with the bride in the Song of Solomon, "I am my beloved's, and his desire is toward me" (Song of Sol. 7:10). Where mutual love exists as God intends it, a wife does not find it hard to accept her husband as the head of the home.

Scriptural Roles for the Husband

A different command is given to the husband in reference to his role. He is to love his wife as "Christ also loved the church" (Eph. 5:25), and to love his wife as his own body (Eph. 5:28). He is to show the same selfish concern for her welfare that he exhibits toward his own person and is to "nourish and cherish" her just as he does his physical body. On the other hand, he is to have the same self-sacrificing love for his mate that Christ has for his bride, the church.

This selfish and self-sacrificing love seems somewhat contradictory until we realize that we cherish most that for which we sacrifice most. Consider the time and attention a young man devotes to his first car, for which he worked and saved over a long period, or the young couple and the first home they purchase after years of saving for the down payment. In real mature love, each partner sacrifices himself and his interests in order to meet the needs of his spouse. The emphasis is not on "me" and "mine," but "you" and "yours."

This kind of love spoken of in the Bible is the antithesis of the popular conception of a selfish "love" that puts the gratification of one's own personal desires above satisfying the needs of the mate. When a man is in fellowship with God and loves his wife as Christ loved the church, he treats her in such a kind, considerate, thoughtful manner that she finds it easy to respect him and submit to him as "unto the Lord." She knows that just as he responds to the needs of his own body and satisfies them for its best welfare, so he responds to her needs and seeks her best welfare since he loves her "as his own body."

The spiritual dimension of the proper roles of husband and wife is emphasized in 1 Peter

3:1–7. The role of the wife delineated in this passage has been previously discussed, but Peter has some specific statements directed to the husband in verse 7: "Ye husbands, dwell with them according to knowledge, giving honour unto the wife, as unto the weaker vessel, and as being heirs together of the grace of life, that your prayers be not hindered." Wuest (1942, 83) comments on this verse, "The husband is to dwell with the wife remembering that she is an instrument of God . . . to be used by Him to His glory. . . . The husband is to pay her honor so that their prayers be not hindered. The word 'hindered' in the Greek text means literally 'to cut in, to interrupt.'" If the husband does not honor his wife, then their prayers will be interrupted and will lack the efficacy they would ordinarily have.

Huggett (1981, 45), referring to headship of the husband, states, "The husband's main aim should be to emulate the love Christ demonstrates for His bride, the church. This kind of loving is not just an emotion: it is an orientation, a chain of choices, a series of actions which are planned to bring about the wife's well-being, happiness, and ultimate wholeness." The fullness of blessing that God desires to bestow upon the Christian home is reserved for the home where the husband manifests his love by obeying the exhortations of 1 Peter 3:7.

At this point it is necessary to refute the argument of the biblical feminists that the traditional view of marriage leads to wife abuse. It is true that some husbands who hold to this view but who do not submit to the lordship of Christ (1 Cor. 11:3) have abused their wives. However, a major study conducted by the University of Calgary investigated the relation between religion and spousal abuse. It was designed to explore "the thesis" that "fundamentalist" men, because they are more likely to subscribe to the biblical interpretation of men being the head of the household and that woman was created to serve him, [a misinterpretation of the verse] would be more likely to violently abuse their partners. This study (1987) surveyed 652 female and 471 male married or cohabiting respondents. They were asked "how often they had engaged in any of eight violent acts ranging from throwing objects to using a knife or gun on the other person in the past year." The researchers were surprised to find that "conservative Protestant women were the most likely to have violently abused their partners." Thirty-seven percent of conservative women versus 28 percent of mainline Protestant women and 24 percent of Roman Catholic women reported committing a violent act against their husbands. The researchers could not explain this finding.

However, they did find that only "18.8 percent of conservative Protestant men reported having committed a violent act, a figure in between the 19.2 percent of mainline Protestant men and 17.2 percent of Catholic men. . . ." When church attendance was surveyed the results were interesting. "Just 10 percent of conservative Protestants who attend church weekly reported committing violent acts, while 64 percent of those attending one to three times a month said they had committed violent acts."

> *If the husband does not honor his wife, then their prayers will be interrupted and will lack the efficacy they would ordinarily have.*

One researcher, Merlin Brinkerhoff, speculated that "the relatively low rate among conservative Protestant men who attend church frequently indicates biblically derived attitudes of male supremacy appear to be balanced by their religious beliefs in the dominion of love." Those who hold to the biblical interpretation that the husband is the head of the household do stress the necessity of loving the wife. Three times in Ephesians 5 Paul exhorts the husband "to love his wife"—as Christ loves the Church, as his own body, and as his own self. It has *always* been the position of those holding (and practicing) this interpretation that a man loving his wife in this manner will exercise leadership in such a way that submission will not be a problem. Certainly a man holding this position and loving his wife as Christ commanded would never abuse his wife (Grand Rapids *Press,* 6 June 1992, B7).

This study does not state what percentage of the male respondents held to the hierarchical view of male leadership. The study assumed that all "conservative Protestant" men do, but many do not accept this interpretation. It would be interesting to see what the results of a survey of only Christian men holding this view would show.

> **The head of the home sets the Christian standards by leading a consistent Christian life that is an example to his wife and children.**

Roles Pertaining Specifically to Christian Couples

The Christian husband and wife share many of the roles common to any marriage. They play the roles of breadwinner, housekeeper, parents, neighbors, as does the secular family next door. Yet some roles are characteristic of their Christian faith. The husband is to be head of the home. This means that he is responsible for making decisions concerning the happiness and welfare of the family. He certainly will seek the input of his wife and family before making any decision affecting their welfare.

The head of the home sets the Christian standards by leading a consistent Christian life that is an example to his wife and children. He conducts family devotions, sees that the family attends services at the local church, and is active in Christian service. The Christian wife has a primary obligation to maintain a home that is distinctively Christian. She gives tender support and submission to her loving husband. Her relationship to her children is marked by love and discipline. She cooperates with her husband in his efforts to provide spiritual leadership in the home. She assumes this responsibility when it is necessary for the husband to be absent. She also engages in Christian service as her time and strength permit. For example, it is often difficult for a young mother to have a role in the local church because of the demands of motherhood.

The woman is "given to hospitality" and uses her home to entertain God's people, and also as a means of witnessing to unsaved neighbors. In Proverbs 31:28, Solomon describes the virtuous woman: "her children arise up, and call her blessed; Her husband also, and he praiseth her." This is part of the reward of a Christian wife for faithfully fulfilling her roles.

The roles of a Christian couple are reciprocal. Swindoll (1980, 41) describes them: "The godly wife asks, 'Lord, how can I show my love to you in the role you have called me to fill?' God answers, 'My dear child, show it in your submissive heart toward your husband.' The godly husband asks, 'Lord, how can I be the kind of man you want me to be . . . ?' God answers, 'My son, your limitless love for your wife shows . . . the kind of love you have for me.'"

Role Conflicts

The misinterpretation of Ephesians 5 has resulted in a warped view of the husband's role in the Christian family. Some Christians seem to read only parts of verses 22 and 23 and fail to read the remainder of the chapter. They feel that the husband as the head is to be an absolute monarch or a dictator in the home, and the wife is to submit to him as his willing slave. The children also are to bow to his sovereign majesty and yield unquestioned obedience to his dictates.

It is apparent that such an interpretation misses the heart of the passage, which teaches that the relationship between husband and wife is based on mutual love and concern; it is not a one-sided power structure. In the home where Christ-like love prevails, where roles are rightly perceived, the husband will have authority and his decisions will be carried out. Love is a much greater motivation to action than fear could ever be. The Christensens (1977, 125) explain, "Headship is a means of *serving* others. That is its essential function. One who exercises headship must understand it first of all as a position from which to serve. . . . [It] is the *service of leadership.* . . . His headship is not meant for domineering and stifling his wife and children, but for leading, protecting, providing, and caring for them."

The ideal concept of the husband-wife relationship is the one found in the Bible. In reality, many factors affect the actual roles in daily living. The changing role of women in our society has made it more difficult for them to accept the traditional role of homemaker and mother (see chap. 1). The average working wife feels she is intelligent enough and contributes sufficiently to the family income to deserve a major part in decision making. If she is among the large number who earns more than her husband, she may feel she should make the decisions.

This should not be a problem for the Christian family, for the wife will play her role of submission to her husband, and he, because of his great love for her, will consider her desires in any decision he makes for the family. Brandt and Dowdy (1960, 52–53) uses a most appropriate illustration of the complementary roles of husband and wife in the areas of submission and decision-making by comparing them to roles played by the president and vice president of a bank who have worked together many years. The bankers interact on the basis of policies that they have mutually determined are in the best interest of their company. Their roles are clearly defined, and when the president is absent, the vice president directs the business. They do not argue or feud over decisions that have to be made; the best interest of the bank is the determining factor in any situation.

> ## The relationship between husband and wife is based on mutual love and concern; it is not a one-sided power structure.

The applications to the roles of husband and wife are evident. They have chosen to work together and the best interests of their marriage should be the major concern of each spouse. Brandt and Dowdy (1960, 53) ask, "Should not the role of the wife be similar to that of the first vice-president? The husband is the head of the wife, but this should be on the basis of friendship, loyalty, goodwill. . . . Selfish interest has no place in marriage . . . both . . . subject themselves to the best interest and objectives of the marriage." Brandt also points out that problems can arise when the couple disagree. He suggests that in case of serious disagreement the husband "carefully make the decision." He "assumes . . . loyalty, and respect, and dedication between a couple." He also sounds a word of warning: "When crises arise repeatedly that cause friction, we must consider that marriage sick and outside help would be indicated." It is apparent that a Christian family, like its unsaved neighbors, can experience role conflict if the partners do not agree, or if either refuses to accept the biblical norm for his or her role.

Dominance-Submission Patterns

Many times role conflicts result because husband and wife are socialized in homes with contrasting dominance-submission patterns. Children ordinarily derive their role concepts from the home. A young man reared in a home where the father is dominant and the mother submissive usually internalizes a dominant role concept. Similarly, a girl reared in this type of home ordinarily wants to play the submissive role. When the young man from this home begins to date as part of the mate-selection process in our culture, he subconsciously seeks a girl who plays the submissive role. If he dates a woman from a home where the mother is dominant, he may have problems, because she usually repeats her mother's pattern and he feels the woman is "too bossy." Instead of permitting him to plan dates and activities, she assumes this role; conflict results and the relationship is broken. In this culture, the male then can continue to date until he discovers a prospective mate who says, "I want my husband to 'wear the pants' in our home and to be the spiritual leader. As far as money matters and things of this nature, I feel we both should discuss such matters together since they are of great importance, and probably the first year I will also be working. Therefore, some of the money I will have earned. But I don't feel I should have the final say in these matters. I am only saying that he should know how I feel about the particular situation." If he marries a dominant woman, there is likely to be conflict.

Children ordinarily derive their role concepts from the home.

Many young men are reared in homes where the mother is dominant and makes the decisions for the family. She may go so far as to pick out and buy clothing for her husband and sons. Many times the mother is dominant because the father refuses to accept his role in the home. The Christensens (1977, 158) make this observation: "It is precisely the *absence* of male authority which plagues American families. Husbands and fathers have abdicated their responsibility. We are fast becoming a matriarchal society. The teaching and discipline of the children, responsibility for upkeep and management of the home . . . all of this has been laid on the woman's shoulders."

When a young man socialized in this type of home begins to date, he subconsciously looks for a girl to dominate him and make decisions for him. He expects his date to plan the evening and to inform him of her plans. If she does not, he is disappointed. After a few dates, or when the relationship becomes too unhappy because of their role conflict, he breaks up with her and seeks another. He searches until he subconsciously finds a woman who likes to dominate her date. If he doesn't, he finally marries a woman from a home with a submissive mother, and they have problems because neither one wants to assume leadership in the home. A student expressed his feelings about the problems in his home in this manner:

> When I marry, I want my home to be different than the one I was reared in. There was continual conflict because neither of my parents wanted to make a decision. My mother expected my father to tell the children what to do, and my father expected my mother to do this. If I asked my mother if I could go someplace she would say, "Ask your father." When I asked him his reply was, "Do whatever your mother said." As a result, I often had to make my own decisions, and if it displeased either of my parents, they would blame the other for letting me go somewhere.

Life in such a home is not pleasant for either the parents or children.

A third type of conflict arises when a person is reared in an egalitarian home where the decision making is shared by the mother and father on a democratic basis. Although democracy is widely used as the basis for family relationships, it is the source for many family problems. If a young man who is reared in a headless family tries to find a prospective mate who wants to dominate him, he will be unhappy in her company. If he dates a woman with a submissive role concept who expects him to assume strong leadership, this also makes him uncomfortable, and he probably will end the relationship. If he should marry either of these types, there is likely to be role conflict. He will be happiest if he marries a woman who wants to share in making the decisions.

Table 4.1 illustrates some of the possible marriage combinations based on role-concept patterns and the probability of conflict or non-conflict.

The opinions of several hundred Christian college students indicate that most of them accept the biblical role concepts, with the men desiring to be dominant and the women wanting to be submissive. Young women do not want an autocrat for a husband, but they do look for a mate who will assume the headship in the home and give due consideration to their opinions. Some young people have difficulties accepting the scriptural position, for they may have had the misfortune of being socialized in homes with one or both parents unsaved, or in homes where Christian parents were not obedient to the Word of God. The confusion engendered in young people reared in such homes is evidenced in the following statement:

My mother became a Christian after she married my father, but he never came to Christ. He is not only unsaved, but also very much against all religion and everything which has anything to do with the church. In this type of atmosphere, my two sisters, my brother, and I grew up, looking mostly to my mother, perhaps mistakenly in some cases, but at other times, simply because of my father's irritation with and dislike of the things which related to Christianity. Neither my mother or father is outspoken, but each spoke for himself. Many times, as children, we simply did not refer to our father when a decision or plans were to be made. We went to our mother, who would therefore probably have had the dominant role, at least with the children. The situation would necessarily have been much different had my father been a Christian also. My mother and father handle the decisions about finances and the home equally, making this portion equalitarian. I do not know how to classify the role relationship in our family.

A young man who grows up in a home where the father refuses to be the head of the household, or where the father submits to a domineering wife in order to have peace in the home, will often rebel against his parents. He will consciously vow to be the leader in his family when he marries. A woman reared in a similar situation occasionally feels so sorry for her father that she also revolts against the role concept of her mother. Thus, she will look for a mate strong enough to be the "man of the house." Even though these young people sincerely want to assume the roles God desires them to play in dating and family relationships, they find it difficult.

However, roles are learned behavior and can be changed, although change usually requires much effort. The young man who has a submissive father will have to consciously assume the leadership in a relationship. He will have to plan the date and activities beforehand, and although decision making will be difficult at first, it will become easier as it is practiced. The woman who is prone to imitate her domineering mother will have to learn to hold her tongue

Table 4.1
Role-Concept Patterns and Conflict

Male	Female	Nonconflict	Conflict
Dominant	Submissive	x	
Dominant	Dominant		x
Dominant	Egalitarian		x
Submissive	Dominant	x	
Submissive	Submissive		x
Submissive	Egalitarian		x
Egalitarian	Egalitarian	x	
Egalitarian	Dominant		x
Egalitarian	Submissive		x

when tempted to make decisions that should rightly be made by her date. There will be mistakes, but the Christian who desires his conduct to conform to the Word of God has the help of the indwelling Holy Spirit to enable him to change in the proper direction.

> # *Roles are learned behavior and can be changed, although change usually requires much effort.*

The question may be asked, "If the dominance-submission pattern is so important for happiness in the marriage relationship, why do many individuals seem to make the wrong choice, resulting in role conflict and unhappiness?" There are many factors involved, but one of the main answers is that many couples become too involved in their physical attraction to one another too early in the relationship. They do not continue the friendship phase of their dating long enough to really get to know one another as persons rather than lovers. Once the physical aspect of the interaction becomes predominant in the relationship, it is easy to overlook detrimental factors since so much pleasurable emotion is received from physical intimacy.

When these couples marry and the physical needs have been satisfied, they must face the difficult task of reconciling the different role expectations that they brought to the marriage. Many more adjustments will have to be made, and often, when the differences seem irreconcilable, the marriage ends in divorce or the couple settles for a lifetime of unhappiness caused by conflicting role concepts. The choice of a spouse with a complementary role concept *cannot* be overemphasized. The quality and success of the marriage will depend on a good match in this area.

Division of Labor in the Home

Earning a livelihood and the division of labor within the home are also part of a person's role concepts. American culture traditionally has defined the masculine role as that of breadwinner and the feminine role as that of homemaker. The preparation for these tasks begins early in childhood. A girl is usually given dolls and dishes as toys to help prepare her for her adult roles as mother and cook for the family. A boy receives toy trucks and guns as preparation for his role of employee and soldier when he matures. If a child adopts the role of the opposite sex, he is termed a sissy and she is labeled a tomboy. Fortunately, most children successfully make the change to their proper role during adolescence, but if for any reason they do not, they face real problems in their relationships with others. A young woman usually prefers a masculine man over an effeminate one, and a young man usually does not enjoy a tomboy as a dating partner.

These traditional roles have been modified since it became popular for wives to work. A survey of several classes of Christian college students indicates about 50 percent of their mothers worked either full or part time. The female students (with one exception) felt it was all right for wives to work until children came or after they left home. They agreed that the mother with children belonged in the home. They did recognize that it might be necessary for the wife to work if the husband were ill and could not be the breadwinner. Occasionally a male student will manifest the traditional position that he does not want his wife to work outside the home under any circumstances. Most Christian men do not mind the wife working when there are no children involved, or when conditions make it necessary to maintain the home.

Concerning the division of labor within the home, the same survey indicated that about 50 percent of fathers helped in the home with such tasks as drying dishes, vacuuming, doing laundry, grocery shopping, and other chores. This is about the same percentage (although not necessarily the same households) of homes with working mothers. It seems to indicate that in Christian homes, husbands are assuming some tasks that wives used to perform. As someone said, "If the wife helps to bring home the bacon, then the husband can help fry it." Since young people do hold differing opinions as to whether the wife should work and whether the husband should help with housework, couples should discuss their expectations in order to avoid problems in this area when they marry.

Achieving Balance in Role Playing

The multiplication of roles for both husband and wife has also contributed to the difficulties faced in many marriages. The husband is not only father and breadwinner, but at the same time he may also be Sunday-school teacher, deacon, youth advisor, leader in Awana, volunteer fireman, and member of the city commission. If he is employed in a second job, the situation is even worse. The wife is not only mother and homemaker, but she also has numerous role demands. She may be a Sunday-school teacher, church organist, choir member, leader of the junior youth group, leader of Awana, president of Women's Missionary Society, secretary of band mothers, member of the PTA executive committee, and chairman of the local Cancer Society fund drive. Some wives attempt to do all this besides having a full or part time job.

Most individuals can play several roles outside the home fairly successfully, but difficulties in role performance arise when the individual attempts too many tasks, with some done poorly, including those within the home. Some people devote too much time to a particular role, and this can be a problem. This is particularly true when the father spends long hours at the office or business and has little time for the family. Pat Williams, a prominent sports figure, and his wife, Jill, are a classic example. In their widely read book, *Rekindled* (1985), they relate how Pat's total devotion to his job and athletics nearly ruined their marriage. By the grace of God and with help of godly counselors, they were able to rekindle the fires and now have a strong, vibrant marriage.

Those in full-time Christian service also need to be careful not to make this mistake. Pastors and other Christian workers can become so preoccupied with their service for Christ that they do not have time or energy for their families.

In discussing this problem of overinvolvement in the local church, the Meiers (1981, 99) comment, "If a child needs attention from his parents, but they are too busy supposedly 'serving God' to meet his needs, he will probably subconsciously blame God for his parents' self-righteous form of ungodliness, and as an adult reject God for taking his parents away from him as a child." They suggest that pastors should help each parent find "one avenue of service that he or she can do well." They should discourage the "overly eager parent" from getting involved in more than "one or two kinds of service."

> *Pastors and other Christian workers can become so preoccupied with their service for Christ that they do not have time or energy for their families.*

The question of the conflict between missionary service and responsibilities to teenage children is not easy to resolve. It is quite common now for a missionary couple to remain home with their children during the troublesome high school years. Others send their children to boarding high schools. Each missionary has to resolve the conflict as God directs, and no one should be critical of them, for they are responsible to God alone and not to anyone else.

Although the primary interpretation of 1 Timothy 5:8, "if any provide not for his own, and specially those of his own house, he hath denied the faith, and is worse than an infidel," refers to the provision for material needs, a secondary interpretation or a logical extension is that a man must also provide the affection, guidance, and discipline needed by teenage children, or else he comes under the condemnation of this verse. After all, Christians believe the things of the spirit to be more important than the material satisfaction of life. Many Christian homes would be healthier if parents would only realize that the spiritual needs of their children are more important than the material benefits they work so hard to provide for them.

Husbands and wives must strive to achieve a balance in their roles. If an individual has too many tasks and cannot do them all well, some must be eliminated. This means learning to say no. Overloading individuals occurs quite frequently in small churches. Someone with a willing spirit and leadership ability continually will be asked to do more and more until finally he or she has more jobs than he or she can do well. The remedy for the situation is to say no so someone else can be found for the job. It is amazing how much unused talent there is in even the small churches.

> # The question of the conflict between missionary service and responsibilities to teenage children is not easy to resolve.

The masculine-feminine roles in American society are becoming more confused as the return of our Lord Jesus Christ draws nearer. The efforts of the women's movement, the influence of radical professors and students, and the propaganda of the mass media all add to the confusion of roles in the minds of our youth. However, the Christian young person has definite guidelines in the Word of God, and he or she can avoid much of the heartache that many marriages suffer if he or she will heed the

Word and choose a mate with compatible role concepts. Those couples who are already married and have fundamental differences in role concepts can seek the help of the indwelling Holy Spirit (Eph. 5:18–21), the Word of God (Col. 3:16–17), and Christian counselors to enable them to work out these differences to the glory of God.

Study Questions

1. Discuss the factors that contribute to the development of a person's role concepts.
2. Why is it important for a couple to have complimentary role concepts?
3. What are some of the positive accomplishments of the secular women's liberation movement? What are some of the negative results?
4. How do you distinguish between a believer's "standing before God" and his daily walk? Discuss Galatians 3:28 in the light of these truths.
5. How do you explain godly men and women who believe in the divine inspiration of the Bible arriving at different interpretations of the same verses?
6. How would you refute the cultural argument for the interpretation of roles in Ephesians 5 and 6?
7. Why is the doctrine of the Holy Spirit so important in discussing biblical role concepts?
8. Describe the manner in which you feel the husband should exercise his headship in the home.
9. What was the dominance-submission pattern in your home? Which type of dominance-submission pattern does your personality fit?
10. Why is it important to have a balance in the number of roles played?

Personality Inventory

What Is Your Role Concept?

Write a short paragraph in answer to each of the following statements or questions. Please be as introspective as possible in order to determine your true feelings about the roles of men and women in marriage.

1. Who is (was) dominant in the families of your paternal and maternal grandparents? In what ways is (was) this dominance manifested?
2. Discuss the dominance-submission pattern of your parents' interaction. Do you approve of this pattern? Why or why not?
3. Is there a sharing of traditional male-female roles by your parents? Do you plan to repeat this type of interaction when you marry?
4. State your views on the women's liberation movement. Compare the evangelical women's liberation movement with the secular women's liberation movement.
5. Give biblical evidence for your view of the scriptural role of husband and wife in the home.
6. Do you think it is important for young people today to be flexible in their role concepts? Why?

Suggested Readings

Bernard, N., and T. O'Neill, eds. 1989. *Male-female roles: Opposing viewpoints.* San Diego, Calif.: Greenhaven. A volume presenting the views of secular writers who hold opposite views on different aspects of the male-female roles. Each of the five chapters ends with a "critical thinking activity."

Christensen, L., and N. Christensen. 1977. *The Christian couple.* Minneapolis: Bethany Fellowship. A sequel to the million-copy best seller, *The Christian Family.* It presents a valid view of traditional husband-wife roles. Refutes the cultural interpretation of the roles in a convincing manner.

Collins, G. 1982. *Beyond easy believism.* Waco: Word. Collins, a psychologist, left his academic field in order to give the reader a challenge to grow spiritually. The reader is exhorted to leave worthless religion founded on atheistic humanism and to "grow in grace and knowledge of Jesus Christ."

Gillham, A. 1982. *Friends and lovers for life: The dynamics of a happy marriage.* Wheaton: Tyndale House. The author presents a traditional view of marriage in which she finds "mutual subservience" as the goal. A most useful volume to compare with Gundry's *Heirs Together.*

Gundry, P. 1980. *Heirs together: Mutual submission in marriage.* Grand Rapids: Zondervan. A presentation of the evangelical feminist position. Gundry emphasizes the importance of culture in the interpretation of Scripture in order to prove her viewpoint.

Lewes, R. A., and M. B. Sussman, eds. 1986. *Men's changing roles in the family.* New York: Haworth. A collection of articles discussing the evidence for the changing roles of the husband and father. Has an extended bibliography and a filmograph listing eleven films on the subject.

MacArthur, J., Jr. 1982. *The family.* Chicago: Moody. Using the theme of God's pattern, the author develops a scriptural presentation of the traditional family emphasizing mutual submission. A good treatment of headship and submission.

Michelsen, A., ed. 1986. *Women, authority and the Bible.* Downer's Grove, Ill.: InterVarsity. This volume is a collection of papers and responses presented at an evangelical colloquium on women and the Bible. They present the evangelical feminist view. There are a few dissenting remarks.

Sell, C. M. 1982. *Achieving the impossible: Intimate marriage.* Portland, Ore.: Multnomah. The skillful use of colorful phrases, (e.g., How to get the cash out of clash) makes this an interesting book to read. At the same time the author treats the usual subjects. His treatment of roles (Can we role into a happy marriage?) is a succinct statement of prevailing views.

Van Leeuwen, M. S. 1990. *Gender and grace: Love, work, and parenting in a changing world.* Downer's Grove, Ill.: InterVarsity. A presentation of the evangelical feminist interpretation by a psychologist. She uses an interdisciplinary approach combining theology, history, biology, and sociology with psychology.

Spiritual Maturity

But grow in grace, and in the knowledge of our Lord and
Savior, Jesus Christ. . . .

—2 Peter 3:18

The Necessity of Maturity in Marriage

The marriage of two young people who are spiritually and emotionally
mature will be much more successful than that of those who have not
matured. Quite commonly Christian young people assume that just
because they are both Christians, they can meet, grow to love one another,
and live happily ever afterward. They assume that their common belief in
Christ will automatically overcome a poor choice of mate or any personality inadequacies brought to the marriage. Seamands (1982, 175) comments that "this does not mean that simply because two people are good
Christians they will necessarily make a good marriage. We all know wonderful Christians who should never have married each other. For philia
[love] includes much more than spiritual unity. It takes in many important facets of personality blending which makes up the rivets in the bond
of matrimony."

It is true that a union in Christ adds much to the stability of a marriage,
but the wise selection of a partner who is spiritually and emotionally
mature will mean greater happiness for even the Christian couple. Christians need to be aware of the factors involved in maturity and to be able
to assess their own level of spiritual and emotional maturation.

The emphasis in American culture on receiving psychological satisfaction or happiness from a marriage relationship stresses the necessity for
maturity in prospective spouses. The Lasswells (1987, 166) make this statement: "Ideally, marriage partners in our society should be two adults who
are physically, socially, and psychologically capable of modifying their
individualities into mutually acceptable patterns that will bring them more
joys than sorrows in their lifelong relationship with each other." This abil-

ity to modify one's behavior to give happiness to another is directly related to one's level of maturity.

> *Christians need to be aware of the factors involved in maturity and to be able to assess their own level of spiritual and emotional maturation.*

The New Birth and Spiritual Maturity

The Bible clearly indicates that a person begins the Christian life by means of the new birth. Jesus said in John 3:3, "Except a man be born again, he cannot see the kingdom of God," and in verse 7, "ye must be born again." The great expositor Albert Barnes (1868, 222) comments on this verse: "the beginning of this new life, is called the *new birth* or *regeneration*. It is the beginning of spiritual life. It introduces us to the light of the gospel. It is the moment when we really begin to live to any purpose. It is the moment when God reveals Himself to us as our reconciled Father. . . ."

A person experiences the new birth, or is born again, by accepting the sacrifice of Jesus Christ on the cross of Calvary, and receiving him as personal Savior. "But as many as received him, to them gave he the power to become the sons of God even to them that believe on his name, which were born, not of blood, nor of the will of the flesh, nor of the will of man, but of God (John 1:12–13).

Eric Liddell, the great Olympic gold medalist who refused to run on Sunday in 1924, later became a missionary to China. While interned by the Japanese he wrote *A Manual of Christ-*

ian Discipleship in which he quotes Leslie Wetherhead (Liddell 1985, 79): "The message of the New Testament is that the most important thing in the world is that we should get our relationship right with God and receive this transforming experience. No hereditary Christianity . . . is a substitute for it, no doing good to others, no life dedicated to humanity . . . will do." The new birth is a supernatural birth effected in the heart of the person receiving Jesus Christ as a personal Savior.

The new birth is only the beginning of the Christian life. The believer in Christ has the responsibility to grow into spiritual maturity. In Romans 8:16 Paul writes, "The Spirit itself beareth witness with our spirit, that we are the children of God," that is, those who have experienced the new birth. In verse 14 of the same passage, he writes, "For as many as are led by the Spirit of God, they are the "[adult] sons of God," indicating that a person's position in Christ is that of an adult. The believer then has a responsibility to submit to the Holy Spirit so that the daily experience gives proof of having accepted the responsibilities that accompany such a high and holy position. In Ephesians 4:12–15 gifts are given to godly people for "the perfecting [maturing] of the saints . . . till we all come in the unity of the faith, and of the knowledge of the Son of God unto a perfect [mature] man . . . that we henceforth be *no more* children . . . but speaking the truth in love, may *grow up* into him in all things, which is the head, even Christ."

The writer of Hebrews expresses the same truth: "For when for the time ye ought to be teachers, ye have need that one teach you again which be the first principles of the oracles of God: and are become such as have need of milk, and not of strong meat. For every one that useth milk is unskillful in the word of righteousness; for he is a *babe*. But strong meat belongeth to them that are of *full age*, even those who by reasons of use have their senses exercised to discern both good and evil. Therefore, leaving the principles of the doctrine of Christ, let us go unto perfection [maturity]" (5:12–6:1).

In his epistles, Peter also emphasizes the necessity of growth for the Christian. In 1 Peter 1:23 he writes, "Being born again . . . by the

word of God, which liveth and abideth forever."
A few verses later in 2:2 he exhorts, "As newborn babes, desire the sincere milk of the word,
that ye may grow thereby." His final benedic-
tion in 2 Peter 3:18 is an admonition, "But grow
in grace, and in the knowledge of our Lord and
Saviour Jesus Christ."

It is apparent from these and other Bible
passages that the Christian is born into the
family of God and is to grow in spiritual knowledge and experience. Consequently, spiritual
maturity is not synonymous with physical
maturity. A person may be thirty years old
physically but only three months old spiritually. The Christian behavior expected from
such an individual will be less than that
expected from a person who is thirty years old
spiritually. The individual who has been saved
for three months will not be expected to know
as much about the Bible and Christian living
as the person saved for thirty years. However,
God expects both to continue to grow so that
daily they become more like the Lord Jesus.

According to Romans 8:29, God has predes-
tined each believer "to be conformed to the
image of his Son," and it is the Christian's
responsibility to live each day with the desire
to be more like Jesus. Wiersbe (1967, 22) writes,
"When you were born again through faith in
Christ, you became a part of the New Creation.
Just as the first Adam was created in the image
of God, so those who belong to the last Adam
are being 'recreated' to the image of Christ."
The hymnwriter aptly expressed this truth, "Be
like Jesus, this my song, in the home and in the
throng. Be like Jesus all day long, I would be
like Jesus."

The process of spiritual growth requires
four elements analogous to those necessary
for physical growth. A normal, healthy body
requires food and water, air, exercise, and rest
for its proper development. In like manner a
healthy Christian life needs a daily portion of
the Word of God, submission to the Holy
Spirit, some service for Christ, and worship
before his throne. It is impossible to develop
spiritual maturity without these factors being
present each day. This means that believers
must develop the practice of private devotions before the Lord in which they read the
Word, pray, and worship the triune God. This

daily experience then motivates them to submit their bodies to the indwelling Holy Spirit,
to be used as instruments in the service of
Christ.

> *The Christian is born into the family of God and is to grow in spiritual knowledge and experience.*

Bridges (1983, 52) asks, "Where can we
find time for quality Bible study? I once
heard that question asked of a chief of
surgery in a large hospital. . . . He looked his
questioner straight in the eye and said, 'You
always find time for what is important to
you.' . . . Is it important enough to take priority over television, books, magazines,
recreation, and a score of activities that we
all somehow find time to engage in?" The
mature young person takes time for daily
prayer and Bible study.

Characteristics of the Spiritually Mature Person

Spiritual growth is manifested in many areas
of the yielded believer's life. "But . . . the fruit of
the Spirit is love, joy, peace, longsuffering, gentleness, goodness, faith, meekness, temper-
ance: against such there is no law (Gal.
5:22–23). According to Small (1959, 67), the
nine different elements mentioned in this passage produce one "fruit": love. He quotes Don-
ald G. Barnhouse's elucidation of these fruits
of the Spirit:

Joy is love singing
Peace is love resting
Longsuffering is love enduring

Gentleness is love's true touch
Goodness is love's character
Faithfulness is love's habit
Meekness is love's self-forgetfulness
Self-control is love holding the reins

All of these are not "fruits" but the "fruit" of love. Wiersbe (1967, 124) writes, "Love is not something that we manufacture; it grows out of our lives as we are united to Christ, the Vine. When something is manufactured, there is noise and effort and dirt; but when fruit grows it is effortless, quiet, and beautiful."

> ## *"Love is not something that we manufacture; it grows out of our lives as we are united to Christ, the Vine."*

The love shed abroad in the believer's heart by the Holy Spirit (Rom. 5:5) manifests itself vertically in love for God and horizontally in love for the Christian brethren and for those who are lost and dying without Christ. The truth of Romans 6 and Galatians 2:20 of the self-life crucified with Christ is experienced daily. A consistent prayer life in obedience to Philippians 4:6–7 results in a life filled with the "peace of God that passeth all understanding," so that the individuals who observe the life of a mature Christian marvel at the equanimity displayed in difficult circumstances.

One of the characteristics of the mature Christian is a definite separation from the world. Strict obedience is given to the exhortation of 1 John 2:15, "Love not the world, neither the things that are in the world. If any man love the world, the love of the Father is not in him." The body is presented as a living sacrifice (Rom. 12:1) and the transformation and renewing of the mind (v. 2) is experienced in the life.

What constitutes worldliness today is debated by many Christians. However, if one remembers that there are just two forces at work in the universe today—those energized by God and those under the direction of Satan—usually it is not hard to determine whether an event, attitude, or amusement relates to God or Satan. In the passage previously quoted (5:14), the writer of Hebrews stated that maturity is marked by the ability to discern between good and evil. In Galatians 6:14, Paul indicated that a definite mark of a life crucified with Christ is being dead to the allurements of the world: "But God forbid that I should glory, save in the cross of our Lord Jesus, by whom the world is crucified unto me, and I unto the world."

Unfortunately, the idea has been propagated in the Bible-believing churches that God has one standard of spiritual maturity for laymen and a higher standard for full-time Christian workers. This is a false concept, for the Bible presents one level, that of likeness to Christ, and God expects every Christian to strive toward that goal. It is easy to see why a spiritually mature young person who has established the habit of daily private devotions, is yielded to the Holy Spirit, is crucified with Christ, who manifests the fruits of the Spirit including love for the brethren and the lost, whose life is filled with the peace of God, and who lives a life separated from the world will make a much better mate than a less mature Christian.

Measuring Emotional Maturity

Intelligence tests, routinely given in elementary and secondary education, provide the means to measure the mental age of a student. In determining mental age, chronological age is always taken into consideration. Measuring emotional maturity is much more difficult. Society links emotional maturity to physical development, chronological age, and mental age. For example, it is permissible for a four-year-old to cry when his wishes are blocked, but it is not appropriate behavior for an eighteen-year-old. A twelve-year-old may change his goals in life each week without censure, but a young person of twenty-four is expected to have a goal in life and be working toward its attainment.

Although there is no one-to-one relationship between emotional maturity and chronological age, it is a fact that it "takes time to grow up." The Lasswells (1987, 166) comment, "The ability to be social adults is almost certainly more widespread among twenty-two-year-olds than among eighteen-year-olds and is almost certainly more widespread among twenty-eight-year-olds than among twenty-two-year-olds. Nevertheless, chronological age is far from a perfect index."

Young people reared in stable environments mature rapidly, while the emotional development of others may be stunted by overprotective or neglectful parents. Maturation occurs more rapidly in some areas of an individual's personality than in others. For example, a student may be childish in handling money. A young woman may exercise leadership in a group, but be so ineffective in her relationships with men that she never has had a date. Even the most mature individual has a few areas in his emotional structure that are underdeveloped. Collins (1985, 96) states that "the pages of history are filled with examples of people . . . who are talented artists, musicians . . . scientists, or statesmen, but who are personally immature, self-centered, bombastic, and unable to get along with people."

Characteristics of the Emotionally Mature Person

Many factors must be considered when determining the emotional maturity of an individual. Primarily, behavior should correspond to the societal expectations for a person of that chronological age. The actions of a college freshman are usually more immature than those of a college senior. A freshman may have difficulty adjusting to dorm life, and this may cause him to fail a course and be placed on academic probation the following quarter. However, for a senior to fail a course is much more serious and may prevent graduation with that class. A freshman without much dating experience may be forgiven some breach of eti-

quette, but a young woman will expect a senior man to know how to act in her presence.

> *Behavior should correspond to the societal expectations for a person of that chronological age.*

The mature young person will discharge responsibilities as they arise, whether they be in the area of study, work, or dating. A student may fail occasionally to meet an obligation, but a pattern develops indicating the person is able to assume responsibility. When failure does occur, it is used as a learning experience rather than accepted as an agonizing personal defeat. This capacity to assume responsibility is an aspect of maturity that is essential in successful marriage. Helms and Turner (1987, 328) list one characteristic of a mature person as "the capacity to assume responsibility for one's choices in life and their consequences. Also, one must be able to renounce unattainable choices and recognize that some variables influencing choices are out of one's control."

One mark of mature persons is the ability to look objectively at themselves and their relationships with others. They are able to examine their own personalities and pinpoint their own strengths and weaknesses. They do not attempt to extend themselves beyond their limits, but try to improve those areas of weakness. Collins (1985, 97) reflects, "As we grow toward maturity, we develop a more realistic view of ourselves." For example, if their athletic abilities are average, they recognize that they will not make the varsity basketball team—but enjoy playing on an intramural team. If they have difficulty in their math courses, they choose a major in a subject area in which they have more ability, even though they enjoy math.

> *One mark of mature persons is the ability to look objectively at themselves and their relationships with others.*

This same type objectivity is applied when one encounters a problem. When mature people meet a problem, they try to place themselves outside of it so they can look at different aspects of the situation in order to find a solution. Reason rather than emotions guides their actions. They learn to separate facts from feelings and try to base decisions concerning the problem on the facts involved rather than on feelings in the matter. In order to seek a solution based on reason, they must be able to control emotions and not become angry, upset, discouraged or defeated when a problem arises. This does not mean that mature people have no feelings or never manifest an emotional reaction to a problem. They may manifest a reaction, but is a controlled one rather than an emotional outburst. The mature individual may be temporarily upset by some happening, but quickly regains composure and makes rational decisions based on objective facts rather than on feelings.

In reference to controlling one's emotions, a distinction needs to be made between controlled emotions and repressed emotions. It is possible for a person to repress certain emotions and deny them expression until such behavior results in psychosomatic illness. The individual has been taught never to express overtly any anger, jealousy, hatred, or other antisocial feelings and keeps them bottled up until a stomach ulcer, a migraine headache, or some other physical symptom of inward stress develops. Such a person is emotionally immature and needs to learn to recognize feelings as being antisocial and seek to relieve them in a socially acceptable manner.

Children who are angry with one another often express their anger by physical aggression (Helms and Turner 1987, 252). When grown adults are angry with one another, however, they are expected to control their feelings. They may not hit each other with fists, but they can find ways to channel their frustrations in more constructive behavior, such as exercise or gardening. Mature individuals learn that society expects them to control their emotions and to release them in a manner approved by the social group. They know that to repress them is not good for themselves or for those with whom they associate. Lester (1983, 60–61) recognizes that "anger, like a stopped-up sewer, backs up until it spills over inside and poisons the self.... Physical disorders that can be caused by internalized anger include cardiovascular problems . . . gastrointestinal disorders . . . and many disorders of the skin.... A major result of . . . self-directed anger is depression."

Dobson (1980, 94–95) lists several ways to "release pent-up emotions": taking the matter to God in prayer, talking to other Christians, showing love to the one who has offended us, accepting God's forgiveness and being willing to forgive those who offend us.

In addition to emotional maturity, another characteristic of the mature person is the ability to understand and to respond to the feelings of others. Most people are able to sympathize or "feel with" another person in a time of loss or tragedy. However, only the mature individual is able to empathize with a person. Santrock (1990, 475) defines empathy as "the ability to understand the feelings of another individual."

The young person who has suffered a broken heart in a love affair knows how a person undergoing such an experience feels and is able to enter into the emotions much better than the person who has never suffered a broken romance. When tempted to make a cutting remark that would hurt another person, the mature individual controls the tongue. The empathetic person is able to get along well with other persons, has the ability to discern their feelings and is able to identify with them. The individual who is always saying something that is later regretted lacks the quality of empathy and certainly needs to cultivate it.

The mature young person is one who is becoming independent from family and friends. Helms and Turner (1987, 329), quoting Allport, refer to this separation as "self-extension." During the process of maturing, the individual is continually reaching out to other individuals such as peer groups and church groups. Eventually, this leads to forming strong bonds with members of the opposite sex and the ability to "share new feelings and experiences with others."

If individuals fail to mature in this area, they are unable to cut the apron strings. Two classic examples of failure in this area are the young person who leaves college the first week because of homesickness, and the young bride who runs home to mother whenever she has a quarrel with her husband.

> ## *Most students benefit by their newly gained freedom from immediate parental supervision.*

In some families the members are close to one another, and the young person has greater difficulty in achieving independence than the young person from a family where the members are not as close. It is easier for the young person to become economically independent in a family where one has learned to work and earn money than it is where the young person has always lived on an allowance.

Problems may arise between parents and young people in at least two areas in this matter of becoming independent. Young people often try to assert independence before they are old enough or mature enough to become independent. For example, the high-school couple who announce they plan to be married even though the fellow has only a part-time job encounters resistance from their parents. The parents believe the couple is not facing reality as mature young people. The parents point out the difficulties such a marriage faces in the areas of finances or personal adjustments, with the hope that the couple will reconsider and postpone marriage until they complete their high-school education or perhaps a year of college. Conflict arises if the couple refuses counsel from the parents. Many young people, in their desire for independence, act rebelliously when their parents feel the young people are not ready for it. On the other hand, problems may also arise if the parents refuse to relinquish control when the young person is old enough and mature enough to become independent. Consider the case of Jane, a college senior:

> My mother and I are having problems because she wants me to come live at home when I graduate, and she wants me to get a teaching position in the local school system that I attended. However, my roommate and I want to get positions in a Western state, and we want to live together in our own apartment. I appreciate what my parents have done in helping to pay my college expenses, but I am twenty-two years old now and feel that I should begin to make my own decisions in reference to employment and housing.

Jane's parents, particularly her mother, are unwilling to accept the fact that their daughter is now a mature young adult who desires to make her own way in life. Wise parents encourage such aspirations of their children. Young married couples may face the same type of problem if they accept financial subsidies from their parents. The couple is not truly independent financially and there may be a tendency for the parental family to attempt to make decisions for their still dependent, though married, children.

Attending college away from home is a maturing experience for many young people because it affords them an opportunity to make decisions by themselves and to meet new friends. Most students benefit by their newly gained freedom from immediate parental supervision and gradually learn to do many things for themselves they formerly expected their parents to do for them, such as writing their own checks or doing their own laundry. Unfortunately, some students merely transfer their dependency from their parents to their roommates and then expect these newly acquired friends at college to help them make their decisions.

A small number of students are not able to adjust to the freedom of college life and use it as an occasion to rebel against parental standards and values that they have submitted to but have not genuinely accepted. They eventually become discipline problems and an embarrassment to their families and to the Christian institution they attend. With appropriate discipline they often mature sufficiently to handle their freedom and become self-respecting members of the college group. A few persist in their rebellion and become a reproach to the name of Christ.

> # *A small number of students are not able to adjust to the freedom of college life.*

Another criterion of maturity listed by Helms and Turner (1987, 330) "is the development of a unifying philosophy of life that embodies the concepts of a guiding purpose, ideals, needs, goals and values . . . such a synthesis enables him or her to develop an intelligent theory of life and to work toward implementing it." Mature Christian young people meet this goal in their commitment to Christ.

They have thought through the Christian philosophy of life and have reached the settled conviction that salvation is only through faith in the atoning blood of Jesus Christ. For them "there is none other name under heaven given among men, whereby we must be saved" (Acts 4:12). Average high-school students encounter enough opposition to their Christian faith so that by the time they reach college they have faced such foes of the Christian faith as evolution, scientism, humanism, communism, and various other "isms." In facing such encounters they discover the Word of God is true and trustworthy and that it contains the answer to all the devil's "isms." They come to realize that faith received at their mother's knee as a child is real and genuine, and it is able to strengthen them in the hour of testing and temptation.

When difficulties come, they have learned to accept them as part of God's will for their life, and they claim the promise of Romans 8:28. Even if God's will should include a lifelong physical handicap, this also is received as from his hand. It is refreshing to the spirit and a challenge to the soul to hear the testimony of mature Christian young people with handicaps whose philosophy of life centers in the Lord Jesus Christ.

Another characteristic of maturity is the ability to defer gratification. One is willing to postpone immediate gratification of some desire so that a more important satisfaction in the future may be achieved. A child comes into the kitchen and asks his mother for a cookie. When asked to wait a minute until the mother finishes her task, the child throws a temper tantrum because the desire for a cookie is unfulfilled. Some young people never mature beyond this stage. Whenever they want something, they must have it now. The young man drops out of high school because he has a well-paid summer job in the factory and cannot give it up to return to school in September. He fails to realize he may be laid off in February, or that it is a job with no future.

The mature young man is willing to sacrifice the money he might be earning in order to get some higher education or some technical training that will prepare him for a rewarding occupation in the future. He is willing to drive the old car in order to be able to go to college, even though some of his high-school class-mates have gone heavily in debt in order to purchase new sport models. In these and many other areas, the mature young person will sacrifice present gratification for increased satisfaction in the future.

A responsible attitude toward sex is also characteristic of the mature young person. One cannot have a proper attitude if not given the correct information about sex. If the parents have failed to give this knowledge, young people must read factual books and pamphlets on the subject so an understanding of sex is not based on misinformation often gained from the peer group. The Bible recognizes sex as God-given and holy within the confines of marriage but immoral outside these bounds, as in promiscuity, fornication, and adultery.

If young people have been reared in a home where affection was shown between husband and wife and between parents and children, they are able to demonstrate affection toward the opposite sex. A young person is aware of the emotional needs of the other person and is able to meet those needs within the bounds of Christian love. They never seek to exploit the opposite sex in order to gratify their own physical desires.

This is one area where young people often manifest their immaturity, since they have not learned to submit their bodies to the control of the indwelling Holy Spirit. Small (1959, 174–75) writes: "The Scriptures say, . . . know ye not that your body is the temple of the Holy Ghost . . . (1 Cor. 6:19). Whatever the standard of the non-Christian, the standard for the Christian is clear. His body is a sacred trust from God, its functions meant to be restricted to and preserved for the ends designed by God. Jeremy Taylor prayed, 'Let my body be servant of my spirit, and both body and spirit servants of Jesus Christ.'"

As young people are able to surrender their bodies to his holy dominion, they are able to distinguish between mere physical attraction and genuine romantic love. The mature young person is aware that much of what the world terms "love" is merely sexual attraction, and a Christian maintains the biblical standards of purity and chastity in his relationships with the other sex.

Mature young people know that sex is for marriage, and will be much more rewarding if they enter the marriage relationship free from the guilt and remorse of premarital experiences. One individual, who learned by sad experience, stated, "Postmarital guilt is one of the best arguments for premarital chastity." However, the mature young couple prepares for marriage during the engagement period by reading one or more marriage manuals so they are informed as to their roles in consummating the marriage relationship.

> *"Postmarital guilt is one of the best arguments for premarital chastity."*

One result of the maturing process is the development of a good self-image. Lamanna and Riedmann (1988, 214) indicate that "the emotionally mature person has high self-esteem. . . ." Since young people are learning to look at themselves objectively, they see their strengths and weaknesses. As they build on their strengths, their self-confidence increases. With increasing spiritual maturity, they have an expanded view of themselves as precious to God, and as having an important part to play in serving the cause of Christ. They are inner-directed by the values which they hold, and though they are concerned about the needs of people, they will not be conformed to the world.

All of these characteristics of maturity rarely are found in one young person. In reference to mate selection, young people should attempt to find as mature an individual as possible. Just as a person may mature more rapidly in some spiritual areas than in others, so emotional maturity may progress faster in some aspects than others. If young people are immature in some area, the important thing is that they should be aware of it and should be attempting to improve in that area. The ability to recognize the area of immaturity is itself a sign of increasing maturity and is a plus factor in assessing the personality.

Maturity for Marriage and Chronological Age

It is evident from the discussion in the preceding section that the spiritual and emotional maturity of a person are more important than chronological age. All states have a legal minimum age at which young people can marry. This minimum age varies from state to state. Most states make exceptions to the minimum age with consent of the parents or a court. State legislatures recognize that a measure of maturity is needed to fulfill the various roles of husband and wife.

> *The spiritual and emotional maturity of a person are more important than chronological age.*

This fact is evident in the high divorce rate of teenage marriages. Young people who marry in their teens are usually not mature enough to assume the responsibilities of marriage. The Lasswells (1987, 162) observe, "Those who marry early . . . find the most difficulty in sustaining intimacy and in carrying out marital obligations, both of which are core elements in marital adjustment. So well-documented is the belief that early marriage sets up a high risk for divorce that early age at marriage is the best single predictor of divorce."

Couples who graduate from college are usually in their mid-twenties when they marry. They tend to have happier marriages than couples who have only finished high school. It cannot be determined whether it is the college experience that contributes to the happiness, or whether it is simply the fact that they are chronologically at least four years older, which gives them that much more time to mature.

Men usually marry women who are two or three years younger than themselves. The theory is that young women mature faster than men. Consequently, many young women are reluctant to date men who are younger than they are. However, some studies have shown that the groom being a few years younger or a few years older does not affect the happiness of the marriage. The important factor is the emotional maturity of the individuals. Thus, a young woman should not hesitate to date a man who is slightly younger if he demonstrates sufficient maturity for his age level.

There is the danger of incompatibility in marriages where there is a large age difference between the two spouses. Twenty years' difference may not appear too great at ages twenty-five and forty-five, but the physiological difference becomes greater after a decade or two as the older partner ages faster. This will be most apparent when the older spouse enters the sunset years of life. The possibility of debilitating and long-term illnesses associated with old age may mean that the younger spouse will spend years as a caregiver while he or she is still in the prime of life.

Age and emotional maturity are also important for young adults who have passed the prime marrying years of the early twenties. The stereotype is that the bachelor or single woman in the early thirties cannot marry and make the needed adjustments in married living. Studies have proven this stereotype to be false, for such couples are able to adjust and to live happily together. One reason is they have lived longer and are more emotionally and spiritually mature than those who marry in their early twenties. Also, when they do marry, they are strongly motivated to make the marriage a success, as they realize that a second opportunity at their ages is not very possible, whereas some young people enter marriage with the idea that if it does not succeed, they can try again. Emotional maturity is the important factor, as it is possible for people in their early thirties to be emotionally immature and incapable of making the adjustments necessary for happiness in marriage.

Maturity and College Marriages

Maturity is especially important in two other marital situations. The first is marriage while attending college. Before World War II, a marriage of college students was a rare occurrence, and it was customary for young people to wait until graduation to get married. The influx of married veterans destroyed the idea that married students could not do as well as single students. Subsequent studies have shown that married students achieve better grades than they did as single students. Many college and universities now provide housing facilities for their married students. Students contemplating marriage while in college need to realize they sacrifice much of the social life that is ordinarily associated with college. Most adult social activities in society at large are for married couples, but college social life is oriented around dating couples; activities for married couples are not as frequent. Unless a couple has had sufficient dating experience and is reasonably sure they will not miss the social activities, they should not consider marriage while in college.

The problem of financing both a college education and a marriage is a real one. The cost of higher education climbs each year, as does the cost of living. If room and board were the only consideration, it is true that two can live as cheaply as one. However, there are other expenses involved, such as automobile costs and insurance, which are usually cared for by parents.

Many couples solve the problem by letting the wife drop out of school and take a full-time job to help pay expenses. The husband goes to school, works part-time, and takes out loans to help pay tuition costs. Other couples have their marriage subsidized by parents for all or part of their expenses. Some parents feel the tuition cost is their obligation whether the student is single or married and agree to pay this expense for the young married couple. Other parents are able to subsidize all expenses so that both the husband and wife can finish their courses and receive their degrees.

Some parents help the couple on a loan basis, particularly if they have younger children who also will need financial aid for college. Some couples insist on paying their own way by only taking as many hours of college work they can afford even though it extends the time they are in college to five or six years. One husband who took several years to complete his college work used to joke that he went through on the "four-year" plan—four years as a freshman, four years as a sophomore, et cetera. Serious thought should be given to the financial considerations by a couple planning to marry while still in college.

Maturity and Military Marriages

Another type of marriage that requires considerable maturity for success is one in which the husband is scheduled to leave for the armed forces. The couple must decide if they should marry before or after the service experience. Assuming they have had a courtship sufficient to test their compatibilities, the deciding factor is the amount of time they have as a married couple before the separation takes place. Many critical adjustments must be made during the first year of marriage, so the couple should have at least a year together before separation takes place. This gives them time to work out any problems that may arise between them as a married couple.

> *The problem of financing both a college education and a marriage is a real one.*

A separation is difficult for any relationship to withstand, for the two persons are undergoing personality changes without the opportunity to adjust to each other. Even though letters are written each day, these are a poor form to communicate changes in feeling and attitudes. It is better for the couple to remain engaged and wait for marriage until the service

89

obligation is fulfilled. If for some reason the relationship is broken, there is no necessity for a divorce with its legal and religious difficulties. Sometimes after the basic training, a serviceman may be assigned to a base in the United States and is allowed to live off base. Marriage under these circumstances is not too different than when the groom holds a civilian job. If the couple is separated during his military service, it is wise to treat the reunion as a second honeymoon where they can have a few days together alone before returning to the routine of everyday life.

Maturity and Successful Marriages

The importance of a young person striving to attain spiritual and emotional maturity cannot be overemphasized. Success or failure in marriage is determined to a large extent by the level of maturity attained. Small (1959, 9) expresses it well: "Spiritual roots are important and cannot be ignored. Emotional maturity will engender emotional unity between a married couple, and in precisely the same way spiritual maturity will engender spiritual unity. . . . Christian marriage offers the way to real oneness by pointing to a unifying center and power outside of the couple themselves."

> ## "Emotional maturity will engender emotional unity between a married couple."

Spiritual and emotional growth continue throughout life. This is what Paul had in mind when he wrote to the Philippians, "Not as though I had already attained, either were already perfect [mature] . . . forgetting those things which are behind, and reaching forth unto those things which are before, I press toward the mark for the prize of the high calling of God in Christ Jesus" (3:12–14). "So let us all who are mature have this attitude" (3:15 *Williams*).

Study Questions

1. How is maturity related to success in marriage?
2. Discuss spiritual growth. When does it end?
3. Is it possible for a spiritually mature Christian to consistently engage in worldly practices? Give scriptural evidence for your answer.
4. What is the relationship between spiritual maturity and emotional maturity? Is it possible to have one without the other?
5. Discuss the difference between empathy and sympathy.
6. How is your philosophy of life related to your Christian experience?
7. What characterizes a responsible attitude toward sex?
8. What is meant by deferred gratification? How is it related to emotional maturity?
9. What is the importance of a good self-image? Compare your self-image to what your best friend might think of your self-image.
10. Discuss the advantages and disadvantages of a couple marrying while both are in college.

Personality Inventory

Are You Ready for Marriage?

Answer each of the following statements or questions with a short paragraph. Please be as introspective as possible to gain insight about your degree of spiritual and emotional maturity.

1. Have you established the practice of a daily quiet time with God? If not, why not?
2. Have you learned to daily yield your life to the control of the Holy Spirit?

3. How important to you is regular attendance at the services of the local church?
4. What forms of Christian service or witness are you involved in?
5. Explain your method of solving problems as they arise in your life.
6. How do you relieve frustrations? Do you need to make any improvements in this area?
7. What do you think is the will of God for your life work? If you are uncertain, why can't you decide?
8. How well do you know your own personality needs? Which areas need improvement?
9. Do you feel that you have had sufficient dating experience to know what kind of marriage partner would be compatible with your personality?
10. Are you still economically or emotionally dependent on your parents or siblings? Will this dependence, if any, create problems if you marry?

Suggested Readings

Collins, G. 1988. *Your magnificent mind.* Grand Rapids: Baker. A professional treatment of the human mind that a layman can easily understand. The control of the mind is important in achieving spiritual maturity. This volume explains how the mind works and how it can be controlled.

Hybels, B. 1991. *Who you are when no one's looking: Choosing consistency, resisting compromise.* Grand Rapids: Zondervan. Written by the pastor of Willow Creek Community Church in the Chicago area. He lists several character traits that are badly needed today and instructs the reader how these may be strengthened. He uses the old definition of character—"You are what you are when no one is looking."

Kuhne, G. W. 1986. *The change factor.* Grand Rapids: Zondervan. A small but powerful book filled with information for anyone wanting to change for the better. The author stresses the part that faith plays in change and indicates how faith is to be utilized to effect change that will result in spiritual maturity.

Lester, A. D. 1983. *Coping with your anger.* Philadelphia: Westminster. A volume designed to enable a Christian to recognize anger as part of God's creation. The author desires the reader to learn the vices and virtues of anger. He gives concrete suggestions on how a Christian can control anger.

Liddell, E. 1985. *The disciplines of the Christian life.* Nashville: Abingdon. The author was the famous star of the 1924 Olympics who refused to run on Sunday. He became a missionary to China. Although the manuscript was written during his internment by the Japanese, it wasn't published until 1985. He writes, "The secret of growth is to develop the devotional life," and this volume is designed for a year of daily devotionals.

McGloin, J. 1988. *Graduating into life.* Grand Rapids: Baker. An excellent volume written to encourage young people to make the right choices and to enable them to grow spiritually and mature in their faith. The author writes, "we prove or disprove both our maturity and our Christianity by the way we choose."

Osborne, C. G. 1986. *Self-esteem: Overcoming inferiority feelings.* Nashville: Abingdon. Many young people have feelings of inferiority. This book is designed to aid them in their battle to overcome these feelings.

Stowell, J. M. 1986. *Fan the flame: Living out your first love for Christ.* Chicago: Moody. The author discusses six principles that are basic to a Christian philosophy of life. If they are practiced when one faces the choices of life, they will enable young people to please God in all their actions.

Swindoll, C. R. 1987. *The quest for character.* Portland, Ore.: Multnomah. Swindoll gives instructions to help individuals build character. He writes that "the quest for character" is a life-long pursuit. Heeding his valuable Bible-based instruction will help in the process of maturing.

Romantic Love

Many waters cannot quench love, neither can the floods drown it.

—Song of Solomon 8:7

Different Kinds of Love

"Oh, Jane, have you heard that I'm in love?" "No, when did this happen?" "Oh, a couple of weeks ago. I met John and he is handsome as a movie star. We hit it off from the very start. I'm so excited I can hardly eat or sleep! I think we'll get married soon."

Is this young woman really in love or is she merely infatuated? Love is an emotion that is hard to describe and define. As a word, it encompasses a broad range of meaning. There is Christian love, which includes love for God, for fellow believers, and for the unsaved; parental love, filial love, puppy love, and platonic love.

Many times the word *love* is used as a synonym for "like," as in, "I love pizza, baseball, tennis, white shirts, antique clocks." There is a difference between love and like. They are both emotional states. Lamanna and Riedmann (1988, 91) distinguish between them: "Liking is not as powerful as loving, and research indicates that liking may be more rational—a result of thinking rather than feeling." They report on the research of Rubin, who found that individuals usually like people who are similar in background and who share common values. Loving involves an emotional intensity directed toward one person who is thought to be "unique and indefinably special." Often liking leads to loving as a relationship develops.

A distinction also needs to be made between love and lust. Lust as commonly used refers to "excessive sexual desire." Much of what is called love in the entertainment world is simply lust. Coleman (1988, 146) comments that "the mass media—including movies, T.V., magazines, novels and popular music—have tended to perpetuate this idealistic view of romantic love in our society." Very often the justification for immorality is that two people are "in love." However, often either one or both partners are motivated by lust.

> # It is impossible to maintain the emotional high that romantic love engenders.

Christensen (1983, 56) reflects, "People say they have fallen in love, when maybe they have only 'fallen into lust.' Physical attraction exerts such a power that someone handsome or beautiful taking an interest in us may sweep us off our feet."

In dating and courtship the predominant kind of love is usually called romantic love. Santrock (1990, 277) defines it as "passionate love or eros, . . . the type of love that involves passion. It is what we mean when we say we are 'in love' with someone, not just 'I love' someone." Santrock (1990, 277) quotes Berscheid as saying romantic love is "about 90 percent sexual desire." However, since it is a desire that can't be fulfilled morally outside of marriage, a longing for consummation with the beloved intensifies until this desire pushes the couple toward marriage and fulfillment of the passion or dissolution of the relationship because of factors that extinguish the passion. As the passion subsides, a deeper form of compassionate or conjugal love develops. It is impossible to maintain the emotional high that romantic love engenders.

DeVault and Strong (1989, 124) suggest that "passion is subject to habituation; what was once thrilling, whether love, sex, or roller-coasters, becomes less so the more we get used to it. Once we become habituated, more time with a person (or more sex or more roller-coaster rides) does not increase our arousal or satisfaction." Huggett (1982, 10) quotes C. S. Lewis as asking, "Who could bear to live in that excitement [of infatuation] for even five years?

What would become of your work, your appetite, your sleep, your friendships?" And Huggett asks, "And who would pay for the phone calls, the postage and love's extravagant trinkets?"

In Christian marriages, the mature love of 1 Corinthians 13 replaces immature, physical romantic love. This does not mean that a good marriage lacks passion, for a wise couple will work at developing the sexual aspects of their marriage so that it improves over time. A good marriage cannot be built on passion, but every good marriage will have a healthy component of passion.

Definitions of Love in the Greek Language

As indicated in the preceding section, the English language is deficient when it comes to the use of the word *love*. The Greek language has several words for love that describe different kinds of love.

Consider first the word *storgē*. Wheat and Perkins (1980, 60) reflect that "this love, referred to several times in the New Testament is the kind of love shared by parents and children or brothers and sisters. . . . *Storgē* love in marriage meets the need we all have to belong. . . ." It is the love of family members who care for and support one another.

The second word is *philio*. R. C. Trench, in his great work *Synonyms of the New Testament*, says, "[philia] without being necessarily an unreasoning attachment . . . is more instinctive, is more of the feelings, implies more passion. . . ." An example of this love as human affection or friendship is found in John 11:3 in the message of Mary and Martha to Jesus concerning Lazarus, "He whom thou lovest is sick."

Eros is another Greek word for love. Lamanna and Riedmann (1988, 89) elaborate: "It forms the root of our word *erotic*. This love style is characterized by intense emotional attachment and powerful sexual feelings or desires. Erotic partners experience an immediate strong attraction upon first meeting." It is the kind of love so often portrayed by the entertainment industry and modern novels. It is a destructive type of love.

Agape is the great New Testament word for love. Morris (1981, 25) indicates that it is "almost the only New Testament word for love." It is the word used for the love of God. DeVault and Strong (1989, 119) emphasize that it "is the traditional Christian love that is chaste, patient and undemanding; it does not expect to be reciprocated. It is the love of saints and martyrs." They also relate that the sociologist John Lee, in describing six basic styles of love based on these Greek terms, did not find any lovers of this type. It is unfortunate that he did not know some Christians, for there are multitudes of beautiful Christian marriages based on agape love. Most do not reach this ideal, but many do, and their children and Christian brethren can bear testimony to this fact. Bogarth (1987, 41) aptly writes, "Agape is the quality of love that stands for and preserves the freedom of the other, even when that freedom is in conflict with one's own self-interest. . . . It is the gift that enables us to make sacrifices for each other so easily and graciously that we don't even know that we are doing it."

There are other Greek words not so common as the previous ones. Lee (DeVault and Strong, 1989) lists "Mania: obsessive love . . . Ludis: playful love, Pragma: practical love." Morris (1981, 117) mentions "eunoia, designating dedicated devotion . . . pothos, desire . . . charis, gratitude and kindness. . . . This enumeration is far from complete."

The English language is not as specific as the Greek. When the word love is used, it may refer to any of the thoughts expressed by these Greek words. It also may represent an idea combining the meaning of two or more of these words. In order to be more definite in English, some descriptive word must be used with "love," such as sensual love (eros), brotherly love (philia), or divine love (agape).

Some terms represent a combination of qualities. Romantic love, for example, could be viewed as a composition of eros, philia, and a small measure of agape. The love that is mature enough for a successful marriage is dominated by the agape element, with the eros factor declining as the couple ages.

Agape love is divine love that God shares with those who accept his Son as Savior and Lord. As the husband and wife are filled with his love, they find that giving love is more important in the relationship than receiving

love. Their desire is not what they can get from the relationship but what they can give. As Christensen (1983, 52) expresses it, "Love should bring you closer to God. The very center of Christian faith is love—for God is love. . . . Such love reveals itself in the physical as well as psychological, for both share a divine element. In one mood love may express itself as a tumultuous passion, and in another a beautiful, calm, mysterious joy. Whatever it is, it is divine." Therefore, the highest, noblest, and happiest conjugal love should abide in the Christian home.

Definitions of Romantic Love

Courtly love, or romantic love, as it is known today, came to prominence in the twelfth century. This was the love of noblemen and knights in medieval times. Murstein (1986, 103–4) traces the development of this type of love through the Renaissance and demonstrates how it filtered down to the middle and working classes of the twentieth century. Johnson (1983, xiii) observes that "modern western society is the only culture in history that has experienced romantic love as a mass phenomenon. We are the only society that makes romance the basis of our marriages and love relationships and the cultural ideal of 'true love.'"

There has been a renewed interest in the scientific study of romantic love in recent years, even though there is no consensus on a definition of romantic love. Friedlander and Morrison (Pope 1980, 27) observe, "A precise and satisfactory definition of romantic love has eluded even those social scientists who have recently risen to the challenge of its scientific study. However, the phenomenon may be identified as an affectively charged subjective experience characterized by an intense longing for and preoccupation with another person."

Branden (Barnes and Sternberg 1988, 220) defines romantic love as "a passionate spiritual-emotional-sexual attachment between two people that reflects a high regard for each other's person."

Hatfield (Barnes and Sternberg 1988, 193) writes of "passionate love" and "companion love." She defines the first as "a state of intense

95

longing for union with another. Reciprocated love (union with the other) is associated with fulfillment and ecstasy. Unrequited love (separation) with emptiness, anxiety or despair. A state of profound physiological arousal."

However, romantic love is an emotion that can be experienced by people of all ages. It is usually characterized by an intense physical attraction. Malcolm (1987, 16) reflects, "When we first meet that special person the sexual, emotional, and interpersonal dynamics are such that we can think of no one or nothing else. Our lives are full of fireworks and grand weddings. Rational thinking and thoughtful decision making tend to be difficult in those high energy days." All the emotions are focused on the lover, who is expected to return them with a similar intensity.

> *A strong physical attraction is a major feature of romantic love and quite often is mistaken for love itself.*

This is the love that makes the heart palpitate on the sight of the beloved. Young people may be fully aroused and find it hard to concentrate on studies or a job; they may also have difficulty in eating or sleeping. Life revolves around the loved one with whom there is total emotional, psychological, and social involvement. Johnson (1983, xii) indicates that "when we are 'in love,' we believe we have found the meaning of life, revealed in another being. We feel we are finally completed, that we have found the missing parts of ourselves. Life suddenly seems to have a wholeness, a superhuman intensity that lifts us high above the ordinary plain of existence. For us, these are the sure signs of 'true love.'"

The wonderful emotional feelings resulting from romantic love are God-given. They are part of his wonderful design to bring a young man and woman together in marriage. Huggett (1985, 31) emphasizes that "the ability to feel drawn to another for sexual contact . . . was dreamed up by God, created by Him. Sexual excitation, like the sex drive, was God's idea. Hormones and erections, tender breasts and ejaculations and the stomach somersaulting with desire, were God's brain-children."

Difficulty arises when these emotions are not kept under control. One of the developmental tasks of young adulthood is learning to love with the mind as well as the heart. Lewis and McDowell (1988, 56) relate a conversation with Gerhard Dirks, one of the developers of the computer while with IBM and who, at that time, held more patents than any other person. Dirks compared computers with the body and mind, and thought that they were programmed in a similar fashion. The basic thesis is that the mind never forgets what goes into it. The authors proceed to state, "your mind is so important—the most important sexual organ you have. And how you program your mind becomes critical. We men need to be especially careful of what we look at. Women need to be careful of what they wear and how they are touched. . . . But if the way you program your mind directly affects your potential for sexual fulfillment, taking precautions is well worth the effort." The young Christian has the help of the indwelling Holy Spirit to help balance emotion and reason.

Since this text is oriented toward young people not yet married, the historical term *romantic love* will be discussed in the following pages.

Components of Romantic Love

It is easier to identify the components of romantic love than it is to define it. A strong physical attraction is a major feature of romantic love and quite often is mistaken for love itself. On the other hand, romantic love cannot exist without a real sexual interest in the partner. God has so constituted human beings that the urge for biological nearness is part of his plan for the formation of new families and the propagation of mankind. This desire for physical nearness is expressed by the sense of touch (Dobbins 1985a, 36). After a couple starts to date, the first physical contact might typically be holding hands. As dating continues and the relationship develops, the next move is to kissing, then to embracing.

In the plan of God, the end result of these normal desires is to move the couple toward marriage so that a new family can be established. These physical intimacies are subject to the moral law of diminishing returns. A couple must proceed slowly in this area, for once they have proceeded to one level of intimacy it is difficult, if not impossible, to return to a lower level. If they start embracing each other, usually they are not satisfied to return to a simple goodnight kiss without an embrace.

It is important that the couple test their compatibilities in other areas before they become too involved in the physical aspect of the relationship. This is necessary because many young people are misled by the popular concept of romantic love—they think a strong physical attraction between a young man and woman is all that is needed to live happily ever after. Movies, television programs, and mass literature convey the impression that if a man and woman have a great physical attraction to each other, they can marry and live happily, for this is all that is needed in marriage. Many young people, Christian and non-Christian, enter into matrimony with this highly romanticized concept of marriage. The marriage fails when the physical desires have been satisfied and the couple discovers that they do not have the basis for a sound marriage (Crabb 1982, 18).

The Wheats (1981, 37) observe that "the Bible gives no indication that the feeling the world calls *love* is to be the foundation for marriage. A marriage built entirely upon this will be characterized by fluctuating feelings as the circumstances change. Result: shaky emotions, shaky marriages! Emotions do not and never will sustain a marriage . . . but . . . commitment binds husband and wife together. . . ."

The intensity of the sexual attraction varies from couple to couple. In the most intense of relationships, the partners may have a great physical attraction from the first date. Just the sight of the other person quickens the heartbeat. The young people may have difficulty eating and sleeping. Thoughts of the loved one so encompass the mind that study and work are difficult until an adjustment can be made to the new status of being "in love" (Blood and Blood 1978, 101).

> # As the husband and wife are filled with God's love, they find that giving love is more important in the relationship than receiving love.

In a less intense relationship, a couple meet and are friends for a long period of time before they have their first date. Johnson (1983, 197) remarks, "When a man and a woman are truly friends, they know each other's difficult points and weaknesses, but they are not inclined to stand in judgment on them. They are more concerned with helping each other and enjoying each other than they are with finding fault." The relationship may develop very slowly until it finally passes an unknown moment when friendship ripens into love. They cannot pinpoint any specific time when they became lovers, but their attraction to each other is definite and unmistakable. Other couples may fall at various points along this continuum of intensity, but for real love to exist, there must be a sexual attraction between the two individuals.

A second feature of romantic love is companionship or desire to be with the person. The Bloods (1978, 95) call this the "social element in love." Ordinarily people choose companions on the basis of similar likes and beliefs. They should have common interests and enjoy each other's company. Two people who marry are going to spend a long time together, so it is important that they choose dating partners who are good companions apart from any sexual interest. If a person enjoys good music or sports, for example, he or she should date someone who is interested in the same things. If people are not good companions, they are merely infatuated physically and must break off the relationship in order to avoid heartbreak and difficulties later. A person should be mature enough to objectively assess a relationship to see it offers good companionship apart from common sexual attraction.

Since church attendance and service are such a large part of the Christian life, the young person who loves the Lord will certainly seek a life companion who has a similar devotion. The Bible asks, "What part hath he that believeth with an infidel?" (2 Cor. 6:15), and it is difficult to understand how a Christian young person can claim to be in love with an unsaved individual or one who does not enjoy the things of Christ.

> ## *The young person who loves the Lord will certainly seek a life companion who has a similar devotion.*

A third component of love is care or concern for the well-being of the partner. Hine (1985, 47) defines care as "concern for another—a desire to affirm, to help, to serve. . . . Here *Agape* comes into play. It is a desire to meet the needs of one's spouse and to reinforce his or her best efforts to achieve fulfillment." As a couple continues dating, they become more interested in the needs and desires of each other. The person who cares for another individual is more concerned about meeting the needs of that individual than about caring for one's own needs. The woman may simply mention that red roses would look nice on her dress for the junior-senior banquet, and her beloved may skip meals in order to have the money to buy a corsage of red roses. She will stay up all night typing his term paper because he needs it the next day. The general attitude is, "Your slightest wish is my command." After the honeymoon, this attitude changes, and her strongest command may not move him from his easy chair to take out the garbage. This change is one of the big differences between romantic love and conjugal love. In courtship, however, true love is doubtful if one individual or the other fails to display this care for the other's welfare.

Another constituent element of love is idealization, whereby one partner projects attitudes and attributes toward the other partner that he does not actually possess. A student dated a very ordinary girl, not especially attractive, but when he returned, he stated to his roommate, "She's so beautiful!" He had enjoyed her lovely personality and attributed qualities of beauty to her that his roommate knew she did not really possess. Quite often a person may ask about a certain couple, "What does she see in him?" or "What does he see in her?" The answer is that the idealization factor of love causes the individuals to see qualities in each other of which the outsider is unaware. This is important, for it enables imperfect human beings to find mates! If everyone waited for the perfect individual to appear, there would be no marriages. As it is, people who have imperfections meet other such individuals, and love develops. As a courtship continues, much of the idealization will disappear. By this time they both realize that, although they are not perfect, they do have a good relationship and are compatible with each other. Of course the opposite can occur and the couple could come to realize they are not compatible and may elect to break the relationship.

A danger in idealization occurs when couples do not date long enough to really know each other, and then enter marriage really thinking the partner has the qualities they have attributed to him or her. If this happens, a disillusionment takes place during the honeymoon when the real selves are revealed and the individuals realize they really did not know each other well. Dobbins (1985a, 46) aptly calls this the "honeymoon hangover." He indicates that "this is the difference between the fantasy person you dated and the real person you married. Many people date fantasies—not persons." This may explain why so many divorces occur within the first or second year of marriage. Idealization is a definite part of romantic love, but it must be tested in personal interaction if the couple are to know each other as persons before they enter into marriage.

An important element of romantic love is commitment. It begins early in a relationship when the persons agree to go steady. They commit themselves to an exclusive relationship with each other. As the relationship grows, the level of commitment increases until the couple becomes engaged. This is the final test of compatibility before marriage. If incompatibilities are discovered and cannot be resolved, then the engagement can be broken. An individual may suffer more than one broken engagement as it is fairly common to break off a relationship at this level.

The final act of commitment occurs when they commit themselves to each other in marriage. This commitment at marriage is for life. Johnson (1983, 103) remarks that commitment binds a man to a woman so that he "will be with her even when he is no longer 'in love,' even when he or she are no longer afire with passion and he no longer sees in her his ideal of perfection or the reflection of his soul." This he calls "the essence of commitment." It is this type of relationship that Smedes (1989, 27) illustrates with the story of Emily and Jason. After ten years of happy marriage, Jason was struck by a virus that rendered him impotent. At the time the book was written, they had continued fifteen more years of blissful marriage because they were committed.

Smedes also relates the story of Eric and Karen. Karen is stricken with Alzheimer's disease, and Eric cares for her as one cares for an infant because he loves her and is committed. This illustration could be multiplied by hundreds of thousands of committed spouses who care for terminally ill mates. Young people approaching marriage and its lifelong commitment need to ask themselves, "If my beloved were paralyzed in an accident during the honeymoon, is my commitment strong enough to care for him or her the rest of my life?" Joni Erickson Tada and her husband are also an excellent example of commitment.

Infatuation and Romantic Love

The various components of romantic love will vary in degree and in intensity with each couple, but they must be present to some degree if love is to exist. For some couples the physical attraction will be strong, but unless the other elements of companionship, care, idealization, and commitment are present, the couple's relationship may not survive. Webster defines infatuation as "unreasoned passion or attraction." The root word means "to make a fool of." Many a young person has admitted after an infatuation he simply made a fool of himself by such unreasoned passion. Huggett (1985, 68) describes infatuation in these words: "Infatuation leaves no part of you untouched. Your mind spins as thoughts of the beloved swirl round vying for attention. The whole of your body tingles . . . your will melts like butter in the sun. And your imagination runs riot . . . feeding on all that the relationship is or seems to be and over-glamourizing what will be." A relationship may begin with an intense infatuation, but as dating continues, the other elements of love should appear and a well-rounded love should develop. This is why it is important for young people with a strong physical attraction to give themselves enough time to really know each other before getting married.

A danger in idealization occurs when couples do not date long enough to really know each other.

In other couples, the companionship element may predominate. They really enjoy doing things together and the physical attraction is minimal, but it must be there or else it is mere friendship. In another situation the element of care is foremost. This is frequently seen in a relationship where a healthy individual is attracted to a handicapped person. The things that distinguishes love from pity is a sexual attraction and a desire for companionship with each other. Love may be a many-splendored thing, but it can be reduced to some basic elements that are fairly easy to distinguish if young people are aware of their existence.

> *Many times lessons are learned in early romances about keeping emotions in check.*

Can a Person Love Two People at the Same Time?

Young people often ask, "Is it possible to be in love with two people at the same time?" This is a problem faced by some of the more popular young people who have many opportunities for dating and courtship. Alberoni (1983, 45) asks, "Is it possible to love two people at the same time? Of course. Is it possible to love one person and fall in love with another? Of course." For example, it is conceivable that a young woman, dating two young men at the same time, could be in love with both of them. She could be physically attracted to them, enjoy the companionship of both, be concerned and care for their welfare, and attribute some qualities to them they actually do not have. Similar backgrounds and other requirements for a successful Christian marriage may be possessed by both young men. In such a case, the young woman, through prayer and the leading of the Holy Spirit, will have to choose one man and nurture the development of their relationship.

When Is a Person Really in Love?

A more frequent problem is faced by the young person who has difficulty in determining whether he or she is really in love with a particular individual. Dating has occurred over a reasonable length of time, but there are doubts as to the future of the relationship. Sometimes the perplexed individual does not feel the passionate emotions the popular culture leads us to believe is an essential sign of love. The solution to the problem, in addition to sincere prayer for God to reveal his will in the matter, is to examine the total relationship. Are all of the elements of romantic love present in some degree? It is necessary to keep in mind that these vary in intensity from couple to couple. Sometimes there is a tendency to compare the present relationship with a former one, and if there is not the same emotional response in the present one, then it is felt it cannot be love. Benson (1971, 117) relates that "if the previous romance was an unhappy one, 'Willard Walter and Reuben Hill (1951) suggest that there may be a certain loss of capacity for love after unhappy experiences. The person develops various protective devices and collects "scar tissue" from romantic wounds, dulling his sensitivity. However, there is no strong evidence that this always or even usually happens.'"

Many times lessons are learned in early romances about keeping emotions in check so that there may be a lesser degree of infatuation in a person's third romance then in the first. Benson (1971, 117) remarks, "it may be impossible to ever again reach the intensity of your very first love affair." He also relates the findings of his research on the question whether the "most intense love affair led to marriage." About one-third of the sample indicated that it did not.

Some degree of sexual attraction must be present if romantic love is genuine, but one must remember the physical aspect of a relationship is not as important as the other elements, since in marital interaction the physical relationship diminishes as companionship and care increase in importance.

Love that is mature enough for marriage requires time to develop, time for infatuation to be tested and mature. This will also allow the persons involved to grow emotionally and spiritually. Butler and Gutknecht (1985, 117) remark that "mature love is 'an ever constant process of personal growth and the awareness of the other's feelings and needs.'" Obviously, mature love can be experienced only by mature people; it involves self-worth, self-love, and self-respect. Many have pointed out that love for others is possible only when one feels love for self. In contrast, with romantic love, which is an undulating series of highs and lows, mature love consists of moderation and is evenly balanced and tempered. This aspect of determining true love might be called the test of time. Present evidence indicates that couples are marrying two or three years later than couples formerly did. This is an encouraging trend.

Another valuable test is that of separation. This is a particularly valid test for college students in love. They have so much time together on campus that a period of separation gives time to assess the loved one and the relationship without the physical satisfaction of being together. The physical may often cloud the good judgment of lovers. A Christian will certainly spend much more time in prayer seeking to know if it is real love or not. Also one must make an objective analysis of the relationship.

Lewis and McDowell (1988, 25–26) list several questions that a person may ask to determine if the man or woman with whom they are in love is the right one: "Ask yourself, 'Do I have a desire and a capacity to meet his or her real needs? Is this person capable of more than merely satisfying my sexual urge, or raising my children, or bringing home the paycheck?' When you date, the search isn't just for someone you can *live with*. Instead, the real search should be for someone you *can't live without*." Marriage is for a long time, and young people need to be sure they have the best love relationship possible.

Love at First Sight

Many young people wonder whether love at first sight is possible. Some couples have had such an experience and believe in such a phenomenon. Where two individuals have in mind an ideal type of person they would like to marry, and these people meet under propitious circumstances, it is quite possible for them to be strongly attracted to each other immediately. Since they represent each other's ideal mate, the attraction will grow and the relationship develop into a harmonious and happy one. This is a rare occurrence and young people should not date with the hope that this will be the manner in which they meet their prospective mates. Most marriages result from ordinary, routine dating and the building of a relationship without the glamor of love at first sight.

Most cases of individuals falling in love at first sight do not stand the test of personal interaction. Many of these people have emotional problems and regularly fall in love in times of stress. It is quite easy for such a person to become infatuated with a new dating partner, to feel that it is love at first sight. The new love experience acts as a release for the emotional stress the person is experiencing. This type of relationship will probably be broken when the interaction between the two reveals incompatibilities that were masked by infatuation.

Malcolm (1987, 16) makes the point that "many Christians have not been taught about the strength of sexual drives and the influence of romantic feelings on their desire to marry. They think that the desire is enough on which to build a relationship that will last a lifetime." Any relationship that starts out as love at first sight needs time to determine if the individuals are compatible and suited to each other for a lifetime of marriage. When this testing of compatibilities yields positive results, then the couple can look back and say, "Yes, it was love at first sight." This will not occur very often. Murstein (1986, 104) points out that "most people do not fall in love at first sight, and in fact, are often indifferent at first to the person they eventually marry."

Dobson (1980, 55–56) takes a different view. He regards love at first sight as a "physical and emotional impossibility. Why? Because love is not simply a feeling of romantic excitement, it goes beyond intense sexual attraction; it exceeds the thrill at having captured a highly desirable social prize.... These temporary feelings differ from love in that they place the spotlight on the one experiencing them. . . . These emotions are motivated by our own gratification. . . . Such a person . . . has *fallen in love with love*." He then proceeds to define real love as something one grows into. "Its nature is that of awareness of needs, unselfish, giving and caring. This kind of love is not the kind of love one 'falls' into at first sight, as though he were stumbling into a ditch."

Is It Possible to Fall in Love?

It is almost impossible to discuss love without some reference to the phrase *falling in love.* The idea conveyed is that of two people who are physically attracted to each other, who can do nothing to prevent their falling in love. With such attraction, it doesn't matter if nothing else in the relationship indicates compatibility as mates. This is part of the false Hollywood type of romance with which most young people are familiar.

> *Rational thought and decision making are just as much a part of love as is the indiscriminate longing of the glands.*

Chapman (1982, 19) compares the experience of falling in love to that of the African hunter who digs a hole and covers it with branches, and then an animal comes along and unexpectedly falls into the trap. He further comments, "We are walking along doing our normal duties when all of a sudden one day we look across the room or down the hall, and there she/he is—*wham-o*—we 'fall in love.' There is nothing we can do about it. . . . Only one course of action is considered. Get mar-

ried! . . . our social, spiritual, and intellectual interests are miles apart. Our value systems and goals are contradictory but we are 'in love.'" The tragedy is that many Christian young people do not realize that physical attraction does not equal mature love, or that they can choose the type of person they wish to love.

McGinnis (1982, 77–78) expresses it in these words: "Some still believe that love is something for which you are fated by the stars and when two people who were intended for each other lock eyes across a crowded room, they will be irresistibly pulled together. . . . All of which is patent *nonsense* [italics added]. . . . Most of us are turned on by lots of people. . . . Your actions do not have to be at the mercy of your glands. You have the choice between nipping your emotions in the bud and fertilizing them."

Rational thought and decision making are just as much a part of love as is the indiscriminate longing of the glands. God created bodies with biological desires, but he also gave them minds to control desires. He expects Christians to use minds as well as bodies in determining God's will in this important task of choosing a life partner. Diehm (1984, 116) comments in a similar manner, "Love is a mental decision, a focusing of the thought processes . . . an intellectual involvement. . . . Love is a decision that involves the mind and all its powers . . . wise persons will recognize the difference between someone who arouses them and someone with whom they choose to live. Arousal can be quickly extinguished."

The Difference Between Love and Lust

At the beginning of this chapter, mention was made of the fact that love is often confused with lust. Confusion also exists in the Christian use of the term *lust.* The dictionary defines lust as "a desire to gratify the senses," but a secondary meaning of "excessive sexual desire" is more prominent in the connotation of the word today. Capps (1987, 53) confirms this: "Most writers on the deadly sin of lust center on sexual desires. They give little attention to the lust for power, or to the relationships between sexual lust and the lust for power."

The term is used by Paul in 2 Timothy 2:22: "Flee also youthful lusts," and Peter (1 Pet. 2:11) exhorts the Christian to "abstain from fleshly lusts, which war against the soul." In 1 John 2:16–17, John commands the Christian to "stop loving the world" and classifies the "lusts of the flesh" as part of that world system dominated by Satan that is to eventually pass away as God's plan of the ages unfolds. It is clear that the obsession with sex that characterizes our society is part of the satanic world system, and the Christian is under divine commands to both flee and abstain from it. The Christian is to submit the body to the control of the indwelling Holy Spirit so that the fruits of the Spirit are produced in the life.

Although these passages make clear the Christian's responsibility, there is a passage concerning lust in Matthew 5:27–28 that presents a problem to many young people as they become aware of their biological desires toward the opposite sex. Jesus said, "Ye have heard it was said by them of old time, 'Thou shalt not commit adultery': But I say unto you, "That whosoever looketh on a woman to lust after her hath committed adultery already in his heart." Jones and St. Clair (1987, 100) state that the word for "lust" in Greek is *epithumia*. "*Epi* means 'over' and *thumos* means 'passion.' Lust means 'overpassion.' . . . Lust is a burning desire for the opposite sex." Anyone who has worked in an office, shop, or factory with unsaved individuals knows by experience how much lusting goes on today. Men see a woman pass by and make lewd and lustful comments among themselves. Many women now do the same. Promiscuity and infidelity are so widespread that some men (and some women) desire (lust) to sleep with anyone. These individuals are guilty of committing adultery in the heart. It seems that society is approaching a state similar to that of Noah's day, when "the wickedness of man was great in the earth, and that every imagination of the thoughts of his heart was only evil continually" (Gen. 6:5).

Christians may be guilty of the same sin if they permit their lower nature to desire or lust after other women or men. Small (1959, 10) remarks, "It is a fine line that separates between the sexual expression of love and the sexual expression of contempt. Lust is not ever far from love in human experience. Men are aroused sexually by visual stimuli much more easily than women, and are prone to mentally dwell on sex."

The obsession with sex that characterizes our society is part of the satanic world system.

Lewis and McDowell (1988, 89) quote Dicks, the computer expert previously referred to, as saying: "Women are basically programmed by touch, and men by their eyesight . . . most women know what's provocative and what's not. . . . What they choose [to wear on a date] sends off all kinds of signals. . . . A guy . . . needs to be alert to what he is doing with his hands. . . . Touch is what turns a girl on, and if you want to be a responsible date, you need to exercise caution in this area." It is for this reason that Paul exhorts the Christian to take "captive every thought to make it obedient to Christ" (2 Cor. 10:5 *Williams*). Jones and St. Clair (1987, 105) comment on the thought life: "If lust catches fire in your eyes, then it spreads to your mind, and your mind is your most important sex organ. If the fire of lust smolders there, you are in trouble. . . . You can renew your mind by replacing the lustful thoughts in there now with the thoughts of God. . . . When your mind begins to wander, immediately replace your lustful thoughts with God's pure thoughts." One good way to do this is to memorize Scripture so that when lustful thoughts come, they can be replaced with a verse that has been learned. The psalmist asked, "Wherewithal shall a young man cleanse his way? By taking heed there to according to thy word. . . . Thy word have I hidden in my heart that I might not sin against thee" (Ps. 119:9, 11).

It is necessary to remember there is a difference between temptation and sin. A man may not avoid seeing a woman in a bathing suit on a commercial, which is a temptation, but he can control his mind so that he does not dwell on the stimulus that could lead to sin. Martin Luther said, "We can't prevent the birds from flying over our heads, but we can prevent them from making a nest in our hair." In a day when revealing clothing is common, a Christian would have to become a hermit to avoid temptation to evil thoughts. Although Christians are in the world, young people do not have to conform to the world but can have their minds renewed and guarded by the Holy Spirit. They may live or work in such ungodly surroundings that they will have to cry out with Saint Augustine, 'Give me thy purity, O Christ,' with the assurance that such a heart cry will be answered."

> *Coupled with a proper understanding of agape love must be the commitment of the will.*

This problem of determining what is lust also arises in dating. Many young males confuse their natural, God-given desires to be with the opposite sex with lust and are filled with regret and guilt when they read Matthew 5:27–28. In that passage our Lord is referring to intense sexual desire that leads to adultery. This is different from desiring to be in the company of a young woman. If Matthew 5:57 were interpreted to include the normal desire to be with a loved one, then no individual with a natural, divinely-given sex drive could enter into marriage without mentally committing adultery during the courtship process. The desire of a male to consummate marriage with the betrothed is far different from the desire to go to bed with every woman he sees.

This does not mean that a Christian man or woman may not be guilty of lust if they are promiscuous in their necking and petting. God expects the young persons to have high standards in these areas and to maintain them with the aid of the Holy Spirit. It is most important that the young person "abstain from all appearance of evil" and make every thought "obedient to Christ."

The Synthesis of Love

The romantic love of Christian courtship that leads to marriage is a blend of the factors found in *eros, philia,* and *agape*. In the early stages of the relationship the erotic aspects may predominate. As the relationship deepens, the companionship features of *philia* and the altruistic characteristics of *agape* must control the relationship. For a couple to marry with anything less than a love governed by *agape* is to risk failure in the marriage.

The man and woman who marry on the basis of love centered in God, who is love (*agape*), will find their personal lives enriched and their marriage relationship fulfilled in a manner that the unsaved cannot understand. Christian young people who wish to have the maximum happiness in their home need to make sure their love consists of the right elements balanced in the proper amount and relationship to each other.

Coupled with a proper understanding of *agape* love must be the commitment of the will. Dobson writes (1980, 71): "My love for my wife is not blown back and forth by the winds of change, of circumstances, and environmental influences. . . . I have chosen to love my wife, and that choice is sustained by an uncompromising will. 'For better, for worse, for richer, for poorer, in sickness and in health, to love and to cherish, till death do us part.'" That familiar pledge from the past still offers the most solid foundation upon which to build a marriage, for therein lies the real meaning of genuine romantic love.

Study Questions

1. How do you distinguish between "like" and "love"?
2. Discuss the different types of love as defined by the Greeks.
3. Is *agape* love demonstrated in your family? Can you think of any friends' or relatives' relationships that are characterized by *agape* love?
4. How does romantic love differ from conjugal or mature love?
5. What elements do you think constitute romantic love? Which one do you consider most important?
6. What verses could you use to prove that sexual desires are a gift of God?
7. Why is the mind the most important sex organ?
8. What are the advantages and disadvantages of idealization in mate selection?
9. Discuss the importance of commitment in marriage.
10. Why is lust such a problem in American culture? How can a Christian overcome it?

8. Do your personalities complement each other?
9. Can you enjoy one another when you are not conversing?
10. Can you share your innermost thoughts and feelings?
11. Does mutual respect characterize your relationship?
12. Do you agree on limits you have placed on sexual intimacy?
13. Does the friendship bring out your best qualities?
14. Are you proud of your friend when you interact with other people?
15. Are you attracted to others while you are dating your friend?
16. Has your relationship pushed out other legitimate interests from your life (e.g., studies, music practice)?
17. Are there things about your friend you would like to change?
18. Is your friend able to accept constructive criticism?
19. Do your disagreements end in conflict?
20. Would you want your friend to become the parent of your children?

Personality Inventory

Infatuation or Love?

A couple who has an intense physical attraction often finds it difficult to know if they are in love. The following questions are designed to help determine whether the relationship is based primarily on physical feeling or if it is mature love.

1. Is the relationship based on a mutual love for the Lord Jesus?
2. Are you good companions apart from sexual interest in each other?
3. Does your friend encourage spiritual growth?
4. Do you share similar values and goals?
5. Do your parents and close friends approve of your relationship?
6. Are you comfortable with the same type of people?
7. Are you satisfied with the dominance-submission roles in the friendship?

Suggested Readings

Alberoni, F. 1983. *Falling in love.* Translated by Lawrence Venuti. New York: Random House. This book was a best seller in Italy. The English translation is not easy to read but it does give the reader a good idea of how a different culture views the subject of love.

Barnes, M. L., and R. J. Sternberg, eds. 1988. *The psychology of love.* New Haven: Yale Univ. Press. This collection of articles attempting to define and discuss love is one of the first to be published since the scientific study of love became fashionable. The readers are asked, "What is love?" and the various contributors attempt to answer the question. There is such a variety of opinions expressed that the reader really doesn't get a clear answer. Maybe it is because one is not possible given the many-faceted nature of love.

Conway, J., W. Trobisch, et al. 1982. *Your family.* Downer's Grove, Ill.: InterVarsity. A collection of articles on problems of young people, written by sixteen different authorities, giving advice to young people on how to share the problems they face with their families.

Huggett, J. 1985. *Dating, sex, and friendship.* Downer's Grove, Ill.: InterVarsity. A helpful volume by an English writer. She deals with these important subjects scripturally and frankly. Chapter 2 on "Be Holy and Sexual" is a good explanation of the difference between sex and sexuality.

Johnson, R. A. 1983. *We: Understanding the psychology of romantic love.* San Francisco: Harper and Row. The first romantic love story was the myth of Tristan and Iseult of the Middle Ages. All Western romantic literature descends from this story. Johnson uses the "principles of Jungian psychology" to interpret the story in order to learn "what it has to teach us about the origins, the nature, and the meaning of romantic love."

Jones, B., and B. St. Clair. 1987. *Sex: Desiring the best.* San Bernardino, Calif.: Here's Life. Written by authors who work with young people. It relates the hard questions that young people often ask about sex. The chapter on "Is Lust Abnormal?" is excellent and worth the price of the book.

Lewis, P., and J. McDowell. 1981. *Givers, takers, and other kinds of lovers.* Wheaton: Tyndale House. A small paperback that is large on content. The authors deal adequately with romantic love. Chapter 5, discussing the mind as the most important sex organ, is very helpful.

Pope, K. S. et al. 1980. *On love and loving.* San Francisco: Jossey-Bass. A collection of articles exploring the psychological aspects of romantic love. Makes a good attempt to define romantic love.

Rubin, T. I. 1990. *Real love.* New York: Continuum. Written for the general public in an attempt to demonstrate that "real love generates real love." Rubin deals superficially with "thirty-one enemies of real love" such as jealousy, envy, perfectionism, and pride.

Whyte, M. K. 1990. *Dating, mating, and marriage.* New York: Aldine de Gruyter. This volume chronicles the results of a survey made in the Detroit area. The author believes that the findings are applicable to the United States in general. The survey tabulates changes in dating, mating, and marriage over three time spans since World War II.

Part 3

Forming a Marriage Relationship

7

Dating

> . . . the way of a man with a maid.
>
> —Proverbs 30:19

Boy Meets Girl

Every society has some legitimate method for men to meet women. In Latin America it may be walking around a central park. In certain parts of Africa young women are bought with a bride price. In some tribes a man must work for the father of the bride for a long period of time to purchase her hand in marriage. In Bangladesh, a Muslim country, parents may use a marriage broker to find suitable mates for their children. The couple may not even see each other until the wedding. In India, brides are often bought while still very young. China passed a law in 1980 outlawing bride price, but Santrock (1990, 273) states that "in rural areas of China . . . bride price payments are still common."

American society has developed a different system called dating. Lamanna and Riedmann (1988, 199) define dating as consisting "of an exclusive relationship developed between two persons through a formal series of appointed meetings. Dating relationships develop into marriage through a carefully orchestrated series of stages: going steady, informal engagement, formal engagement. Evolving, progressive commitment is expected, along with greater emphasis on sexual exclusivity."

This system gives young people great freedom in choosing a life partner. They do not have total freedom, for the culture places certain restraints on the choice.

Dating and Social Class in America

The social class system in America is different from that in Europe because it developed from a frontier culture. The early colonists rejected much of the class systems of their European ancestors. However, a class system did evolve but with much more freedom to move up or down in the system. Today, some sociologists recognize three main categories—upper, middle, and lower. Each of these can be further subdivided into three levels so that nine different classes can be arbitrarily identified.

Each class has its own patterns of speech, dress, cultural values, and child-rearing methods. Since there is not a single standardized pattern of child-rearing methods, the result is a great variety in the patterns of personality development in children. Our dating system has evolved to allow young people with different personalities to test their psychological compatibility. By dating many different persons, the young person is able to select a mate whose personality is compatible with his or her own.

> **Our dating system has evolved to allow young people with different personalities to test their psychological compatibility.**

Christensen and Johnson (Henslin 1985, 21) state, "A person is much more likely to date and select a marriage partner from his own general social class position. . . . The great attention attracted by the rare Cinderella marriage illustrates the lack of cultural prohibition against them (our value system favoring equality) and the force exerted by the status placement function of the family which almost precludes its occurrence." This matching of personalities is most important. The success or failure of a marriage in the United States is judged by the amount and quality of personal satisfaction received from the interaction between the couple. By contrast, in an African tribe where women are not highly esteemed and family problems are settled by male dominance, the matching of personalities becomes a moot point.

In Bangladesh, there is little husband-wife interaction, so little attention is paid to how well the personalities complement each other. Their roles are well defined by the Muslim society, and each spouse is able to fulfill the role without much regard to personal interaction. The system of mate selection in these cultures is not obliged to match personalities. The success or failure of the marriage is judged by other criteria. The ability to produce children to provide for the couple's old age is of primary importance in those cultures.

In American culture, with changes taking place in the family structure, great emphasis is placed on the psychological satisfaction that each partner receives from the marriage. It is necessary that young people have the opportunity to test their personalities with those of many different individuals. The goal is to find a match that promises to yield the greatest happiness to each partner. Our system of dating and mate selection is a trial-and-error method, but if properly used it can produce good results.

In his marriage manual, Christensen (1983, 21) observes, "We need outlets for the pleasure that our senses and our bodies can bring to us; we need to feel worthwhile and worthy. No relation more pleasurably and adequately meets these needs than the committed marriage." Dating is the process that leads to the wonderful state of matrimony.

Dating—A Learning Experience

Dating usually follows a logical progression, moving from random dating through steady dating to engagement to marriage. In random dating partners are chosen without any thought of serious emotional involvement. Such dating may begin in junior high school and is quite common in senior high school. This type of dating should be the norm for young people during senior high and the first two years of college. Nelson (Murphey 1984, 21) describes it in these words: "Dating is an end in itself where casual interest in the person is sought primarily for an evening of social activity. Sometimes we call this 'playing the field' to differentiate it from more serious involvement in the social interacting of persons."

The purpose of the system is to allow young people to meet different people of the opposite sex in order to test whether their personalities are compatible. They should try to meet as many people as possible in order to discover the type of person with whom they feel most comfortable. Dobbins (1985a, 17) comments, "Random dating is the most important phase of our mate selection process. Don't neglect it! You can make several important discoveries by having a variety of dating partners." During these dating experiences, young people come to know and understand better their own personalities. They encounter strengths on which they capitalize and discover weaknesses that they need to correct. They see certain traits in the opposite sex that they want to avoid when deciding to choose a mate.

Santrock (1990, 272) indicates that "dating is part of the socialization process in adolescence—it helps the adolescent to learn how to get along with others and assists in learning manners and sociable behavior." Learning how to ask for a date or to respond to an invitation to date is a difficult task, especially for a shy person. It is a skill, and like other skills it becomes easier with practice. He discovers it is easier to ask for a first date with someone that he has already met in a class, a club, or some other social activity. He learns that on a first date, it is easier to take the girl to a party or concert where there are planned activities so that their conversational abilities are not strained. She learns to give him little clues that she is enjoying the evening and thus relieves some of the strain that accompanies a first date, since both are trying to make a good impression. He also learns to differentiate between a girl's polite excuse that indicates she does not want to date him and a "raincheck" response that indicates she is interested but

has a bona fide reason for not being able to accept his invitation.

DeVault and Strong (1989, 147) observe, "It is as difficult for some women to turn a man down as it is for some men to ask a woman out. 'I don't want to hurt his feelings' is a common problem expressed by women who find themselves going out on a date with somebody they don't particularly like."

> *During their dating experiences, young people come to know and understand better their own personalities.*

During these formative years of dating, the young Christian is seeking God's will in regard to a vocation and realizes the necessity of finding a life partner who has the same desire to do the will of God. Young people become more aware of the values they hold, and how a mate is needed who holds to similar values. One girl related her experiences concerning values as follows:

I dated a fellow when I was confused in the area of life's goals, and this hurt our relationship. This guy valued money . . . it was important to him. I have never cared much for money. It seems of little importance to me, probably because it matters greatly to my mother.

This girl recognized the young man's values concerning money differed greatly from her own and could be a source of conflict if she continued dating him.

Dobbins (1985a, 18–19) suggests several other advantages of random dating: the feeling of being attractive to the opposite sex; to satisfy one's need to have fun; the opportunity to compare potential partners. Dating helps young people form a realistic view of the kind of mate they desire to marry. It is easy to see why random dating is such an important step in our mate-selection process.

Dating and Personal Standards of Conduct

When dating begins, the young man or woman has to decide what his or her standards of conduct will be in relationship to the opposite sex. Christian youth face temptations involved in necking, petting, and premarital relations because they live in the same sex-suffused society as do the unsaved.

> *Purity of mind and body takes on a divine dimension, for God said, "Be ye holy, for I am holy."*

Unsaved youth may subscribe to the so-called new morality, but Christians may not: they are conscious that they live in the presence of God and that the Word is their foundation of truth and values. Although the world may condone sin and even encourage it, they realize that sin is sin and is under the judgment of God. They know their bodies are the temples of the Holy Spirit (1 Cor. 6:19) and are to be kept pure and chaste in order not to grieve the indwelling Holy Spirit. Alcorn (1985, 58) emphasizes this point: "Biblical Christianity is an intrinsically and intensely moral religion. Sexual morality is by no means the whole of morality. . . . The acceptance or endorsement of any immoral practice is ultimately an attack on the faith. More fundamentally, it is an attack

on God Himself, whose holy character is the basis of biblical morality."

The manner in which a Christian youth responds to the God-given biological urges that are manifested at puberty will largely depend on the way in which sex was presented in the home and church. An erroneous attitude still prevails in our society, and even sometimes in our churches, that sex is sinful and dirty and not to be openly discussed.

This distorted view may have arisen because the Bible so sternly warns against sexual sins. God knows that stable family life is essential to any orderly society, and that nothing is more disturbing to the family than fornication and adultery. Consequently, he is careful to instruct and warn the human race to avoid such perils. The false view that sex is sinful and dirty prevents an adolescent from recognizing sexual desires as God-given and holy and may result in problems of adjusting to interaction with the opposite sex.

The Penners (1981, 31) suggest that the negative attitude toward sex may be a result of the Victorian era, during which people frowned on anything pertaining to sex. They state that "since sex involves intense emotional feelings . . . there has been a tendency to view the subject as a private dimension of our lives. The indirect message has often been that there is something basically sinful about our sexual natures—that this is part of the lust of the flesh." Huggett (1985, 28) relates that a young woman she was counseling finally cried out, "This conversation will have to stop. It's making me physically sick. It's just not wholesome to talk about sex." Huggett continues by saying, "It was not that the conversation was in any sense smutty or distasteful. It was just that she could not bear to think of herself as a sexual human being."

Another, more accurate, scriptural interpretation includes the prohibition against sexual sins, but teaches that sexual desires are divinely given, are holy, and are to be satisfied and enjoyed only in marriage. Leman (1981, 13) expresses it in these words: "God created us as man and wife. He sanctified the institution of marriage. He is the one who taught us first that sex belongs only in marriage and that sex is a vital part of marriage." Children and young people are taught the dignity of the human body as the temple of the Holy Spirit. The dangers and virtues of sex are openly discussed between parent and child, pastor and young people, so that healthy attitudes toward sex are developed.

In this view the submission of the body to the control of the Holy Spirit is stressed, rather than mere self-control. Chastity of the body then becomes much more than the simple preservation of one's virginity for the prospective mate. Purity of mind and body takes on a divine dimension, for he said, "Be ye holy, for I am holy." Those who approach dating with this attitude will find it much easier to face the challenge to their values they will encounter during dating and courtship.

The greatest threat to Christian standards of sexual behavior comes from the so-called new morality, which is nothing more than the old immorality with a new title. This philosophy teaches that there are no divine moral absolutes, but every act is judged by whether or not it is done under the guise of love. Joseph Fletcher, who wrote *Situation Ethics,* is thought to be the author of this philosophy, but he merely stated what has been practiced for some time.

Alcorn (1985, 56) observes, "The popularity of 'Situation Ethics' (which became a synonym for the 'New Morality') should come as no surprise given the moral climate of the sixties. Many who wanted to taste the forbidden fruit of immorality were not prepared to directly reject the Christian faith. Now they were told they didn't have to. They could violate biblical standards . . . and still be good Christians."

Abraham (1985, 55) relates how he used to begin his seminars by proving that America was in "the midst of a major upheaval of our sexual values. Today that is not necessary. 'The Sexual Revolution,' as it has been called, has been so successfully pulled off its coup, it is no longer considered revolutionary. The so-called New Morality has been with us for so long, it now seems old hat."

The new morality was the result of two generations of religious liberalism in our churches and the teaching of John Dewey's relativity of morals (i.e., there are no absolutes) in public schools. In an earlier day the hedonistic philosophy of Hugh Hefner would likewise have failed, but the moral climate has been altered by the failure of our churches ("God is dead") and the dissemination of the philosophy of the relativity of morals. Thus, the new morality was not a creation of the 1960s but was merely the full manifestation of the secularistic tendency already prevalent in American society.

Since the Christian subculture is influenced by the national cultural pattern, young people in Christian churches have been affected by the morality practiced by their peers. Although the vast majority hold to the biblical standard prohibiting sexual relationships outside of marriage, many individuals justify their petting on the basis that it is all right if the couple "loves" one another. If they are not "in love," they do not have the social approval of their peer group and the girl is labeled "promiscuous." This peer-group approval, and the fact that the young woman remains a "technical" virgin, in the sense that she has never had a sexual relationship, are aspects of the "petting complex." However, from a Christian viewpoint, such a young woman is guilty of breaking the spirit of the moral law even though she has kept the letter of the law.

> *The new morality was not a creation of the 1960s but was merely the full manifestation of the secularistic tendency already prevalent in American society.*

Necking is usually defined as contact above the neck; light petting as contact between the neck and waist, and heavy petting as contact below the waist (Dobbins 1985, 36). Huggett

(1982, 87–88) writes, "This kind of heavy petting without intercourse preserves a girl's *technical* virginity, but is it really keeping the rules? If so, whose rules? Certainly not God's. It may be keeping to the letter, but certainly not the spirit of God's requirements."

One young woman with guilt feelings from such an experience wrote, "I engaged in some necking and light petting with a fellow I planned to marry. We then were separated for a semester. After we parted I felt guilty, and wondered how many others I might possibly 'love' before I married. I may still marry him, but I have made up my mind to refrain from such activities until I am married."

> ## The increased intimacy engendered by steady dating exposes the couple to temptations to transgress their standards.

Unfortunately, some young couples who engage in petting cannot stop short of the sexual relationship, and pregnancy results. Quite often they attempt to justify such behavior on the basis that they are "in love." Trobisch (1987, 133) gives a penetrating answer to such a couple who asked, "Isn't all that matters is that it was done in love? I answered, 'Love? Love to the baby for whom no proper home is prepared? Love to your partner whose professional career is now messed up? . . . Maybe you solved one problem—you released the sexual tension. But you created new ones—wedding, home, support, profession. . . . Love?'" He proceeds to say, "Love is hurt when it is not protected by divine will. Sex can hurt love. Therefore God protects love by confining sex to marriage." Christian young people need to be

very careful not to reject the new morality in one area but by the same philosophy attempt to justify other behavior that is displeasing to God.

Problems of Going Steady

As young people engage in the process of dating, they eventually begin to go steady with one particular person. In the early years of dating, it is a form of social security whereby each person knows he or she has a date for social events. In the later years going steady becomes a step in the mate-selection process that leads to engaged to become engaged. It involves an agreement not to date others and often leads to a commitment to marry each other. Santrock (1990, 275) reflects, "the longer a couple goes steady, the more likely they are to consider marriage."

The increased intimacy engendered by steady dating exposes the couple to temptations to transgress their standards in the area of sexuality and is one of the big disadvantages of this type of dating. This is particularly true when couples date before they are mature enough to handle the emotional pressures of prolonged physical contact. Many of the difficulties couples face could be averted if they avoid compromising situations, such as parked cars, where they are tempted to engage in necking and petting. Often Christian couples do not intend to violate their standards in this area, but do so when their emotions get out of control while in some compromising situation.

Most couples do not know that there is, as Small (1959, 165) states, a "moral law of diminishing returns" in physical relationships. A couple who has progressed from holding hands to kissing cannot return to the less intimate level and be satisfied. If they have started petting, it becomes difficult to regress to kissing as the only means of physical contact. As the petting continues, more and more intimacy is required for satisfaction, and the couple unwittingly faces increasing temptation. At this stage it is easy for the emotions to get out of control, with regrettable results that can also affect their families and friends.

When faced with temptation, Joseph said, "how can I do this great wickedness, and sin against God?" (Gen. 39:9). He knew that sexual indulgence is sin against God, and he did not want to displease Jehovah. This is still one of the best motives for purity of life. Young people also need to remember that many relationships are broken and they should ask themselves, "Would we be ashamed of this act if we broke up, or will we be sorry for it once we are married?"

The desire to touch and caress the partner is a definite part of romantic love, but it should be kept in its proper perspective in the total relationship. If it becomes the dominant factor in a dating situation, then the more important function of dating to test psychological compatibility will be obscured. When the physical aspect is dominant in a relationship and a couple cannot proceed to engagement or marriage because of their youth or finances, the biological pressures may build up until they break a relationship that might have otherwise become a happy marriage. Even if the relationship does not break up, the individuals are filled with guilt feelings because they know they are misusing their bodies, and they have taken that which God intended to be holy and sacred and lowered it to the level of the sinful indulgence of the flesh.

Many of the problems of necking and petting can be avoided if the couple plan their dates so that little time is available to spend alone. The situation is helped by thoughtful parents who set realistic hours for their young people to be home. Meier and Meier (1981, 82) suggest that "standards for dating should be discussed: whom to date; a plan for permission to date; where to go on a date; when to be back home."

It is difficult to begin this if young people are already accustomed to coming in whenever they please. It is much easier if parents assume this responsibility when sons or daughters begin to date so that from the beginning they know they are to be home at a particular hour. This is particularly helpful for the young woman, because in our culture she is expected to draw the line in relationship to necking and petting. It is not fair to give her all this responsibility, for the Christian man ought to realize his obligation to the Lord to keep himself pure

and holy. Many young men do hold such a standard:

> I like to neck, but I am strictly against petting. My girl and I have not talked about it and made any kind of agreement; I just assumed responsibility myself for drawing the line, or controlling the situation. We kiss and embrace, but each kiss and embrace is kept to a very short time (ten–twenty seconds?). . . . My aim is to keep us from getting passionately involved, or "turned on."

> *Many of the problems of necking and petting can be avoided if the couple plan their dates so that little time is available to spend alone.*

There are those whose conduct is not what it ought to be and who will seek to exploit the dating partner for the selfish gratification of their own desires. The young woman who agrees to "park," whether it be in the lovers' lane or the driveway at home, is inviting difficulty that could easily be avoided, and society (including church members) will hold her responsible if moral standards are transgressed.

Danger of Dating Unsaved Persons

The old cliché "every date is a prospective mate" contains much truth. Whether it be a junior-high date or a college date, the first one can lead to the second. The many individuals who marry childhood sweethearts support this fact. Consequently, it is best for Christian young people to date only born-again individuals. If there is no first date with an unsaved individual, there will be no opportunity for a mixed marriage to materialize.

It is best for Christian young people to date only born-again individuals.

This standard of dating only Christians poses a real problem for girls, particularly in small churches where they usually outnumber the males. Consequently, many girls are left with the choice of no dates or dating the unsaved. If they choose the former, they miss some of the learning experiences that dating provides, and if they choose the latter they run the risk of marrying outside the will of God.

There are some who take an opposing viewpoint. They say that Christian young people should date unsaved boys and girls as a ministry of witnessing. If unsaved youth are not witnessed to, then the possibility of being saved is limited. Therefore, it is legitimate to date an unsaved person. However, if no witnessing takes place on the first or second date, the relationship should be broken. Further dating may lead to emotional involvement, and the Christian faces the temptation to become entangled in an unequal situation. Persons taking this approach have to examine their motives carefully. Is the desire to date a certain unsaved person really to witness? Or is it because that person is particularly attractive or a leader in the peer group? The situation is fraught with danger.

Wilkerson (1983, 103) writes, "I've had kids argue . . . and say, 'Look, I'm not planning to marry the guy—I just want to date him!' Famous last words! Ask the woman who is married to an unbeliever; have her describe for you the agonies she has endured, the bitter pain, the disappointment, unfaithfulness, drinking,

and involvement in a life-style that is entirely out of step with . . . Christian beliefs." He makes a strong case for Christian young people never to date the unsaved.

Kageler (1989, 80) also warns against this type of dating: "What does a date at sixteen have to do with being unequally yoked in marriage? Maybe nothing. But potentially a great deal. 'Missionary dating' rarely results in non-Christians becoming Christians. Most youth workers can readily tell about a strong Christian teenager who innocently began dating a non-Christian. . . . Most of these stories *don't* [italics added] have happy endings."

Age and Dating

The age at which dating begins is important. Santrock (1990, 272) observes, "Most adolescents have their first date sometime between the ages of 12 and 16. Less than 10% have a first date before the age of 10, and by the age of 16 more than 90% have had at least one date." A survey of Christian college students show that some girls have their first date at the age of twelve, and most of those who date had their first date by the age of fourteen. There were some who indicated they have never had a date. Among the males, dating began a little later, with thirteen being the youngest age, while the largest number had their first date at fifteen.

This trend means that the time span for dating is longer now than it was in the past. The average girl who begins dating at age fourteen and who marries at age twenty has a six-year period of dating. If a young man decides to wait until he has finished his professional education, there may be a ten-year period during which he must delay marriage until he reaches his goal. Very often he will marry and pursue his education at the same time. Consequently, in our culture there is a relatively long time during which Christian young people must control their biological desires until the actual marriage.

Conflicts arise when adolescents and parents differ on how old young people should be before they begin to date. Many parents feel that since they did not date until they were seventeen or eighteen years old, their children should not date before that age. They fail to realize that dating begins much earlier today, as indicated by our survey of Christian a college students. Some parents do not consider that each child is different and that some mature earlier than others. One daughter may be perfectly willing to wait until seventeen to begin dating, but her sister may be mature enough to start dating at fifteen. Kageler (1989, 77), a dedicated youth worker, comments, "How do you decide with your teenager when to allow dating? Is your son or daughter ready to date? The answers to these questions will vary. . . . To determine what's right for your teenager, talk about such issues as dependability, maturity and responsibility. . . . By deciding together when to begin, teenagers feel like they are part of the decision." The wise parent will attempt to maintain good communications with the children and work out a plan for each child individually rather than setting uniform age limits at which dating can begin.

Parental Roles in Dating

It is also wise for parents to establish some other guidelines in regard to dating. Certain rules should be agreed upon concerning the use of the family car. It is embarrassing for Junior to plan to use the car for a date on Friday night when Dad must use it to leave town on a business trip. This can be avoided if there is an understanding that Junior talk with Dad before he makes a date involving the use of the car. The use of the family living room by sister and her date may conflict with mother's entertaining unless there is good communication between them. Most parents enjoy having their children bring their friends home with them, but the parents also lead a social life that occasionally requires entertaining their own friends.

Although some young people may disagree, parents have an obligation to counsel with their children in reference to their choice of dating partners. Parents have a moral obligation to correct their children when they err. Parents also must be aware of their own limitations and not project their own preferences and desires upon the children. Just because

Dad preferred redheads to brunettes does not mean that Junior will also prefer redheads.

> *Parents have an obligation to counsel with their children in reference to their choice of dating partners.*

Sometimes young people will be justified in rejecting the advice of the parents if there is no valid reason for the parents' objection. Paul exhorts children to obey their parents "in the Lord" (Eph. 6:1), but the time comes when children reach maturity and must make their own decisions concerning the will of God for their lives. If disagreements arise between the parent and the young adult as to what constitutes the will of God, then the young person must prayerfully make the decision based on God's will. As adults, they are responsible before God, and God will not hold the parent responsible for the actions of an adult son or daughter. The case of Mary and John illustrates this fact:

Mary and John met during their freshman year of college. Mary was very pretty, a superior student, and had received a full scholarship. John was handsome, an average student but had musical talent and played in one of the college trios. Both were sincere in their dedication to Christ. Their relationship developed and Mary took John to her home for vacation. It was an unhappy time as her parents rejected John and made it quite clear they did not like him. They intended for Mary to finish college and then acquire graduate training in her field, so from their viewpoint marriage was out of the question until her education was completed. Perhaps the parents were projecting their own unfulfilled ambitions upon their daughter and expected her to achieve goals which they had not gained. John was a fine Christian man and there was no rational reason for their rejection. John and Mary were very much in love and tried for two years to gain her parents' approval. Their disapproval continued through Mary's junior year, at which time they decided to marry in spite of her parents' feelings. The marriage was to take place in John's home church. At this point her parents realized that the couple was sincere and they changed their attitude. John and Mary were married in Mary's home church. Eventually a good relationship was established between the couple and Mary's parents. However, John's and Mary's courtship had many unhappy moments because of the parental opposition to John.

The Rapid Development of College Relationships

The case of John and Mary also illustrates another point concerning dating in college. In the average Christian college where young people are not limited to seeing each other at specific times, the couple may have much more interaction than they ordinarily would if they were living at home and following usual dating patterns. This type of dating can be called greenhouse dating, since the relationship grows so much more quickly due to the amount of interaction between the man and woman.

> *Parents are often disturbed when a college couple who has been dating only a year desires to be married.*

At college the couple can have morning devotions together, go to breakfast, attend classes, eat lunch, study in the library, have dinner, attend a basketball game or other social function, and finally have devotions at the close of the day. This togetherness can be repeated day after day, and after three months, they have had more testing of personal compatibility than the couple at home would have had in a year or two of ordinary dating. Unless the couple is careful to keep their emotions under tight control, they will be ready for marriage much sooner than they expect.

Parents are often disturbed when a college couple who has been dating only a year desires to be married. They feel they have not known each other long enough, since they are unaware of how much time the couple has actually spent together during the year. Parents need to be aware that it is only normal that a relationship between a couple develop to a point when they are biologically and emotionally ready for marriage. If for some reason marriage is not possible, the couple then face the danger of biological pressures tempting them to transgress their moral standards, or else these pressures subconsciously cause conflict that may eventually destroy the relationship.

Another possibility exists: the couple see each other so often that interest is dulled and the relationship is broken. A college couple who are in each other's company from morning until night can see each other more than the average husband and wife, since the husband is employed for eight or nine hours per day. College couples have often been counseled to limit their interaction to once a day, or every other day in order to recapture some of the vitality that their relationship has lost because they have been seeing each other too often.

Why Some College Students Do Not Date

Many young people have no difficulty in dating; others arrive at college without ever having had a date.

Although Bible schools and Christian colleges are facetiously spoken of as "match factories," the truth is that they do bring together marriageable young people who have many things in common. There is no better place for a young person to find a mate with similar beliefs, goals, and values; and a multitude of happy Christian marriages have resulted from courtships on Christian campuses. If a man or woman leaves the campus without a mate or prospective mate, he or she will never again have such a wide selection of possible mate choices. There may be eligible bachelors and single women back home in the local church, but the opportunities will be much fewer than they are on campus.

It is important then that young people learn to date, as it is the initial step in the mate-selection system. Many students, however, give reasons why they do not date. Some of these are valid, such as "dating someone back home," but others indicate personality inadequacies that the individual needs to remedy. The following additional reasons are not discussed in any necessary order of importance.

Some students do not date because they intend to get as much as possible out of their expensive college education. They realize that graduate education is important in today's culture, so they want the best undergraduate grade-point average possible. They do not date because they know this may lead to serious involvement and marriage.

The returning GIs of World War II demonstrated that marriage may not hinder a person's studies but may help them. Other surveys have also demonstrated that students may do better after marriage.

Parents often contribute to this pressure by telling the student they will help them with college expenses only if they remain unmarried. This attitude might be proper if they send the son to a school attended only by men or the daughter to a college for women. It seems unfair for parents to send young people to a coeducational college where they will be surrounded by members of the opposite sex and then expect them to refrain from dating and courtship. It also displays an ignorance on the part of parents of the functional role of the college in mate selection in American culture. Most parents, however, are aware of this role, and such parents usually are willing to help the young couple to complete their education.

A small percentage of students come to college already involved in a relationship with someone back home. This is a legitimate reason for not dating if the two agree not to date others during the separation. The facts are that most of these relationships are broken by the separation, for although "absence makes the heart grow fonder," it usually makes it grow fonder for someone closer at hand.

Many students come from small churches where the number of prospective Christian dating partners is limited, and when they arrive at college they are often pleasantly surprised at the large number of persons available to date. The partner back home begins to seem less favorable in the light of all the young people in the college setting, and many such relationships are broken during the first quarter or semester of college. When such relationships do not dissolve, it may be because the couple had a long period of dating before the partner left for college, so that a very strong bond developed between them that separation could not break, or else the college was located close to home so that frequent visiting was possible.

> *It is important that young people learn to date, as it is the initial step in the mate-selection system.*

It is unfortunate that on some college campuses there is social pressure against random dating. Young people may tend to think of a specific person as "the only one" and thus they decline to date anyone else. Or they may assume that some couples are "steadies" and thus not ask for or accept a date with one of those persons. Students on such campuses miss the opportunity to date with lovely personalities, and they perhaps end up with less than the best as a choice for a mate. They are unaware of the value to themselves of random dating and of the part it plays in the mate-selection process.

Some students do not date because they have no desire to do so. Even at college age they have not matured to the point where they have a normal, active interest in the opposite sex. Sometimes such individuals have been conditioned against marriage by the example of unhappily married parents. Anyone who has counseled young people for a long period of time is aware of the large number of miserable Christian homes, and it is not surprising that children reared in such circumstances will occasionally have such a negative reaction that they resolve never to get married. Thus, they have no interest in dating.

> *Some individuals are shy by nature, while others may have painful experiences in childhood that caused them to withdraw into themselves and avoid reaching out to others.*

Young people in this situation need to realize that though their home was not happy, there are many examples of fulfilling Christian marriages. If they will look around the church they will find a family that is happy, and who can serve as a model for their own marriage. They may then be able to substitute the positive view for the negative one. Individuals are not responsible for the environment in which they were reared, but they are obligated to change unhealthy ideas and attitudes that are not pleasing to God. They have all the promises of the Word of God, and the strength imparted by the Holy Spirit so they can say with the apostle Paul, "I can do all things through Christ who strengtheneth me" (Phil. 4:13).

Many students do not date in college because they are shy and lack self-confidence. Usually they did not date in high school for the same reasons. Some individuals are shy by nature, while others may have painful experiences in childhood that caused them to withdraw into themselves and avoid reaching out to others, for fear of being hurt again. With respect to dating, a shy young man may not ask a girl for a date for fear that she will refuse. This would be another hurt for an already bruised ego, so he avoids the situation.

If a man calls a bashful woman and asks for a date, she may refuse because she feels she cannot carry a conversation. These individuals may be intelligent and capable in many areas, but they have not developed socially. They may have the normal desires to date, but are unable to break out of their shells.

Social skills in dating can be learned only by practice, and the shy individual who is attempting to improve his self-confidence might begin to date. It will be helpful if at first a man dates individuals he knows so there are some common interests that can serve as a focus for conversation. The use of the telephone is especially helpful in asking for a date since it avoids the face-to-face interaction that makes the shy individual nervous. The shy woman may have to develop some social skills by learning to converse with other women before a man will notice her and ask her for a date. Shyness is a learned behavior and can be overcome with the help of the Holy Spirit.

Confidence in one's self can be improved by conscious effort. McGinnis (1987, 15–16) gives the illustration of a shy college sophomore who was challenged by a professor to change the way he thought about himself. He accepted the challenge. That young man with an inadequate self-concept is known the world over today as Dr. Norman Vincent Peale! McGinnis (1987, 27), a family therapist, gives "Twelve Rules for Building Self-Confidence":

1. Focus on your potential instead of your limitations.
2. Determine to know the truth about yourself.
3. Distinguish between who you are and what you do.

4. Find something you like to do and do well, then do it over and over.
5. Replace self-criticism with regular, positive self-talk.
6. Replace fear of failure with clear pictures of yourself functioning successfully and happily.
7. Dare to be a little eccentric.
8. Make the best possible peace with your parents.
9. Determine to integrate the body and spirit.
10. Determine to live above neurotic guilt.
11. Cultivate people who help you grow.
12. Refuse to allow rejection to keep you from taking the initiative with people.

After 178 pages of excellent counsel, McGinnis (1987, 178) makes the further point that "it is from loving and being loved that confidence best emerges, and ultimately it is divine love that sets this all in perspective. . . . It is the love of God that provides the foundation of our identities, and because we are then given such a peaceful center . . . we are able to turn and give ourselves to others . . . and suddenly one day we awake to realize that we are confident and rather happy."

The success or failure, not only in love but in life itself, depends to a great degree on one's self-confidence. It is important for each young person to study books, seek counseling, and do everything to have the best possible self-image and self-confidence.

Physical problems prevent many young people from dating. In our culture there is the extreme overemphasis on physical beauty. Individuals who, by accident of birth or some combination of genes, lack beauty as defined by the culture are at a serious disadvantage in our dating system. Whereas in one tribe in Africa, the young bride-to-be is placed in a "fattening room" for three months prior to the wedding, our culture stresses thinness as a most desirable physical trait. The young woman who is obese is sometimes rejected as a dating partner even though she may have a beautiful personality. Likewise an overweight young man may encounter difficulty getting dates with desirable young women. Since there is a shortage of young men, he will generally be more apt to find a marriage partner than his female counterpart. Young people who are overweight will need to make a concerted effort to lose weight and to develop pleasing personalities so that they may attract dating partners.

The overemphasis on physical beauty in our culture is reflected in dating. It begins in infancy when babies are judged as pretty or not so pretty. It continues through childhood into adolescence, when the lack of physical attractiveness is most critical since it can affect the self-esteem of the young person. When one begins dating, the chief factor considered is physical attractiveness. Santrock (1990, 276) asks and answers the question, "Why do adolescents want to date attractive individuals? . . . It is rewarding to be around physically attractive individuals. It provides adolescents with consensual validation that they too are attractive. As part of the rewarding experience, the adolescent's self-image is enhanced. It is also aesthetically pleasing to look at physically attractive individuals."

Young people need to remember that the physical characteristics of a person will change but the inner self, the real personality will change little. In selecting a mate for a lifetime, the choice should be based on the real person—not the body he or she lives in.

> *In selecting a mate for a lifetime, the choice should be based on the real person—not the body he or she lives in.*

On the other hand, dating poses problems for beautiful women and handsome men. Dobbins (1985a, 8–9) indicates that the attractive young woman may find it hard to determine whether her date sees her as a person or merely a sex object. The handsome man faces a similar problem. All kinds of women will be drawn to him, and he will have to determine which woman is genuine, sincere, and would make a good wife.

Earles (1984, 82) has some good advice for those who are beautiful or handsome. "For those who may be fond of their looks, here are five words of truth: beauty is only skin deep. There is much more to personhood than the skin you see in the mirror. Pride over good looks is dumb, because your basic makeup was not created by you. It was done by God. . . . Develop the real you before the world convinces you that being one of the beautiful people makes you better than others."

Physical infirmities can also hinder some young people from dating. People with acne, for example, sometimes feel so self-conscious about their condition, they are paralyzed socially.

> *It appears that the dating relations between young men and women have become more friendship-oriented and egalitarian.*

Compatible goals in life pose a problem for some young people who date, particularly people who have a well-defined goal or calling. They realize the necessity of finding a mate who will eagerly share such a lifework. These are important values, for many a man has had to leave the ministry because of a wife who could not accept her husband's role and her own role. Some men called to the mission field have been sidetracked into God's second best because of a wrong mate choice.

The rating system deters many from dating on some campuses. In every school there are always those students who because of beauty, masculinity, or personality are rated as desirable dates. Some students are so ego-centered they will not date at all if they cannot date a person they perceive as highly rated. A corollary of this is the social pressure exerted in some dormitories whereby a young person may be ridiculed for dating someone who is not rated highly by the friends in the dorm. The tragedy of this is that many individuals with winsome personalities and deep spiritual commitments are passed over as prospective dates because they do not have physical beauty.

Some young men may not date because they do not have money or a car. It is true that higher education is costly today. Even where parents tried to plan a program of savings to help their sons or daughters through college, they may not have realized the havoc that inflation causes to the best-laid plans. On the average Christian college campus there are numerous opportunities for inexpensive dates, such as athletic games, concerts, and church activities that need not require a car nor a lot of money. A young man with a low budget may still date if he is able to plan well and make a sincere effort to do so.

There are also some males who are normal heterosexual individuals but prefer the company of other young men. They find more enjoyment in playing a game of touch football than having a date. When they do date, the girl often finds herself playing second fiddle to his friends. Unless a young woman enjoys being alone much of the time, she should not marry that type of young man; even after marriage, he may still prefer his friends' company to hers.

The chief reason women do not date is that they are not asked. Except for a few special events, women in our culture are not permitted to ask for dates. This problem is compounded on some campuses where the women outnumber the men. There is not too much a woman can do in this situation except be warm and outgoing in her casual relationships with males until they may get to know her personally and then may ask for a date. She should avoid always being with a group of women since many young men might have difficulty asking for a date under normal circumstances and would hesitate to ask her in front of a group of young women. She should avoid appearing too eager, as this may turn a male off as quickly as being too shy.

A number of young women may have such a high ideal for their prospective mate that they may never find a man who measures up to their standards. It is good to have an ideal, but it should be tested by actual dating and adjusted to reality as needed. Some women spend a lifetime looking for a perfect partner, never realizing their own imperfections.

Some young people do not date because they are preoccupied with studying, to make the highest honor roll. It is difficult to determine if these people are attempting to avoid dating because they lack the necessary social skills, or whether they are not asked, since men prefer to date women less intellectual than they are.

The feminist movement has had an influence on dating in the society at large. Korman and Leslie (1985, 344) observe: "Little empirical evidence on dating has been gathered over the past decade, but it appears that the dating relations between young men and women have become more friendship-oriented and egalitarian. . . . Now, neither sex is dependent on the other. Males and females alike initiate dates. Either partner may drive or they both may take their own cars and meet at the chosen locale. If this egalitarian view becomes prevalent on the Christian college campus, then it may make it easier for young women to secure dates.

Indications of Dating Incompatibility

A definite feature of a trial-and-error dating system is the dissolving of relationships. Most young people will go through one or more experiences of breaking up. The emotional results may vary with the extent of the time the relationship has been in progress and the intensity of the emotional involvement of the partners. Onc couple may go together a short while, not feel too deeply toward each other, and break up one week and be dating someone else the next. Another couple may suffer a traumatic emotional experience when they dissolve the relationship after a long and intense period of dating. They may not recover from their broken hearts and date again for several months.

Many times there are danger signals that a relationship is in difficulty, and young people need to be aware of these as they often indicate that the relationship is not the best one possible. Most dating couples will occasionally have a quarrel, after which they may experience great emotional satisfaction as they make up. These quarrels are a normal part of the adjustments that two people make in learning to interact closely with one another. However, if the disagreements and quarrels are numerous and often intense, this is a warning that something may be wrong in the relationship. The couple should analyze the situation and try to determine the cause of the friction. If they discover they have irreconcilable differences in the important areas of goals and values, then it may be best if they part company. It may be that one partner uses quarreling as a neurotic release, and if not treated, it is unlikely one would want to go through life married to such a person.

> *Many times there are danger signals that a relationship is in difficulty, and young people need to be aware of these.*

Couples who frequently break up and then get back together should be aware that such behavior indicates there may be some serious incompatibility in the relationship. They might do well to examine their interaction to discover any area or areas where disagreement occurs. They might then seek to modify their behavior in these areas to see if helpful adjustments could be made. They must be careful not to sidestep disagreeable issues by thinking it will be different after they are married. For example, if they have strong differences over the use of money while dating, the conflict could become worse after marriage. Avoiding issues to avert dissension will only lead to greater frustration and conflict at a later date. Mature young people will probably closely examine their compatibilities, and if agreement cannot be reached, they may do well to end the relationship. They could then be free to seek a more compatible dating partner.

A lack of interest and concern for the dating partner may be a sign that something is wrong in the relationship. Many relationships are continued long after one partner has lost interest. It is the very nature of a person in love to be concerned about the loved one and to desire to communicate as frequently as possible with that person. Anyone who has experienced the frustration of placing a call to a college dormitory during the evening hours is familiar with this aspect of love.

> # *Many relationships are continued long after one partner has lost interest.*

It is absurd for a man who has been going with a woman for two years to tell her he loves her and then fail to communicate with her during the summer. In like manner, a young man who does not give a woman a gift on her birthday or some other special occasion may be demonstrating a lack of love for her, for it is the nature of love to give. Of course there may be extenuating circumstances, but if this is the case, he certainly will explain. If she is in love with him, she will understand. A repeated lack of concern is an indication that the relationship should be reexamined.

A relationship may also be in trouble when one partner wants to go further in the area of necking or petting than the other partner. Since it is believed that males have the stronger sex drive, it usually means that he will be the one who wants to transgress in these areas. Since they are "in love" there may be the tendency for the woman to lower her standards, but she may do well to remember this does not justify such behavior. If she does give in to his desires, he may lose respect for her and eventually the relationship may break up anyway.

There is a real problem on secular college campuses today involving violence such as slapping, punching, and pushing in dating. The ultimate violent act is date rape. Korman and Leslie (1985, 353) report one study where "fifty-six percent of the women reported that they had been subject to forcible attempts at intercourse and six percent to aggressively forcible attempt at intercourse that involved threats or the infliction of pain."

Such behavior is foreign to the norms of dating on a Christian college campus. However, Christian college students can still allow themselves to be controlled by the flesh rather than the Holy Spirit. In such a case, it is conceivable that violence could occur on a date. When dating partners allow the Holy Spirit to control their emotions and actions, they need not fear violence in their interaction.

Another situation occurs often on Christian college campuses where individuals engage in intense dating from morning to night. If after a year of such dating, a person is not willing to commit himself or herself to the partner in some understanding about marriage, then it would seem doubtful that there is much to be gained in continuing the relationship. Self-revelation typically will unfold rapidly under such dating intensity, so a couple ought to know after several months of such interaction whether they are compatible or not. They should have enough knowledge of each other to know if they should proceed toward marriage.

Breaking a relationship is usually a painful emotional experience, but young people should realize that dating is for testing psychological compatibilities. When incompatibilities cannot be reconciled, it is proper to end a relationship and start over with another partner. This process can be repeated numerous times until in the will of God the best possible partner is found. "The name of the game is dating," and if the game is played rationally and well, it can lead to happiness in marriage.

Study Questions

1. Compare dating as a means of mate selection with the methods used in Bangladesh and rural China.
2. How does the American social class system influence dating?
3. What is the major criterion used to judge success in American marriage? How is psychological compatibility related to this?
4. Discuss the importance of random dating to the mate-selection process.
5. Did you receive any biblical teaching about sexuality in your home church? If not, how would you initiate change in this area?
6. List advantages and disadvantages of going steady.
7. Discuss the "moral law of diminishing returns."
8. What are some parental obligations in relationship to the dating of their young people?
9. What is meant by greenhouse dating? What are its disadvantages?
10. What are some danger signals that young people need to be aware of in a dating relationship?

Personality Inventory

Are You a Good Dating Partner?

1. How often do you date? How do you account for either your frequency of dates or your lack of dates?
2. Discuss the importance of random dating in the mate-selection process.
3. Do you lack social skills in dating? If so, what steps can you take to increase these skills?
4. Why is it so necessary to follow the rules of etiquette on a first date?

5. Do you need to improve your physical appearance in order to be a better date? What are you doing to enhance the image you present to others?
6. Discuss your feelings about this statement: "It is the young woman's responsibility to draw the line regarding physical contact."
7. Do you usually enjoy double dates? Why or why not?
8. What was the nicest date that you can remember? Analyze the situation to discuss the factors that made it such a great time.

Suggested Readings

Dobbins, R. 1985. *Narrowing the risk in mate selection.* Akron: Emerge Ministries. A small booklet filled with information designed to help take some of the risk out of selecting a mate in American culture.

Earles, B. D. 1984. *The dating maze.* Grand Rapids: Baker. This book has forty short chapters that touch on most of the factors involved in dating. He suggests that for casual dating it should be permissible for a woman to ask a man for a date.

Friesen, L., and J. R. Maxson. 1980. *Decision making and the will of God.* Portland, Ore.: Multnomah. The subtitle, *A biblical alternative to the traditional view,* indicates a new approach to determining the will of God. The authors present a plan of decision making that they term "a biblical approach to guidance." Two very helpful chapters on making the right decisions concerning marriage are presented. Every young person will profit from reading this volume.

Hartley, F. 1980. *Dare to be different: Dealing with peer pressure.* Old Tappan, N.J.: Revell. A booklet written by a young pastor who relates how he dealt with peer pressure. He gives practical methods whereby young people can withstand peer pressure.

Kageler, K. 1989. *Helping your teenager cope with peer pressure.* Loveland, Colo.: Family Tree Group. A most helpful book written by a successful youth pastor. He defines the problem and gives four keys "to resisting peer pressure." He deals with pressures young people face in dating.

McGinnis, A. L. 1987. *Confidence: How to succeed at being yourself.* Minneapolis: Augsburg. In his practice McGinnis encountered many people who lacked self-confidence. He uses case studies to illustrate the principles that can be employed to bolster one's self-confidence. Should be required reading for college students.

Richards, L. 1979. *How far can I go?* Grand Rapids: Zondervan. A classic presentation of the problem faced by those of dating age. Scriptural basics and practical advice help young people know where to draw the line.

Sanders, B. 1986. *Tough turf: A teen survival manual.* Old Tappan, N.J.: Revell. An excellent volume that encourages young people to achieve the highest in life. The chapter on building self-esteem has thirteen practical suggestions.

Santrock, J. W. 1990. *Adolescence.* Dubuque, Iowa: Brown. This is a standard textbook that is widely used. However, it is easy to read and most informative. The average young person will learn many things about himself or herself. It has a helpful section on dating.

Stets, J. E., and M. A. Pirog-Good, eds. 1989. *Violence in dating relationships.* New York: Praeger. This volume is a scholarly but sad commentary on the American college scene. It is a collection of articles on physical and sexual abuse in dating relationships.

The Engagement, Wedding, and Honeymoon

. . . Rejoice with the wife of thy youth. . . . And be thou ravished always with her love.

—Proverbs 5:18–19

Engagement in the Bible

Engagement has been a part of marriage customs in many countries for centuries. Most Christians are familiar with Jacob's agreement to work for Laban seven years in return for the hand of Rachel, and those seven years "seemed unto him but a few days, for the love he had to her" (Gen. 29:20). He was deceived by Laban on the wedding night and had to serve another seven years for his beloved Rachel.

The New Testament story of the engagement of Joseph and Mary is well known (Matt. 1:18–25). According to the custom of the time, a written contract of engagement was signed under oath and then the bride returned to her home for a few months before the actual wedding. In this interval she received instruction in the home on the duties of a good Jewish wife. Thus, the engagement period aided her in preparing for her responsibilities as a wife and mother. If unfaithfulness on her part occurred during this time, the husband-to-be had the choice of having her stoned to death or giving her a bill of divorce (Alford n.d., 4). Joseph decided on the latter course of action, and that is when the angel appeared to him with the announcement that Mary was to be the mother of the Messiah.

Engagement as a Social Ritual

Many Christians have heard missionaries from various countries tell about the puberty rites that adolescents of various cultures pass through. Sociologists speak of these as "rites of passage." The society has a ritual to help the person move from one status to another, particularly when the second status involves more responsibility than the first.

American society has rituals in high-school and college graduation ceremonies and in rituals associated with marriage, birth, and death. Engagement in our culture is different from that of the New Testament Jewish culture in that it is not as permanent or binding, but engagement serves as a rite of passage to help prepare young persons for the responsibilities of married life.

> *American society has rituals in high-school and college graduation ceremonies and in rituals associated with marriage, birth, and death.*

The man giving the woman a ring, the announcement of the engagement in the newspapers, and the various showers given for the bride-to-be are all part of the ritual associated with engagement (Lewis 1981, 20). It may not be necessary for a ring to be given for the couple to be engaged; in fact, many couples are informally engaged for some time before a ring is given. Although a ring is not essential, it may be so important to the engagement ritual that a woman feels "more engaged" if she has one.

Whyte (1990, 37), in his study of marriages in the Detroit area, discovered that 90 percent of the women were formally engaged before they were married. This figure had not changed significantly over three generations. Nearly 74 percent of the women recently married had received a ring. Although many couples are choosing cohabitation, the evidence indicates that those entering marriage are following the usual courtship pattern.

Functions of an Engagement

An important function of engagement is to give the couple a final opportunity to test their psychological compatibility in a more intimate relationship. In random dating little of the self is revealed. In the dating process, young people reveal their true selves gradually. However, as couples continue to date and become seriously interested in one another, more self-revelation takes place.

When the relationship develops to the point where a young man asks a woman to marry him and they become engaged, they enter into a much more intimate phase of courtship with a large increase in self-revelation. Huggett (1982, 27) amplifies this idea with a chapter on "Getting to Know You." She indicates that self-revelation is a part of "love's beautiful curiosity" whereby lovers like to talk with each other. Couples need to know each other well before marriage, especially their family background, spiritual and intellectual compatibility, interests in recreation, habits, emotions, and ability to forgive. She discusses each of these areas. During this time most couples adjust to this increased knowledge and the relationship solidifies. For others, the increased intimacy may reveal facets of personality that were unknown before and to which the partners cannot adjust, and the engagement is broken.

If the maladjustments result in irreconcilable conflict, the engagement should be broken, as it would be difficult to build a happy marriage from such a relationship. Although broken engagements and the heartaches that accompany them are difficult to endure, they are accepted by church and society without reproach. Couples should give themselves enough time during engagement to get to know each other well. If their compatibility passes this final test, they should not be afraid to consummate the engagement in marriage.

Another purpose of engagement is to give time to plan for the wedding. The type of wedding may determine the amount of time needed. A large, formal church wedding followed by a lavish reception necessarily takes more time to plan than a simple wedding in the home or church. It is unfortunate that the wedding ceremony in many churches becomes a status symbol. Each family tries to surpass the size and cost of the last wedding, and much of the money might better be given to the newlyweds to help establish their household. Nevertheless, even a simple wedding ceremony can be quite involved, and the engagement period should allow sufficient time to prepare for a well-planned wedding day. Lewis (1981, 27–48) has a well-designed calendar the couple can use to assure all the details are completed on time.

The engagement period may also provide time for the couple to attempt to reconcile any differences they may have with their future in-laws. The number of parents who object to the choice of a spouse is not great. Whyte (1990, 49–50) discovered that 80 percent of parents approved a daughter's choice, and 85 percent of parents approved a son's selection. If one set of in-laws is against the marriage, the announcement of the engagement may serve notice that the couple is really serious about marriage, and the in-laws may intensify their attempts to destroy the relationship. This opposition could serve as a warning signal to the couple that it might be wise to examine their relationship in a mature, objective, and prayerful manner to determine if deficiencies exist of which they are unaware. It is possible for young people to be so emotionally involved with each other that they cannot see problems that may be obvious to their friends and relatives.

If there is strong opposition to a marriage by one set of future in-laws, or by other relatives and friends, the couple should see a red flag. Diehm (1984, 108–9) observes that "obstacles often heighten the experience of mutual love. You might consider this advice: Be aware of friends and relatives who do not like your new friend. Their dislike may cause you to be unnaturally attracted to him or her." It may prove helpful for the couple to seek counsel of a godly Sunday-school teacher, pastor, youth leader, or other Christian leader who can give them an unbiased, objective appraisal of their relationship. If the counselor has some of the marriage prediction tests available, it would be helpful to see if there are areas of possible incompatibility. The counselor can then alert the couple to areas in their relationship which

may require extra attention in order to make a good adjustment. Many counselors use the Taylor-Johnson Temperament Analysis. Lewis (1981, 25) states that "it is especially useful. It reveals nine personality traits, and shows you not only how you see yourselves, but also how you see each other. There are no right or wrong answers—just insights."

The will of God for the particular couple is the important matter. If after much prayer and godly counsel, couples feel they should proceed with the wedding, they should make every reasonable overture to the objecting in-laws for a reconciliation prior to the wedding. If this is still impossible, they are duty-bound to do what they conscientiously feel is the will of God for their lives.

There are some situations in which it is most difficult for Christian parents to consent to and bless the proposed marriage of a son or a daughter. Since the union of a believer with an unbeliever is in clear violation of 2 Corinthians 6:14–18, a Christian parent cannot be expected to sanction such a marriage, for it is contrary to the Word and will of God.

> *There are some situations in which it is most difficult for Christian parents to consent to and bless the proposed marriage of a son or a daughter.*

A similar situation exists where Christian parents have strong convictions against divorce, and a son or a daughter wishes to marry a divorced person. Christian parents in such circumstances cannot approve of the desired marriage because of their own convictions concerning the will of God. Certainly the parents will counsel the son or the daughter to be obedient to the Word in such cases.

If the individual still insists on marrying outside the will of God, the parents have done their duty and there is little purpose in opposing the wedding. The task then is to seek to establish some relationship with the couple in order to try to win the unsaved person to Christ in the future.

> # The engagement period gives the couple time to communicate with each other about many aspects of their future married life.

Parental opposition may be faced by the Christian young person who plans to marry someone with a different ethnic or socioeconomic background. Even though both are Christians, the parents may feel the cultural differences are too great for the couple to overcome and that a happy marriage cannot be achieved. They may also be exhibiting their prejudice against the nationality or social class of the intended spouse. In this case, the couple must reassess the relationship, seek counsel, and then do the will of God in spite of parental objection. The engagement provides time for making these reconciliations, for the couple who has the blessing of both sets of in-laws has a greater chance for happiness in marriage.

Where there is no opposition of in-laws, it is good for them to give their blessing to the new couple. Swindoll (1980, 29) writes, "More and more I am including the parents in the wedding ceremony, asking them to stand and publicly agree to release their parental authority

and entrust their offspring to the new home beginning that day. This, I believe, cements the decision and makes it permanent in everyone's mind."

The engagement period also gives the couple time to communicate with each other about many aspects of their future married life. Decisions that will affect the future of the relationship need to be made during this period. The couple should discuss and come to a mutual agreement about such things as the roles they expect to play in marriage, their financial goals and methods of handling money, the number of children and how they are to be spaced, and their spiritual goals in life and how they expect to attain them.

With the increase in divorce among Christians today, Trobisch (1982, 118) asks three very important questions the engaged couple should answer: "Have you discussed divorce and your feelings about it? What will you do if your marriage reaches a real point of crisis? Does one or both of you see divorce as an option at that point?" Facing such questions realistically will help to insure stability to the marriage when difficult times arise in the future. Divorce ought never be an option, and if either individual thinks it is, it would be better to break an engagement now rather than face the trauma of divorce in the future.

Inability to talk about important issues should be considered a warning signal that the undiscussed area is a potential source of incompatibility. If individuals cannot agree on the use of money during engagement, they will not be in harmony after the wedding ceremony. If they cannot solve the problem of family planning before marriage, they can temporarily get by without really facing the issue. However, once they start on the honeymoon trip, it will have to be faced in a realistic manner.

Conflicts in an Engagement

Most problems young people face in engagement have a solution, unless they involve a clash of incompatible values or goals. For example, if a young man feels called to full-time Christian service, and the partner feels she could never fulfill the role expectations of a pastor's or missionary's wife, then the best solution is to break the relationship and look for a spouse who shares the same goal. On the other hand, a conflict over the use of money can be solved if the individuals are adaptable enough to compromise their views in order to reach a mutually agreeable settlement. If such an agreement cannot be reached, it indicates the individuals are not flexible enough to compromise and therefore it may be wise to dissolve the relationship.

Two Christian young people who have the inspiration and help of prayer and the Word of God can more easily reach satisfactory agreements than can the unsaved couple who lacks such aids for daily living. In either case, the couple must be able to communicate with each other during engagement if they expect this interaction to be characteristic of their married life. If they are successful in establishing communication, their engagement should be successful, increasing the chance their marriage should be successful.

Confessing the Sins of the Past Life

Engaged couples who establish good communication often face the problem of how much of their past life they should reveal to each other. Sometimes there are skeletons in the family closet that the partner needs to know about, since they may have an influence on the marriage itself. In this day of permissiveness and going steady, young people quite often transgress their moral standards concerning necking, petting, and premarital sex and often feel the need to tell the engaged partner of their failures.

In Christian youth these experiences usually leave the person with a burden of guilt, and in an attempt to be honest with the present partner, they feel they should tell about their previous experience. Usually it is best not to tell unless the individual has been so promiscuous that it is common knowledge, or if there has been such consequences as venereal disease or an illegitimate child. However, sexual sins, if confessed and forsaken, are forgiven like other sins (1 John 1:9), and should be forgotten, for God forgets them: "for I will forgive their iniquity, and I will remember their sin no more" (Jer. 31:34).

If a young person has been guilty of such sins and cannot find release from the burden of guilt, even though he confessed the sin to God, he should seek out a counselor, pastor, or teacher and talk to that person rather than confessing his past to his loved one, who may be terribly hurt and disillusioned by such a revelation. A counselor is familiar with such confessions and can be objective in his viewpoint, but to confess such sins to a fiancée may be too much strain for the relationship to bear. The engagement may survive such a revelation, but the memory may prove to be a real deterrent to good sexual adjustment in marriage. In other words, there is little to be gained and much to be lost through such a confession.

> *Engaged couples who establish good communication often face the problem of how much of their past life they should reveal to each other.*

McDowell (1985, 97) states that if the reason for silence is fear of rejection by the fiancée, then the past should be shared so that their love can be tested. He also quotes the advice of Mace, who suggests that if the confession is made to a trusted counselor who suggests it is best not to confess, the individual should let it go. If there are future disclosures he can recount the advice of the counselor and explain that he did not confess to her because he thought it was the most loving thing to do at the time.

In view of God's attitude, it is not proper for young people to pry into each other's past romantic life. One phase of love is accepting a person as he or she is, and if the partner is acceptable, what value is there to be gained from probing into the past? Paul's exhortation in Philippians 3:13 is applicable here: "forgetting those things which are behind, and reaching forth unto those things which are before. . . ."

Premarital Counseling

The engagement period also provides time for the couple to seek premarital counseling and medical examinations. If the couple has had the advantage of a good high-school or college course in marriage and family living, then counseling will not be necessary unless there are problems in the relationship. Such individuals should be aware of the many adjustments they will have to make during the honeymoon and first few months of married life. Other couples who have not had the benefit of a course in marriage and family living can obtain new information and attitudes from a trained counselor who can help prepare them for their new roles as husband and wife.

Many pastors require premarital counseling before agreeing to perform the wedding ceremony. Some parents pay for the couple to receive premarital counseling at a Christian counseling center. They consider this a part of the normal wedding expenses.

> *Some parents pay for the couple to receive premarital counseling at a Christian counseling center.*

Ketterman (1984, 23–24) makes the valued observation that many young people are growing up without the model of a loving Christian home. She suggests, "If you happen to be one of those young people without a model, and with scars from neglect (or even abuse) in your childhood, you will need special help. I strongly urge you to seek Christian counsel. Through this and through prayer, you may find healing for these hurts and wisdom to create your own unique model."

Each partner should visit a physician for a premarital examination. Before the visit, the couple should read a good marriage manual so they may ask the doctor any questions that need clarifying concerning the marital relationship. The visit should be made sufficiently in advance of the wedding to provide time for any minor surgery that may be necessary. The doctor will also discuss the various methods of family planning and will make a recommendation if asked to do so. Although most physicians in America are busy, they will usually take time to counsel and help young people in order that they can get a good start in their matrimonial life.

The Length of the Engagement

The length of the engagement varies from couple to couple. Many young people have a private understanding that they are engaged to be married and may interact on this basis for many months prior to making a public announcement. In his study, Whyte (1990, 37) found the average couple had dated 2.6 years before the wedding. For such a couple, a long public engagement is not as necessary as it is for those who have known each other for only three months. Knowing each other such a short time does not give sufficient opportunity for the two persons involved to really get to know each other well.

Huggett (1982, 41) reflects, "Discovering whether you fit cannot be done in a hurry. . . . You need plenty of time to learn to understand one another. Understanding is one of the prerequisites of marital love. It comes with hours of patient talking and listening. That is why couples who marry after a brief courtship often have a precarious introduction to marriage."

Young people are better prepared for marriage if they have an engagement of a year or more. However, if the young people are separated and see each other only on a few special occasions, little self-revelation will take place. Thus, they do not test the relationship and they have no great advantage in determining compatibility over the couple with a short engagement.

It is also possible for a couple to have a lengthy engagement and still miss the benefits that should result from such a period. A couple may continue to see each other through the idealization of romantic love and subconsciously refuse to bring their real attitudes and feelings to the surface. However, after marriage, time will eventually permit real feelings to manifest themselves. These real attitudes and feelings may be a source of incompatibility if they concern basic values or goals in life. Ordinarily the passing of time in the engagement permits additional self-revelation to take place so that potential areas of conflict are discovered and the necessary adjustments made. If these cannot be made, the engagement may be broken. Unless the engagement period is used for self-revelation, a long engagement may not be any more useful than a short one.

Usually a couple should not announce their engagement until they are able to set an approximate date for the wedding. An engagement that is too long can be as detrimental to the relationship as one that is too short. However, studies have shown that of the two choices, lengthy engagements more often result in happier marriages. "Burgess and Cottrell found that the ratio of couples with 'poor' adjustment declined from 50 percent for engagements of less than three months to 11 percent for those of twenty-four or more in duration" (Williamson 1966, 307). This may be partly explained by the fact that the added time allows the couple to make many of the adjustments to each other during the courtship period. When they finally do marry after an engagement of two or three years, they are so well adjusted to each other they do not have many of the conflicts which characterize most marriages that follow short engagements.

There are two major perils to a relationship during a long engagement. The first is the possibility that the long waiting period may cause the relationship to stagnate, that is, the partners lose interest in each other. This loss of interest may be mutual, but most often one partner grows weary of waiting and breaks the relationship. Small (1959, 210) describes such a situation: "Lovers get on each other's nerves when there is exclusive preoccupation with themselves, yet with no workable goals to demand their thought and ingenuity."

> *Young people are better prepared for marriage if they have an engagement of a year or more.*

The second danger is the possibility of becoming too intimate physically. By its nature, the engagement period is one of greater intimacy than merely going steady. The normal God-given biological desires that find their fulfillment in marriage increase during this time. If this period is too long, the couple faces the possibility of transgressing their standards in the matter of necking and petting.

Huggett (1982, 88) gives several suggestions to help people control their passions. It is her opinion that the couple should avoid the kind of touching and love-play that lead to intercourse. Better to use touching that is an end in itself. Also, the couple should avoid "provocative dress, undressing, lying together and over-stimulation of erogenous zones." Avoid being alone too much, thus reducing the opportunity for extended periods of petting. Physical contact should not replace other means of communication. She realizes that this advice is easier to give than to follow and recommends the study of Galatians 5:13 and following verses so that the couple may learn to live in the power of the Spirit rather than of the flesh.

Sometimes there is the insidious temptation for the couple to reason, "We are going to be married soon; why should we wait?" There are several good reasons. The most important is that such behavior before marriage is sin in the sight of God, and the Holy Spirit will bring conviction of sin and guilt to the heart. The act may cause the loss of respect for the partner and destroy the love between the couple. It may certainly rob them of the joy that should be theirs on the honeymoon.

> ## Sometimes there is the insidious temptation for the couple to reason, "We are going to be married soon; why should we wait?"

Diehm (1984, 91) remarks, "That supreme moment of excitement that comes with the first sexual contact needs to be preserved for the memory of the honeymoon night. . . . If they wait, all the excitement of sexuality will be concentrated in the honeymoon period, and they won't have to pay the price of bad memories or jaded sex." The Frylings (1977, 48) add, "We have never met a couple who regretted waiting, not just for intercourse, but for other intimate demonstrations of affection; but we have met many couples who regret having had too much physical intimacy before marriage. . . . Keep reminding each other that the best is yet to come. . . . What a wonder and a joy on your wedding night to be able to say to one another, 'This is what we have been waiting for.'"

It is estimated that more than 50 percent of the people who marry have been engaged at least once before (Abraham 1985, 66). Having sex during the engagement may be a decision especially regretted if the engagement is never consummated by marriage.

Ken Abraham, a youth pastor, (1985, 65) tells the story of Tim and Judy, two consecrated Bible college students each with real talents to serve the Lord. On the way home from weekend ministry, they began to engage in heavy petting and finally in intercourse. They rationalized that they would soon be married. However, they broke up, a traumatic experience for both. Judy left college in the middle of her senior year and gave up her prospective singing career. Tim said, "Even after I knew I was forgiven by God and by Judy, the pain was still there. . . . We thought sex was okay because we were engaged. Man, were we wrong. After we broke up it was awful. . . . We were both virgins before she and I started dating. If we had waited, we'd probably be together today." Abraham (1985, 66) relates that Tim also told him, "There is really something about sex that binds two people together. A man and a woman who have shared such intimate oneness were never intended to be separated." Abraham comments that this experience will affect the two people the rest of their lives. The moral is WAIT.

Sometimes couples engage in premarital sex thinking it will strengthen the relationship; on the contrary, it usually weakens it or leads to a break. Diehm (1984, 88) writes that "premarital sex for the Christian is a violation of our codes of conduct. If persons too easily violate codes of conduct before marriage, there may be suspicion that they will too easily violate them after marriage. So for two people to build a long future of faith and trust, it would be wise to consider waiting." This same suspicion can carry over into marriage; the spouse may feel, "If he or she had sex with me, then she or he may have it with others." Hauer (1983, 53) tells the story of Ted and Sylvia, who decided not to wait. The experience devastated Sylvia. "Suddenly there is no more room for the wonderful tenderness and erotic tension that characterized earlier times together. . . . Their magical closeness together has been sacrificed to their preoccupation with sex." Sylvia ended the relationship.

The possibility of pregnancy and the resulting shame of a baby arriving too early certainly make it worthwhile to wait. In the secular world much of the shame of having a baby arrive too early or illegitimately has been removed (Whyte 1990, 52). In most churches there is still a stigma attached to an illegitimate birth or the too-early arrival of a baby. Someone has said there has been no improvement in contraceptive devices as far as engaged couples are concerned, for so often they do not plan to engage in premarital sex but get carried away with their emotions. The result is an unplanned pregnancy. These are some of the valid reasons for saving physical intimacies until after the wedding ceremony.

Breaking an Engagement

Since engagement is a final testing of a relationship, it is only reasonable to expect some to fail the test. There are no reliable statistics, but estimates for young people in general indicate that from one-third to one-half of all engagements are broken. Coleman (1990, 50) offers the following advice to couples faced with the need to break off a relationship: "This was a vow that should not have been made. . . . Acknowledge the fact that you were naive and romantic to give that promise. Wish the other person God's blessing, and ask for forgiveness. Having concluded that you are not in love, do the person a favor and leave. . . ."

The high divorce rate suggests that it might be better if more relationships were broken during engagement rather than starting a marriage doomed to failure. The functions of an engagement for the Christian are the same as those for the non-Christian, but Christian young people must prayerfully discern the will of God before committing themselves to an engagement. Small (1959, 198) suggests, "Much that is usually relegated to the engagement period should properly be incorporated into courtship preceding engagement."

Many young people experience premarriage jitters or doubts about the relationship as the wedding day approaches. "For some individuals the feeling of mental and physical distress as the wedding day approaches generally signifies to the individual the momentous step he [she] is taking" (Williamson 1966, 306). Since marriage is a lifelong commitment for the Christian, it is easy to understand why young people might have doubts. The only way to determine whether the doubts have a legitimate basis is to objectively reexamine the entire relationship. An examination of this type

should demonstrate whether there are basic incompatibilities that threaten the future marriage. If the overall relationship is judged to be a good one, the doubts should be put out of the mind and be replaced by a positive attitude toward the impending ceremony. If the appraisal indicates there are serious incompatibilities and the couple cannot resolve the difficulties, then it is better to break the engagement.

> *There are no reliable statistics, but estimates for young people in general indicate that from one-third to one-half of all engagements are broken.*

A couple may hesitate to take this step if showers have been held and numerous gifts received. It is much better to suffer the embarrassment of returning gifts than to enter into a relationship that is less than the best for the two individuals concerned. Life is too short to spend it in an unhappy marriage simply because the bride-elect is afraid to send back gifts.

Occasionally one hears of a bride or a groom who does not show up for the wedding. Even this embarrassment, crushing as it is, is better than consummating a union that results in unhappiness. Such an experience indicates the couple had unresolved problems.

Frequently young people have doubts about their engagement if they feel a physical attraction to someone other than the partner. Many young people (and older ones as well) do not understand that it is possible for a person to be physically attracted to a person of the opposite sex without becoming involved or even acquainted with that person. When this attraction comes to a mature person, it is put out of the mind as simple a passing fancy. This type of problem is common on the college campus where young people are in close contact daily with many other attractive persons of the opposite sex.

> ## The Christian couple can make the engagement period a time of great spiritual blessing and growth.

Coleman (1984, 20) uses the term *tingles* as a synonym for "infatuation." He writes, "We may have the tingles with many people of the opposite sex before we meet the one we should marry. Many Christians would testify that it is possible to feel the tingles for someone other than your mate even after you are *married. . . .* In His power, we commit ourselves to our partner. . . . The tingles are temporary and should never dictate our actions." During a lifetime, a person will be brought into contact with many very attractive persons of the opposite sex, but it is his/her responsibility to keep thoughts and emotions under control, realizing that the love is pledged to the spouse.

Not all experiences have a happy ending, for many engagements are broken because one of the partners becomes interested in someone else. The fact that there is no cultural bias against breaking an engagement serves to help young people decide to sever an incompatible relationship. Usually they have the encouragement of relatives and friends, particularly if the courtship has been noticeably unhappy. Some may resort to "Dear John" letters, but this is not in good taste if a personal encounter is

possible. Since the individuals have spent much time together, the least they owe one another is a personal meeting to explain why they want to break the engagement. Certainly a person wants to do the will of God, but it is not proper to blame him for the breaking of a relationship without valid reasons for doing so. Marilyn had an unhappy experience of this type:

Jim and Marilyn met during his sophomore year while she was a junior. They had many things in common such as their aim to become teachers. At the end of the year they had reached a private understanding of engagement, but early in the summer Jim was drafted into the army. He corresponded and telephoned regularly while in basic training. Near the end of his first leave he purchased a ring and gave it to Marilyn with a pledge of undying love. The next day he left for an army base in a neighboring state. A week went by and Marilyn did not hear from Jim. This was very upsetting as Jim had been such a good correspondent during the basic training. After two weeks she telephoned him and he was very apologetic and promised to write. The promise was not kept and she phoned again. This time he told her he was not sure it was God's will for them to be married and did not want his ring back, but could give no logical reason for his indecision. Eventually, Marilyn sent the ring to him. It later developed that Jim had met a woman in the local church and had wanted Marilyn to keep the ring until he solidified his relationship with the new woman, whom he married two months after receiving the ring back. He attempted to blame the will of God for his own infatuation.

"Honesty is the best policy" is a good maxim in breaking a relationship. Coleman (1990, 51) reflects, "If we made a mistake . . . it would be foolish to turn that into a forty-year mistake." It is much better to break an engagement that should be broken than to enter into a marriage that might eventually lead to a broken home.

The Christian couple can make the engagement period a time of great spiritual blessing and growth. The practice of reading the Word of God and praying together accentuates their growth toward spiritual oneness in Christ and lays a firm foundation for continued spiritual growth in their marriage. Problems arising due to the increased self-revelation of engagement are prayed about and worked through to a mutual adjustment. The favor of God is invoked upon all the plans for their life together. His guidance is sought in daily activities, and for their lives in the future. During engagement the Christian couple can begin to appreciate the oft-repeated truth: "Each for the other, and both for the Lord."

The Marriage Ceremony

The successful engagement culminates in a wedding. This is a public declaration of the leaving, cleaving, and becoming one flesh that is spoken of in Genesis 2:24—"Therefore shall a man leave his father and his mother, and shall cleave unto his wife; and they shall be one flesh." The ceremony is usually held in the church as the couple take their vows before God. It is holy matrimony. It is a recognition that the couple is ready to assume their responsibilities to demonstrate to the world that Christian marriage is a reflection of the love that Christ has for his bride, the church. In so doing they testify that their marriage is a lifetime commitment. The assembly of relatives and friends witnesses that the couple is assuming new roles and obligations that have significance for the community at large. It is also a statement to the church and society that the new husband and wife have pledged themselves to a life of sexual fidelity.

In this day of widespread immorality, this is an important function of the wedding. By having the ceremony in the church, the couple is accepted by the church and accepts the faith of the church. The exchange of rings binds the couple to each other, and they find a freedom only found in the marriage bond. When the pastor pronounces the couple to be husband and wife, the process of leaving, cleaving, and becoming one flesh that began with the first date is two-thirds completed. The one-flesh union will be the completion.

Occasionally a couple elopes and avoids the planning and expense of a wedding, but most Christian couples have their marriage solemnized in a church ceremony. Some parents may object to the expense involved in a lovely church wedding, but it is interesting to note that a higher percentage of happily married couples were married in a church than those who were not. Undoubtedly other factors may account for the higher happiness rating, such as the religious commitment of those having church weddings. It does help to give a good beginning to a marriage when the blessing of God is invoked upon it.

> *The assembly of relatives and friends witnesses that the couple is assuming new roles and obligations that have significance for the community at large.*

Traditionally the bride and her family plan and pay for the wedding, and the groom assumes the responsibility of the honeymoon. Whyte (1990, 57) discovered an interesting fact: only 38 percent of the weddings were paid for by the bride's parents. The bride and groom shared the expenses with the bride's parents for 18 percent of the weddings. The bride or groom or the groom's parents paid the expenses in 37 percent of the cases. Lewis (1981, 49–57) has an extensive budget worksheet to aid the couple in figuring the expenses of the wedding and reception. Although the bride often chooses to have the ceremony in the parsonage, in her home, or on the lawn or garden of the home, the majority prefer the traditional service in the church sanctuary. The families of the bride and groom may make suggestions, but it is the bride's day and her wishes should override the desires of all other individuals connected with the wedding.

Numerous etiquette books deal with the details of the actual wedding, so it is not necessary to repeat them. The wedding should be carefully planned within the budget of the family, and should not be a display of conspicuous consumption or used as a status symbol. The Jeverts (Hendricks and Neff 1988, 118) suggest, "Keep your wedding plans in perspective. . . . Your wedding is not your marriage. . . . Enjoy this special day, and cherish the memories the rest of your life."

> ## It is the bride's day and her wishes should override the desires of all other individuals connected with the wedding.

The actual ceremony will be largely determined by the pastor who officiates, although most men will be considerate of the wishes of the bride. The selection of the music and vows to be spoken can be mutually agreed on by the pastor and bride and groom.

There is a tendency in today's wedding ceremonies to leave out parts of the traditional ceremony. It is occasioned by the fact that the permanence of marriage is being questioned. Willimon (1979, 67–74) writes, "Mere keeping of one's marriage vows will not a marriage make. But without the total, permanent, life-long commitment that those vows represent, there is little possibility of a deep relationship. . . . Married couples must make deliberate, intentional, persevering efforts in order to achieve true union and must continually *work* [italics added] to keep alive . . . the vision of the kind of marriage they want."

As the traditional ceremony states, such vows are not to be taken "unadvisedly or lightly" since they are taken before the living God who will hold the one who vows responsible for their fulfillment. Swindoll (1980, 152) cautions, "Remember those words you promised before God? . . . Did He take such vows seriously? Read for yourself, 'When thou vowest a vow unto God, defer not to pay it: for He hath no pleasure in fools. Pay that which thou has vowed' (Eccles. 5:4). Yes, He takes them seriously, He remembers them permanently. A vow is a vow. . . . We are to fear God. He says so. We are to keep our word."

DeSanto and Williams (1988, 41) elaborate further on this thought: "As Christians we believe that commitment means something. . . . Commitment calls for unconditional love. . . . When a problem arises, we ask ourselves, 'What can I do to resolve it to our *mutual* satisfaction?' not 'How can I get *my* own way?' or 'How can I escape?'" A deliberate commitment to the wedding vows will enable the couple to overcome every obstacle their marriage faces.

Many dedicated Christian couples desire that the ceremony contain some gospel witness to the unsaved who are present, many of whom only attend a church for a wedding or a funeral. Often the pastor can weave the plan of salvation into his remarks to the congregation or to the couple; however, the pastor must use tact and wisdom, remembering that it is a wedding and not an evangelistic service. Some couples use a printed bulletin that includes the testimonies of the bridal couple, and an invitation for the reader to recognize his own need of the Savior if he does not know him.

The value of retaining some parts of the typical ceremony may be questioned. For example, the sentence, "If any man can show just cause why they may not lawfully be joined together, let him speak now, or forever hold his peace," may be superfluous when a young couple reared in the church are married, but it is a safeguard for the minister when one of the individuals has been married before. Wyman Ritchie relates that on one occasion he halted the ceremony because of a valid objection to the wedding. The event occurred when a woman whose husband had disappeared and had been legally declared dead was to be married to a second husband. When the invitation "to speak now or forever hold your peace" was given, the woman's first husband stood and declared his identity. He explained that he had endured marriage with the woman for several years. In order to save his sanity, he had deserted her but lived close enough to know what she was doing. He explained that he did not want any other man to have her even though he could not live with her himself and keep his sanity. So there are occasions when this seemingly outdated exhortation is worthwhile.

Marriage is "until death do us part" for the Christian couple, and the wedding ceremony should be one happily recalled on the golden wedding anniversary.

The Reception

Most weddings are followed by a reception that provides an opportunity for the guests to personally congratulate the bride and groom (Whyte 1990, 57). If it is a church wedding, the reception may be held in a church facility or in a rented hall if the church does not have a place. If it is a home wedding, the affair may be held in the home, on the lawn, or in the garden, depending on the location of the ceremony.

Photographs of the bridal party are often taken before the ceremony to avoid a delay between the wedding ceremony and the reception. If photos are taken after the ceremony, music is usually provided to fill the interval. Others utilize this period by having friends open the gifts so they can be admired by the guests.

The food served at the reception may range from wedding cake with a beverage to a full meal served at tables or an elaborate buffet. This is often the most costly part of the wedding, but it should be within the budget of the family. The cutting of the wedding cake by the bride and groom is the high point of the reception. After greeting the guests, the newly married couple are free to prepare to leave on their honeymoon.

The Honeymoon

After the original wedding in the garden of Eden, there was no need for a honeymoon. Wheat and Perkins (1989, 32) paint an imaginary picture: "It was a perfect honeymoon, for in the sunlit and starbathed delights of marriage in the Garden, both were naked and were not ashamed. No barriers existed between them: there was nothing to hide, nothing to overcome. What liberty to love and become one, without the conflicts which tear at us while we painfully learn our lessons in oneness."

> *Photographs of the bridal party are often taken before the ceremony to avoid a delay between the wedding ceremony and the reception.*

Two people starting on a honeymoon will discover they do not know each other as well as they thought they did. The honeymoon has developed to enable the newlyweds to begin their new roles as husband and wife in privacy. A great amount of self-revelation takes place at this time, as there are many facets of personality that can be discovered only in the intimacy of marriage itself.

Swindoll (1980, 71) even proposes a new name for the honeymoon. He suggests "*adjustment period*. How unromantic can you get? . . . That's exactly what it is! It's the beginning of a whole new lifestyle. . . . If a couple begins this adjustment period with all four feet firmly fixed on reality, it's doubtful they will suffer many sudden disappointments." There are many adjustments to be made in the first few days of marriage. These include a whole set of practices—sharing the same bed and bathroom, dressing and undressing, ordering or preparing breakfast—and the need for flexibility in roles and habits. The couple can make these adjustments better apart from relatives and friends. A pleasant honeymoon experience does not just happen but requires careful planning and preparation on the part of the couple.

> *The important thing is that the honeymoon be taken immediately after the wedding, for if it is delayed even a few days, it is no longer a honeymoon—the functions provided by the honeymoon have already been accomplished.*

The honeymoon should be planned to fit within the budget. Many couples feel this is a once-in-a-lifetime experience, so they should really live it up. Some borrow money, go into debt for an expensive honeymoon trip, and begin their married life with economic problems. They return home without money to pay the first month's rent and may have to borrow money from their parents for groceries. This is evidence of immaturity, but it happens more often than it should. The mature couple will use the engagement period to plan their honeymoon and save enough money to pay for it. If necessary they should change their plans to fit their budget.

The location of the honeymoon should be acceptable to both partners. In some areas, such as the Pocono Mountains in Pennsylvania, hotels specialize in providing accommodations for newlyweds. Upper-class and upper-middle-class couples often choose Bermuda. Most couples choose a hotel or motel not too distant from the place of the wedding. They should not plan to spend much of their time traveling, as this is tiring.

It is better to select one place where the couple can spend most of their time getting to know each other better. This does not prohibit some local sightseeing, which is far different from spending a two-week honeymoon traveling by car from New York to California and back. Most couples like to keep the location secret to avoid practical jokes that some people like to play, or to avoid an overprotective parent such as the mother who called her son three times on his wedding night. However, parents or other close relatives should be informed so they can locate the couple in case of an emergency, such as serious illness or the death of a relative or close friend.

The length of the honeymoon will depend on several factors, such as the amount of time off from employment and budget limitations. An ideal period might be one week, with an absolute minimum of three days. This gives the couple time enough to adjust to each other before returning to the routine of daily life. If the honeymoon is too long the couple may get anxious to be in their new home, and this anxiety may have a dampening effect. The important thing is that the honeymoon be taken immediately after the wedding, for if it is delayed even a few days, it is no longer a honeymoon—the functions provided by the honeymoon have already been accomplished. Martinson (1970, 260) states, "It is better to have a honeymoon of three days . . . than a postponed trip of three weeks." If circumstances prevent an extended honeymoon, it is imperative that the couple leave for at least a day or two so they have some time together in privacy.

A central feature of the honeymoon is the self-revelation involved in completing the marriage through physical intimacy. Wheat (1977, 48) quotes Deuteronomy 24:5, which states that the groom was to be free of all major responsibilities for one year so that he might "cheer up his wife whom he hath taken." It is impossible for a man to take off a year, but Wheat further remarks, "the first few weeks of marriage are a crucial time for the young couple. To 'cheer up' the wife means literally in the Hebrew 'to know sexually and understand what is exquisitely pleasing to her' in the physical relationship." In most states the marriage is not considered a bona fide marriage if the couple does not or cannot enter into a sexual relationship, and the union can be annulled by a court of law.

If the couple has planned well and is considerate of each other, the first sexual relationship need not be the traumatic experience that one often reads about in case histories of marriage counselors' files. A couple who has read a good marriage manual or who has had good premarital counseling should encounter no great difficulty if they do not expect too much from the first experience. There are several Christian marriage manuals available (*Intended for Pleasure* by Dr. Ed Wheat, and *The Act of Marriage* by Tim and Beverly LaHaye). These books will help the couple to understand that the area of sex adjustment is one that often requires varying periods of time to achieve a mutually satisfying adjustment.

> ## Many couples have few or no problems and the honeymoon for them is the peak of sexual enjoyment for the entire marriage cycle.

If the couple is mature, they will have a realistic view of the sexual relationship and will not be greatly disappointed if the first union does not produce all the thrills and sensations that our culture leads many young people to expect from a sexual relationship. Dobson (1987, 67) warns, "Don't be surprised if sexual intercourse is less intense than anticipated on the honeymoon. For those who have saved themselves

for that first night, their level of expectation may exceed reality by a wide margin. . . . For one thing, the transformation from 'Thou shalt not' to 'Thou shalt, regularly and with great passion' is not so easily made by some people."

One study of consecrated Christian couples quoted by McDowell (1985, 102) indicates that 78 percent adjusted sexually within a week. Many couples have few or no problems and the honeymoon for them is the peak of sexual enjoyment for the entire marriage cycle.

Mature Christian couples who have wisely chosen to use the engagement period as a final pretest of the marriage, and have planned the marriage ceremony and honeymoon carefully have laid the best foundation possible to enter into their married life together and to enjoy the blessing of God upon their union.

Study Questions

1. How does engagement in American culture differ from the New Testament concept of engagement?
2. What should a couple do if their relationship is opposed by one or both sets of future in-laws?
3. Discuss the amount of self-revelation that takes place in random dating, going steady, engagement, and the honeymoon.
4. List ten areas that a couple must discuss during their engagement.
5. Why is psychological compatibility in marriage more important than physical compatibility?
6. Under what circumstances should a person reveal his or her past erotic involvements to the partner?
7. Why is premarital counseling so important for a person from a single-parent home or from a home where there was physical or sexual abuse?
8. List the advantages and disadvantages of a long engagement.
9. Discuss four reasons why a Christian couple should have a church wedding.
10. What are the requirements for a successful honeymoon?

Personality Inventory

Analyzing an Engagement

The following questions should prove helpful in assessing either an informal or formal engagement. The mature young person should examine objectively a relationship and determine whether it has the potential for a successful Christian marriage.

1. How long have you gone together? How long do you expect your engagement to last before you are married?
2. Have you been separated for any length of time? What effect, if any, did the separation have on the relationship?
3. Have you ever given serious thought to breaking the engagement? If so, why?
4. Are you able to communicate freely on all subjects, or are there areas that you avoid discussing because you disagree?
5. List the factors in your background that will contribute to compatibility in your marriage.
6. What areas in your background are potential sources of incompatibility? What adjustments are you making in these areas?
7. Discuss the values and goals that you have in common. Any areas of disagreement or conflict? If you have disagreements, how do you intend to reconcile them?
8. Do you consider your knowledge of sex adequate for marriage? Do you have any attitudes toward sex that might prove a hindrance in your marriage? Have you read a marriage manual?
9. Have you discussed and reached agreement on such important subjects as the use and handling of money; the number, spacing, and discipline of children; the family altar, etc.?
10. Do your families and friends approve of your engagement? If not, how valid are their objections? Have you discussed these objections with a counselor who was impartial in his appraisal of the situation?
11. If you have arrived at the time where you are making wedding plans, do both partners agree on the details?
12. Are your plans for a honeymoon realistic according to the time and money that you have available?

Suggested Readings

Coleman, W. L. 1991. *Cupid is stupid: How to fall in love without falling on your face.* Downer's Grove, Ill.: InterVarsity. A clever title and an intriguing theme. The author discusses the "cupid mentality" so prevalent in American culture. It says that love is something we cannot manage if it comes. Coleman's thesis is that love *is* manageable and can be controlled. Excellent treatment of the entire subject of love.

Diehm, W. J. 1984. *Finding your life partner.* Valley Forge, Penn.: Judson. The title tells the purpose of this book. It is filled with good suggestions on how to meet people and how to interact with them. It includes a test for romantic feelings and also one to discern compatibilities. Engaged couples will benefit from taking these tests.

Fryling, A., and R. Fryling. 1977. *A handbook for engaged couples.* Downer's Grove, Ill.: InterVarsity. A small but helpful booklet for the engaged couple. It is available in Christian bookstores.

Hauer, G. 1983. *Longing for tenderness: Responsible love before marriage.* Downer's Grove, Ill.: InterVarsity. Translation from the German of an excellent treatise on love before marriage. Hauer deals competently with the question of "why wait?" and gives solid reasons for waiting. The book illustrates that young people throughout the Western world face many of the same problems.

Huggett, J. 1982. *Growing into love before you marry.* Downer's Grove, Ill.: InterVarsity. InterVarsity Press has done a real favor to America's youth by publishing the writings of Joyce Huggett. Although she is British, she frankly deals with problems faced by teenagers and young adults in either her country or the United States. Her solutions are biblically based.

Ketterman, G. H. 1984. *Before and after the wedding night.* Old Tappan, N.J.: Revell. Written by a medical doctor, this volume gives much valuable information, particularly in reference to the honeymoon. The sexual organs are pictured and described and information given for sexual intercourse.

Lewis, K. O. 1981. *Your Christian wedding.* Old Tappan, N.J.: Revell. A complete handbook that covers almost everything a couple needs to know in planning a Christian wedding. Suggestions are given for those who wish to formulate their own vows.

McDowell, J. 1985. *The secret of loving: How a lasting intimate relationship can be yours.* San Bernardino, Calif.: Here's Life. The author gives suggestions for improving one's self in order to be able to love. The second half is devoted to a description of mature love.

Wheat, E., and G. Wheat. 1981. *Intended for pleasure: Sex technique and fulfillment in marriage.* Rev. ed. Old Tappan, N.J.: Revell. A marriage manual designed to instruct newlyweds in the various aspects of the sexual relationship.

Willimon, W. H. 1979. *Saying yes to marriage.* Valley Forge, Penn.: Judson. Written by a pastor who has seen firsthand the many problems of marriage today. He attempts a "fresh look at an old institution." He succeeds by presenting marriage as a revolutionary activity in today's culture.

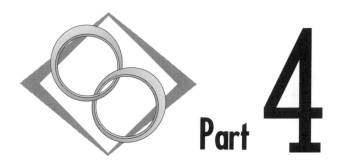

Part 4

Fellowship in Marriage

Communication in Marriage

Let your speech be always with grace.

—Colossians 4:6

Importance of Communication

Joanne turned on the dishwasher, then walked through the dining room and into the living room where she sat down on the couch next to her husband. She asked, "Did you have a good day at the office?"

"Uh huh."

"Did the big order come in that you were praying about?"

"Uh huh."

"Do you think they will recall some of the men who were laid off?"

"Uh huh."

"Did Johnny show you his report card with two As on it?"

"Uh huh."

This type of conversation occurs so often in American homes that marriage counselors list lack of communication as a primary problem in marriages. One study of clients undergoing counseling found that 86 percent of them cited "failure to communicate" as their main problem. Yet every aspect of home life depends on the ability of husband and wife and parents and children to communicate with each other.

Several studies in recent years have attempted to discover the traits of a healthy family. One of the pioneers in this area is Nick Stinnett of the University of Nebraska. He and his colleagues studied more than three thousand strong families in several nations. The researchers discovered six main qualities of strong families: they "are committed to each other, spend time together, have good family communication, express appreciation for each other, have a spiritual commitment, and are able to solve problems in a crisis" (Rekers 1988, 38). They found that strong families talk much to each other and also listen to each other.

Curran (1983, 31–58) approached the study of healthy families from a different angle. She surveyed 551 professionals who work with families. Of 56 choices to select from, her respondents chose "communicating and listening" as the number one trait of healthy families.

> ## The goal is to develop communication that is open, honest, straightforward, caring, and responsible in an atmosphere that is loving and accepting.

Identifying the changing function of the family helps to explain the importance of communication. In previous generations the husband was the breadwinner and the wife the homemaker. The performance of these roles was the important factor in providing satisfaction in the marriage. Today, as Curran (1983, 33) remarks, "the major function of family is relational. Our needs are emotional, not physical. . . . We need to know that we are needed and appreciated. We want to share our intimacies, not just physical intimacies but all the intimacies of our lives."

The success or failure of a marriage (chap. 3) is determined by the amount of emotional and psychological satisfaction received from the interaction between husband and wife. Fitzpatrick (1988, 38) in her study of marital communication writes, "Marital satisfaction is central to marital success. Scholars debate the very best way to measure this important concept, although most now agree that communication is strongly related to marital happiness." Communication is the tool that enables one spouse to show love, care, concern, acceptance, and other emotions and attitudes that create a positive emotional response in the other spouse. The result is happiness in the relationship. Thus, strong families list it as one of their predominant traits.

The opposite is also true. When one spouse cannot convey positive emotions and attitudes, the other spouse will tend to be unhappy. The result is that this lack of communication becomes the number one problem that marriage therapists encounter.

Couples need to work at improving their communication skills if they are to avoid this problem. The goal is to develop communication that is open, honest, straightforward, caring, and responsible in an atmosphere that is loving and accepting. The apostle Paul (Eph. 4:15) instructs the believer to "speak the truth in love." This is possible only when a couple totally accepts each other so that each is free to speak without fear of criticism, ridicule, or rejection. Each one is free to express thoughts and emotions knowing the other will accept them in the loving spirit in which they were given.

Communication Defined

The average person may think of communication as talking. Much more is involved. In many homes much talking takes place but no communication occurs because no one is *listening*. Even if a person is listening there is no real communication unless the message is *understood*.

Ketterman (Rekers 1988, 109) includes these three ideas in her definition: "Effective communication is the successful transmission of information and feelings from one person to another. It involves the assurance that whatever is stated by the communicator is reasonably similar to that which is heard and understood by the listener or recipient."

H. Norman Wright, one of the early writers in the field of communication in marriage has a similar definition (1974, 52): "Communication is a process (either verbal or nonverbal) of sharing information with another person in such a way that he understands what you are saying." This statement adds an additional factor that is important to note. Communication may be either verbal or nonverbal. The wink of an eye, the touch of a hand, a smile or a frown, an arched eyebrow, outstretched arms, plus hundreds of other bodily gestures convey messages usually understood by those who observe them (McDonald 1977, 72).

Many people think that most communication is on the verbal level. However, "studies have shown that fifty-five percent of communication is through body language; thirty-five percent through tone of voice; two percent is intuitive, and only eight percent is through words" (Snyder and Snyder 1988, 129). Consequently, people who are near each other communicate even though they are unaware that communication is taking place. In such circumstances it is impossible not to communicate. For example, strangers in a supermarket will look away from each other to indicate they do not want to recognize the other's presence. The husband who hides himself behind the newspaper at breakfast communicates to his wife that he does not want to talk to her. The spouse who gives his mate the silent treatment is communicating his displeasure of some action she has taken. Even the distance between the speaker and the listener relays the speaker's attitude toward the listener. A person may acknowledge an acquaintance's presence by a simple nod of the head. In each case the action communicates the level of the relationship between the two individuals.

Noller (1984, 3) suggests nonverbal communication performs three functions: conveying interpersonal attitudes, expressing emotions, and handling the ongoing interaction "by indicating interest in and attentiveness to the person with whom one is interacting." Fitzpatrick (1988, 37) quotes a study of the communication patterns of happily married couples that indicated they exhibit "more positive nonverbal cues" and have a "consistency in their use of nonverbal cues." This stresses the necessity for a couple to learn to understand the body language of a spouse as well as his or her spoken words, for as Chapian states

(1986, 158), "Perhaps, of every language in the world, body language talks the loudest."

The Importance of Listening

Listening as a part of communication needs to be emphasized because it is so much easier to talk than to listen. In courtship, listening would seem to come naturally; the couple is trying to learn about each other. They are intensely interested in every aspect of each other's lives: their daily experiences, their plans for tomorrow and for the future. Then it is easy to listen.

> *In courtship, listening would seem to come naturally; the couple is trying to learn about each other.*

After the honeymoon is over, listening becomes more difficult. More self-revelation has taken place, the couple knows each other well, and living becomes a daily routine. Unfortunately, in too many marriages the couple take each other for granted and communication breaks down. Although they talk, they no longer listen to each other. Small (1968, 20) comments, "Having come from two different worlds, the married partners return to two different worlds, and much to their own surprise are saying, 'We seem to have so little to talk about any more. We speak to each other only when necessary.'" Such couples may seek a divorce if they do not receive counseling to help resolve their problem.

Most people find it easier to talk than to listen. Some shy individuals listen more than they talk. Such an individual tends to marry a person who will prefer to talk rather than listen.

Small (1968, 106–7) discussed why most people prefer to talk rather than listen. He states, "Speaking is a means of self-assertion; listening is not." He explains that individuals have a "primary need for self-assertion." Individuals discover their identity by talking about their ideas, opinions, and feelings in a social situation. Consequently, this primary need is met more readily by talking rather than by listening.

Since listening is more difficult than speaking, it must be consciously practiced in order to enhance the ability to hear what the other person is saying. Jesus was cognizant of this fact. On many occasions he exhorted his audience, "If any man have ears to hear, let him hear" (Matt. 11:15; 13:13; Mark 4:9, 23; 7:16). Listening requires attention to the speaker. By listening attentively to the speaker, the listener pays respect to that person and indicates the speaker is important: the listener is willing to respond. Listeners can even guide the conversation by the questions they ask.

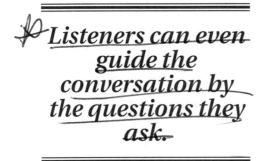

Listeners can even guide the conversation by the questions they ask.

Wright (1986, 20–23) gives several suggestions for learning to listen more effectively. He suggests that the person listening give feedback to the one speaking by using such phrases as, "What I hear you saying is . . . ," "If I hear you correctly, you are saying . . . ," or "Do you mean that . . . ?" This technique clarifies the communication and eliminates misunderstandings. He also suggests one should "listen with empathy," that is, to try and feel as the speaker feels. He uses Romans 12:15 as an example where Paul exhorts the believer to "Rejoice with them that rejoice, and weep with them that weep." Curran (1983, 43) quotes Dr. Jerry Lewis, "There is probably no more important dimension in all of human relationships than the capacity for empathy."

"Listen with openness" is another criterion of effective listening. Wright proposes that the listener think of the speaker as from another country and speaking another language that the listener must understand in order to comprehend what is being said. This is particularly true in marriage where two different individuals unite from two different subcultures (male and female). Each spouse has learned the language of the gender subculture, a fact that often makes it difficult for the spouses to understand each other.

In every culture, boys typically grow up in the company of other boys, and girls tend to be reared in the presence of girls. Consequently, they are prone to think and communicate as they have been trained in their subculture. Van Pelt (1989, 166–67) observes that girls prefer small groups and especially a best friend with whom to share secrets. The friendship depends on the ability to share intimacies. Boys tend to play in large groups and time is spent in activities rather than in talking. "Rather than sharing secrets, boys engage in king-of-the-mountain play and can-you-top-this stories to prove masculinity." As a result, men tend to think of sharing activities with a woman rather than talking. It may be no problem to the man if there is no sharing of secrets.

"Listen with awareness" requires the person to judge the consistency of the speaker's message. In this situation the listener must decide if the words, tone, and body language match up. The eyes of the listener are involved because the nonverbal signals must be observed to see if they are congruent with the verbal. Wright states (1986, 93), "The more observant you are, the more sensitive you will become, and the better you can communicate."

This sensitivity involves more than just body language. It also includes listening with the heart or the emotions. The listener must be alert to the emotional state of the speaker and be able to identify with and to understand the mood of the speaker (Rekers 1988, 113). When the listener says, "I know how you feel," it informs the speaker that he is being understood.

Barriers to Communication

The average person does not realize how difficult it is to communicate with another person. Smith (Hendricks and Neff 1988, 292) identifies at least eight steps involved in communication:

1. What the husband intends to say to the wife.
2. What the husband actually says to the wife.
3. What the wife hears.
4. What the wife says to herself about what she has heard.
5. What the wife intends to say back to the husband.
6. What the wife actually says to the husband.
7. What the husband hears.
8. What the husband says to himself about what he hears.

This process occurs not only between husband and wife but between two or more individuals who are trying to communicate with each other. It is easy to see how misunderstandings can occur. A breakdown in communication can develop at any stage of the process. The complexity of this procedure caused someone to say, "I know you believe you understand what I said, but I'm not sure you realize that what you heard is not what I said." Couples must strive for clarity in their speech in order to avoid the misunderstandings that come from failure to clearly state their ideas.

Young people are rarely taught anything about the complex process of communication. Osborne (1970, 63) comments that learning to communicate is more difficult than learning to drive a car or to type. He makes the salient point that we would not expect a young person to use a computer without some instruction. Yet our culture expects two young people, when they marry, to interact through communication and establish a happy home without any teaching about the fine art of communication. The purpose of this chapter is to help

those anticipating marriage, or already married, to be able to interact more successfully than those not exposed to such instruction. Since marriage is for a lifetime, it is incumbent on newlyweds to make a more detailed study of what is involved in good marital communication.

A major barrier to communication in marriage is that men and women differ physiologically. Smalley and Trent (Yorkey 1990, 16) describe several studies that demonstrate these differences. One study carried out in a nursery showed that girl babies had more lip movement than boys. A Harvard study wired a playground for sound and discovered that 100 percent of the sounds from little girls were recognizable words. Only 63 percent of the boys' sounds were words. The rest were "either one-syllable words like 'uh' or 'mmm' or sound effects like 'varoom,' 'yaoooh,' and 'zooooom.'"

> *"I know you believe you understand what I said, but I'm not sure you realize that what you heard is not what I said."*

Van Pelt (1989, 25) writes concerning the discovery of the difference between the right brain in females and the left brain in males. Medical researchers discovered that between the sixteenth and twenty-sixth week of pregnancy, the brain of the male fetus is bathed with testosterone and other sex hormones that destroys some of the corpus callosum, the connective tissues between the right brain and the left brain. The right side recedes slightly so that the male baby becomes more left-brain-oriented. "The hormonal bath gives a specialization to the male brain that might be called logical linear isolation, which females don't tend to get. Left brain is more logical and the right brain more intuitive or emotional. This explains what is called 'woman's intuition.'"

> ## "Left brain is more logical and the right brain more intuitive or emotional. This explains what is called 'woman's intuition.'"

The right side controls language and communication skills, so that women tend to be more verbal than men. Thus, men may be at a disadvantage when they engage in verbal sparring with women. Smalley and Trent (Yorkey 1990, 20) conclude their discussion by stating, "If a woman truly expects to have meaningful communication with her husband, she *must* activate the right side of his brain. And if a man truly wants to communicate with his wife, he *must* enter her world of emotions."

It is apparent that God made men and women to complement each other in this area. This does not mean women cannot think logically or that men cannot become emotional. Persons use both sides of their brain but some differences do exist between men and women. Van Pelt (1989, 26) writes, "How incredibly creative of God to put dominance of logic in the male and dominance of feeling in the female. Each of these perspectives is needed in order to be *whole* or *complete*."

This information should aid couples in understanding why they derive different answers from the same data. Boys and girls not only think differently because of psychological differences, but they tend to be reared in separate subcultures that teach them to think and speak differently.

Another barrier to understanding one another is poor communication. Near the top of the list is failure to listen properly. Very often the listener is mentally forming a response to what is being heard. At other times the listener hears the first part of the conversation and then assumes he knows what will follow. Most often these assumptions are wrong, and the reply frustrates the speaker, for the message has not been understood.

Very often a speaker will fail to engage the listener's attention before beginning to speak. The classic example of this is the husband reading the paper who fails to realize his wife is speaking. On the other hand, there is the compulsive talker who continues to chatter whether anyone is paying attention or not. Listening takes effort and the speaker should have something worthwhile to say if one is expected to listen.

A major problem in some marriages occurs when a spouse gives the mate the silent treatment following a confrontation. The offended spouse refuses to speak to the offender. Chapian (1986, 128) emphasizes, "I don't think I've ever seen any behavior as destructive as the silent treatment." The refusal to hear and speak may last for three days or three weeks. Such behavior evokes negative emotional responses in the person receiving the silent treatment. The average person will endure such a response for a limited period. If professional counseling is not received to help change the pattern, there is great possibility the relationship will be destroyed.

Mistakes can also be made by the speaker. Failure to speak distinctly or with clarity make it difficult to be understood. Avoiding issues by saying something irrelevant or contradictory causes confusion in the listener's mind. A common complaint is that the speaker does not speak loudly enough. People with soft voices need to cultivate the habit of projecting their voice. On the other hand, there are others with strong voices who may need to lower their voices in order to communicate pleasantly.

A common barrier is the failure to adequately and honestly express true feelings. If a person says, "I don't care" but does care, the listener has no way of interpreting what the speaker really feels. Or a person may say, "It's not important" when it is important. If honest feelings are not expressed, the listener cannot respond as the speaker expects. The tendency then is to condemn the mate for failing to respond as the speaker expected. This type of interaction breeds conflict. When a spouse is uncertain of his or her own feelings, this should be conveyed to the other mate. Exploring the speaker's feelings together can enhance the communication. Each spouse needs to be free to express feelings and thoughts without fear of ridicule or censure.

A person who constantly jokes hinders effective communication. Although a spouse usually learns to judge what the mate is saying most of the time, the speaker risks being misinterpreted by his joking or sarcasm, with confusion and even conflict as the almost inevitable result.

One of the greatest barriers to marital communication is failure to take time to talk to each other or to the children. People cannot communicate well if they do not spend time together. Stinnett (Henslin 1985, 308–10) found that the second quality of a strong family is that they spend much time together. He discovered that they "structured their life-styles so they could spend time together. It did not 'just happen' but they made it to happen. And this togetherness was in all areas of their lives—eating meals, recreation and work." Since strong families do spend much time together, Stinnett found they also had good communication patterns. They had time to talk and listen to one another.

Americans live in an age of labor-saving devices. There are computers, microwaves, frozen foods, household appliances for every task, yet time for communicating with each other is lacking. Welch (Yorkey 1990, 65) reports that a survey of working women by the *American Sociological Review* found they spent an average of twelve minutes a day talking to their husbands. Another study (Greeley 1991, 44) relates that the median number of hours per week that husbands and wives talked was twenty hours. This same study states that 43 percent of the married men and women talked to each other "without interruption often."

The fact is that families are not spending enough time together, and when they do, they do not talk. A common complaint of wives reveals that some husbands come home and usually pick up a newspaper. When dinner is over, they watch television until bedtime. An earlier survey of children stated the comment "they most often hear from their fathers is, 'I'm too tired,' Next is, 'We don't have enough money,' and the third is 'Keep quiet!'" (McDonald 1977, 71). The pace of life has increased since the study, but it is doubtful if the comments have changed in the intervening years. Professional men such as pastors, counselors, and physicians have demands made upon them that intrude upon family life. Wives and children are often neglected because of the desire or necessity to achieve professional goals.

> # One of the greatest barriers to marital communication is failure to take time to talk to each other or to the children.

The solution to this time problem is not easy. Kessler (1984, 122) suggests several possible solutions. First, the couple must sit down and discuss the problem. If they cannot solve the problem, a visit to a professional counselor may help. They must agree that time for talking is a major priority. As such, it is worth the effort it takes to set time aside for it. It may be that there are activities they have been doing separately that they could do together. If he washes the car while she does the dishes, then she could help him with the car and he could help her with the dishes. If he puts the children to bed while she does the dishes, then these activities can be done together. His final suggestion is for the couple to arise early before the children, make a pot of coffee, read the

Bible, pray together, and have a time for uninterrupted talking.

Professional people may have to allot time in their daily schedule for the spouse or family. One therapist, after a crisis in his marriage because of neglect of his family, scheduled an hour (4 to 5 P.M.) for them. He arrived home early and spent the time rebuilding the broken relationship with his family.

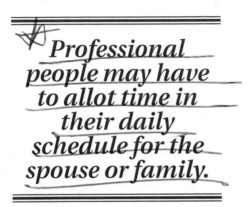

> *Professional people may have to allot time in their daily schedule for the spouse or family.*

Inevitably there will be some families whose time together will not result in satisfying communication. There will be some men who will just not talk to their wives or children. There will be danger signals in the courtship indicating that the prospective mate cannot communicate, but in the heat of romantic love these signals will be ignored. Some wives will not share the interests of their husbands and will be unable to communicate with them. If professional counseling does not help, the affected spouse may have to learn to adapt this lifestyle. Women can find an outlet by initiating friendship with other women but the danger always exists that one spouse will find a "listening ear" who "understands" and a triangular love affair may develop and lead to a broken marriage.

Communication and Conflict in Marriage

In 1 Corinthians 13:4 and 7 Paul states that "love suffereth long" and "beareth all things." This is easily done in courtship but becomes difficult in the increasing intimacy of marriage. When two people from different backgrounds and subcultures are united in marriage, there is the possibility of disagreement and conflict

as they learn to live together. Personalities need to be merged into a pattern of creative growth and fulfillment. As the various stages of the marriage cycle unfold, new challenges to the relationship must be overcome. The increasing intimacy reveals weaknesses that can be exploited by a spouse in a time of conflict. Life is more complex today, and this fact amplifies the opportunities for disagreements. The pressures of limited time and stress on individual rights and personal assertiveness all contribute to the possibility of conflict.

These pressures are real and are reflected in a large number of cases of spouse abuse and child abuse. Husbands and wives who cannot control their anger risk physically and emotionally abusing each other. Parents abuse children physically, emotionally, and sexually. (Cargan 1991, 147) states "that more than six million children and three million spouses are severely assaulted each year." Social service agencies and the criminal justice systems in our cities have separate departments to deal with these problems. Most cities have arranged special facilities for abused women and their children. The extent of this social problem is not fully known, for many cases are never reported to the authorities.

Christian families are not immune to these problems. Christians are subject to the same frustrations and temptations as unbelievers. If the resources of Christian faith are not utilized, Christians are vulnerable to these same situations. It is heartbreaking to read of a Christian worker who abuses his wife or who is guilty of sexually abusing a small child. One reads of these crimes all too often in the newspaper.

Managing Conflict in Marriage

Conflict is inevitable in marriage. Occasionally a couple who have been married as long as fifty years state they have never had a conflict. It is possible to live this long without one, but it is more probable that after fifty years they have forgotten many things that took place in their early years together.

Even strong families have conflict. Stinnett (1985, 310) discovered that they became angry at one another, but they had the communication skills to resolve their differences. They were able to talk about them, to share their feelings openly, and to come to a resolution of the problem. He comments (Henslin 1985, 310), "These strong families have learned to do what David and Vera Mace (1982) have reported to be essential for a successful marriage—making creative use of conflict." Since confrontation is inevitable in marriage, it is necessary to consider some ideas to help prevent and overcome it. Most conflicts start out when a couple disagree on some subject. Each spouse takes a defensive position and the disagreement becomes a quarrel. This creates tension between them and perhaps some hostility. The inability to find a solution to the disagreement and the intense feelings that it generates distinguish a quarrel from a discussion.

For a couple with poor communication, confrontations may serve a useful purpose in that they force the couple to face problems that they otherwise would avoid. It would be much better if the couple would establish open lines of communication so they could discuss their problems rather than quarrel about them.

Certain guidelines for arguing may be helpful to some couples, but as in many areas of conduct, it is easier to make rules than to follow them. A quarrel is indicative of some underlying difficulty in a relationship, and the first task is to discover what is at the base of the issue. For example, a wife is accused by the husband of spending too much money on clothing. This couple must determine what is normal for a wife in her social stratum to spend in order to dress appropriately. It may be that due to the difference between the gender subcultures in relationship to clothing, the wife is not overspending. It is merely the case of a husband not understanding the wardrobe needs of a woman.

If it is established that she is spending too much, then they must determine her motivation. Does she have subconscious ego needs that she needs to deal with? She could have an inferiority complex and overspend on clothes to compensate. If the husband handles the money and the wife buys clothing on charge accounts, perhaps she is subconsciously striking back at his exclusive control of the family money, and her spending becomes an attempt to control part of it for he must legally pay her

bills. Only after the basic problem has been isolated can the couple take constructive steps to settle the difficulty. If they do not seek the source of the difficulty, they will continue to argue about symptoms rather than settling the underlying problem. It may take much prayer, soul-searching, or even professional counseling to find the source of the argument, but the Christian couple has all the resources of their faith in Christ to help discover a solution.

Once an issue has been discovered and discussed and a solution found, then it should be permanently settled. It should not be brought up again. It is unfortunate that some couples are unable to settle controversies and each time they have a quarrel they exhume old problems to add to the new one. Such couples obviously experience a great deal of unhappiness. It is imperative that young couples establish the habit of finding solutions to their differences so they do not go through life arguing about them.

> *The inability to find a solution to the disagreement and the intense feelings that it generates distinguish a quarrel from a discussion.*

When a couple quarrels, they should not attack each other's personalities. As a couple live together, they learn each other's weaknesses and it becomes easy to hurt the partner during an argument. For example, he knows she bitterly resents being compared to her mother, so in the heat of a quarrel it is easy for him to say, "You are just like your mother!" She knows he is sensitive about his inability to handle money so it is easy for her to say, "You never have a dime in your pocket!" The couple should learn to leave personalities out of the discussion and concentrate their time and energy on solving the fundamental issue.

Each partner has certain basic personality traits and habits that may become a source of quarrels. Many of these are really not important, but may be given more attention than they deserve. Blood (1978, 142) calls these irritants "tremendous trifles." He says, "Any problem that is tremendously significant to the injured party but merely a trifle to the innocent one is a 'tremendous trifle.'" He indicates that they arise because of the "intimacy of marriage." In living together under the same roof, the partners are exposed to the seamier aspects of each other's lives.

> # *Differences between the husband and wife typically should never be discussed when other people are present.*

The classic illustration is the couple who quarrels about squeezing the toothpaste tube. He likes to carefully roll up the tube and she just grabs it in the middle and squeezes it. Every time he brushes his teeth he resents her squeezing the tube and this habit becomes a source of friction. In reality, it does not matter how the toothpaste is pressured out of the tube as long as all of it is used up. For the Christian, the grace of God (2 Cor. 12:9) is sufficient for such trifles, but often the couple forgets to apply their Christianity to the practical aspects of adjusting to everyday life.

Some times are more appropriate than others for discussing problems. Differences between the husband and wife typically should never be discussed when other people are present. It is not wise to bring up some problem when either spouse is tired or hungry. It is better to wait until both are well fed and rested. The Conways (1991, 75) suggest that "forcing communication when there isn't sufficient time or interest may damage the overall outcome. If your mate wants to talk when you're not ready, be courteous to set a later time. Then prepare yourself for a positive and profitable encounter."

Some couples set aside a particular hour each week for a family conference when they may discuss any aspect of their relationship or their family that needs attention. Others find this too mechanical and prefer to discuss matters as they arise. The important factor is that the couple keeps the communication lines open at all times and makes an honest attempt to solve problems as they arise.

When facing a disagreement, sometimes one partner may withdraw from the area. David Mace (1982, 14), in a frank discussion of some of the problems he and Vera faced early in their marriage, relates that fleeing the scene was his way of dealing with conflict. He would disappear for long periods of time. When he returned, he was unable to tell Vera what was wrong. This led her to conclude that he was a moody person. Fortunately, they learned to control their anger and describe the solution they found in *Love and Anger in Marriage.* They devised a three-step plan in which they agreed to immediately tell each other of their anger, to recognize it was acceptable to be angry but not acceptable to attack the other person, and both would work through every anger situation that threatened their relationship. This made anger a process of growth rather than deterioration of the relationship.

Richard and Mary Strauss (Yorkey 1990, 22–27) also openly shared their early struggles to resolve conflicts. Originally, he fought to win whenever there was a disagreement. The result was to drive Mary farther from him. Eventually they solved their problems by developing "love fights" that not only resolved the conflict but led to greater love for each other. They list six steps in a love fight—adopt a learner's posture so that both can grow and learn through the experience; listen with the heart so feelings are understood; keep emotions under control; keep short accounts by confronting problems when they arise; think before speaking; and focus on one's own part of the blame.

There are several other ways in which couples come to an agreement over differences that arise between them. The most important means is simple compromise. The couple who has established good communication is able to talk over a problem intelligently. The Christian couple desires the will of God in every phase of their marriage and prays for God's guidance in the situation. Each gives in to the other so that both are satisfied and happy with the solution. Neither partner get his or her own way, but each person benefits since now they function as a unit rather than as individuals with separate viewpoints. Blood (1978, 253) suggests that compromise is not always possible. If a man has a choice between a new job in a distant town or his present one, no compromise is possible. He must choose one or the other. Compromise as a method of settling differences is necessary in all human relationships and is indispensable in the intimacy of marriage if the marriage is to be successful.

In some marriages there are some areas where the couple cannot agree to compromise. In this case they agree to disagree and each holds to his own viewpoint, even though the other partner is unhappy or may even harbor some resentment against the mate for refusing to compromise. They reach a state of accommodation similar to labor and management, who cooperate with one another to achieve production although neither organization trusts the other. Needless to say, in matrimony such a method of resolving differences is not a happy one. Christians should be able to pray about such matters and seek the mind of God, then follow his leading. Some people take a position and then refuse to change regardless of prayer or the will of God.

A similar situation occurs when the couple have a difference between them and they agree to disagree but genuinely respect each other's viewpoint. There is no desire to change the other person. In the realm of politics, one spouse may be a Republican, the other an independent, and each allows the other the privilege of retaining their views in marriage. This toleration of each other's view does not hinder the happiness of the relationship in any way since they respect each other as genuine persons. Toleration is different from accommodation in that it is a positive solution, whereas accommodation has a negative effect.

> **Toleration is different from accommodation in that it is a positive solution, whereas accommodation has a negative effect.**

Differences also may be adjusted by assimilation when one partner accepts the view of the other. This usually follows prayer and discussion of the issues involved. One spouse changes and accepts the position of the other. Often one individual so respects and admires the partner that it is easy to accept the opinions and judgments of that person. Where such a condition prevails, there will be little disharmony and much happiness.

Often problems can be solved by careful analysis. The major source of potential conflict in marriage is the use of money. Perhaps it might better be stated, "the lack of sufficient money." Most families lack enough to satisfy the needs of both husband and wife. The disagreement is over whose needs are going to be met. The solution is to analyze the money situation, set up a budget that will meet the needs of the family, then compromise on how the disposable income can be used to satisfy the needs of both partners. Such a solution requires the effort of both spouses to live within the budget so that a surplus is available.

Conflict in marriage is inevitable but it can be overcome if the couple will consider each disagreement as a means of growth and enrichment of their marriage. Wright (1979, 139) states, "Through conflict a person can share his differences with another individual. Facing conflict is also a way of testing one's own strength and resources. Each person in a conflict situation will bring one or more alternative choices to the discussion." Each partner is revealing himself or herself in a manner that only conflict can display. This self-revelation can help the partners to understand each other better. As conflicts are amiably resolved, growth takes place in the relationship.

On the other hand, if conflict is not managed properly, it becomes destructive, and the ultimate end is the dissolution of the relationship. The high divorce rate indicate that many couples do not learn how to handle conflict. Christian young people make a lifetime commitment so it is necessary to develop skills to manage conflict. This not only assures the stability of the marriage but helps to provide the happiness that marriage is designed to provide.

A relationship is begun, nourished, and maintained by communication.

A relationship is begun, nourished, and maintained by communication. Howe emphasizes with the analogy that "dialogue is to love, what blood is to the body. When the flow of blood stops, the body dies. When dialogue stops, love dies, and resentment and hate are born" (LePeau and LePeau 1981, 29). A couple must learn and then practice all they can about the art of communication. It starts in courtship, will assume different forms over the life cycle of the marriage, but it must never stop flowing.

Study Questions

1. What is the relationship of communication to a healthy family?
2. Define marital communication.
3. How does verbal communication differ from nonverbal?
4. Why is listening more difficult than speaking?
5. List several ways a person may increase his or her ability to listen.
6. How does the differences between men and women affect their communication?
7. List several barriers to communication and suggest ways to overcome them.
8. Suggest several ideas a family may follow in order to have more time together.
9. Discuss the statement, "Conflict is inevitable in marriage."
10. Discuss several methods that couples may use to solve conflict situations.

Suggested Readings

Borisoff, D., and L. Merrill. 1985. *The power to communicate, gender differences as barriers.* Prospect Heights, Ill.: Waveland. The authors were concerned about the difficulties faced by women in the marketplace. The book investigates the characteristics of male and female communication so both sexes can understand each other better.

Fitzpatrick, M. A. 1988. *Between husbands and wives: Communication in marriage.* Newbury Park, Calif.: Sage. This is a technical book based on a study of couples. The author discovered she could divide the couples into three different classes, each having its own way to communicate. Technical but interesting.

Howell, W. S. 1986. *The empathic communicator.* Prospect Heights, Ill.: Waveland. This book was written as a textbook to teach interpersonal skills in communication. It is an excellent source of information for those interested in developing their abilities to communicate.

Mace, D. 1982. *Love and anger in marriage.* Grand Rapids: Zondervan. David and Vera Mace were pioneers in the fields of family-life education and marriage counseling. In this volume David Mace shares how they overcame conflict in their relationship and gives constructive help to those involved in conflict.

Miller, S., E. W. Nunnally, and D. B. Wackman. 1979. *Couple communication I; talking together.* Minneapolis: Interpersonal Communications Programs, Inc., 1979. This book was written to serve as a textbook for classes in couple communication. These seminars are designed to teach the basic skills of personal communication to enable couples to enjoy greater satisfaction in their marriages.

Pearson, J. C., and B. H. Spitzberg. 1990. *Interpersonal communication: Concepts, components and contexts.* 2d ed. Dubuque, Iowa: Brown. A textbook designed to cover all aspects of interpersonal communication. It is well organized. The chapters on "Self-Disclosure" and "Self-Assertion" are very informative.

Snyder, B., and C. Snyder. 1988. *Incompatibility: Grounds for a great marriage.* Phoenix: Questar. Designed to illustrate the qualities

brought to a marriage by two people who are different. The husband and wife share their experiences and feelings in learning to love and live together.

Timmons, T. 1982. *Stress in the family.* Eugene, Ore.: Harvest House. Since much of the conflict in families is caused by stress, this book is designed to aid families to recognize it and to deal with it. It has a chapter on "The Body Language of Stress" that is most informative. Every family should read this book.

Wright, H. N. 1974. *Communication: Key to your marriage.* Ventura, Calif.: Regal. H. Norman Wright succeeded Dwight Small as the instructor of Christians in the field of marriage communications. He is an able writer who presents the material in a readable fashion.

———. 1986. *Energize your life through total communication.* Old Tappan, N.J.: Revell. A more recent volume by Wright that emphasizes the importance of learning the language of the spouse in order to communicate effectively.

Intimacy in Marriage

"My beloved is mine, and I am his . . ."

—Song of Solomon 2:16a

Intimacy Defined

Psychologists say that one of the greatest needs of individuals is to have a close relationship with one or more persons. Hillerstrom (1989, 35) writes, "The need for emotional closeness and intimacy is inherent in human nature. Everyone wants to be loved for who they are, not just for what they can do or give to someone else." God said that it "was not good that man should be alone." He created Eve to be a companion to share all of Adam's life. It is this sharing of another's life that provides the basis for intimacy. Webster's dictionary indicates that the word *intimacy* is derived from the Old Latin *intimus,* which means "innermost."

Intimacy may be defined technically (Derlega 1984, 14) as "a relational process in which we come to know the innermost, subjective aspects of another, and are known in a like manner." To be intimate means one is able to reveal one's innermost thoughts about oneself to another, and to expect that person to reveal himself or herself in a similar fashion. The individuals are willing to share their beliefs, fantasies, interests, goals, and backgrounds. They are able to confide in one another and to give each other sympathetic understanding.

In common parlance intimacy may be thought of as closeness. A continuum of a personal relationship might begin with "stranger" on the left, and progress to "intimate" on the right. Two strangers meet and the relationship develops as the individuals disclose more and more of their "self" to each other. This self-disclosure is a prerequisite for love to develop. A person who refuses to reveal himself fully and honestly to another will find it impossible to love another. The other person will find it impossible to love him. Derlega (1984, 72) quotes Jourard as saying, "Effective loving calls for knowledge of the object. How can I love a person whom I do not know? How can the person love me if he does not know me?"

> ## *To be intimate means one is able to reveal one's innermost thoughts about oneself to another, and to expect that person to reveal himself or herself in a similar fashion.*

In casual dating, for example, little self-disclosure typically takes place. Each step of the courtship process requires more self-disclosure for the relationship to deepen. On the honeymoon a large amount of the self is revealed because the manners of dating are replaced with the realities of daily living. All the facades are removed and the newlyweds are exposed to each other as they really are.

This process of self-disclosure continues throughout the life cycle of the marriage. It will be related to the changes the couple experiences. It concerns every aspect of their relationship. The ability of the couple to reveal their true thoughts and feelings to each other will to a large degree determine the extent of their intimacy and therefore the happiness of the marriage. If they cannot share their innermost thoughts and feelings, they will not be drawn closer together and may drift apart. Studies have been made of the relationship of self-disclosure and marital satisfaction. These indicate that the greater the self-disclosure, the happier the marriage is rated (Derlega 1984, 73–74).

As a couple becomes more intimate, the more they learn to trust each other. This leads to a greater commitment to the relationship. This increased trust causes individuals to continue the process of self-disclosure. This enables the persons to give each other the emotional support they need in facing the difficulties of daily life.

Marriage is not the only relationship where intimacy can develop. Before marriage, most people develop friendships with either their own or the opposite sex. If the appropriate amount of self-disclosure occurs, the friendship may develop into an intimate one. After marriage, intimate friendships should be limited to the same sex or the marriage may be threatened. Most spouses cannot handle the mate having an intimate friend of the opposite sex. Derlega (1984, 89) relates the story of a young man who had been married four years. While he was attending graduate school, he met a girl with whom he became friendly. They worked on assignments together and had lunch together several times a week. It was a platonic friendship. The man commented, "I don't think that I can ever tell my wife how close I felt to this other girl. She couldn't accept the fact that I might be interested in someone else. She'd be too jealous." Derlega (1984, 90) continues, "Husbands and wives are supposed to be interested in each other—exclusively—and they should *never* go out alone with the opposite sex. They are also expected to share all their activities and relationships with each other."

Subcultural Barriers to Intimacy

Since approximately 95 percent of men and women will marry, they need to learn how to build greater intimacy into their marriages. Young people are not given any education on how to develop intimacy in a relationship. In courtship it seems to come naturally, but in the closeness of marriage many adjustments have to be made in order for increased intimacy to occur. Couples are unaware of the need for adjusting to each other, and may not be prepared to make the adjustments that contribute to intimacy.

LeMasters (1957, 488) says that many of the adjustments are necessary because marriage marks the first real intimate union of two persons reared in the separate male and female subcultures. He indicates that young people are socialized according to their sex, which creates a subculture for each sex. It is possible for a man to have been reared in a home without sisters, and without even a mother, if the father is divorced or widowed. A young man reared in such a home is at a disadvantage in relating to young women in comparison to one reared with a mother and sisters. The latter is somewhat acquainted with women and some aspects of their subculture, such as their emotions and interests.

In a similar manner a young woman may be reared in a home without a father or brothers. A survey of classes in a marriage and family course at a Christian college indicates that approximately one-fourth of the students were reared in homes where there were no siblings of the opposite sex. Thus, when she marries, a young woman without brothers comes into intimate interaction with the male subculture for the first time. She may not be aware or fully understand male interests and emotional needs, and this can create conflict situations in the marriage.

The male and female subcultures are noticeable in areas other than the home. They are also evident in the school system. Benson (1971, 58) observes that elementary-school children now engage more in heterosexual relationships than they did in past generations. Consequently, a boy learns to think about himself in reference to girls, but his "main sense of *male* identity before reaching adolescence is interaction with other boys." The same observation may be made of girls; that is, most of their interaction is with other girls and women.

It is important that young people be informed as to some characteristics of the subculture of the opposite sex. This is especially true if they do not have siblings of the opposite sex. The male subculture, for example, is characterized by an interest in athletics, either as a participant or a spectator. The television programming for any New Year's Day will be dominated by football. One woman became so disgusted with her husband for his excessive watching of football games on television that she offered the set *and her husband* for sale in the classified ads. Some women are termed golf widows. Athletics, according to LeMasters (1957, 491), function as a symbol of adult manhood in high school and college, a fact that helps to explain the inordinate emphasis given to these activities by these organizations. This interest does not cease when men leave school and is perpetuated by adult leagues in the various sports. For this reason, young women may need to adjust to this interest in athletics or look for a mate who is not typical in this respect.

> ## Marriage marks the first real intimate union of two people reared in the separate male and female subcultures.

The typical male interest in automobiles and racing events is also difficult for some women to understand. In many areas the automobile functions as a status symbol even at the high-school level, and the girls are sometimes more interested in a young man's car than in his qualities as a person. Consequently, a young male is anxious to buy his own car, even though it may impose severe financial problems for him or his family. This interest in cars may not cease when the young man enters marriage. If he marries a woman unfamiliar with the expense necessary to buy and maintain a late-model auto, she may be shocked at the large percentage of the family income consumed by such expenses. The potential for conflict over money spent on cars is tremendous, but it may be lessened if the wife is fully aware of the part cars play in the male subculture or if the husband outgrows the immature need for a car as a status symbol to bolster his ego.

One feature of the female subculture that the average male finds difficult to understand is the different clothing needs of women. This is the subject of many cartoons that picture a woman looking into a closet filled with dresses and saying, "I don't have a thing to wear!" Although males are giving more attention to their dress than they formerly did, they still do not have the same needs women do. Before they are married, women have to dress well in order to compete for husbands, and after they marry, they have to dress to reflect their husband's social position.

The different male and female subcultures may also be manifested in marriage by the manner in which men and women spend money. In American culture men may like to spend money for cars and to support hobbies. Many women do not realize how expensive a hobby such as golf, woodworking, or photography can be. Women may like to use money to purchase clothes and home furnishings. If the husband wants to buy a new car or recreational vehicle and the wife wants new carpeting instead, there is likely to be conflict.

> **The different male and female subcultures may be manifested in marriage by the manner in which men and women spend money.**

The couple must be aware of each other's ego needs in these areas. A man may receive his status from the car he drives. The wife may derive hers from the way she furnishes and keeps up her home. A man should not have such a weak ego that he needs a new car every year or two, nor should the wife have to keep up with the Joneses by purchasing new furniture often. Many of the material things that a family "needs" may be merely wants when the motivations are closely examined. A mature couple ought to realistically assess their needs for transportation and home furnishings and then plan ahead so that the ego "needs" of both spouses are met.

A man may think that he will never really understand women. This may be true to some extent, but he should be familiar with some of his difficulties in relation to the female subculture. A woman may also never fully understand men, but the effort should be made to comprehend how the culture operates to mold them. A mutual attempt to understand the opposite sex should make it easier to achieve intimacy in a marriage.

Physical Barriers to Intimacy

Certain biological differences may also make adjustment difficult. Dobson (1980, 410–11) lists a number of physical differences between men and women. They differ in the chromosome combinations that determine their sex; women have stronger constitutions and live longer but men have 50 percent greater brute strength. Because the wife cannot compete on the basis of physical strength she may use verbal fluency instead. The woman's thyroid is larger: "she laughs and cries more easily." Heart disease is much more common among men, even though a female's heart beats eighty times per minute compared to a male's seventy-two times.

After marriage, men must adjust to certain aspects of the female physiology such as menstruation and pregnancy. Most males may not realize how complicated the female reproductive system really is. They may have a vague understanding that there are changes in moods and feelings during certain periods, but in marriage they face the reality of the situation. Pregnancy also requires many adjustments. Some young women have no problems at all, while most experience some morning sickness. In a few cases the wife may be sick the entire term of pregnancy. During this experience the husband may need to extend an extra measure of kindness and consideration to the wife.

Psychological Barriers to Intimacy

The partners in a marriage may be generally well suited but they still have individual personalities that need to be harmonized so they can function as a family unit as well as individuals. "Each partner needs to provide a new anchor for the other—an anchor of intimate associations to replace the parental anchor. If the partners can do this, they become the *primary resource persons* [italics added] for satisfying each other's personality hungers" (Clinebell and Clinebell 1970, 110). In a long courtship many of the adjustments between the personalities may be made so that the couple experience less unhappiness after the wedding (see chap. 8).

Regardless of the length of courtship, marriage adds a new and much more intimate dimension to the relationship. Living together twenty-four hours a day may be far more demanding on the partners than merely seeing each other for a few hours at various times during the week. Many marriages fail because the individuals may not have tested their psychological compatibility sufficiently and cannot adjust to the demands of living together in such an intimate relationship. Mature young people recognize that changes must take place and are willing and able to alter their habits and behavior so that their personalities begin to harmonize rather than clash with one another. Conflicts are inevitable but they should be few and constructive in nature.

Change is inevitable when two young people unite in marriage. Both must be willing to change in order for intimacy to develop. Differences in habits, thought patterns and a dozen other aspects of personality need to be discussed and resolved so that the relationship can be improved. Honestly facing the need for change may hurt, but modifying behavior for the sake of the loved one usually leads to a closer relationship. Changes must be shared by both spouses. A relationship is in danger when one mate is expected to make all the changes.

Fear of suggesting a desired change to a spouse is one of the major problems encountered by marriage therapists. When John arrives home from work worn out from speaking to customers all day, he is met by Mary, who begins to recite all the problems of her day. His response is to ignore her and bury his head in the newspaper. Instead of asking Mary to wait until he has had time to recoup from the hassles of the day, he continues his behavior, which in turn discourages Mary. Eventually they end up in the counselor's office because of their inability to share their inner thoughts and feelings. Sharing can lead to constructive changes and greater intimacy.

> *Regardless of the length of courtship, marriage adds a new and much more intimate dimension to the relationship.*

When contemplating changes, sometimes there may be an attempt by a spouse to remake the mate into a carbon copy of himself or herself. This must be avoided for each spouse is an individual and as such will always retain those features that constitute individuality. Each spouse needs some separateness in which to adapt to the other. Since young people are marrying at a later age, they have more time to form habits before marriage than was true formerly. Many have lived a single life for an extended period, and marriage requires the merging of two separate lifestyles. When one is used to his or her own bed, bathroom, and privacy, it may require real effort to adapt to sharing these with a spouse. It is important to honestly and lovingly explain one's feelings to the partner so that an understanding may be reached.

Men and women also differ in their emotional lives. A man who grows up with sisters has some understanding of female psychology, but the man reared without sisters is at a definite disadvantage. In our culture, women are permitted to cry whenever the occasion or their pent-up emotions demand it. A boy or man is not allowed to cry other than for reasons of physical pain or in a time of bereavement. Since men have little experience in crying, it is difficult for them to understand why women shed tears so easily. In reality, it is well that women can find emotional release in tears, for crying relieves the buildup of emotional pressures. At first a husband may feel that some act of his may be the cause of tears, but he soon discovers that usually his wife's tears have no relationship to his actions. His best response is to give her a shoulder to cry on and a handkerchief to dry her tears.

> ## *A man who grows up with sisters has some understanding of female psychology, but the man reared without sisters is at a definite disadvantage.*

Men and women have the same overall level of intelligence, but data suggest that they do think differently, which may cause adjustment problems.

It was God who designed the male and female. He made them different in order that they might complement each other. The task in marriage is to discover and learn to appreciate these differences. Men need to be masculine and women need to be feminine, but these needs are modified to enhance the total relationship.

Time Necessary to Achieve Intimacy

The adjustments between two personalities and other necessary changes take time and will not be accomplished on the honeymoon. Christian newlyweds may think they do not have to make many adjustments because of their common faith in Christ, but they too bring different personalities to the marriage and have to work at achieving adjustment between them. The Harts (1983, 45) observe, "Intimacy is, in many ways, the key challenge and deepest joy of marriage. It is the challenge of sharing our life and our world with another." The Christian couple has an advantage over the unsaved couple since they have spiritual resources to help them make adjustments in achieving intimacy. Many authorities feel many of these adjustments are made during the first year, making it a critical period in the life of a marriage.

God recognized the importance of this stage in marriage, for in Deuteronomy 24:5 we read, "When a man hath taken a new wife, he shall not go out to war, neither shall he be charged with any business, but he shall be free at home one year, and shall cheer up his wife which he hath taken." The newlyweds were not to be separated, nor was the husband to have any extra responsibility. These provisions insured that the couple could make the necessary adjustments in their new marriage. Wheat and Perkins (1980, 135) indicate that "'to cheer up' meant to delight his wife, to know her, and to discover what is pleasing to her." This was to be a time for laying the foundation of the marriage in an atmosphere as free from distractions as possible. As the first year is crucial in God's sight, then it should be lived with care and forethought.

Newlyweds enter marriage to assume the new roles of husband and wife for which they have received little or no specific education. Many times they have been reared in Christian homes where the parents have been poor models of what a Christian husband or wife should be. Consequently, they must learn these new roles as they interact with each other after the wedding. The Clinebells (1970, 111) say it this way: "Becoming a need-satisfying and adequate husband or wife—what Jolesch calls

166

learning appropriate spouse roles—is the developmental task of the first years of marriage."

If the partners have established good communication with each other during their engagement and have discussed the type of roles each expects to play, then the adjustments should be easier and the partners should be able to be more patient and understanding (bear and forbear) with each other when mistakes are made. Since it is difficult enough to learn to play these roles well, it might be wise for the couple to postpone having their first child to avoid having to assume the roles of mother and father before they are accustomed to the roles of husband and wife. LaRossa (1977, 18–19), writing on the first pregnancy as a crisis in marriage, indicates that some couples wait several years before they begin a family. This allows them to first enjoy the companionship of their marriage.

Sometimes the wife is pregnant at the time of marriage. DeVault and Strong (1989, 272) indicate that "twenty percent of all women are pregnant when they marry." These couples have little time to learn their roles as husband and wife before they face the crisis of the birth of the first child. They must learn the roles of mother and father before they have adjusted to each other as husband and wife. The stress is too great and many such marriages fail.

In the critical first year some couples have the problem of adjusting to the basal metabolism of the partner. One person may always be too hot and the other too cold. An adjustment has to be made and it usually means the cold-blooded individual will wear a sweater year round. A similar situation exists when a man whose metabolism is slow in the morning has difficulty arising but then stays up late at night, and is married to a woman who likes to rise early and go to bed early. One possible medical explanation was given by Lois Baker, R.N., who states that the adrenal gland gives off a spurt of cortisone at regular intervals twice a day. The time at which this cortisone is released determines whether a person is an early-to-rise-early-to-bed individual or the opposite. Since these habits not only are learned behav-

ior but also are linked to the body's metabolism, it is not easy to change them.

> *The time at which cortisone is released determines whether a person is an early-to-rise-early-to-bed individual or the opposite.*

Another factor that aids newlyweds in adjusting to each other is commonly referred to as the honeymoon attitude. Although the actual honeymoon may only last a few days, the chief concern of each spouse is to please the other, and the primary interest is to meet each other's needs. This attitude does not end with the honeymoon; it is particularly strong during the important first year of marriage when the couple has many changes to make in themselves and in their relationship. In a really good marriage, this honeymoon attitude will be the prevailing one throughout the years. In many marriages a state of accommodation is reached in which the partners refuse to make any more changes and expect to be accepted as they are. In the large number of marriages that end in early divorce, the honeymoon attitude apparently is not strong enough to help the couples to resolve adjustment problems.

Sexual Intimacy in Marriage

The sexual relationship between husband and wife is the most intimate interaction they experience. It is in sexual intercourse that the maximum amount of closeness is achieved. For this reason intimacy is often equated with sexual intimacy, whereas sexual intimacy is only one factor in the total intimacy of the couple. In this relationship they most uniquely and fully express their love for each other and fulfill the one-flesh dimension of the marriage. In most states, failure to complete the sexual union constitutes grounds for the annulment of the marriage.

> # Why do Christians enjoy the sexual relationship? They subscribe to an agape *love, an unconditional love, that receives pleasure in giving rather than in taking.*

A Christian couple recognizes that their sexual natures are a gift from God. If they have been taught that sexual relations are sinful and dirty, they must go back to the Bible and study what God has to say about the subject. Hebrews 13:4 informs us that the marriage bed is undefiled. In 1 Corinthians 7:2–5 Paul plainly indicates the spouses do not have control of their own bodies but each exists for the pleasure of the other. First Corinthians 6:19 reveals that the body of the believer is a temple of the Holy Spirit. The Harts (1983, 90) write, "The body is a sacred place, where God dwells and is manifested. The body's beauty and mystery are prominent in the sexual expression and celebration of love. God is there." For the Christian, the sexual union is not only a physical act but should be an act of worship and celebration of God's love and goodness.

The media often portray Christian women as having a so-called Victorian and prudish attitude toward sex in marriage. McDowell (1985, 100–101) cites several studies that prove such views to be false. A survey of twenty-six thousand men and women concluded that "women with the strongest positive feelings about religion tend to have very good sex lives." Women with strong anti-religious feelings were "the likeliest to have unhappy sexual relationships." A *Redbook* survey of one hundred thousand readers revealed that "the greater the intensity of a woman's religious convictions, the likelier she is to be *highly* [italics added] satisfied with the sexual pleasures of marriage." This same report concluded that "the greater sexual pleasure for the religious woman may be simply a manifestation of an overall greater happiness with life in general." This is quite a compliment from a secular magazine.

At the same time the *Redbook* survey was being made, Tim LaHaye surveyed approximately seventeen hundred Christian couples. This is the largest survey of the sexual practices of born-again Christians ever made. The respondents answered ninety-five questions and the answers are tabulated in *The Act of Marriage* (LaHaye and LaHaye 1976, 212–30). He summarizes the results by stating, "We are quite satisfied that our survey has established that over the long years of matrimony, Christians do experience a mutually enjoyable love relationship, and that they engage in the act of marriage more frequently and with greater satisfaction than do non-Christians in our society." These studies should encourage newlyweds to enjoy their sexual relationship and to make every effort to insure that it gives the greatest satisfaction to each other.

Why do Christians enjoy the sexual relationship? They subscribe to an *agape* love, an unconditional love, that receives pleasure in giving rather than in taking. The emphasis is on satisfying the spouse rather than one's self. The unbeliever emphasizes the satisfaction of personal needs rather than the needs of the spouse—"What can you give me?" not "What can I give you?" *Agape* love is divine love that thrives on giving rather than receiving. The LaHayes (1976, 218) comment, "The more love an individual has from God to give to his [her] partner, the more fulfillment he [she] will give and receive in marriage." Christ promised the believer a more abundant life (John 10:10), so satisfying marital sexual relationships would seem to be included in that life.

Another important reason is that believers attempt to live their Christian faith in the home. If they succeed, the home will be filled with love and kindness. It is what goes on in the brain, the primary sex organ, during the day that determines the quality of lovemaking at night. A wife who is loved, respected, and shown kindness during the day will be able to respond to overtures for love at bedtime. Men can be aroused easily through visual stimuli whereas women are aroused more slowly through romantic experiences that include loving approaches throughout the day.

A couple anticipating a lifetime of satisfying sexual intimacy needs to prepare for it. During engagement and as the marriage approaches, they should read together a good marriage manual. *The Act of Marriage* by Tim and Beverly LaHaye and *Intended for Pleasure* by Ed Wheat are two excellent volumes by Christian writers. McDowell (1985, 102) relates one study that indicated that 97 percent of the Christian couples surveyed had discussed complete details of their plans for their sexual life when they married. By so doing they knew what to do and what to expect from the spouse.

A person may subscribe to a magazine for golf enthusiasts and read a manual explaining the game, but that will not make him a great golfer. So it would follow that premarital counseling and reading marriage manuals will not insure sexual pleasure on the honeymoon. Studies show, however, that most people do enjoy their first attempt. McDowell (1985, 102) records one survey that demonstrated that 78 percent of couples achieved sexual adjustment within a week, and 12 percent within two weeks. Thus, 90 percent had adjusted during the honeymoon period. The other 10 percent required more time.

Much is written in the popular press about what constitutes good sexual adjustment. The ideal presented in the marriage manuals is for the husband and wife to achieve orgasm at the same time. Ideals are not always attained, although McDowell (1985, 102) observes that 41 percent of the couples surveyed had orgasms together all or most of the time and 38 percent had orgasms together some of the

time. Some couples are frustrated if they do not achieve all the results listed in the marriage manuals. The Wheats (1981, 88) make the salient observation that "while arriving at orgasm at the same time may be a goal for lovers, it is not nearly as important as aiming at mutual enjoyment. . . . What does matter is that both partners be fully satisfied in each sexual encounter." The believer is aware that 1 Corinthians 7:3–5 teaches that one's body belongs to one's spouse, and the fulfillment of the spouse's needs is the primary goal of coitus.

> *One survey demonstrated that 78 percent of couples achieved sexual adjustment within a week, and 12 percent within two weeks.*

Some couples claim to have satisfying sexual relationships even though the wife seldom or never experiences an orgasm. For many wives the context of the relationship is more important than coitus itself. They are more concerned that their husbands express genuine affection, concern, and gentleness during sex. The LaHayes (1976, 227) comment that "many nonorgasmic women testify that they enjoy the closeness, excitement, and affection that lovemaking provides and that sex is pleasurable without orgasm." Also, most women do desire to experience orgasm. In the survey (1976, 227) more than 81 percent of wives in their twenties "regularly to always" experience orgasm, 11 percent "periodically," and only 3 percent "never." If a wife is able to enjoy making love without achieving orgasms, the husband should not insist that she do so. Dobson (1975, 124–25) emphasizes that this puts the wife into an "unresolvable conflict." If the husband persists, the wife has only three choices—"lose interest in sex altogether . . . she can try and try and try—and cry; or she can 'fake' it." If she fakes it, then she must continue to do so to please her husband, which might lead him to think "she's on a prolonged pleasure trip, when in fact her car is still in the garage." Open and honest discussion, with sympathetic understanding by the husband, contributes greatly to a satisfactory solution.

> *Many young wives find it difficult on the wedding night and during the following weeks to discard the inhibitions built into their psychic superstructure over the years.*

Factors Hindering Sexual Intimacy

Good sexual adjustment is not the most important role in marriage (as the culture would present it), but it is still important in the total relationship between husband and wife. If one partner is unhappy with the sexual adjustment, the spouse should strive to meet the needs of that partner. Most often the wife encounters problems, and the husband must remember that the wife has been conditioned since childhood by society against having sexual relationships outside of marriage. The Landises (1968, 45) state that "girls are likely to be impressed more than boys with sexual taboos. . . . Many parents solve the practical problem of protecting a daughter by overimpressing her with the dangerous aspects of sexual activity. All such policies may create emotional attitudes that later handicap sex adjustment."

Consequently, many young wives find it difficult on the wedding night and during the following weeks to discard the inhibitions built into their psychic superstructure over the years. The wife must be aware of the cause of her attitude, and the husband needs to be patient and prayerful. Given a little time, the problem can be solved. However, if the problem is too great, or if it is not solved over a period of time, the couple should seek professional counseling.

The informed young couple also realizes that the sexual relationship, the most intimate of their marriage, reflects the attitudes and moods of the total relationship. DeVault and Strong (1989, 215–16) indicate that "sex is a barometer for the whole relationship." Dobson expresses this truth by stating (1980, 436), "marital conflicts occurring *in bed* are caused by conflicts occurring *out of bed*." Ignorance of this fact has caused some to blame poor sexual adjustment for the dissolution of many marriages, whereas in fact the inadequate sexual relationship was simply a mirror of disharmony between the spouses. For example, a couple cannot expect to quarrel all day about money matters but find everything to be harmonious when they retire for the night.

Smalley (1988, 20) writes, "Harsh or abusive treatment can easily remove [a woman's] desire for sexual intimacy for days at a time. When a woman's emotions have been trampled by her husband, she is often repulsed by his advances." It is evident that a couple with a problem in sexual adjustment must first examine their total marital interaction patterns to make sure their relationship is free of differences in other areas.

If the wife is not experiencing a good sexual response, it may be caused by failing to use the pelvic muscle named the pubococcygeus. This muscle is located beneath the vaginal passage about one to two inches from the opening and has pressure-sensitive nerve endings. The LaHayes (1976, 147–64) describe how Arnold Kegel of the Kegel Clinic at Los Angeles County General Hospital discovered that the tone of the pubococcygeus muscle is directly related to feminine response in sexual intercourse. The tone of the muscle can be improved by simple exercises each day for a period of two or three months. Once in tone, it remains so. The result is that many women enjoy their marriage relationship after doing the exercises and learning to use the muscle during intercourse.

It is evident that every wife (not just those experiencing difficulties) should learn to use the pubococcygeus muscle (P.C.) since it is the key to feminine response. The LaHayes (1976, 147–64) devote most of a chapter of *The Act of Marriage* to a description of and suggestions for the development and use of the P.C. muscle. He feels that it is worth the time and effort for the wife to learn to utilize the muscle, for such use can bring a lifetime of increased sexual fulfillment.

Difficulties in sexual adjustment are caused by many other factors. For example, privacy should be assured for the greatest enjoyment. A wife may not be able to relax if she is afraid of interruptions, or that others will hear their lovemaking sounds.

Fatigue of one or both partners may interfere with sexual adjustment. Young couples who both work and study often have several roles to play that do not leave much energy for the sexual relationship. The young mother is often exhausted after caring for children all day, particularly when they are small and need much time and attention. The thoughtful couple is considerate of each other and endeavor to find a time such as early morning when both are refreshed. It is better to wait a few hours than to risk a frustrating experience because of fatigue. As sex is an integral part of marriage, time must be made for it. The Penners (1981, 218) emphasize that "making sure you have time together is the responsibility of both partners. It takes forethought, planning, effort and recommitment. . . . If there is time together—you will have to make it."

Until after menopause, when the possibility of pregnancy has ceased, the fear of conception prevents some wives from readily responding to and enjoying sex in marriage. Each couple needs to prayerfully consider the will of God in family planning. Most couples choose some form of contraception to aid them in this planning. If a wife still has fears while using one type, the couple may consider using two types at the same time. This practice

may help her conquer her anxieties so she can respond adequately in the relationship.

> *Each couple needs to prayerfully consider the will of God in family planning. Most couples choose some form of contraception to aid them in this planning.*

However, a time usually arrives when the young couple desires to start a family. The psalmist wrote, "Lo, children are an heritage of the Lord . . . happy is the man that hath his quiver full of them" (Ps. 127: 3, 5). In a rural economy children were an asset because of the labor they could provide, but they may become an economic liability in our industrialized society. The apostle Paul stated, "But if any provide not for his own, and especially for those of his own house, he hath denied the faith, and is worse than an infidel" (1 Tim. 5:8).

A Christian couple should plan and pray for the number of children they will be able to provide for adequately. They must remember that in American society this includes more than just food, clothing, and shelter, for the parent is also responsible to provide an emotional climate for the child's healthy development and many other material benefits such as medical care and education. This also includes some form of higher education, which is very expensive.

Many sincere Christians today desire to limit the number of children, not because of economic reasons, but because of environmental concerns. The pressure of population upon our land and natural resources is acknowledged as a serious problem. A corollary of this is the pollution caused by too many people. Some couples, instead of having children of their own, are adopting children. Others, after having one or two children, adopt additional children when they desire to increase their family.

The area of family planning is one where Christian liberty prevails, for there are no clear statements in Scripture delineating it. Each couple must arrive at their own convictions as to which method of family planning they wish to use. Even with the best methods of family planning, there are unwanted pregnancies. Nevertheless, if a couple communicates well and is conscientious in the use of contraception, they can achieve great control over the number and spacing of children.

> # *The area of family planning is one where Christian liberty prevails, for there are no clear statements in Scripture delineating it.*

A newlywed couple has a number of optional methods of family planning available. Some of the more commonly used are oral contraceptives (the pill), a diaphragm plus vaginal jelly, vaginal foams, condoms, intrauterine devices, and the rhythm method (Cargan 1991, 195). The couple should discuss the type of family planning with a doctor during the engagement period, for some methods are available only through a physician. After a couple has the desired number of children, sterilization is the favorite method. In 1986, 32.7 percent of couples were using it, with 21.9 percent of the wives and 10.8 percent of the men having been sterilized. This made it the most

widely used method of birth control. Only 28.6 percent of couples used the pill, which used to be ranked number one and still is for those couples who have not completed their families.

Sterilization for women (tubal ligation) involves cutting or tying off the fallopian tubes to prevent the egg from reaching the womb. In men, a vasectomy diverts the sperm cells from the prostate gland to the bloodstream, which deprives the male semen of sperm. The Wheats (1981, 175) warn, "Never depend on your vasectomy for conception control until you have had at least one sperm-free specimen examined." Immediately after a vasectomy, other contraceptives must be used for six to eight weeks to insure that all of the sperm are eliminated (Wheat and Wheat 1981, 174–77).

One of the newest methods of contraception involves surgically implanting hormones under the skin of the wife. This method is supposed to prevent conception for five years. However, for many, it is cost prohibitive.

Some individuals adopt a fatalistic attitude: if children come, then it is God's will; if a pregnancy doesn't occur each year, that also is God's will (Hess and Hess 1989, 23). The individuals absolve themselves of any concern for bringing more children into the world than they can support. The exhortation of Paul in Ephesians 5:17 seems appropriate in this type of situation: "Wherefore be ye not unwise, but understanding what the will of the Lord is." God desires the Christian to seek his will in all matters of life, and this certainly applies to the number of children and the spacing of time between their arrivals. Not only the bearing of children but also the caring for them must be considered.

Another difficulty is faced by some couples when the wife has a subconscious hostility toward her husband. This may be caused by the wife's attitude toward her father, which is projected onto her husband when she marries. This problem can often be recognized if she will review her feelings toward her father as she grew up. If she harbored a hostile attitude toward him, then she is likely to do so toward her husband. Other cases may require the services of a professional counselor to help the wife discover her real attitude toward men, including her husband.

When a Christian couple encounters a problem in sexual adjustment, they should take advantage of every available means of medical and other professional help to enable them to reach a satisfying sexual relationship. The husband and wife can aid each other by maintaining an attitude of love, concern, and tenderness. The Christian philosophy that it is more blessed to give than to receive applies to every phase of a couple's marriage and includes their sex life.

In the early years of marriage, the sexual relationship may assume more importance than it does later in the marriage cycle, yet it is important throughout the life of the couple. Most couples enjoy intercourse until their drives diminish with old age. A couple should be willing to make every effort in the first few months to sexually adjust and thus lay the foundation for a lifetime of rewarding sexual enjoyment. Since a good sexual adjustment helps to make a happy marriage, it is worth all the prayer, time, effort, and professional help necessary to achieve.

A final note of warning is necessary to remind young people that a marriage cannot be built on good sex alone. Miles (1963, 123) states, "In order to have happiness in marriage, all the phases of total life experience (the spiritual, the mental, the social, the emotional, the moral, the physical, and the sexual) must work as a cooperative unit." The challenge facing every young couple taking the marriage vows is to blend their separate lives into one in many different areas. They should attempt to balance these areas so that all positive factors may operate as an aid in binding all the areas into one harmonious unit.

Spiritual Intimacy in Marriage

A husband and wife who are truly born again and who desire God's will for their lives individually and as a couple have a foundation on which to build a marriage characterized by spiritual intimacy. The closer they get to God, the closer they draw to each other. National studies of healthy families (Curran 1983; Stinnett 1985) discovered that members of such families share a faith in God and practice it in their daily experience. The results are manifested in the quality of the relationships within the family.

God has given believers the means of grace in order to enable them to live as he desires. In addition to regular church attendance, the believer must maintain a devotional life of prayer and Bible study. A man and woman must continue to do this after they are married. A close walk with God enables them to perform their roles as determined in Scripture. A man who is not loving his Savior will find it difficult to love his wife as Christ loved the church. A wife who lacks a warm relationship to Christ will find it hard to play her role in a Christ-honoring manner. Kessler (1984, 450) indicates that only 5 percent of all Christians have a quiet time with God. Can this be a contributing factor in the increasing number of Christians seeking a divorce? It takes real self-discipline to maintain a regular quiet time, but the rewards are worth the effort.

Couples must also develop the habit of daily devotions together. The Christian is to live the Christian life at all times, and the place where this is most important is the home.

> *The Christian is to live the Christian life at all times, and the place where this is most important is the home.*

It is just as necessary to manifest the fruits of the Spirit (Gal. 5:22–23) in a gracious Christian life in the home as it is in the office or factory. The husband and wife who desire to please the Lord at all times will also find it easier to please one another. When differences or disagreements arise between them, it will be easier to pray and seek the Lord's will in the matter. Krutza (1974, 40) comments, "Bringing God honestly into your marriage via honest conversation with him is one of the greatest things that can happen. . . . As you open yourselves up to him, trusting in the forgiving love of Jesus Christ, you'll soon notice how quickly you can open up yourselves to each other." Since each spouse has experienced the forgiving grace of Christ (Eph. 4:32), it will be easier to forgive each other when a mistake has been made. This forgiveness must take place before they can pray, for they cannot approach the throne of grace while harboring resentment or ill-will against each other (Matt. 5:23–24; 1 Pet. 3:7).

The home is where husband and wife are called upon to display the *agape* love described in 1 Corinthians 13. It is amazing how many Christians think of this love in reference to those outside the home but fail to acknowledge that it has an application to those within the family. This love "suffereth long . . . [is] not puffed up . . . not easily provoked . . . beareth all things, believeth all things, hopeth all things, endureth all things" (1 Cor. 13:4–7). The couple filled with the love of God and with love for one another should find it easy to be long-suffering or patient with one another. During courtship individuals are not easily provoked, but after the honeymoon period (first year) is over, often it does not take much to provoke one another. This will not be true of the couple who daily read the Word of God together, are reminded of his great love, and bring each other before the throne of grace petitioning the heavenly Father for aid in resolving differences between them. Such individuals will know the fullness of blessing in a successful Christian marriage.

The old cliché, "the family that prays together stays together," is true. Shedd (1965, 154) cites statistics he heard that "one marriage in four ends in divorce." However, for those families that are regular in church attendance, "the ratio is one to fifty-four," and for those "who pray together, the ratio is one to five hundred." After hearing these figures Shedd began to analyze his own counseling records and made the amazing discovery that out of two thousand cases covering twenty years, he had

"never had one couple or one member of a marriage come to me with their troubles if they prayed together. There were a few, perhaps a dozen, who said, 'We used to.'" This testimony should encourage every young couple to begin the habit of having devotions together during courtship, so that it becomes an important part of their relationship. It will be natural for them to continue this fellowship with God when they become husband and wife. This devotional life together will become the basis of family devotions when children come.

Family Devotions

Some Christian parents believe that taking or sending a child to the services of the church is sufficient for religious education. Parents must assume the leadership in this area or disaster may result. The question may be asked as to what age a child should be led to Christ. It varies from child to child, but the maxim is that when children are old enough to love their parents, they are old enough to love the Lord Jesus and to place their faith in him as their personal Savior from sin. Some children are saved at a very early age, even as early as age four, and others take much longer to come to the point of decision for Christ. The parent needs to be sensitive to the working of the Holy Spirit in the child's life and be ready to help the child when he or she indicates a desire to be saved.

Children and young people should also be taught the doctrine of the indwelling Holy Spirit. One reason so many second-generation Christians are weak and powerless and often defeated in their experience is that they have been taught the norms of the Christian life, but have not been instructed concerning the necessity of yielding their bodies to the domination of the Holy Spirit. They attempt to live the Christian life in their own strength. They sincerely love the Lord Jesus and do not understand why they fail in their attempts to please him. Once they learn to submit their lives daily to the control of the Holy Spirit, they come to know the joy of victory in their lives. Wiersbe says, "Doing the will of God is not a burden, nor a battle to the believer whose will is yielded to the Spirit" (1967, 116). This important truth should be taught to the child by the parents, not the Sunday-school teacher or the pastor.

The church reinforces what has been taught in the home. Family devotions are one of the great aids to help parents meet their children's spiritual needs. Some families may meet at bedtime when children are small, then change to meeting around the dinner table as they grow older. It makes little difference when a family meets, as meeting *consistently* is more important than the time. In some families parents take turns reading the Bible and praying, while in others the father reads the Word and prays. As children become old enough to pray and then to read, they participate also. This enables them to pronounce many of the more common proper names and the old English words in the King James Version. There are many ways of conducting family worship, and it should be varied so that it does not become a mere routine or ceremony. Books on how to conduct family worship are available.

The devotional period is a time when children are free to ask questions about the Bible or a doctrine they might be too shy to ask of a Sunday-school teacher or youth worker. It is also an excellent place for children to learn the value of prayer and how to pray. They can pray about daily needs such as school problems and the salvation of playmates. This helps children see that Christianity has a very practical application to daily life, and is not merely the formality of attending many church services a week. The reading of the Bible can be interspersed with reading a short chapter from a missionary biography. This serves a dual purpose of informing children of missionary history and also helping to create interest in missions. This interest can be increased by gleaning prayer requests from mission board publications and making these a definite matter of prayer. One of the children can be the secretary and record answers to prayer.

The family prayer time is also an excellent way for the family to memorize Scripture verses. The psalmist said, "Thy word have I hid in my heart, that I might not sin against thee" (Ps. 119:11). This is one way in which parents can help strengthen children to live in the sinful world surrounding them. Verses should be learned on the subject of personal soul-winning so that children can be effective witnesses to their playmates in the neighborhood and school. Local churches often sponsor Scripture memorization programs such as those promoted by Bible Memory Association and Awana.

> ## *There are many ways of conducting family worship, and it should be varied so that it does not become a mere routine or ceremony.*

Family devotions can be one of the most effective aids in the religious education of children. It can give the family a sense of unity and help to cement family ties. When children leave home, they are aware that the family is praying for them daily, an encouragement as they face the problems of college and employment. Having devotions together as a family takes time, effort, and planning, but it is worth it all since eternal dividends result. The Shedds (1984, 123), write, "Talking together—listening together— this is the number one plus for Bible Study together." Father, mother, and children talking to and listening to God will provide a spiritual intimacy that will enrich every day of their lives.

Conclusion

Although many functions that the family formerly performed have been taken over by other social institutions, they can never fulfill the need people have for intimacy. The universal need for closeness and companionship is best found in marriage. Intimacy does not occur automatically when man meets woman, but it must be developed through self-disclosure. Through honest and open communication two individuals make themselves vulnerable to each other in exchange for that feeling we call intimacy. In a similar manner, intimacy is developed with God as they commune with him on a daily basis. As children are born, they too will come to know the delights of intimate family relationships and spiritual fellowship. For God said, "It is not good that man should be alone."

> ## *Intimacy does not occur automatically when man meets woman, but it must be developed through self-disclosure.*

Study Questions

1. Why is intimacy so important in interpersonal relationships?
2. What is the basic definition of intimacy? How many intimate friends do you have?
3. How is self-disclosure related to intimacy? Give an example where you experienced self-disclosure.
4. Why is an understanding of the male and female subculture so important in the attempt to achieve intimacy in marriage?
5. List five physiological differences between men and women. Why is it necessary to recognize them in order to achieve intimacy in marriage?
6. Discuss and illustrate the statement, "Change is inevitable in marriage."
7. Why is the first pregnancy considered a crisis in the marriage?

8. Discuss several reasons why born-again Christian husbands and wives receive greater pleasure and satisfaction in the sexual relationship than non-Christians.
9. Explain the importance and use of the P.C. muscle in the sexual relationship.
10. Explain how spiritual intimacy is related to intimacy in marriage. Do you regularly have a quiet time with God?

Suggested Readings

Chapian, M. 1986. *Growing closer: The intimacy of love and friendship.* Old Tappan, N.J.: Revell. Chapian describes intimacy and then discusses different kinds of intimacy. She describes obstacles to intimacy and also presents strategies for growing closer to people.

Conway, J., and S. Conway. 1991. *Traits of a lasting marriage.* Rev. ed. Downer's Grove, Ill.: InterVarsity. This volume is based on a survey of 186 couples who shared what they thought were the ingredients of a strong marriage. The survey showed that a mutually satisfying sex life was important in providing stability in marriage. The book has a good chapter on sexual intimacy.

Crabb, L. 1991. *Men and women: Enjoying the difference.* Grand Rapids: Zondervan. Dr. Crabb illustrates how self-centeredness can hamper a relationship. He then proceeds to discuss the traditional and egalitarian viewpoints, both of which he rejects. He proposes a new interpretation of headship and submission as "mature and loving expressions of our distinctive sexuality in the marriage relationship."

Derlega, V. J. 1984. *Communication, intimacy, and close relationships.* Orlando, Fla.: Academic Press. A selection of articles designed to show how intimate relationships develop and how they can be maintained. The critical role of communication is emphasized.

Derlega, V. J., and A. L. Chackin. 1975. *Sharing intimacy: What we reveal to others and why.* Englewood Cliffs, N.J.: Prentice-Hall. The theme is self-disclosure, which is central to any form of intimacy and is discussed in relationship to friendship and marriage.

Hershey, T. 1990. *Go away, come closer.* Dallas: Word. The author believes that everyone can achieve intimate relationships, but there is a price to pay. Intimacy doesn't "just happen"—it is achieved through hard work and perseverance. It involves self-acceptance, vulnerability, and honesty.

LaHaye, B., and T. LaHaye. 1976. *The act of marriage: The beauty of sexual love.* Grand Rapids: Zondervan. Written by Christians for Christians, this marriage manual presents a scriptural view of the sexual relationship of the Christian couple. It records a survey of seventeen hundred couples who answered a questionnaire concerning their sexual lives The chapter on the pubococcygeus muscle is very helpful.

Minirth, F., and M. A. Minirth, et al. 1991. *Passages of marriage.* Nashville: Nelson. The authors list five stages in the marriage cycle. They describe each and indicate problems that are encountered. Case histories include solutions to the problems. The first phase is "Young love, the first two years." Newlyweds will profit from studying these chapters.

Shedd, C., and M. Shedd. 1984. *Bible study together.* Grand Rapids: Zondervan. Charlie Shedd is well known for his *Letters to Karen* and *Letters to Philip.* In this small volume he and Martha relate the difficulty they encountered in finding a time to worship together. They finally devised a method of individual Bible study with a weekly meeting to discuss their findings.

Wheat, E., and G. O. Perkins. 1980. *Love life for every married couple.* Grand Rapids: Zondervan. The subtitle reads, "How to fall in love, stay in love, rekindle your love." The Wheats reveal the principles they have discovered in the Bible that enable them to stay in love. The chapter on "Prescriptions for a Superb Marriage" is based on the acronym BEST—blessing, edifying, sharing, and touching.

The Extended Family

One generation shall praise thy works to another.

—Psalm 145:4

Marriage and the Extended Family

In American culture, marriage is into the extended family, with a network of kinship within the respective families. Because Americans move frequently, the extended family in urban areas is much weaker than in the rural areas. Some children are reared hundreds or thousands of miles from their nearest relatives. However, most couples maintain rather close ties with the parental family even though they may not have too much contact with other relatives such as aunts and uncles.

The extended family is not the influence it was a generation or two ago, but it still has value for the young family. Malcolm (1987, 103) suggests that "the extended family makes at least three important contributions." For example, the family always has a need for a model and the extended family can provide this. Many Christians can testify to the influence godly parents or aunts and uncles had on their lives. She observes that the "nuclear family or single adult finds sustenance in the larger branch of the family tree." The extended family can be a source of strength and healing for the family that has been traumatized by divorce. She comments, "The gospel can turn the black death of divorce into a blessing for children who are surrounded by aunts, uncles, and grandparents who can help fill the void left by a father or mother."

Single-parent families leave many children without adequate role models for their socialization. The boy without a father in the home or girl without a mother may find a role model in an uncle or an aunt. For example, Jane had two boys without a father but Uncle Dave took a real interest in them and became the pattern for their social and spiritual development. The same relationship can develop between a motherless daughter and an aunt. Children from a single-parent home can also find a role model of a good marriage in the extended family.

However, when God instituted marriage and before there were children from the union, he ordained that the newly married couple were to separate from the parental family. God in his infinite wisdom knew this method was best for the happiness of all the families concerned. Although there have been many changes in family life, it is still best for the newlyweds to start their own home separated from the parental families.

> *Although kin ties are maintained with both families, they tend to be closer with the bride's family.*

This does not mean that the parental relationships are severed. Some couples who experience difficulties with their prospective in-laws think that at marriage they can ignore their parents or forget them. This is impossible; no marriage ceremony can sever emotional and legal ties. The Walkers (Petersen 1977, 223) comment, "Now and then a man will say to his prospective bride, 'But I am marrying you, not your family.' He is about as far from the truth as he can get. She is linked to her family by emotional ties that keep her in its orbit . . . and [she is] sensitive to what happens back home. Both he and she marry a collection of peculiar relatives when they stand at the altar to be joined in holy marriage." Hine (1985, 74) indicates "that one marries the whole family of the spouse. . . . Knowing this, the newly married couple need to discuss openly and honestly how relations with other family members will be handled, for such handling will have much to do with the progress of the marriage."

Although kin ties are maintained with both families, they tend to be closer with the bride's family. In Whyte's study (1990, 139), he discovered that 49.4 percent of the families in the Detroit area maintained "very close" ties and 38.4 percent "somewhat close" ties with the wife's family. The corresponding figures for the husband's family were 35.4 percent ("very close") and 42.7 percent ("somewhat close"). Only 12.1 percent of the wife's families were "not close," whereas 21.9 percent were "not close" to the husband's family. He concluded that wives attempt to maintain kinship ties more than husbands do. The figures also indicate that the average American family is not as isolated from the extended family as is often depicted. The Hirnings (1956, 413) point out that marriage enlarges the social contacts for some people. "The social life of a young person often is expanded when he marries a mate who has brothers and sisters. Under favorable circumstances, the newcomer is welcomed and, in turn, the mate's siblings are accepted as friends. In such cases, the union between husband and wife becomes closer, is strengthened, and made secure. . . ."

This extension of social contacts can be harmful to couples if they do not establish good relationships with all the siblings and their mates. This may be true in a large kin group that stresses unity in the family. If one sibling and his mate do not get along with a set of in-laws, then the harmony of the family gatherings is marred. The happiness of the newlyweds can be helped or hindered by their ability to relate to the many sets of in-laws in an extended family.

The basic problem of in-law adjustment is how to separate from the parental families and yet maintain harmonious relationships. If the couple does not break away sufficiently, there may be difficulties. If they ignore the parental families, then serious problems arise. The problems are compounded if a partner in either the parental family or the young new family is neurotically attached to a child or a parent and refuses to give the other individual freedom to play the necessary role. For example, a mother may cling to her daughter and interfere with her married life, or a daughter may cling to the mother and hinder emotional bonding with her husband.

In-Law Problems Caused by Parents

The mother-in-law is blamed for many in-law difficulties. James (Wheat and Perkins 1989, 161) comments, "The term *in law* can immediately conjure up every bad mother-in-law joke you have ever heard and bring visions of your mate's family dissecting you, just hoping to find something wrong. Every insecurity that you ever felt suddenly rears its ghastly head because you know *they* are going to see the worst in you." Hine (1985, 74) relates that "studies show that most problems occur between the wife and her mother-in-law; the second highest number of problems is between the wife and her sister-in-law. Other studies indicate that the number of conflicts with the mother-in-law are surprisingly few. Most young couples have good relationships with the extended family (Whyte 1990, 139). Although the mother-in-law is involved in in-law difficulties more often than other family members, there are different conditions where either in-law can create real obstacles to happiness for their children.

A common situation occurs when parents think so much of their children that they feel no one is good enough to marry them. Whenever the young person is dating, they continually find some reason for rejecting the suitor and they endeavor to break the relationship. Even if a young woman were to find Prince Charming himself, such parents would find fault in him and advise their daughter against marrying him.

The opposite case occurs when the parents have rejected a child. For young people reared in good Christian homes where they have received much affection, it is hard to realize that thousands of children's births were not planned by their parents and the children were rejected. One young mother of two small children became pregnant and gave birth to twins. Since their birth occurred only ten months after that of the second child, she was burdened with caring for three infants at once. She totally rejected the twins, and their personalities were warped by such treatment.

> *The basic problem of in-law adjustment is how to separate from the parental families and yet maintain harmonious relationships.*

The mother who rejects a daughter may also refuse to accept the man she marries. In extreme cases of rejection, a neurotic mother may try to win the affections of the daughter's suitor. In a case known to the writer, a forty-four-year-old Christian woman divorced her husband and married an eighteen-year-old youth who had been courting her daughter. It is difficult enough to understand this kind of behavior in an unbeliever, but it becomes almost incomprehensible when a Christian mother does this.

Some Christian parents are unhappily married and adopt the attitude that no one else can be happily married. Such parents continually examine the relationship of the young couple, looking for any situation they can exploit to prove their fears. Then they tend to blow out of proportion any little thing that happens between the young couple in order to prove their point. The solution for such in-law difficulties is for the young couple to move away where the in-laws cannot interfere. If this is impossible, the young couple must consciously try to preserve their union by recognizing this type of behavior when it occurs and agreeing to carefully examine the motives behind the comments made by the in-laws.

There are occasions where in-laws reject a son-in-law or daughter-in-law because they do not like some facet of his or her background. Such is the case when only one child in a family is a believer and marries another Christian.

Quite often the unsaved family rejects the young Christian family because of its stand for Christ. Although it is difficult to find someone to take the place of the real mother and father, it is possible for the Christian couple to find wonderful fellowship in the local church with people of God. The psalmist said, "When my father and my mother forsake me, then the Lord will take me up" (Ps. 27:10).

> # The couple must recognize that advice from parents, if it is solicited, may be helpful, but it is not binding.

A similar situation may exist when the child marries someone from a lower socioeconomic class. Class distinctions are part of American culture, and many people are not aware of the great influence that class pressures exert in their lives. James (Wheat and Perkins 1989, 163–66) relates the difficulties she encountered when she married David, who was from a higher social class. She writes about her introduction to David's family at a birthday celebration for him: "David didn't think to warn me that his family celebrated birthdays (and all traditional occasions) more formally than I was used to. My first thought when I saw the dining room was, *This is a three-fork family, and I'm a one-fork woman.* At least I hadn't worn my jeans and tee shirt!" She proceeds to emphasize how important it is for the couple to understand each other's background in order to deal constructively with in-law relationships. She did not have the ability to communicate her feelings and suffered a complete break in the relationship with her mother-in-law. However, this story has a happy ending. One day their relationship was reestablished by talking out and working out their problems, and they became real friends.

Domineering parents can create great problems for their married children. Such parents desire to continue their domination after the child marries, and the mate resents this behavior. A mother who has always made decisions for her daughter may attempt to make them for her after marriage. She tells her what kind of drapes to hang or what style of furniture to purchase. A father may insist that the son purchase a home in a particular neighborhood. In either case, the spouse may object to such advice and demand that his or her voice be heard before a decision is made on drapes, furniture, or neighborhoods. The couple must recognize that advice from parents, if it is solicited, may be helpful, but it is not binding. They must learn to make their own decisions.

The Walkers (Petersen 1977, 224) offer this advice: "Start making your own decisions and choices together independently. You need not consult either family every time you turn around. Consult each other, think together, pray together, and plan together." They indicate that if the couple has a relationship of independence from the parents, they may want to consult with them. If the parents tend to dominate, then the couple should make their own decisions and merely report them to the parents. This type of parent is easily recognized before marriage, and an individual should avoid marrying a person dominated by his or her parents unless the spouse can live comfortably with such domination, or unless the couple plans to live a great distance from the in-laws.

Overattachment of a parent to a child can be just as damaging to a marriage as domination is. It is possible for both parents to be overly protective and neurotically attached to a child, but more frequent is the case of a widowed or a divorced mother who rears a child without a father. The Selfs (1989, 97) draw attention to the "potentially dangerous situation . . . when the husband is the only son (or favorite) of a widow. Often the mother and son are very close, and the mother may feel left out of the new relationship. The son doesn't want to hurt his mother, but he may face a difficult situation with his wife. However, it is up to the new husband to act on the fact that his new wife is now the most important person in his life." A similar situation exists when an unhappily married wife gives all her affection to the children instead of her husband. Children from such a home may also encounter in-law problems.

The child reared in such a home has great difficulty in breaking the ties because the mother will make her children feel guilty whenever they share affection with someone of the opposite sex. Some mothers try to prevent their son or daughter from marrying so they can continue to enjoy the adult child's company. Swindoll (1980, 29) points out that "leaving father and mother is a difficult decision for some. In fact, it keeps many a person from cultivating a serious relationship with the opposite sex." Some parents cling to the children for social security in that they expect the single son or daughter to care for them in their old age. They attempt to make life so easy and enjoyable at home that it becomes difficult to think of giving up such a delightful existence for the weighty responsibilities of married life. In reality, such a parent is being selfish, for he or she fails to realize that the son or daughter will be left to a life of loneliness after the parent's death.

Young people who marry mates from such homes should be prepared to share the spouse's affection with his or her parent. One such mother inveigled herself into accompanying her son and his bride on their honeymoon trip! In these types of cases the symptoms of in-law difficulty are experienced during the courtship stage and should be considered a warning signal in the relationship.

Some in-law situations are caused by the rejection of the parents by the spouse or of the spouse by the parents for no apparent reason other than incompatible personalities. They may be good Christians, of the same social class and political party, but yet they will express an open dislike for each other. Social interaction between the parental family and the young family is virtually impossible because of these attitudes. This situation is sometimes helped by the birth of grandchildren, but they may be rejected also. The spouse of the rejected in-law needs to be sympathetic

and understanding with the mate. To condemn the mate does not help the matter. If attempts to change the situation fail, the couple must accept the situation and draw closer to one another to compensate for the failure of the in-laws to play their role effectively.

> ## *Some mothers try to prevent their son or daughter from marrying so they can continue to enjoy the adult child's company.*

In-Law Problems Caused by Married Children

The exploitation of parents by young couples is the cause of many in-law problems. Many times the couple get themselves into financial difficulty and expect their parents to come forth with a gift to help save them from financial disaster. Couples who get into such financial straits do not know how to handle their money, and when in-laws come to their rescue, they do not help the basic cause of the problem. Part of the problem may be due to failure of the parents to teach their child how to manage money. The young couple may take advantage of the fact that no loving parent is going to stand by and see children or grandchildren go without food or be evicted from their home, or go without needed medical care. Some parents may subconsciously enjoy helping their child because it keeps the child dependent upon them.

The problem can be solved only by the young couple learning financial responsibility. A first step in this direction would be for the couple to learn to make a budget and then to live on it. The parents may refuse further financial help until the couple makes a real effort to learn to live within their means. This may result in some temporary hardship for the young family, but it may have permanent results if they make a sincere effort to manage their funds wisely.

> ## One maxim of good in-law adjustment is that the newlyweds must never live in the home of an in-law.

Another source of difficulty may occur when the young family tries to take advantage of grandparents by asking them to baby-sit the grandchildren. Most grandparents do not mind this activity and actually enjoy caring for their grandchildren on occasion. However, if young parents are inconsiderate and expect grandparents to babysit the children several times a week, they usually object to such expectations. One daughter regularly took her children to her mother every afternoon, then came for them just before dinnertime. This did not give the grandmother any afternoons for herself. Finally she had to tell her daughter she would babysit only one afternoon or evening a week since there were many things she would like to do herself. This awkward circumstance could have been avoided had the mother made such a statement when the daughter first began imposing on her. If the grandparents reside close enough to become involved with babysitting, it is wise from the beginning, to have an understanding in this matter.

Major Periods of In-Law Adjustment

There are two periods in the marriage cycle when in-law adjustments are particularly necessary. The first is in the early years of the mar-

riage when the young couple is becoming independent of the parental family. This is a difficult time, for in American culture the young family is expected to emancipate itself from the families of orientation, yet society does not lay down any guidelines for the families to follow.

The changes in the American family life also affect in-law relations since many young families are fully or partially subsidized while the young husband and wife complete their educations. This complicates the emancipation process, for the young family does not assume a fully separate and independent status. The same difficulty faces many teenage couples who are forced into marriage by premarital pregnancy and must live with one of the in-law families while they complete their secondary education. Couples in these circumstances will encounter many more adjustment problems than will couples who are financially independent and able to separate from the parental families.

One maxim of good in-law adjustment is that the newlyweds must never live in the home of an in-law. There are enough adjustments to be made between themselves as they learn their new roles of husband and wife. They must be free to adjust to each other without the interference of any third party. If necessary, it is better for the couple with limited means to live in a one-room furnished apartment and to accept a lower standard of living than to move in with in-laws. The Walkers (Petersen 1977, 225) tell of a young couple who refused the parents' subsidy and lived in a "single room where they ate, slept, and cooked. 'We don't have much,' she remarked without apology, 'but we have each other and we're having a wonderful time.'"

If during the courtship, there are indications there may be difficulties with the in-laws, it is wise for the newlyweds to move to another town to establish their home. A long distance between the two families may be a great aid to good in-law relationships! Pursley (Wheat and Perkins 1989, 143) relates how he and his wife received premarital counseling from Tim LaHaye, who strongly suggested, along with other items, that they "should move one thousand miles away from each set of parents for at least the first year of marriage." Perhaps LaHaye was being facetious, for such a suggestion has bad points as well as good ones. If there are difficulties during the engagement, however, it might be a good suggestion. Most couples enjoy their in-laws and many receive helpful insights and services from them. The important fact is that newlyweds need to start their own home separated from the parental families.

Many difficulties can be avoided in the first years of marriage if both the parental families and the young family recognize a change of status and role takes place at marriage. Prior to the wedding the bride and groom were dependent children in their respective families. At the wedding a new family is established, and the bride and groom take a new status of husband and wife in a new family that is on a par scripturally, legally, and morally with the parental families. They are no longer dependent children but now have the roles of husband and wife and are equal to those of their parents.

Although the parents still have the role of parents, the relationship is changed, and it is helpful also for the young family to think of their parents in the role of good friends. As such they are free to seek the advice of their parents, but they are not duty-bound to accept it. Wesley and Elaine Willis (Hendricks and Neff 1988, 370) tell of their experience in seeking advice from Elaine's parents shortly after they were married. "They later told us that whether or not we took their advice was irrelevant; they deeply appreciated the fact that we respected them enough to include their opinion as part of our input. It only makes sense to draw on the wisdom and insight of mature relatives. And God has instructed us to seek wise counsel." Such advice should be carefully weighed, as the parents have twenty-five or thirty years of experience, and their wisdom should be considered in any decision where counsel is needed.

The parental family must avoid giving advice unless it is asked for. Simply because parents have more years of experience does not give them the right to impose their view on the younger couple. They should let the newlyweds know they are available for advice and help if needed. Hine (1985, 74) relates the case history of a couple who had a problem caused

by the wife's parents, who continually gave gifts to the couple. "If the parents saw anything missing in the way of appliances, clothing or food, they would be quick to supply it." The young husband resented this, as he wanted to supply the needs of his young family "without outside help."

> *At the wedding a new family is established, and the bride and groom take a new status of husband and wife in a new family that is on a par scripturally, legally, and morally with the parental families.*

Difficulty may also be caused if the new family is too sensitive to suggestions or advice from the parents. In their desire to become independent, the couple may interpret any offer from the parental family as an attempt to retain some control over them. It is true that some parents use monetary gifts and loans in an effort to influence and perhaps even control the young family. Thus, if they want the son to live in the same area, they may offer the gift of a lot on which to build a new house on the condition that the couple buys near the parents. This is clearly an unfair interference in the decision-making process of the couple. Many couples appreciate parental help in purchasing a home, but the wise couple will refuse such offers if unfair restrictions are placed on them. On the other hand, the offer of a gift or low-interest loan to purchase a home can be a real blessing to the couple, for it may help them to

185

begin acquiring equity in a home much sooner than if they had to first save for a down payment.

> ## *Many couples appreciate parental help in purchasing a home, but the wise couple will refuse such offers if unfair restrictions are placed on them.*

Financial aid to complete a person's education is also helpful if unrestricted. It is certainly unfair and unwise for a parent to offer to help only if the young husband agrees to follow the career chosen by the parent. Parents who wish to help their married children can do so by making unrestricted gifts at appropriate times such as birthdays, anniversaries, and Christmas. It is customary to give gifts on such occasions, and the couple should not be embarrassed by these gifts. Conversely, they should recognize that these are gifts and should not expect them on every occasion, or be too disappointed if an event passes without such a gift. Many parents do help the couple get established in one way or another, the amount depending on the financial status of the parents. Even though parents may make mistakes from time to time, the young couple needs to remember that parents do have the best welfare of the couple at heart, and thus be forgiving and understanding in their attitudes toward the parents. The Willises (Hendricks and Neff 1988, 370) suggest, "When in-laws register any differences or foibles, we often become intolerant and irritated . . . in-laws have needs and feelings too. Some needs

include communication and a sense of being valued."

Most problems are with the parental in-laws but another difficulty of the early years involves adjustment to a brother-in-law or a sister-in-law. Many times a mate resents the favored treatment by the spouse's parents of a sibling. For example, a parent with two married daughters may be more generous toward one, and such partiality may be resented by the husband of the less-favored daughter. Similarly, one daughter may exploit her parents for financial reasons, and this type of conduct causes resentment by the sister and her husband who manage their money well. The actions and attitudes of unmarried siblings still at home may also cause animosity. In addition, great differences in personality, religion, or political views may cause friction with brothers- or sisters-in-law, and if siblings cannot avoid conflict, a couple may have to forego visits with them.

Nearly every young couple will have to determine where they will spend holidays and vacations. Hudson (1981, 87) relates, "As a counselor every year at holiday time I see some horrible example of in-laws who offer problems about who stays where, when, and how long." Both parental families desire the company of the young family. It is easier if they all live in the same area and both sets of in-laws can be visited the same day. However, if extensive travel is involved, a choice has to be made.

Elaine Willis (Hendricks and Neff 1988, 369) faced this situation because her husband's family spent Christmas with relatives. They did this "even though it has meant traveling many miles . . . and our boys have deeply appreciated the times we spent together. We made sure, however, that we spent roughly equal time with both sets of relatives." Spending equal time may not always be possible but if it is done whenever feasible, it will make for happier in-laws.

If the couple lives at a distance from both parents, the question of where to spend vacation may also become a problem. Compromise in this situation will also be necessary.

The time will come, as the family matures, when young parents will want to begin their own traditions. The change from spending time with grandparents will have to be done little by little so they are not offended. If there is good communication between the families, the change should be effected with few problems.

The second major period of in-law adjustment occurs when parents become old and often infirm, and the children must assume their care. If the Lord tarries, the task of providing for parents should become less of a problem in the future since many more people are covered by private retirement plans as well as Social Security. However, many of the present generation who went through the Great Depression are forced to live on Social Security benefits that are inadequate to meet all their needs. High rates of inflation (which lower buying power) or low interest rates for savings also make it difficult financially for retired parents. Consequently, the children may find it necessary to help with support of the parents.

This provides an opportunity for children to fulfill their scriptural obligation to care for parents, and also to help repay them for the care and help provided earlier in life. The apostle Paul wrote, "But if any widow have children or nephews, let them learn first to show piety at home, and to requite [pay back] their parents: for that is good and acceptable before God." Problems may arise over such things as sharing equally in the support, where the parents should live, or failing to visit the parents.

When parents are well, gerontologists usually feel it is best for them to live in their own home when feasible and as long as it is wise. There are times when it is not wise: an aged couple living in a twelve-room house, or parents unable to care for their home or themselves. When a move becomes necessary, many couples go to warmer climates such as California, Arizona, or Florida. Some prefer the security of an apartment or a condominium in a retirement colony where many services are provided. Others who are well prefer individual homes. Many find that mobile-home living has much to offer. Some prefer an apartment near one of the children.

A real decision must be made when a parent becomes too ill to live alone and yet not ill enough to be hospitalized. One of the children must take the parent into the home to provide nursing care, or else the parent must be placed in a nursing home. Taking them into the home is difficult and often impossible in a small home. Nursing homes are very expensive, and many are dreary places for an ill person to live. Some church groups have homes for their aged, providing a wholesome environment for them. Gish (*Encyclopedia* 1982, 333) mentions the necessity of involving all the family members when it becomes necessary to change living arrangements of parents. Usually one person becomes involved as a caretaker but actually "caretaking should involve all the family members according to some equitable plan." With the increase in life expectancy, more and more families will have to face the issue of caring for aged parents. The Lord leads when such decisions must be made, and the Christian couple can depend upon his leading when faced with such situations.

> *The second major period of in-law adjustment occurs when parents become old and often infirm, and the children must assume their care.*

Conclusion

Good in-law relationships can add much happiness and be a help to a Christian marriage. The relationship of Ruth and Naomi is an example of this. The women of Israel gave expression to this fact when Obed was born: "thy daughter-in-law, which loveth thee, which is better to thee than seven sons, hath borne him" (Ruth 4:15). Many a Christian parent has experienced something of the same feeling when a son-in-law or daughter-in-law has become as precious to them as their own child.

Mace says, "The goal to be aimed at was well expressed by the mother who said, 'When Tom married Peggy, I thought I lost a son. But what actually happened was that I gained a daughter'" (1966, 70). Like Ruth, many a daughter-in-law has come to love the mother-in-law with the same affection she feels for her mother.

Young people must remember that when they marry, they marry into an established family, but their new family is on an equal level with the parental families. When difficulties arise, husbands and wives must always act as a family unit, realizing that loyalty and affection for the spouse take precedence over that for parents. Malcolm (1987, 108) has a fitting tribute to the value of the extended family. She indicates that the materialism of today tends to separate the extended family. People are offered bigger salaries to move to new locations where they can have a higher lifestyle. She writes, "Instead of leaving our families to get rich, I believe God is calling us to make great investments in each other—investments of time, money and emotional energy in order to keep the generations together." The love and support of the extended family can contribute immensely to the happiness of a Christian couple.

> *When difficulties arise, husbands and wives must always act as a family unit, realizing that loyalty and affection for the spouse take precedence over that for parents.*

Study Questions

1. Why is the extended family important to the newlyweds?
2. How should a newly married couple treat a parent who is neurotically attached to one of the spouses?
3. Discuss the subject, "Most newlyweds will encounter problems with the mother-in-law."
4. When and why is it wise for the young family to move a great distance from the in-laws?
5. In what ways are the parental in-laws often exploited by a young family?
6. When are warning signals of possible in-law difficulties significant enough to break an engagement?
7. What role changes in reference to parents take place when a couple is married?
8. How should a young family handle the problems of holidays and vacations?
9. In which two periods of the life cycle of the marriage are in-law problems most likely to occur?
10. What basic principle should guide a young family faced with an in-law difficulty?

Suggested Readings

Hudson, R. L. 1981. *Now that our kids have children.* Waco: Word. This volume, written by a counselor and grandparent, offers helpful advice both to young families and to grandparents. He gives helpful suggestions on how to deal with many common in-law problems including those of holidays and vacations.

Malcolm, K. T. 1987. *Building your family to last.* Downer's Grove, Ill.: InterVarsity. The author makes frequent references to her parents, who were missionaries in China. As a schoolgirl she was interned by the Japanese for three years. Although it is not stated, her desire for readers is to have a family relationship emblematic of the wonderful family from which she came and the family of procreation to which she now belongs.

McCubbin, H. T., et al. 1988. *Family types and strengths*. Edena, Minn.: Bellwether. A study by University of Wisconsin Family Life researchers who surveyed families to discover family strengths in the areas of hardiness, coherence, family traditions, celebrations, and routines. Although it is a technical study, the case histories provide ideas for the extended family in reference to celebrations and traditions.

Owens, V. S. 1990. *If you do love old men*. Grand Rapids: Eerdmans. This delightful story was written by a granddaughter about her grandfather in East Texas. It is a picture of an extended family with its pleasures and pains. So well written that it is a joy to read.

Rossi, A. S., and P. H. Rossi. 1990. *Of human bonding: Parent-child relations across the life course*. New York: Aldine de Gruyter. A cross-generational technical study made in the Boston area. One significant finding was that children reared in homes where parental affection was warm and demonstrative tended to have homes with similar qualities.

Self, C. S., and W. L. Self. 1989. *Before I thee wed: A guide to help engaged couples prepare for marriage*. Old Tappan, N.J.: Revell. This book resulted from the experiences the Selfs had in teaching a class for "nearlyweds." It encourages couples to examine their emotions and then to prepare to meet the problems they will encounter. After the couple is married, they then enter a class for newlyweds. The book has two short chapters dealing with in-laws and family traditions.

Wright, H. N. 1985. *So you're getting married*. Ventura, Calif.: Regal. A discussion of marriage based on commitment. The chapter on "Commitment to Build Positive In-law Relationships" is one of the best available treatments of the subject.

Christian Parenthood

And, ye fathers, provoke not your children to wrath: but bring them up
in the nurture and admonition of the Lord.

—Ephesians 6:4

The Biblical Model

Why do people want children? There are several reasons, including continuing the family name, establishing oneself as an adult, and bringing change and fulfillment to an otherwise routine life. More importantly, children give their parents love and affection and in turn become objects of love. In an increasingly bureaucratic, impersonal, and mobile society, children keep parents from becoming bored and lonely (Palkovitz and Sussman 1988). Having a family is special and most married adults look forward to it.

For Christians, there is a more important reason for having children. Being a parent becomes an opportunity to demonstrate who God is and what he is like. Having children is a high calling, a sacred trust, and a ministry of evangelizing and discipling (Dobson 1987; Wright 1989). Children are a heritage and a gift from the Lord (Ps. 127:3, 5) and parents have an awesome responsibility to demonstrate the relationship humans can have with God. How a parent relates to a child has a direct bearing on how the child will relate to God. By learning love, trust, and discipline from his parents, the child will be able to transfer these concepts in his relationship to God (Meier and Meier 1981; Narramore 1979; Sears 1991).

The Bible describes God as a parent. God calls us his children (1 John 3:1) and his family (Eph. 3:15). Scripture uses the words *child, children, father,* and *fathers* more than three thousand times. God presents himself as the perfect parent and human parents need to understand who God is, to properly teach and model the same character traits for their children (Narramore 1979).

Spiritual growth in the New Testament is found in the concept of maturity (Eph. 4:13; Phil. 3:15; Heb. 5:14; 6:1; James 1:4). Applied to parenting, this concept means parents help their children mature not only spiritually, but physically, emotionally, and intellectually as well. As children mature, they become capable, competent, and independent, preparing for the day they grow up, leave their parents, and start their own family (Gen. 2:24; Eph. 5:31; 1 Thess. 4:12). As this takes place, young Christian adults transfer their dependence from their parents to dependence upon God (Prov. 3:5, 6). The method parents use in establishing a child's maturity is that of empowerment. To empower children is to give them the skills to be competent, capable individuals. Parents who empower their children are actively involved through teaching, guiding, modeling, and caring (Balswick and Balswick 1989; Wright 1991).

> *Having children is a high calling, a sacred trust, and a ministry of evangelizing and discipling.*

Empowerment takes place best in a nurturing family environment. To nurture means to give the best care possible to cultivate and sustain life. The apostle Paul describes the role of a nurturing parent: "As ye know how we exhorted and comforted and charged everyone of you, as a father doth his children, that ye would walk worthy of God" (1 Thess. 2:11–12). Successful Christian parents provide a nurturing environment, built on biblical values, where children can grow and mature into secure and competent adults. They will, their parents hope, become mature Christian adults, manifesting healthy attitudes and godly character traits. But children are born in sin, with a

free will, and may choose to reject God's values as revealed in the Bible and demonstrated by their parents. Providing a godly, nurturing home does not guarantee children will become born again, but it does provide an opportunity for them to become Christians. Christian parenting is indeed an important spiritual ministry entrusted by God.

The Importance of Values

Values are the compass that guides a family through life. A great deal of research points to the role parents play in the character development of children. Month after month, year after year, children observe what their parents stand for and what is important to them (Havener 1983; Ward 1989). Although community, school, and church environments are important influences in a child's life, parents, especially fathers, have the greatest power in shaping values (Dobbins 1985). Character is still shaped in the home and parents are the primary communicators of values (Strommen and Strommen 1985). Unfortunately, many children in America are growing up with fuzzy ideas about values. Many children grow up valuing only self-enhancement and pleasure, as many parents do not have any other values to pass on (Havener 1983).

Parents' values tend to be the result of their own upbringing. They have adopted the life priorities and beliefs their own parents and surrounding culture deemed important while they grew up (Narramore 1979). Such values may or may not be biblically correct. One of the most profound examples of transferring bad values is the commonly recognized fact that most child abusers come from homes where they were abused (Ketterman 1989). Children are easily molded to accept any values, good or bad, as normal, and it is mainly parents who teach them or reinforce them. If children hear their parents talk about, or see them act toward different ethnic or social groups as being inferior or bad, they will tend to accept the same prejudice, thinking it is truth.

The Bible has much to say about transferring God's values to the next generation. The Lord instructed the children of Israel: "And these words, which I command thee this day, shall be in thine heart: And thou shalt teach them diligently unto they children, and shalt talk of them when thou sittest in thine house, and when thou walkest by the way, and when thou liest down, and when thou risest up" (Deut. 6:6–7). Earlier in Deuteronomy, he commanded, "but teach them to thy sons, and thy sons' sons" (Deut. 4:9). Dobson (1987) believes these verses are the most important verses in the Bible on parenting.

Values are important because moral judgments are made on the basis of principles (Ward 1989). If a family does not adhere to biblical principles, then the correct moral framework that children need is lacking. Values are also important because a direct connection exists between values and behavior. What a parent believes will show in his actions. Research has shown moral values are learned more by observing a parent's actions than by his words. Children are quick to recognize hypocrisy when parents say one thing but do another.

A major key to successful parenting is discovering, agreeing upon, and refining a basic set of values used in building a family. Two sets of values are needed and both should be biblically correct. First, the parents must determine the principles they themselves will personally live by. Second, they need to agree upon certain values in raising children. Parents usually learn skills and values concerning child rearing from their own parents. Again, such values may or may not be appropriate. Prospective parents should discuss their own experience of what their parents' parenting styles were and what beliefs they held about parenting.

Once values are agreed upon, they are to be taught to the children. Sizemore (1989) notes two common mistakes made in teaching values. First, parents should not use fear or guilt to teach values. Second, a distinction should be made between fundamental life values and nonessential life preferences. A moral value is one that affects the well being of another individual. A preference is personal and does not hurt another person. For example, if a mother chooses to dress her child in a certain color of coat, it is her personal preference. If she does not dress her child in a warm coat in freezing

temperatures, it becomes a moral issue since she is endangering the child's health.

Preparation for Parenthood

It is not unusual for Christian couples to be unprepared for parenthood. Once the wife discovers she is pregnant, the couple usually embarks upon a nine-month crash course in parenting. Parenting is an important ministry and requires more than just good intentions. Quinn (1986) states that the difference between successful and unsuccessful parents lies in their effectiveness in showing love and care. This requires knowledge and skill. Producing competent, self-assured children requires parents who have skills and competence in parenting.

> *Values are important because moral judgments are made on the basis of principles.*

One way a couple can prepare is by studying the many good books available today on the Christian family. Taking a course in child development and child psychology is also valuable. Engaged couples or newly married couples should get experience by babysitting different families and by working together in the church nursery. Teaching children in Sunday school is a way couples can learn how each partner deals with children. It gives opportunities for each to see how the other handles children, copes with the stress of being with children, and enjoys being with them. Learning to parent is a lifelong process. Children differ because of their gender, personality, birth order, talents, and preferences. There are no guaranteed formulas that work for every child; each has different needs, level of needs, and interests (Dobson 1987; Sears 1991; Ward 1989).

Preparation also means understanding the increasing and decreasing responsibilities occurring throughout the family life cycle. There are four stages to the family life cycle: prechild stage, child stage, adult child stage, and role-reversal stage. The prechild stage is a time when the newly married couple establishes their marriage and career choices before having children. In this stage, the key word is adjustment, as the couple further discovers and clarifies roles and values. This is a critical time of settling in, and there is a danger that couples may have children too soon, before their careers and marriages are established (Dobson 1987).

> *There are four stages to the family life cycle: prechild stage, child stage, adult child stage, and role-reversal stage.*

The second stage of having children is also a crucial period in the married couple's life. Becoming a parent is a great psychological transition requiring entry into new roles, relationships, and responsibilities (Palkovitz and Sussman 1988). Having a first child is such a dramatic change in lifestyle that it is not unusual for couples to divorce after the birth of their first child. Becoming a parent means increased responsibility because neither the parent nor child is free until the parent helps the child learn how to manage his or her own life (Dobbins 1985b). The key word for this stage is *nurturing,* as the parent cares and prepares children for adulthood.

Another transition occurs in the third stage as children grow up, leave home, and establish a new independent relationship as adult children. The parents' role changes from nurturing to helping as they assume roles as grandparents and helpers to their adult children. A fourth stage evolves when parents become elderly and are unable to take care of themselves. The roles reverse and the adult children begin taking care of their parents. Sometimes called the sandwich years, these times can be stressful years for the adult children as they simultaneously take care of their own children and their elderly parents.

Couples anticipating parenthood need to discuss and agree on basic values and preferences. The first issue deals with family planning, whether to have children or not, when to have them, how many, and of which sex. Spacing of children is important because having children spaced too closely together can be quite stressful, especially in the early years. The couple should discuss birth-control preferences, birthing options, infertility and adoption, deformity or handicap, and abortion. Although conservative Christians view abortion as immoral and as an act of murder, the couple should still study for themselves why the Bible opposes abortion.

Another issue is balancing career and family responsibilities. The couple should discuss the extent of the father's involvement in childcare in light of his career obligations. The current trend is for fathers to have more involvement in childcare, especially if the wife works outside the home. Another legitimate question is whether or not the wife will have a career outside the home. According to a major research study sampling 350,000 households, more than half of mothers working outside the home believed being a full-time homemaker was better than working outside. They told researchers a full-time mother has the advantages of having more influence in guiding her children's morals, spending better quality and quantity of time, and giving more consistent discipline. They also felt children were more secure when a mother is full time in the home, and full-time mothers felt less guilt about leaving their children than career mothers did. The study concluded that most mothers believed a mother should be at home, wants to be at home, and would be a better mother if she is at home

(Genevie and Margolies 1987). Mothers have a great opportunity to make an enormous impact on their children. Abraham Lincoln once said, "All that I am or hope to be, I owe to my mother."

A major question a mother needs to ask herself is whether she is working outside the home primarily for economic reasons or for personal satisfaction. It may entail financial sacrifice to be a full-time mother, but the intrinsic rewards of seeing children grow and mature may more than offset the benefits of a higher standard of living. Nevertheless, a couple may still choose for the wife to have a career outside the home. In this case, they need to discuss whether her career should be full-time or part-time, if job sharing is possible, and what options they are comfortable with regarding babysitting and day care.

Another decision area deals with family leadership and home life. The couple should discuss which parent will lead spiritually. Sometimes the father is too busy or is not interested in leading in family devotions, praying before meals, and going to church. Often the mother has to assume spiritual leadership out of necessity. This is unfortunate as sons may think spiritual matters are only for women or may think being spiritual is really not that important. The Bible is quite clear that the father is to be the head of the home and spiritual leadership is his responsibility.

Another important question is, "Who will be responsible for training the children before they attend school?" Perhaps the couple will divide the learning activities between them. Once children are school age, a major concern is whether they will attend public school, private school, or home school. Other questions regarding family life include methods of discipline, family traditions, visits with in-laws, and where holidays will be spent.

A final area of discussion involves family support. As unpleasant as it may be, the couple must discuss contingencies in case a wage-earning spouse dies or becomes disabled. The couple should decide in advance what to do with life-insurance proceeds and who would watch the children if the remaining spouse was forced to work outside the home. Legal matters regarding wills, trusts, and guardianship should be taken care of once the marriage is stabilized and at least by the time the first child arrives.

> ## *The couple must discuss contingencies in case a wage-earning spouse dies or becomes disabled.*

All of these areas are important to discuss so that the couple comes to agreement before becoming parents. At the same time, it does not mean decisions, choices, and preferences will not change over time. As parents mature through family living, they may change their minds about certain preferences. For instance, they may have agreed earlier to have only two children but find they enjoy children so much they want more. They may also want to keep having children until they have one or more of each gender. Flexibility in nonmoral issues is healthy.

Parental Responsibilities

Successful parenting is a complex job requiring deep commitment and a variety of skills. At different times a parent serves as provider, helper, nurse, moral guide, disciplinarian, teacher, communicator, counselor, encourager, confidant, facilitator, motivator, coach, mentor, cheerleader, chauffeur.

Primarily, a parent's responsibility includes being a provider, role model, teacher, and leader. As providers, parents have a responsibility to supply all the needs of their children (Narramore 1979). The Bible specifies meeting physical needs (2 Cor. 12:14; 1 Tim. 5:8), emotional needs (Isa. 66:13; 1 Thess. 2:7), and spiritual needs (Deut. 11:18–19; 32:45–46; Josh.

24:15). Meeting spiritual needs is especially important as children need to see genuine Christianity practiced in their parents' lives. Children should see their Christian parents studying their Bible, praying, and growing in their Christian walk. Unfortunately, too many Christian parents open their Bibles only on Sunday morning.

Children need a healthy emotional environment provided by well-adjusted, happy parents. The emotional health of parents directly affects the emotional health of their children. It is unfortunate that children from Christian homes often rebel against God and their parents because their emotional needs are not met (Narramore 1979). Positive, supportive home environments are created by positive, nurturing parents who are mature enough to learn and work at it (Quinn 1986). A parent is the most important person in a child's world, and it is crucial for that adult to take responsibility for guiding a child in a positive way (Carter 1991). Life should be viewed as exciting and challenging, not futile or depressing.

> **Fathers model emotional intimacy to their sons by how they treat their wives.**

Coping with Stress

Parents also have the responsibility of coping with parental stress. The modern family is subjected to a great deal of stress as it tries to function in a demanding and complex society. The potential for burnout is real. Parents are sometimes so exhausted and overwhelmed that they may emotionally withdraw from their children, allowing them to suffer (Dobson 1974; Quinn 1986). Caring for children takes an enormous amount of physical time, energy, and effort, especially when they are young. Par-

ents are on duty twenty-four hours a day, seven days a week, year after year. At the same time, tending to children is just as much, if not more, draining emotionally, especially as they get older (Michaels and Goldberg 1988). As parents become stressed, they become absorbed with themselves, trying to meet the demands of career, marriage, and social life, leaving little energy and time to meet their children's needs (Elkin 1988). It takes hard work for parents to provide a nurturing environment without letting the pressures of life interfere with their family.

Role Modeling

Secondly, parents serve as important role models to their children. As they mature, they look for role models as patterns for their own behavior. Children are natural imitators, and role models can be one of the best teachers they can have (Hausner 1990). By expressing genuine love, parents model how a person can love God, their spouse, and others. A husband and wife who do not love each other can have a detrimental effect on several generations (Meier 1977).

Fathers model emotional intimacy to their sons by how they treat their wives. If a father treats a mother harshly or is impatient with her, he teaches his sons it is all right to mistreat girls and women. Sons learn how to gain control in a marriage relationship through intimidation rather than genuine love. Years of attitudes and behavior between parents are observed by children, and their future marital relationships are greatly influenced by their parents' marriage (Williams 1991).

At the same time, mothers model to their children how a man should be respected and treated. Research has shown that mothers are the basic filter through which children view their father's personality, character, and integrity. Children interpret their father the way their mother thinks and feels about him. If she respects her husband, they will respect their father (Dobson 1987). The same is true for fathers as they interpret for their children the value of their mother. If a mother follows the biblical pattern of submission, she teaches her family the important value of the father being the respected head of the home. Not submitting to her husband has a harmful effect on children. Meier (1977) states that a great majority of neurotic children he has treated have a home environment with a weak, passive, or absent father and a domineering, smothering, overprotective mother.

Parents model integrity and honesty in parent-child relationships. Trust is both the glue holding the family together and the lubrication making it run smoothly. It is the cornerstone of emotional health. For children to develop trust requires a home where consistency is modeled daily. It shows children the world is a predictable and safe place. The betrayal of trust between a parent and child can emotionally cripple a child for life (Quinn 1986). Trust is the foundation for healthy parent-child communication and if parents do not keep their children's secrets, little real communication can take place between them (Sizemore 1989).

A further responsibility parents have is modeling fairness and equality. Favoritism can only damage relationships with children who are not receiving special treatment. Many children grow up resenting the parent, along with the sibling who has received preferential treatment, and their view of life may be distorted because of continual unfair treatment. Conversely, a favored child also develops a distorted view of life, often expecting special treatment from everyone. A wise parent is one who can acknowledge each child's talents and achievements while still showing equal love to all of the children (Williams 1991).

Modeling communication skills is an important role. Communication is useful in conflict resolution as it helps clarify conflicting or confused expectations between father and mother, parent and child. Loving, firm communication builds a nurturing environment while mean, unkind words hurt relationships. A parent's words are powerful and can build a child's self-esteem or destroy it. How a parent communicates pleasure or displeasure can strongly affect the motivation and morale of a child (Quinn 1986; Wright 1991). Parents are often guilty of not spelling out their expectations for their children, leaving them unsure of their roles and responsibilities. Parents and children should talk out their differences, and parents should listen attentively to each concern of the child. If children feel understood, they will cooperate more and have greater respect for their parents (Carter 1991).

Teaching

A third responsibility of being a parent is teaching. Before a child ever enters a school, several years of teaching have taken place already. Although there is a danger of demanding too much learning (Elkin 1988), there is also a danger of not teaching a child enough before school. Because of the pressures of parenting, some children live in an intellectual wasteland when they could have a head start on school. Teaching values is a primary role of parents. Shaping the moral and spiritual values of children is the responsibility of the parent, not others (Deut. 6:1–2). For children to grow up with values compatible with their parents, it is required of parents—not surrogate parents—to be the main role model of values (Hausner 1990).

> *Research has shown that mothers are the basic filter through which children view their father's personality, character, and integrity.*

The only way parents can ensure they are the main teacher of values is to actually spend enough time teaching their children right moral and spiritual values. Learning values requires quality and quantity time. Children learn values in a variety of settings by observing how parents respond to different life experiences and how they interact with others who have different values. Spending sufficient time with children gives parents opportunities to answer questions that naturally arise at the most unexpected times (Williams 1991). If parents do not spend enough time teaching their children their own values, they should not be surprised if they adopt different values espoused by other adults or peers. What some call a generation gap may in reality be a values gap (Sizemore 1989).

> *Children learn values by observing how parents respond to different life experiences and how they interact with others who have different values.*

Leadership

A fourth parental responsibility is family leadership. Effective parents demonstrate leadership by managing time in an organized fashion, making confident decisions, and controlling their emotions when faced with conflict. They allow for different opinions, listen to viewpoints of other family members, and admit their own mistakes. They express leadership by delegating family responsibilities according to individual capabilities and by offering plenty of compliments and rewards (Carter 1991). Parents with effective leadership skills create a stimulating, confident environment that provides opportunity for children to assume responsibility and learn from their own mistakes.

Special Role of Fathers

As societal changes and economic conditions propel more women into the work place, fathers are often forced to help in the home. Moreover, research reveals contemporary fathers actually want more of a role in child rearing and are more satisfied with themselves and their marriages when they are involved (Berman and Pederson 1987). This is a comforting trend, as fathers play an important leadership role in helping a family function normally.

Fathers have a scriptural mandate to lead their family spiritually. In Deuteronomy 6–12, there are nine references to fathers being responsible for passing on the religious heritage of the nation of Israel to the next generation (Clinton 1988). The father models who God is like and his children's perception of God is often based on their view of their own father. Children who have cold, passive, or absent fathers often believe God is also cold, distant, and indifferent. On the contrary, children whose fathers are warm, loving, accepting, and accessible usually have a healthy concept of God (Meier and Meier 1981).

In the *Encyclopedia of Christian Parenting* (1982), Wolf explains how a boy does not know what it means to be a man without a strong father image. Every boy needs a mentor to learn how to identify and be comfortable with his masculinity (Williams 1991). A father can introduce his son to the delicate balance of being strong yet gentle. By watching his father interact with his mother, sister, and other women, the son learns how a man properly behaves toward women. Fathers especially need to teach their sons to be sensitive to the opposite sex, since boys are socialized in a male subculture typified by machismo and toughness. For a father to be strong and gentle, he must be secure in himself. If a father is insecure, it is likely his son will be also.

Nurturing fathers strive to include and affirm their sons through regular interaction. Researchers studying homosexual men have discovered problems often exist in a homosexual's relationship with his father. Usually both the father and homosexual son reject each other. The father rejects the son by not approving him or ignoring him while the son rejects the father by refusing to identify with him. If a father likes his son, his son will like himself (Williams 1991). A father has a profound influence on the development of his son's self-image and sexual orientation.

A father's relationship with his daughter is just as important. Research points to the value of a continuous and positive relationship between a father and his daughter. Daughters with positive father-daughter relationships have better self-concepts, higher self-esteem, greater moral maturity, and lower rates of unwed teen pregnancies. They also exhibit more self-confidence in personal relationships and social interactions (Clinton 1988).

In addition, a woman's sense of femininity and competence is affected by her relationship with her father, and this, in turn affects her future love relationships, work, and self-esteem. A father shapes a daughter's perception of men and how men should treat her. He has a unique influence in preparing her for a special role as girlfriend, fiancée, and wife (Wright 1989).

It is imperative for a father to be emotionally involved with his daughter by consistently expressing his feelings. If a father emotionally withdraws, especially as a daughter reaches puberty, that withdrawal can have a devastating effect. Research has indicated a strong link between a father's emotional withdrawal and a daughter's eating disorders. One study revealed thirty-six of thirty-nine girls suffering from anorexia had lost their father's affection when reaching puberty (Wright 1989).

Fathers often neglect their daughters in favor of their sons. In general, research shows that fathers give more attention to sons than to daughters (Wright 1989). Fathers must demonstrate to their daughters a consistent pattern of giving and receiving affection, giving equal time between daughters and sons, expressing the same expectations for daughters' success as they do for their sons.

Research reveals the necessity for fathers to have regular interaction with their children. In one study, the periodic absence of the father had the same emotional results as if the father had died. A chronically absent father can lead to low motivation for achievement, juvenile delinquency, and low self-esteem in his children (Clinton 1988). The vast majority of neurotic children and adults grow up in families where there is no father, or the father is chronically absent, weak, and uninvolved, leaving a domineering mother in charge (Meier 1977). Williams (1991) asks all fathers a poignant question: "When a father is on his deathbed, will he look back and wish he had received more money and promotions, or spent more time with his family?" It may be more important for a father to choose a career that is conducive to spending time with his family, even if it means sacrificing status and compensation.

> ## *Research points to the value of a continuous and positive relationship between a father and his daughter.*

What makes a father an excellent father? Researchers, asking eleven hundred mothers, discovered an excellent father is one who is patient, spends free time with his children, expresses affection often and freely, and puts his children's needs first. The excellent father also shares responsibility for both the good and bad aspects of parenting. He also believes his role as father is just as important, if not more so, than his role as breadwinner (Genevie and Margolies 1987). All in all, an excellent father is one who takes fathering seriously, creates a nurturing environment, and seeks to strengthen his family's relationships. Being a good father is one of the most important contributions a man can make with his life.

The Well-Adjusted Child

A major goal of successful parenting is raising well-adjusted children. Preparing children for adulthood is a crucial element of parenting. A person's attitudes and behavior as an adult is often a result of what they learned as a child. Habits begun in childhood usually carry over into adulthood. Children with unresolved conflicts and problems will become adults with unresolved conflicts and problems, often with adult-size consequences (Quinn 1986).

What characterizes well-adjusted children? Well-adjusted, healthy children are those who are able to handle life's problems effectively, manage their anxieties, and have a high level of self-esteem (Quinn 1986). They feel good about themselves and others. The parent's own attitudes and self-esteem directly affect the self-esteem of children. Producing well-adjusted children requires competent, well-adjusted parents.

> ## A parent must prepare a child to develop certain competencies necessary for success in life.

Parents can help children become well-adjusted in two ways. First, a parent's outlook on life must be confident, positive, and proactive. In their study, the Goertzels found highly successful adults had grown up in homes where their parents had a physical exuberance for life, a tenacious drive toward goals, and an intense love for learning (Havener 1983). A parent's zest for life and learning carries over into the children.

Second, a parent must prepare a child to develop certain competencies necessary for success in life. Well-adjusted children are characterized by flexibility, resilience, security, and trust. They bounce back from disappointments and failures, believing things will ultimately work out. They have confidence in themselves and in others (Gordon and Gordon 1983). A competent child is able to show affection, trust others, feel self-worth, accept responsibility, and have effective social skills (Havener 1983).

Another important area of parenting is helping children feel good about their bodies and teaching them to take care of their bodies; that is, personal hygiene, proper grooming, regular exercise, good nutrition, and sufficient rest. In addition, children need intimacy, most often expressed by touching (Quinn 1986). Children need and like to be held, touched, and hugged. As children mature, they need to be taught about their sexual development. This is a primary responsibility of parents and should not be delegated to the school, church, or peers.

Building Social Skills

Children need to learn acceptable social skills and this begins with the child being a functional, integral part of the family. Developing social skills in conversation, manners, poise, and conflict resolution starts in the home and prepares children to be confident outside the home in their interpersonal relationships.

Developing Good Habits

An important tool for teaching children competence is having a plan for regular routines and habits (Wright 1991). One way children can become organized is to teach them the value of goal setting. This can easily be done by keeping daily checklists of chores and duties. Meeting daily goals can motivate children to behave properly if meeting the goals results in receiving a special privilege or gift after the children have several perfect or near-perfect checklists. Checking off lists and earning privileges can be a powerful way for children to learn good habits; this practice reinforces acceptable behavior.

Learning Responsibility

Children have a basic need to learn. Parents should teach them facts, values, and world views. As they achieve success in learning, they will want to learn more. Children develop character by learning to be sincere, honest, and trustworthy. Being disciplined and industrious are important habits children should learn early. Learning responsibility is crucial to maturing into healthy adults. In the Goertzels' study of eminent doctors, lawyers, and scientists, it was discovered that most of them had responsibilities thrust upon them early in life. A study of adolescents in Israel also revealed that those who had learned to accept responsibility early in childhood had the most stable personalities (Havener 1983). Each year as children grow and mature, they should accept more and more responsibility, preparing them for becoming independent of their parents (Dobson 1974).

Self-Esteem

Building emotional strength, managing emotions, and developing a positive view of the self is essential to healthy personal development. The basis of most psychological problems and psychiatric disorders stem from a lack of self-love and self-esteem (Dobson 1974; Meier 1977). Consequently, children with low esteem get into trouble by either not managing their resentful feelings or by being too conforming and yielding (Havener 1983). Parents cannot begin too early in this regard, as by eighteen months the foundation of a child's personality has begun to form, and by the age of three, the child's temperament is set (Ketterman 1989).

Having high self-esteem means a child has confidence in the ability to cope with the basic challenges and problems of life. Children with high self-esteem believe they have a right to be happy, have feelings of worth, and believe that they deserve to have their needs and wants met. They are not driven to be superior to others, nor are they constantly proving their worth by measuring themselves against some comparative standard. They enjoy being who they are rather than being better than someone else (Branden 1992).

Children with high self-esteem feel good about themselves and trust others. Such persons are not threatened or paranoid of what others say or do to them. They have a sense of humor yet not at others' expense. They do not exploit other people but genuinely care for them. A person with high self-esteem forms mutual relationships easily and gets along with others.

> *Self-esteem in children is best understood through the parents' self-esteem.*

If children constantly judge themselves according to outside standards that they cannot control, their self-esteem will be in chronic jeopardy. Unfortunately, society is bombarded by values that the media and corporate world claim are important to self-esteem. The three main values of this faulty value system are beauty, intelligence, and money. A child learns early that some people are considered valuable if they are good looking, smart, and have more money than others. It is important for parents to teach their children that God created them the way they are, the way they look, and in the social status of their family and that he has a plan and purpose for them (Branden 1992; Dobson 1974; Meier 1977).

Parents have a major role in the development of their child's self-esteem, for it simply cannot be delegated to others. As mentioned, society will not reinforce a healthy self-concept, so it is imperative that parents take responsibility for it (Dobson 1974). Self-esteem in children is best understood through the parents' self-esteem. Parents set the example in exhibiting self-esteem. If parents have a high level of self-esteem, it will be easier for the child to pick up those qualities. If parents feel worthy, take pride in their work and home, make an attempt to dress and look attractive, then their child will also feel good about parents and home life (Ketterman 1989).

How can parents build self-esteem in their children? First, they provide a home where children feel the security of belonging. A secure home is characterized by parents showing unconditional love and consistent behavior and making every effort to include and support the child in enjoyable family interaction (Havener 1983; Ketterman 1989; Lewis 1985). Second, children need to feel the satisfaction of achievement. Nurturing parents provide opportunities for their children to explore, create, and achieve. When children succeed in their efforts, they should receive plenty of praise and hear their parents praise them to others as well. Wise parents honestly accept their children's limitations and direct them into projects they are capable of accomplishing without becoming frustrated or discouraged (Hausner 1990; Ketterman 1989).

One way to defend a child's ego from faulty value systems is the encouragement to counterbalance weaknesses with strengths. By compensating for weak areas, children will be less susceptible to feeling inferior about their weaknesses, especially if the weakness is in an area that society considers important. Learning compensating skills becomes increasingly significant as a child matures. If a teenager enters the difficulties of adolescence without feeling competent in at least a few areas, it can have devastating effects on self-esteem as peer acceptance is at a critical stage (Dobson 1974).

A third way parents can build self-esteem is having children feel the joy of being valued. They value themselves according to how the significant people in their lives value them. If parents treat their children with respect, they will in turn respect themselves and others (Gordon and Gordon 1983). Research has shown that children with the highest levels of self-esteem usually came from homes typified by parental warmth, fair controls, and respect for the child (Narramore 1979).

Destroying self-esteem is much easier than building it. All a parent has to do is continually criticize and ridicule a child by pointing out failures and imperfections. Another way to destroy self-esteem is to always make decisions for the child, intimating that he or she is not worthy enough to make his or her own decisions (Lewis 1985). Research reveals that parents who are directive (issuing lots of commands) often have low-esteem children (Havener 1983). Children need the freedom to learn from their own mistakes by making decisions on their own.

> # God expects parents to teach their children the basis of all self-esteem.

Spiritual Development

Contrary to the value system of man, God expects parents to teach their children the basis of all self-esteem—the fact that humans are created in the image of God himself and that the source of real self-esteem is found in a relationship with God. Children can feel worthy, not because of looks, intelligence, or family background, but by knowing they are important to God. Christian values parents should teach include worshiping God, obeying his commandments, respecting authority, loving mankind, exhibiting self-control, and having a humble spirit (Dobson 1974). But the most important thing parents can do for children is to model a Christian life pleasing to God, demonstrate godly traits, and let children know they are valuable because God values them. Children have a need to develop spiritually by knowing and loving God in an intimate way through accepting Christ as Savior, having a faithful prayer life and reading God's Word.

Principles of Discipline

A caring, nurturing parent corrects the child when it is necessary. Just as the Lord corrects those he loves (Prov. 3:12; Heb. 12:6; Rev. 3:19), so the loving parent must do the same. According to the Bible, discipline is a command of God that gives a child life and hope (Prov. 19:18; 23:13). It is good training to teach children to respect others (Heb. 12:9, 11). Failure to discipline a child leads to dire consequences.

Meier (1993) believes the worst thing a parent can do is to spoil a child, never discipline, create complete dependence on the parent, and never teach the acceptance of responsibility for wrong behavior. The result is a child who develops dependent personality disorders, including alcoholism, drug addiction, eating disorders, mental disorders, and sociopathism. Dobson (1974) notes that parents who allow their child's will to be untamed encourage the child to develop an extreme self-will, resulting in a child useless to others and to God. Narramore (1979) points out that if children are not disciplined, it will be more difficult for them to learn to respect other authority.

The purpose of discipline in the home is to promote proper Christian behavior that honors God and others. Through parental discipline, a child learns self-control, self-discipline, and self-respect. Children are commanded by God to obey their parents (Eph. 6:1–2), and as they learn to obey their parents, they learn to obey God. Furthermore, when children are disciplined, they develop a conscience, learning to distinguish right from wrong. Research indicates that the development of conscience is correlated with the nurturing warmth of the mother, how much the child identifies with the father, and the way parents and child communicate after a child breaks a rule (Havener 1983).

Several principles provide a foundation for delivering good discipline. First, good discipline should enhance a child's self-worth. Proper discipline is always conducted in love, not in an attitude of spite or hostility. The parent is careful to explain to the child that the action or behavior is bad, not the child. This is based on the theological concept that God hates sin but loves the sinner (Ps. 45:7; Rom. 5:8).

Another theological distinction a parent should realize is the difference between punishment and discipline. In the Bible, God, in righteous anger, punishes unrepentant sinners to satisfy his justice. In contrast, God disciplines his children to promote their growth, maturity, and respect. God has a different attitude toward his children, for he corrects in love. Just as God's discipline encourages Christ-like attitudes and behavior in his children (Heb. 12:10), so parental discipline encourages children to pursue correct and responsible behavior (Narramore 1979).

> *Through parental discipline, a child learns self-control, self-discipline, and self-respect.*

A second principle of good discipline is balance. Parents should be neither too lenient (Prov. 13:24) nor too strict (Eph. 6:4). Being too lenient leads to uncontrollable behavior, whereas being too strict can cause rebellion, depression, and discouragement (Ketterman 1989). Both extremes can damage self-esteem, as neither extreme shows respect for the child as a person. During the early years of childhood, the goal is to shape the will, not neglect it or crush it (Dobson 1978). Parents need to search for a balance between demanding too much and expecting too little.

Third, good discipline is fair. The parent ought to give discipline equal to the misconduct. To not discipline enough makes a mockery of the disciplinary process. To discipline too much is to anger and provoke the child (Eph. 6:4). If more than one child needs disciplining for the same infraction, all children should be disciplined to the degree of their involvement. If a child confesses a misdeed before it is found out, discipline may still be necessary but may be reduced to reward the honesty inherent in the confession. Being fair also means giving discipline appropriate for the age of the child.

Methods of discipline change as children get older and more mature. Dobson (1992a, 64–66) suggests spanking with a neutral object (e.g., a switch or a paddle) as an appropriate means of discipline for children ages eighteen months to twelve years. However, most corporal punishment should be "finished prior to the first grade (six years old). It should taper off there and stop when the child is between the ages of ten and twelve." He indicates that some people do not approve of the use of a neutral object since it can lead to child abuse. However, the hand "should be seen as an object of love—to hold, hug, pat and caress" and ordinarily should not be used in spanking a child.

> # *Children should know and understand the boundaries of acceptable behavior.*

Spanking should not be used to discipline children for acts that are appropriate for their age, such as a small child spilling a glass of milk. It should only be used when the child's will is pitted against the parent's will. The child must learn to obey the authority of the parent. Failure to obey parents will result in failure to obey other authority figures such as teachers and law-enforcement personnel.

Spanking should never be used to discipline teens. Dobson (1992a, 72) writes, "Teens desperately want to be thought of as adults, and they deeply resent being treated like children. Spanking is the ultimate insult at that age, and they are justified in hating it. Besides, it doesn't work." Revoking privileges for adolescents is

more effective. He suggests that parents be creative in devising other forms of discipline. The value of discipline should match the degree of misbehavior.

Corporal punishment is a subject debated in American culture. Some schools have prohibited it. There is a movement to make it illegal, even for parents (as has already happened in Sweden). Since there is a possibility of child abuse, some parents should *never* spank their children. Dobson (*Christianity Today*, 8 February 1993, 69) warns, "Anyone who has ever abused a child . . . [who] has ever felt themselves losing control during a spanking . . . who has had a violent temper that at times becomes unmanageable should not use that approach." He proceeds to state "that's the minority of parents, and I think we should not eliminate a biblical approach to raising children because it is abused in some cases." Every parent should read and heed the advice given by Dobson in *The New Dare to Discipline*. He makes it clear that he does not *"believe in parental harshness."* He believes children "deserve to grow up in an environment of safety, acceptance and warmth" (Dobson 1992a, 12–13).

Children should not be humiliated in front of their peers, especially as they become older (Dobson 1992a, 26). The parent should respect children by not letting them lose self-respect. The old adage of "praise in public, criticize in private" still holds true. By being corrected in private by parents, the child will learn to handle interpersonal differences as an adult in private as well. Too many adults mistreat others in public without learning to respect the biblical injunction of going first in private to a person who has caused an offense (Matt. 18:15).

A fifth principle is that children should know and understand the boundaries of acceptable behavior. Parents should explain what commands need reasonable obedience and then make sure children obey them (Dobson 1974). Children should know in advance what the boundaries are, and once they know, that knowledge will provide security, for the rights of the child and others are protected in a structured environment (Dobson 1978).

A sixth principle of good discipline is that parents need to always have a united front, with both husband and wife in control of disciplinary situations and in agreement with the form and intensity of discipline. If one parent disagrees, that parent should not disagree in front of the child who has broken the rule. Children are quick to play parents against each other if they detect their parents do not agree. It is important for each parent to back up the other one, for otherwise children learn to manipulate parents to get out of trouble (Havener 1983; Meier 1993).

Finally, good discipline is consistent. This is perhaps the most important principle as it affects all the other principles. In other words, parents should be consistent in the degree of strictness and fairness, and in their ability to maintain a united front. They should consistently enforce the boundaries and limits, consistently discipline immediately, and consistently discipline to enhance self-worth. Inconsistency is confusing to children and causes them to misbehave, to test and stretch the limits. This can lead to neurotic behavior later on (Ketterman 1989). Being consistent disciplinarians requires parents to be disciplined themselves. When parents make a threat to discipline a child of any age, they must follow through or else the child will know the parents are not serious. Consistent discipline is hard work.

The whole family benefits from good discipline. Through discipline, children gain freedom from their parents. In turn, parents get back freedom from their children (Dobbins 1985b). Good discipline teaches children to behave, respect others, feel secure, and be responsible, and most of all, good discipline glorifies God.

Signs of Dysfunction

Although the goal of successful parenting is to empower their children in a nurturing, caring environment, there is an alarming trend of dysfunctional families. Such a family has a home environment where family members are mistreated, either through abuse or neglect. To abuse means to mistreat or harm someone through insult or violence, whereas neglect means to mistreat someone through insufficient care. There are three targets of abuse and

neglect—child, spouse, and elder (Janosik and Green 1992).

Parents play a leading role in whether a family will be functional or dysfunctional. The quality of family life is reflected in the quality of the marriage relationship, and generations can suffer from a husband and wife who do not properly love each other (Meier 1993). The quality of family life is also reflected in the skills and competencies parents bring to it. The most important element a parent can bring to the family environment is a good self-concept (Carter 1991). If parents cannot cope with problems, do not like themselves, or cannot get along with a spouse, it is unlikely the children will be able to cope with the challenges of life. The child's basic need is for security, and if parents are unstable or unable to cope with the demands of life, their problems will emotionally overwhelm the child (Quinn 1986). Neurotic parent-child relationships often develop because a neurotic husband-wife relationship already exists. It is not unusual for a therapist to treat a parent or both parents and then see the child's problems go away on their own (Meier 1993). As parents go, so go the children.

> *The most important element a parent can bring to the family environment is a good self-concept.*

Of the two parents, again, the father plays the most important role. Often a dysfunctional family is the result of a dysfunctional husband-father (Wright 1989). A father has a key role in providing emotional support; when he does not provide this, his wife and children suffer (Lamb 1987). When a marriage fails, the husband often withdraws emotional support, and even if he does not move out of the house, he is still estranged emotionally and intimately from his wife. Out of neglect and lack of romance, the wife turns her affection on to her children, smothering their natural desire for independence and making them dependent upon her (Dobson 1974; Wright 1991). When a home is dominated by a smothering, overprotective, emotionally starved mother, and the father is weak, passive, and emotionally withdrawn, the children often develop neuroses needing clinical care (Meier 1977).

It is in such an unhappy home that child abuse and neglect can take place. There are different kinds of abuse. Physical abuse takes place when a parent harms the child, with or without an implement. Sexual abuse includes molestation, rape, and incest. Emotional abuse involves verbal abuse (threatening, belittling), attempted physical or sexual assault, or confinement. Child abuse leaves physical and emotional scars that the child may carry for life (Ketterman 1989).

> ## As Christian parents try to cope with an increasingly pressured lifestyle, their children are in grave danger of being neglected.

Research has discovered that parents of abused children are often immature, impulsive, self-centered, dependent, and rejecting. They are usually low on coping skills and do not tolerate frustration well. It is not unusual for abusive parents to have poor social skills and not able to function well as neighbors (Mayhall and Norgard 1983). Research also reveals child abusers are often young parents living on tight budgets or parents who have less than satisfactory sex lives, who had poor relationships with their parents, and who believe

children exist only to satisfy parental needs (Havener 1983).

While most Christian parents would never dream of physically or sexually abusing their children, they may be prone to emotionally abuse them. Verbal abuse is apparent when a parent uses degrading, caustic, or judgmental words to hurt a child. It is unacceptable for a parent to belittle, blame, or find fault with a child. When a parent attacks a child's appearance, intelligence, or competence with hurtful words, the attack is emotionally damaging. Nurturing parents strive to communicate and correct their children by building them up and supporting them (Wright 1991).

Child neglect has various forms as well. Physical neglect means a parent does not care for his child and may neglect to provide proper clothing, hygiene, health care, and nutrition, or neglect to attend to a child's safety needs. Emotional neglect results when a parent gives inadequate nurturance and affection, permits socially unacceptable behavior, and refuses to allow treatment for emotional problems. Educational neglect results when parents fail to enroll their children in school or fail to educate them adequately (Mayhall and Norgard 1983). Another form of neglect not mentioned in secular literature is spiritual neglect. Parents who neglect to teach their children about God are in direct violation of the commands given in Deuteronomy. They should seek to lead their children to Christ at an early age.

As Christian parents try to cope with an increasingly pressured lifestyle, their children are in grave danger of being neglected. This is especially true of children whose parents are engaged in helping careers such as medicine, counseling, and full-time ministry. With parents always on call, they often have little emotional energy left to give their best to their children.

Nurturing parents express genuine love for each other and their children, have their personal lives under control, and find a balance between their work, social, and family responsibilities. It requires personal discipline in their own personal life, spiritual life, and family life (Meier 1993).

The difference between a healthy, functional home and a dysfunctional home is found in what is lacking. A dysfunctional family lacks the acceptance, care, love, and togetherness of functional families (Wright 1989). In other words, a dysfunctional home is not a nurturing home.

Developing a Nurturing Environment

Because of their experience in a family, children learn whether they are likely to be loved and cared for, or neglected and abused. Children have basic needs and when these are not met, they develop feelings of inferiority, anxiety, humiliation, and disillusionment. A child's experience in the home will determine ability to adjust to the challenges and sorrows of life (Janosik and Green 1992).

Today, there is a clarion call for Christian parents to provide a genuine loving, nurturing home built on biblical values. Wright, in the *Encyclopedia of Christian Parenting* (1982), defines nurturing as giving the best possible care. It means parents provide a home environment where children can develop to their greatest potential, through maximum possibilities. Nurturing parents do not try just to get by, but go out of their way to provide the best for their family.

A nurturing family is one that meets a child's needs. As those needs are met, the child grows, matures, and eventually becomes a responsible adult. The following list describes twelve needs that children have:

1. A personal relationship with Christ and an understanding of biblical truth and principles.
2. A moral framework with consistent values and beliefs.
3. Genuine role models who exhibit integrity in their lives.
4. Christian parents with disciplined, balanced personal lives who put Christ first in all that they do.
5. Parents who are emotionally stable, secure in themselves, with a strong, loving marriage relationship.
6. Parents who give thoughtful guidance to help their children cope with the demands of growing up.
7. Warm, stable home life with family traditions and memories.
8. A secure, predictable home environment that serves as a refuge from the world.
9. Feelings of personal worth, significance, and acceptance through parent's love, affection, attention, trust, praise, approval, and affirmation and the opportunity to develop personal competency, leading to achievement and recognition.
10. Respect for authority through consistent discipline and fair, equal treatment.
11. Creative growth environment with freedom to communicate, interact, learn, and explore.
12. Regular routines with clear, appropriate roles and responsibilities.

By meeting a child's needs, a parent makes a great impact upon who that child will become. A child's relationship with the parents, along with home life, are the two greatest influences molding a child's personality. Both of these influences need to be healthy and functional (Quinn 1986). The best thing parents can give their children is a nurturing home, built on solid biblical values, in which the husband and wife truly love each other. In an environment such as this, a child can learn to know and love God for who he is.

> *The best thing parents can give their children is a nurturing home, built on solid biblical values, in which the husband and wife truly love each other.*

Study Questions

1. Why do couples want children? What is the most important reason?
2. How do parents develop character in children?
3. What is the difference between a moral value and a preference? Give an example from your own experience.
4. List several ways in which parents serve as role models.
5. Why is a father so important in rearing children?
6. How can parents help children to have self-esteem?
7. Why is it important to discipline children?
8. Discuss several principles of discipline.
9. Define a dysfunctional family. List several factors that result in a dysfunctional family.
10. List and discuss several needs of children that are met by a nurturing family.

Suggested Readings

Dobson, J. 1974. *Hide or seek.* Old Tappan, N.J.: Revell. A Christian classic on developing a child's self-esteem. A major theme is children learning to excel with strengths to compensate for their weaknesses.

———. 1992. *The new dare to discipline.* Wheaton: Tyndale House. A revision of a best seller first published in 1970. It is required reading for all parents who are concerned about using a biblically based method of discipline.

Dobson, J., and G. Bauer. 1990. *Children at risk.* Dallas: Word. The authors are concerned about "the battle for the hearts and minds of our children." They warn the family of the liberal forces in society that are determined to destroy today's children. They plead for a return to the traditional structure and values of the family.

Ketterman, G. H. 1989. *Understanding your child's problems.* Old Tappan, N.J.: Revell. A practical, comprehensive guide to dealing with many of the problems parents face. Offers preventative and remedial techniques for solving childhood problems.

Meier, P. 1993. *Child-rearing and personality development.* 2d ed. Grand Rapids: Baker. A biblically supported guide for developing good mental health in children. Covers all stages of child development from conception to late adolescence.

Narramore, B. 1979. *Parenting with love and limits.* Grand Rapids: Zondervan. A fine treatment of parenting from a solid biblical and theological basis. Emphasis on the responsibilities of parenting.

Quinn, P. E. 1986. *The well-adjusted child.* Nashville: Nelson. An insightful book on nurturing emotional health in children. A good overview of common parental mistakes.

Wright, H. N. 1991. *The power of a parent's words.* Ventura, Calif.: Regal. A guide to recognizing dysfunctional communication patterns often learned from one's own parents. Sound methods of communication are provided to nurture child maturity.

Part 5

Family Finances

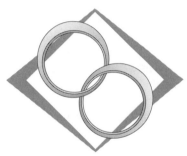

13

Stewardship and Budgeting

His lord said unto him, Well done, thou good and faithful servant.

—Matthew 25:21

Money and Conflict in Marriage

John looked up from his desk where he had been writing checks to pay the monthly bills. "Jane, how are we going to pay the phone bill this month? You made three long-distance calls to your mother that added nearly forty dollars to the bill, and there is no money in the budget to pay for them."

"You'll just have to let some other bills go this month. You always find the money when you call your parents."

"That's different! I call mine once a year and hold it to ten minutes."

"Yes, but a ten-minute call to Hawaii costs more than a half dozen calls I make."

John and Jane are arguing again because they don't have enough money to pay all their bills. Before the argument is over, they undoubtedly will say things they don't really mean, and Jane probably will end up crying. One hopes both of them will be able to forgive each other, kiss, and make up.

The chief cause of conflict in American families—Christian or non-Christian—is the use of money. Burkett (1989, 8–16) indicates that half of all first marriages fail and 80 percent of divorced couples between twenty and thirty list financial difficulties as the primary cause of their divorces. This is an alarming statistic that proves the need young couples have for instruction and assistance in the area of family finances. For this reason, two chapters of the text are designed to aid students in making rational decisions in financial matters.

Many families, like John and Jane, do not have enough money left over when the bills are paid to meet the desires of both the husband and the wife. When the husband is the breadwinner and the wife pays the bills, the husband often wonders where his hard-earned money went. In one such family, the husband received a raise. After a few paydays, he asked his wife why there wasn't more income left after the bills were paid. She replied that the extra income from the raise was being used to pay a larger car payment they incurred when he traded for a newer automobile.

Dual-income families may also face similar problems if there is not a solid agreement on who is to handle the money and how it is to be spent. Some dominant husbands insist on controlling all the income, a circumstance that leaves the working wife resentful, if not rebellious toward his attitude. Many times a dual-income couple will go deeper into debt because of the extra income.

> *The chief cause of conflict in American families— Christian or non-Christian—is the use of money.*

Many marital problems are confined to just one period in the life cycle of the marriage. In-law problems, for example, usually occur early in the marriage as the families learn to adjust to each other and also possibly late in the marriage when the care of elderly parents can create conflicts. On the other hand, money problems can occur at any time—from the beginning of the honeymoon up to the retirement years (Blood and Blood 1978, 523). One retired couple had difficulties because the husband wanted to use some of their ample savings for a trip abroad and the wife refused to go.

A high level of expectations can be another reason young couples encounter financial problems. They "try to accumulate in three years what took their parents thirty years to accumulate" (Burkett 1989, 75). They are pressured by advertising to start out with a new car,

new furniture, and a new home. Easy credit makes the beginning of such a lifestyle possible, but the maintenance of the debt creates real difficulties. Instead of starting out with a simple lifestyle and acquiring some savings as a reserve for emergencies, the couple is burdened with payments that often cannot be met. These are the couples who often let debts destroy their marriage.

Some conflicts over the use of money arise from different backgrounds of the spouses. A husband may have been reared in a family that stressed saving money for a rainy day. Havemann and Lehtinen (1990, 311–12) compare this person to the ant who stows away food for the winter. The wife may have grown up in a family that enjoyed living for the day with no thought of tomorrow, like the grasshoppers. They each bring to the relationship an attitude toward money that will inevitably lead to conflict.

Crosson (1989, 32–33) points out that different backgrounds will affect many areas of the use of money. Spouses will have different ideas about stewardship and giving; the type of lifestyle the couple should live; the places where they should vacation. The solution is that each spouse should be sensitive to the other's background. He writes, "The more sensitive you become to your spouse's ideas, and the source of them, the greater the mutual understanding and harmony in your marriage. It is easy to communicate your expectations about money and make sure that any decision you make contributes to harmony."

Other individuals stress saving money to compensate for deprivations in their earlier lives. Such persons may find it hard to spend money even for necessities and need professional counseling to help them "understand the basis of their money habits" if they are going to solve conflicts over money (Jauncey 1966, 122).

A husband who is not sure of his masculinity is threatened if he permits his wife to handle any money. He insists in controlling the money and gives his wife only what he thinks she needs to run the household. Even if his wife works, a husband may insist that she give her paycheck to him so he can have complete control of the finances. Such a person will demonstrate this need for control during courtship. Unless a woman is willing to submit to this type of personality, she should not marry him. Conflict after marriage because of his attitudes can be solved only as the husband gains insight into the relationship between money and his personality.

People who have an unmet or unresolved emotional need or conflict may spend compulsively in order to satisfy that need. Juroe (1981, 24) gives the illustration of Susie, who said, "Shopping for me, I have discovered, is an addiction. It soothes my nerves. It usually makes me happy, may even make me high. . . . If I am hurt or despairing, I go out and buy myself a present because I deserve it." Some young people buy expensive items to make them feel better because they have something their friends lack. These possessions give them a sense of self-worth— although a false one. Many of these emotional problems connected with money will show up during the dating period and should be considered a danger signal in the relationship. For some, the emotional needs may be so deep that only professional counseling can help.

Since so many factors are involved in the use of money, it is easy to understand why conflict can occur. Couples need to examine themselves and their attitudes toward money during courtship to see if there are areas of disagreement that cannot be easily resolved. It is better to break a relationship than to enter marriage with incompatibilities in this important area. The large percentage of divorces listing financial problems as the primary cause indicates that many of these couples should never have married in the first place.

The Christian couple who has unresolved conflicts over money should seek outside help to solve the problem. There are many available sources, ranging from books and tapes to professional financial counselors. A combination of professional help, the power of the indwelling Holy Spirit, and a proper attitude of love and concern for one another can solve most if not all financial conflicts.

The Christian couple who has unresolved conflicts over money should seek outside help to solve the problem.

Stewardship or Tithing?

A Christian couple can avoid much unhappiness caused by conflict over money if they have a correct understanding of Christian stewardship.

The use of money by Christians is an important aspect of their lives, about which the Bible has much to say. Blue (1986, 19) quotes MacArthur, who says that "sixteen out of thirty-eight of Christ's parables deal with money; more is said in the New Testament about money than heaven and hell combined, five times more is said about money than prayer; and while there are five hundred verses on both prayer and faith, there are over two thousand verses dealing with money and possessions."

The Bible also teaches that all that is in the world belongs to God. Exodus 19:5 reads, "for all the earth is mine." God said to Job (41:11), "whatever is under the whole heaven is mine." The psalmist quotes God as declaring, "for the world is mine and the fullness thereof" (Ps. 50:12). The basic thesis of stewardship is that a believer's possessions are gifts from God's bounty to be used for his glory. Blue (1986, 23) defines stewardship as "the use of God-given resources for the accomplishment of God-given goals." He also states that this definition "acknowledges God's ownership over my possessions and His direction of my use of these resources." This encompasses the life and abilities as well as the material benefits that God bestows upon the believer. The Christian is merely a steward (or in modern terminology, a manager or a caretaker) of these resources that are to be used to bring glory to God.

Pierson (Petersen 1971, 345), a godly Bible teacher of a past generation, once wrote, "Not only money, but every gift of God is received in trust for His use. Man is not an owner, but a trustee, managing another's good and estates, God being the original and inalienable owner of all." God expects each Christian steward to be faithful (1 Cor. 4:2) in the employment of money and will hold each believer accountable for its use. "For we must all appear before the judgment bar of Christ, that each may get his pay for what he has done, whether it be good or bad" (2 Cor. 5:10 *Williams*). Blue (1986, 21) expresses this truth by writing, "I don't understand it, but I do know that somehow my eternal position and reward is determined irrevocably by my faithfulness in handling property that has been entrusted to me by God."

Stewardship and consecration are invariably linked.

Stewardship and consecration are invariably linked. Foster (1985, 19) quotes Martin Luther as saying, "There are three conversions necessary; the conversion of the heart, mind, and the purse." A Christian cannot be conscientious in the use of money until there is the realization that all one possesses, belongs to Christ and must be yielded to him. In 1 Corinthians 6:19–20, Paul writes, "What? Know ye not that your body is the temple of the Holy Spirit . . . and ye are not your own? For ye are bought with a price; therefore glorify God in your body, and in your spirit, which are God's." The believer has been redeemed "with the precious blood of Christ" (1 Pet. 1:19), and as such is to present the body as a living sacrifice to do the will of God (Rom. 12:1–2). Foster (1985, 41–42) comments, "God's ownership of all things enhances our relationship with Him. When we know—truly know—that the earth is

the Lord's, then property itself makes us more aware of God. . . . We are only temporary stewards of things that belong to Another."

Not only do many Christians fail to use money wisely as a good steward of God, they actually permit money to dominate them. Money is simply a medium of exchange. We exchange our labor for dollars. We exchange the dollars for food, clothes, and shelter. Crosson (1989, 11) points out "that we have elevated money to something other than it is. We seem to think it is not only a medium of exchange, but power, prestige, and worth. We view it as an end rather than a means to an end."

The Bible gives us examples of both those who were dominated by money and those who used money as a trust from God. The parable of the rich fool (Luke 12:16–21) warns against the danger of being slaves to material things without regard for spiritual values. The rich fool said to himself, "Soul, thou hast much goods laid up for many years, take thine ease, eat, drink and be merry." But God said unto him, "Thou fool, this night thy soul shall be required of thee; then whose shall those things be, which thou hast provided?" The Lord then warns, "So is he that layeth up treasure for himself, and is not rich toward God." The lesson is clear: material things must be used for the glory of God.

The Macedonian believers, however, are good examples of wise stewards of God's resources. Paul writes in 2 Corinthians 8:2–5:

> How that in a great trial of affliction the abundance of their joy and their deep poverty abounded unto the riches of their liberality. For to their power, I bear record, yea, and beyond their power they were willing of themselves. Praying us with much entreaty that we would receive the gift, and take upon us the fellowship of the ministering to the saints. And this they did, not as we hoped, but first gave their own selves to the Lord, and unto us by the will of God.

The Macedonians had accepted the most important principle of stewardship: yielding the self and will to do the will of God. Baldwin and MacGregor (1984, 34) summarize this thought by stating, "In view of God's double ownership of us [he made us (Ps. 100:3) and he bought us (1 Cor. 6:19–20)], the only reasonable thing to do is to present ourselves to Him. And when we present ourselves, He owns all that we are and have." In view of this fact, he observes that we possess, but God owns; we earn but God enables; we are God's, so all we have is God's.

In American culture today the prevailing philosophy is materialism. The Bible teaches in Luke 12:15 that a "man's life consisteth not in the abundance of the things which he possesseth," a teaching directly opposed to materialism. The Christian is surrounded by a culture that continually emphasizes the acquisition of new homes, new furniture, new cars, new boats, new campers, ad infinitum. They are encouraged to use easy credit, until they, like those in the world surrounding them, are only one paycheck from bankruptcy. Crosson (1989, 26) warns the believer, "If you give your life in the pursuit of money, and the things money buy and neglect your posterity, you will be unable to leave a mark on the next generation. What a travesty of God's plan!" The Christian must always be on guard against the intrusion of materialism into one's life. Jesus warned against the danger of materialism and promised, "But seek ye first the kingdom of God and his righteousness, and all these things shall be added unto you" (Matt. 6:33).

Improper teaching of tithing, rather than Christian stewardship, may have contributed to materialism in our churches because many Christians have the mistaken belief that if they give a tenth of their income to the Lord, they are free to use the remaining nine-tenths for their own gratification. Davis (1984, 63) states, "I find no evidence in the New Testament that tithing should ever be taught as the final goal for Christian giving. When we teach this, that's where Christians stop growing in their giving." It never occurs to them that the Lord might want them to give two-tenths or three-tenths of their income to his work. In a day of great affluence with many Christians having two incomes, churches, Christian schools, and missions continue to suffer great needs because the vision of giving is limited to a mere tithe. Foster (1985, 74) recommends the concept of

the graduated tithe. A couple decides on a standard of living and then gives 10 percent of that amount. For every thousand dollars of additional income, they give 5 percent more. When a substantial sum (eighteen thousand dollars) over the basic standard is reached, then 100 percent of additional income is given. If this form of tithing were taught and practiced in our churches, Christian organizations would have the money they need and missionary appointees would not have to wait years to raise their support, outfit, and passage funds.

This does not mean that tithing is wrong. Millions of Christians, including the writer, can give testimony of the financial blessing of God because of the practice of tithing. Tim LaHaye (1968, 30–31) observes, "You can literally accomplish more financially with God's blessing on the expenditure of the 90 percent than you can the 100 percent without God's blessing. I have never known a couple that was not blessed by tithing." The point is that most Christians do not get beyond giving 10 percent because they believe that is all that belongs to God. The Bible teaches that *all we have* belongs to God and in this affluent society many Christians ought to be giving much more than merely 10 percent.

The Bible teaches *that* all we have belongs to God.

It is perfectly scriptural for a young couple to decide on a tithe (10 percent) as the basis for their Christian stewardship *early* in their marriage. Foster (1985, 73–74) observes, "with glad and generous hearts let us give proportionately, *beginning* with a tithe of our incomes. Neither Jesus nor any of the apostles confined giving to the tithe—they went beyond it. The tithe . . . is not a rigid law, but a *starting point* for organizing our economic lives." Baldwin and MacGregor (1984, 45–57) give several illustrations of couples who were in debt and relate how they made a commitment to tithe and were able to get out of debt within months. In his seminars he challenges couples to tithe for three months. At the end, if they have unpaid bills equal to the amount of tithe they gave, he offers to pay those bills. After several years of such an offer, no one has sent him any bills to pay! However, it must be emphasized that the tithe is only the beginning of real Christian stewardship and should not be considered the norm for Christian giving as is often taught in churches.

> ## *The Christian couple must learn to use in the wisest possible manner the resources that God entrusts to their care.*

Foster (1985, 42) comments that "God's ownership of everything also changes the kind of question we ask in giving. Rather than, 'How much of my money should I give to God?' we learn to ask, 'How much of God's money do I keep for myself?' The difference between these two questions is of monumental proportions." Many examples could be given of individuals who have increased the proportion of their giving to God and the blessings that resulted. The stewardship of R. G. LeTorneau, who learned to live on 10 percent and give 90 percent to God, is an example known to many Christians.

Sometimes Christian couples are given the idea that if they tithe they will experience little conflict over money and will be relatively free from financial problems. Crosson (1989, 6) comments, "We need to be faithful to manage wisely the money God entrusts to us—that is stewardship. But our faithfulness is no guarantee that we will have lots of money."

It is possible for a family to tithe and be conscientious about giving but still make poor financial decisions. For example, the car of a couple already heavily in debt needs repairs costing two or three hundred dollars. They can either have it fixed or buy a different one, incurring additional debt of several thousand dollars with large monthly payments. For a family already overburdened with debt, the latter decision probably would not be a wise one and would create additional strain on an overloaded budget. The fact that a couple tithes generously does not necessarily mean they will always make sound financial decisions. If they do not use good judgment, they can suffer the same results of such poor judgment as those who do not tithe or have faith in the principles of Christian stewardship. The Christian couple must learn to use in the wisest possible manner the resources that God entrusts to their care.

There are, however, many fine Christians who have a real burden to give to the cause of Christ. It is the purpose of this chapter and the following chapter to educate and encourage this generation of young people who are dedicated to learning and applying the principles of Christian stewardship.

Another basic principle of Christian stewardship is that in order to give more, one must have more. In the parable of the talents in Matthew 25:14–30, there was an unequal division of the talents by the master. The servants were judged on the basis of their faithfulness in the use of the talents, but the servants who had more to begin with were able to gain more than the one with just one talent. The master condemned the unfaithful servant for not giving the money to "the exchangers" so that it would have at least earned some interest. This passage clearly teaches the use of money to increase the amount of money. Referring to this parable, Foster (1985, 4) states, "Christians are to immerse themselves in the world of capital and business. That is a high and holy calling. . . . Some are called to make money—lots of money—for the glory of God and the larger public good."

One of the problems in evangelical Christianity today is that few individuals are able to give substantial gifts to sustain and enlarge

Christian organizations. One of the problems in the early church at Jerusalem was that members sold their houses and lands (their capital assets) and spent the proceeds. Then the apostle Paul had to take up collections from the churches in Asia Minor to send to the "poor saints . . . at Jerusalem" (Rom. 15:26). It is necessary for the believer to accumulate capital in order to increase his ability to give more funds for the work of the Lord.

Burkett (1975, 65) defines accumulation of wealth as "making, using, and spending money." He continues by stating that the purpose for a Christian to accumulate wealth is to have a "ministry of giving." He emphasizes that "if you have the ability to make money, you *must* have the ability to share money."

In accumulating wealth, the believer must take care to follow the will of God and maintain devotion to Christ in the midst of a materialistic generation. This is difficult to do, and many sincere Christians have backslidden because they could not stand prosperity. Henry R. Brandt (1960, 36) writes that over the years different men have come to him with plans to acquire wealth and thus aid the cause of Christ. He relates that two of those who came to him were successful but became absorbed in using their money to make more money. They did not currently give because their capital was tied up, but expected to give generously sometime in the future when their capital was freed up. Burkett (1982, 76) states that "if part of your ministry is the ability to make money and give it, you need an investment reserve." He indicates that funds need to be retained from each investment to make new investments, but not 100 percent because God needs money for his ministry today. He concludes, "Many investors will be disappointed when, after having kept the Lord's money for years and never grasping the opportunity to share in His work, they realize it's gone."

Young people should not be discouraged by these examples of men who failed the Lord. Many successful Christians are faithful stewards and give generously to the work of Christ, which indicates that financial success and spiritual growth are compatible goals in life. Blue (1986, 217) tells of a physician and his wife who came for financial planning. The physician was fifty-two years old and had a net worth of three hundred fifty thousand dollars. They stated a desire to give a million dollars to the Lord's work before they died. With careful planning they were able to give that much and more. God does not expect every Christian to become wealthy, but all must be faithful in the use of the money entrusted to them. God will judge them on the basis of how faithfully they use what is given to them. The words of the Lord to the servants in the parable of the talents were, "Well done, thou good and faithful servant; thou hast been faithful over a few things, I will make thee ruler over many things; enter thou into the joy of thy Lord" (Matt. 25:21).

> *Funds need to be retained from each investment to make new investments.*

Who Should Handle the Money?

This question should be settled during the engagement period so the couple will be able to plan effectively for the honeymoon and the first few weeks of marriage. It does not make much difference whether the husband or the wife handles the money so long as the most capable person does it and the arrangement is agreeable to both partners. Some men believe it is part of their role to care for the finances and their masculinity is threatened if the wife does it. The husband may be the one to do it if this is mutually agreeable, but if he is a compulsive spender, it would be unwise for him to assume the role of money manager. Likewise, if the wife is an impulsive buyer, better that the husband take the job even though he may not like to do so. One wife had spent her husband into bankruptcy once and was well on the way again when the creditors suggested she see a counselor. Burkett (1982, 84–85) states that "wives are the bookkeepers in over ninety per-cent of the homes." Some couples decide on a division of labor whereby the husband pays for taxes, insurance, car and house payments, and the wife buys clothing, groceries, and sundries. There must be consensus in this area for the couple to succeed in their stewardship for Christ.

Even with a division of labor it is possible for misunderstandings to arise. If the husband handles finances outside the home (e.g., investments) and the wife takes care of bud-geting and check writing, they must coordinate their tasks (Rushford 1984, 148). Rushford (1984) retells her own experience: her husband handled investments and she took care of household accounts—but they didn't keep each other informed and eventually accused each other of overspending. By sharing in each other's tasks, they solved their problem. In every family it is important for both husband and wife to be fully informed about family finances. In case of illness or death, the sur-viving spouse will be able to carry out the financial plans of the family.

> ## The family that practices good financial management from the beginning should never have to deal with creditors over delinquent bills.

Some Bible teachers insist it is the husband's role to control and handle all the family's finances. Burkett (1987, 17–18) observes, "God usually puts opposites together. If a wife has the ability to manage home finances, there is nothing unscriptural about her doing so." He indicates the financial planning for the family should be done together, but that the wife should not be compelled to make all the deci-sions. He emphasizes that in case of debts, the husband, as the authority in the home, should deal with creditors and "bear the emotional pressures of creditor harassment." However, the family that practices good financial man-agement from the beginning should never have to deal with creditors over delinquent bills.

Blue (1986, 19–20) indicates that if the basic thesis of stewardship is that God owns every-thing a Christian possesses, then "three revo-lutionary implications" follow. The first is that "God has the right to whatever He wants when-ever He wants it." God, as the owner "has *rights,* and I, as a steward, have only *responsibilities.*" The second implication is that not only is giv-ing to the Lord's work a spiritual decision, "but *every* spending decision is a spiritual decision." Buying groceries, a home, a car, paying taxes are all spiritual decisions.

The third implication of God owning every-thing is that it is impossible to fake steward-ship. Your checkbook reveals all that you really believe about stewardship. Blue reflects that Christians may fake prayer, Bible study, and other Christian activities, but their checkbook is a written record of goals, priorities, and con-victions. He suggests this may be the reason people "are so secretive about their personal finances."

In view of these solemn facts, and the greater fact that every steward will stand before the Master at the judgment seat of Christ, it is incumbent upon all Christians to know all they can about the use of money in reference to their personal and family lives. This includes making a financial plan for the future.

Financial Planning

If a family had an unlimited amount of money to spend, a plan for spending it would still have value. But the vast majority of us have a limited amount to spend, making a plan for spending it essential.

Before a financial plan can be started, a cou-ple must know what they owe and own. This is determined by compiling a financial statement. Most financial institutions have forms available to list the family's assets and liabilities. Rosefsky (1983, 86–87) has used one prepared by a Santa Monica bank. Assets and annual income are listed on one side and liabilities and annual expenditures on the other. Subtracting liabilities from assets equals the family's net worth. The form also has spaces to list investments, properties, and insurance policies. Financial institutions use these statements to determine if they wish to grant a requested loan.

A financial statement should be made out each year to enable the family to see its progress or lack of growth. Theoretically, the net worth should increase each year. Rosefsky (1983, 85–88) gives several advantages of the net worth statement. It acts as a safety valve against incurring too much debt since debt has a tendency to creep up. It helps the family keep reins on credit. It also helps to protect against loss by keeping insurance equal to current values, and it alerts the family to increase or decrease life insurance coverage. It also is a tool for estate planning, as certain assets or liabilities may need to be taken out of the estate for tax benefits. It is apparent that preparing such a financial statement is necessary for establishing a sound financial plan. New Year's Day is a good time to review the past year to see what changes have taken place.

In formulating a financial plan, the family's next step is to set some goals. The Fooshees (1980, 113) relate that of five thousand couples with financial problems, the number one problem was the failure to set goals.

Blue (1986, 100–103) gives four reasons for setting goals and four barriers to goal setting. The first reason for setting goals is to "provide direction and purpose." When goals are set, decisions are made to reach those goals. Second, goals should be written out to enable the couple to establish their priorities. They should have well planned objectives to pursue. Goals also provide personal motivation. If a family has a clear-cut objective, then they can make the sacrifices necessary to achieve that objective. Christians seek to do the will of God, and goals become "a statement of God's will" for the family. It is important that the husband and wife agree on these goals if they expect the blessing of God on their finances.

One barrier to goal setting is the fear of failure. This fear is part of our fallen nature. We rationalize that if goals are not set, then failure cannot occur. Another barrier is the false idea that setting goals takes a lot of time. A family spends much time on unimportant things. Goal setting should be a high priority; the time, effort, and prayer expended is a worthwhile investment. The third and fourth barriers are that many people do not know what goals to set or how to set them. Today, there are excellent books written by knowledgeable Christian writers such as Ron Blue and Larry Burkett that give detailed instructions in goal setting. Blue's *Master Your Money* is "a step-by-step plan for financial freedom" designed to help the average person set up a sound financial plan. Every couple early in the marriage should consult these books and set goals for the family. The couple needs to pray and ask God what his will is for them in the area of finances. God's plan will be different for every couple, but the important issue is to determine his will and then establish a method to accomplish it.

In goal setting, the couple needs to think in terms of short-term and long-range objectives. Rosefsky (1983, 70) uses the terms "today's dollars" and "tomorrow's dollars" to identify these two categories. These goals must also be listed according to priority.

> *In goal setting, the couple needs to think in terms of short-term and long-range objectives.*

Short-term goals include such items as the day-to-day expenses of the home, insurance, education, travel, contributions, emergency fund, medical care, and transportation. These items will be included in the family budget. However, it is wise to project what these expenses might be one or two years in the future.

> ## A person who defers gratification for the short term can experience greater satisfaction over the long term.

Long-term goals (Blue 1986, 29) might include financial independence, college education for children, paying off large debts such as the home mortgage, major lifestyle changes such as a larger home, a second home, or a car, major charitable giving, and owning a business. Rosefsky (1983, 79) suggests additional long-range goals of providing for retirement, care of elderly or disabled parents, a "stake" for your children, and "big rainy day" expenses.

Money can be set aside for the long-term objectives only if there is a surplus after the short-term expenses have been met. The easiest way to do this is to be sure that the expenses are less than the income. This is the secret of financial success. Blue (1986, 13–14, 38) relates the interesting experience of meeting an eighty-year-old retired pastor who had never earned more than eight thousand dollars a year. He had accumulated more than six hundred thousand dollars in cash, money-market funds, and certificates of deposit. He also had invested ten thousand dollars in the stock of a new company, an investment that had increased to about one million dollars. When asked the key to his financial success, the pastor replied that he had "never spent more than he earned," and that he had tithed, paid his taxes, and lived on the rest. Blue concludes by stating that the only way to achieve

"long-term financial goals is to spend less than you earn over time."

Blue (1986, 39) also emphasizes deferred gratification as a means to achieve the surplus of income over expenses. This concept teaches that a person who defers gratification for the short term can experience greater satisfaction over the long term. The main area of near-term expenses that can be cut are those connected with the family's lifestyle. A secular family's lifestyle is characterized by conspicuous consumption. Such a lifestyle is usually maintained by acquiring large debts. A Christian lifestyle "is an organized way of life with one's commitment to Christ at the center of life" (Davis 1984, 58). It exhibits "biblical principles and values." It should be marked by simplicity in stark contrast to the luxurious character of the secular lifestyle.

Burkett (1987, 9) discusses the matter of "indulgence" and defines it as "anything we buy that has little or no utility to us." Whether a possession has utility or not is determined by our lifestyle. God does prosper some individuals more than others, and what is utilitarian in one lifestyle may not be in another, depending on the level of prosperity. The problem in America is that our society is so status-conscious that Christians get caught up in seeking higher status levels and miss out on the blessing of using their money for the work of God. Blue (1986, 114) writes that "the biggest financial mistake I see is . . . *a consumptive lifestyle.*" He defines this as "spending more than you can afford, or spending more than you should, given your other goals and priorities." This lifestyle is encouraged, he states, by "a hedonistic philosophy, 'Enjoy yourself . . . Live it up. You owe it to yourself.'" Blue notes the power of advertising to influence one's lifestyle in proportion to how much time one watches television and by how much time one spends in shopping malls.

What level of lifestyle should a Christian enjoy? Blue (1986, 39) gives a formula for determining the money available to finance a lifestyle: take the total income, then subtract the tithes, all taxes, debt repayment, and savings for long-term goals; the balance funds a lifestyle. The problem is that American culture, through high-pressure advertising and easy credit, encourages people to live a lifestyle beyond their means. He states that "only by the grace of God" can a Christian family live a lifestyle that will create a surplus to finance the long-term goals of the family.

Dual-Income Couples

There are several ways the family can obtain surplus funds for long-range goals, some of which can affect the family's lifestyle. Many husbands take a second job (moonlight) to increase the family income. This has the big disadvantage of limiting his roles as husband and father. However, in the majority of families the wife works outside the home in order to augment the family income.

The traditional role is for the wife to be a mother and homemaker. Burkett (1987, 15) takes the position that "no biblical references prohibit a wife from working outside the home, provided the other areas of family life are in balance. However, just because the Bible does not discourage it, that doesn't automatically imply the Bible encourages it. That decision has to be made by each couple." He points out (1987, 13) there can be wrong motives for a wife to work outside the home. It is wrong if she is working because the family "needs" the money, for until they learn to live on the husband's income, they will never have enough. Second, if the wife is working "to fulfill her ego" it is wrong and can "lead to divided loyalties between the job and home."

When polled, most Christian young women indicate a preference for the traditional role, but they also desire to work for a year or two before children come. Almost without exception they want to be home when they have children. Again, the couple should be in firm agreement as to the specific role the wife is to play. Most men do not object to the wife working for a while, although there are some who believe she should only work if the male breadwinner is ill. On the other hand, there are husbands who will insist that their wives work. Agreement on this issue before marriage is absolutely necessary or the union may be filled with conflict.

The number of married women working outside the home has been increasing since World War II. The majority of mothers with preschool or school-age children are now working outside the home. It is apparent that an increasing number of women feel they can play the role of employee in addition to those of wife and mother. It may be necessary for some college-educated wives to work in order to pay off college loans. Due to the high cost of a college education today, these can be substantial. Other wives believe they should utilize the expensive education they received and work in their chosen field for a year or two after marriage. Later in the marriage the wife may go back to work to help pay for children's college expenses. Some wives also return to work as therapy during menopause or when the children leave home.

> *Saving the wife's income can provide the basis of financial security for the family and for increased Christian giving.*

If the wife works before children are born and there are no educational loans to pay off, the couple should save the wife's entire income after tithes and offerings. They should discipline themselves to live on the husband's salary from the beginning. There are two reasons for this. The first is that the couple will be oriented to live on one salary if the wife becomes pregnant and cannot work. Many couples get accustomed to living on two salaries and face real hardship when the wife cannot work.

The second reason is that saving the wife's income can provide the basis of financial security for the family, and for increased Christian giving throughout the life of the marriage. A substantial down payment can be made on a home, thus lowering the monthly payments and allowing more current income for family needs and Christian stewardship. Some of the savings can provide an emergency fund so that future savings can be invested in such forms as mutual funds or common stocks, which will provide for capital gains as well as interest on savings.

There are also some disadvantages to the wife working. Often the husband must help with traditionally female tasks of cooking and housekeeping—and some men do not enjoy this. However, the increasing number of egalitarian marriages find the husbands helping to care for the home and children. Occasionally the husband will assume the primary care of the home while the wife provides the family income. Malcolm (1987, 40) tells of her brother who married a pediatrician. Their lives became complicated with both pursuing careers. They believed at least one parent should be with the children. The solution was for the father to stay home with the children while the mother continued her medical practice. While children are a mother's primary responsibility, they are the chief concern of both mother and father. One of them needs to be with the children.

> # *The mother is the primary person in the formation of the child's personality.*

Marriages that have been organized around the wife's career have been termed "wife-as-senior-partner" or WASP (DeVault and Strong 1989, 345). Such marriages may be perceived as "deviant by friends, relatives, and co-workers" and tend to be under considerable stress. Wives generally considered being the major breadwinner a disadvantage, while husbands believed the wife's time away from home was the main problem.

When the wife works and the couple use both salaries for living expenses, the birth of children may be postponed entirely, and they become what is popularly called a DINK family—dual income, no kids. When these couples do have children they often become parents at an age when most couples are becoming grandparents.

The care of children is a major problem for mothers who work. Small children are cared for by relatives, nonrelatives in the home, family day care homes, or group care facilities (DeVault and Strong 1989, 350). There is strong pressure for the government to finance such facilities on a national basis. This desire for government funding has been resisted because of the belief that mothers should care for their young children. Many corporations provide day care for their employees.

The permanent effect of day care upon infants and small children is constantly being debated. Crosson (1989, 85) observes, "More and more studies are showing how important it is to have a mother at home, especially with young children, for bonding and long-term security and stability in their character, not to mention the inculcation of values." He proceeds to discuss the studies of Willard Gaylin, a psychiatrist, who concludes that a child's "capacity for love, capacity for tenderness, affection, morality, and conscience can be destroyed by the way it is treated in those first few years." Crosson finished his chapter on "The Myth of the Working Mother" by listing ten facts that a mother should consider before deciding to work outside the home. They can be summarized by stating that the mother is the primary person in the formation of the child's personality and that day care may have a negative impact on the child's personality.

The care of children between the ages of six and thirteen is also a problem when the mother works. It is estimated that there are between two million (DeVault and Strong 1989, 352) and ten million (Malcolm 1987, 41) children who care for themselves between the time school is dismissed and the arrival home of a parent from work. These children often carry their house key around their neck, thus the name *latchkey kids*. Malcolm (1987, 41) quotes Robert Vernon, a police officer from Los Angeles: "Neither mother or father is there to welcome the children home from school, to give them the guidance, encouragement, and love that is needed during the formative years . . . neglected children—little ones who feel insecure and rejected—are the ones who pay the price for our 'good life.'" He indicates that rebellious children are often the result of such neglect.

DeVault and Strong (1989, 352) point out that studies of latchkey kids have contradictory results. Some studies show such children are not adversely affected. Others demonstrate the opposite. The maturity of the child, the stability of the family, and the safety of the neighborhood seem to be the major factors impacting the children. Each family needs to consider these facts when deciding on self-care for their children.

The fact still remains that scripturally the main role of a Christian wife and mother is in the home. Paul wrote in 1 Timothy 5:14, "I will therefore that the younger women marry, bear children, rule the house, give none occasion to the adversary to speak reproachfully." Women who hold to this traditional, biblical role generally find their greatest fulfillment and happiness in being with their children rather than in employment outside the home. Crosson (1989, 82) mentions a survey that found "eighty-four percent of mothers employed full or part time agreed that they would rather be home with their children."

There are times when wives work to provide extras for the family they could not otherwise afford on the husband's salary. In many cases more careful budgeting may provide some of these extras and the mother must weigh the possible results of her absence from the home against the worth of the other extras her employment provides. Julie Crosson (1989, 195) makes a cogent statement: "I am convinced that God does not hold me responsible to help my husband afford a larger house, a nicer car, and more expensive clothes. He will ask me how I did on my job description. . . . One of the best ways for me to help my husband is to be content." Very often working mothers in such situations may attempt to assuage guilt feelings by giving lavish presents to the chil-

dren to compensate for failing to give them more time and attention.

Other mothers feel they cannot stand the routine of homemaking, so they take employment and hire a babysitter to care for the children and do some of the housework. The housewife and homemaker is constantly denigrated by feminists and the media. She does not receive pay for her work; consequently it is considered unproductive and of little value. This is a false view, but it has been accepted by many Christian women.

Fulfillment for the Christian is found in doing the will of God (1 Cor. 10:31). The believer's identity is based on a relationship with Jesus Christ, not on a job title. Hof (1981, 231) writes, "In the Christian scheme, there is room for both women who work at home and women who work outside of it. The primary work directive for the Christian is that everyone work. . . . What all this means is that the Christian woman or man has fulfillment apart from job or any temporal source." Consequently, the wife and mother who chooses to be a full-time homemaker should attempt to avoid feeling threatened or intimidated by the attacks of feminists upon her role. The role of homemaker and mother is noble and indispensable for "the hand that rocks the cradle is the hand that rules the world."

It is also important to examine whether there might not even be an economic disadvantage to the wife working if it places the couple in a higher income bracket. After the work-incurred expenses and added tax are calculated, real profit may be small. The Fooshees (1980, 103–11) devote an entire chapter to "Seeing the Working-Mother Squeeze" in which they give figures to show that little income is added to the family funds if all expenses are carefully and honestly tabulated. The amounts figured are not current, but any wife contemplating working outside the home might do well to use their procedure to calculate just how much surplus money would be made available.

Burkett (1987, 15) also states, "A working mother may actually spend more than she makes if she has to pay for day care, transportation, and a work wardrobe, not to mention the taxes on her income." The income of a mother who works to help pay college expenses may move the family income into a category that eliminates the students from certain grants and loans.

The disadvantage most often cited by working wives and mothers is lack of enough time and energy to devote to their husbands and children. They expect also to fulfill the traditional roles of caring for their family and feel guilty when they cannot live up to their own expectations. An employed wife still does most of the household duties. Although the present generation of husbands and fathers does more work in the home than the previous generation, the wife still does most of the household chores. The presence of diaper changing stations in some men's public restrooms indicates that younger fathers are helping more with child care.

An employed wife still does most of the household duties.

DeVault and Strong (1989, 342–43) list various studies that confirm the fact that men do not share equally in housework. The conclusion is "the husband's contribution to household work does not significantly increase if his spouse is employed." The best part of the day and the greatest amount of energy are expended outside the family. This can leave the employed woman feeling resentful as a wife and guilty as a mother because her family's needs are unmet emotionally. The Fooshees (1980, 109–10) ask some pertinent questions of the working mother: "Is your working worth the cost? Your cost is the taxes and expenses. Your cost is having someone else spend those fleeting hours with your children. Your cost is being a part-time helper to your husband. Your cost is busy, busy, busy. What do you think?"

Working outside the home may also limit the spiritual growth of the mother and the family. She does not have time for periods of devotion with the Lord. "Starved spiritually, they have little time to read and meditate on the Word, little time for a mature prayer life . . . too busy to lead souls to Christ. In addition, their associates on the job may be a detrimental influence. When these same women go home to be with the Lord, they will be strangers to their own Savior" (Narramore 1963, 57–58). However, some mothers who are well organized do find time to develop their spiritual lives and are capable witnesses for the Lord.

If the wife feels she should work, then she might also seek some kind of work she can do in the home. Perhaps she can do babysitting for others and remain with her children while earning extra income for the family. Those with art and musical skills often give lessons in the home. The creative mother can usually find some work she can do in the home if she feels she must supplement the family income.

Home-based employment is an "explosive phenomenon" according to an article in the Dayton *Daily News* (27 July 1992). The article noted that more than thirty million households had home offices, mostly men who own their own businesses. Many are accountants, architects, stockbrokers, computer programmers, and consultants. The technological revolution with computers, modems, and fax machines make it possible for many men and women to work productively at home. The article detailed the experience of a young mother, an assistant to an executive, who wanted to spend more time with her year-old son. Her employer refused to give her flexible hours or job-sharing, so she quit, since spending time with her son "was far more important to me than any job or any salary." She contacted a former business professor who owned a software company. He provided her home office with a computer, printer, fax machine, and business phone. He closed down his traditional office and moved it into the basement of his home. He now has seven home-based employees who earn thirty thousand dollars to forty thousand dollars annually with a 10 percent bonus of the company profits. The plan saves the employer overhead costs and enables mothers to be with their children.

Other mothers have started craft projects in their homes. Telemarketing and word-processing can also be done in the home. The desire for home-based employment has given rise to fraudulent schemes that are widely advertised, such as stuffing envelopes, addressing envelopes, or making small objects to be bought by the company selling the parts. Most of these are scams to be avoided. Rosefsky (1983, 125) warns, "The postal fraud authorities and the Council of Better Business Bureaus agree: they have never seen a work-at-home scheme that worked, except for the promoters."

Some professional women, such as teacher and nurses with school-age children, find employment where their working hours coincide with the school hours of their children. This enables them to be home when the children are. Of course, all working mothers still must face the problem of having sufficient energy for the responsibilities of home.

If a young couple enters marriage without large education debts and can save all the wife earns until the children come, their financial situation should not require that the mother work, assuming, of course, they learned to budget the husband's income and make wise financial decisions. Any mother with small children facing a decision to return to work outside the home should ponder the words of Burkett (1987, 15): "a family has to learn to get along on the husband's salary. During a child's first five years, basic attitudes are developed, and a mother's influence is the greatest. . . . Mothers of older children know that once those early years are lost, they can never be recovered. Many mothers would later trade a hundred times what they earned to be able to have a greater influence on their teenagers."

Crosson (1989, 83) appeals for couples to model the biblical family for the next generation. To do this the men must provide and the women must "nurture and provide domestic support." He states that "the comment, 'We *have* to have two incomes' is not really true. It is a matter of *values* and *priorities* [italics added]. It is deciding whether we want God's best for our marriage, or are content to settle for second best." He indicates the purpose of his book, *Money and Your Marriage,* is to help

people think correctly about money, and when they do, they will be able to live on one income.

The Family Budget

Financial planning can be enhanced if a family defers purchases or has two incomes. Another tool to ease financial planning is a family budget. A budget to control family funds ensures that the income is always greater than the expenditures.

Most families have a limited amount of income. This money must provide for present and future needs and wants in the most satisfactory manner. If it is mismanaged, the family acquires debt, which often leads to difficulties. The Fooshees (1980, 113) found that the average young couple had been married two or three years but had incurred debts totaling between eight thousand dollars and ten thousand dollars. This may happen to couples who do not have a spending plan for their limited income. Juroe (1981, 154) indicates the primary reason people are in debt is the absence of a reasonable budget. They don't know where the money has gone.

> *The primary reason people are in debt is the absence of a reasonable budget.*

Some kind of budget is "recommended by all family experts" (Havemann and Lehtinen 1990, 312). A budget "is simply a financial plan for the home" (Burkett [1979] 1982, 4). It enables the family to be good stewards of that which God entrusts to them. Blue (1986, 115) considers "a budget to be one of the most financially freeing things you can have. A budget guides you and tells you are on course, just as a roadmap does when driving in an unfamiliar area." Baldwin and MacGregor (1984, 14) cite the old adage, *"If you are going to manage your assets properly, you don't ask where the money went; you tell it where to go."* A budget is not something to be feared or dreaded, but is to be welcomed as a basic tool in achieving financial security for the home.

The Christian family needs to make sound financial decisions in order to have a strong testimony for the Lord. A family that is always in debt or is not able to provide adequately for the needs of the children usually does not command the respect of unsaved people. Occasionally, in the providence of God, a family may suffer financial reverses or a chronic and expensive illness that can result in poverty and distress but still maintain a good testimony for the Lord. The blessing of God ordinarily implies the ability to meet the financial needs of the family according to the particular social level of the family in the community. A budget is one device that will help a family manage its income in a way that pleases the Lord.

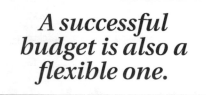

A successful budget is also a flexible one.

Crosson (1989, 120–21) lists four "barriers to having a system" of control or a budget. The first is that many people do not understand why a budget is needed. It is needed to make sure the family lives within its income and this in turn will promote "harmony and unity in the marriage." (Remember, the number one problem in marriage is conflict over the use of money.) The second barrier is failure to take time to set up a budget and to work out its shortcomings. It may take a year or two to get a plan working smoothly. The problem here is determining realistic amounts for each item in the budget. It takes real discipline for each spouse to make the system work. The third obstacle is "developing a system that is too complicated." One should not try to keep track

of every dime spent or try to write down every expenditure. This is all right in the beginning but may not be necessary as the couple becomes accustomed to the new spending habits.

The fourth barrier is "the husband's fear of failure." Men feel they should know all about money and don't need a budget. They usually are not as given to detail as their wives, and keeping a record of all a man spends may make him uncomfortable. He may view the fact that a budget is needed as a reflection that his income level is not sufficient to allow the family to spend as they wish. In such a case, the wife must assure her husband she is content with his income and that the best reason for a budget is that the income can be utilized as wisely as possible.

The first step in preparing a budget should be to determine the short-term and long-term financial goals of the family (Burkett 1975, 48). The short-term goals will consist of certain expenses that are relatively fixed each month, such as tithes and offerings, rent or mortgage payments, insurance premiums, and certain installment payments. Long-term goals will include a fund for emergencies, savings, vacations, children's college education, and retirement. The fixed expenses and long-term expenses are added up for a month and subtracted from the monthly income. What is left is available for the day-to-day expenses such as groceries, clothing, recreation, and hobbies. This should provide a guideline for distribution of income each month.

A successful budget is also a flexible one (Blue 1986, 140). The partners must agree to it, but it should be flexible enough to take care of unexpected needs. The emergency fund is built up over a period of time and may serve to meet needs for such items as clothing or auto repairs. However, the major purpose of the fund is to take care of larger items such as loss of income due to temporary unemployment or illness of the breadwinner or unusually large medical bills.

There are several systems of handling money in a budget. Some couples prefer the envelope system whereby the money for each item is deposited in an envelope after payday, then used as needed during the month. This system makes it fairly easy to determine how much money is available in any category at any time.

Other couples prefer a bookkeeping journal to list disbursements each day, which are then totaled at the end of the period to see how money was spent and whether or not the expenses conformed to the budget. Office-supply companies and stationary departments of larger stores carry reasonably priced home-budget records that are sufficient for the average budget. Printed columns for each month of the year, plus several pages for financial records, simplify budget keeping for the average couple. The disadvantage of this method may be the obvious bookkeeping involved and the necessity of each partner to keep track of money paid out. Spreadsheets for home financial management are a modern technological version of the bookkeeping method. The family with a home computer can use these to generate budgets and statements in a matter of minutes. The cost of a spreadsheet program is many times that of a bookkeeping ledger, but the time and effort saved may be well worth the added cost.

The third method widely used is the checking-account system (Burkett 1987, 30). The money is deposited each payday into a checking account. Then the partners pay all bills and make purchases by check. A check is written for the savings account. One check is cashed to provide spending money. The check stubs provide a record of spending for the period. The disadvantage here is that the couple must be sure to carry a checkbook at all times, as little cash is used in this system.

The couple should remember the purpose of a budget is to help them manage their money more efficiently to the glory of God. Whenever spending habits have been established, it may be possible to dispense with a formal budget. In like manner, if the techniques of keeping a budget become a source of friction between spouses, it would be better to give up the budget system. However, the couple must have some kind of spending plan or they may encounter financial problems.

The purpose of the budget is to enable the family to spend less than it earns so that it can achieve the long-term goals of its financial plan. Blue (1986, 33–41) indicates that financial independence is possible if income is more than outgo over a long period of time. He explains the "magic" of compounding interest, whereby the interest you earn begins to earn interest itself; savings then grow faster than mere deposits. He states that a young person saving one thousand dollars each year for forty years at 12.5 percent interest would have total savings of one million dollars due to compound interest. (This does not figure the tax implications.) On page 35 he records a chart showing how money multiplies at various time increments and percentages.

> # *Financial independence is possible if income is more than outgo over a long period of time.*

It requires discipline to live within a budget and accumulate the surplus that is needed to fulfill plans for giving and for savings (Burkett 1987, 33). Both husband and wife must be committed to the short- and long-range goals of the family's financial plan. When they practice self-discipline and self-denial, the couple will be pleasantly surprised how much they have to give to the Lord's work.

Stewards as Consumers

Wise Christian stewardship and good budgeting require that family members be informed consumers. Knowing how to buy wisely can add many dollars to the family's surplus.

Every library has volumes on consumer education and personal finance that contain information to help the consumer make wise decisions. Popular magazines such as *Consumer Reports* and *Consumers' Research, Inc.*

Magazine may be subscribed to or consulted in the library. *Consumer Reports Buying Guide* and the *Consumer's Research Annual Guide* are published each year and cover items tested in prior years. The informed consumer will consult these magazines or guides before making major purchases. The *Consumer's Resource Handbook* is a free publication available by writing to U.S. Consumer Information Center, Dept. 579L, Pueblo, CO 81009.

The greatest source of savings will be in day-by-day purchases. DeVault and Strong (1989, R–44) suggest that the first step for the consumer is to decide what the actual need is. Then a list of criteria such as "necessity, size, long life, color, dry-clean, warmth, resale possibilities" should be used to determine what quality and price range is acceptable for the article. Whenever possible it is wise to comparison shop. Value is more important than price. A bargain is not a bargain if it is not needed.

> ## Credit is part of good financial planning, but it must be used carefully.

The federal government and state governments have bureaus such as the Food and Drug Administration (FDA) and the Federal Trade Commission (FTC) designed to aid the consumer (Rosefsky 1983, 136–40). Any reference librarian can provide the name of the proper organization to contact in order to resolve complaints. Each community of any size has a Better Business Bureau. It should be consulted before doing business with any company that is unknown to the buyer. The BBB is paid by legitimate businesses to keep track of complaints against a company. It takes time and effort to become an informed consumer, but the potential dollars that may be added to the family's surplus over time will undoubtedly be worth it all.

Stewards and the Use of Credit

The American economic system is based on the widespread use of credit, and wise Christian stewardship necessitates a proper understanding of credit and how to use it. It is estimated that about 40 percent of American families are in debt each year. They have borrowed money and cannot make payments they owe. Many borrow more money to make payments on the money they already owe (Burkett 1987, 78). This is not the situation that God wants his children to be in. Credit is part of good financial planning, but it must be used carefully.

Some individuals prefer to save their money and pay cash for everything they buy except a home. This has the advantages of enabling the person to buy when things are on sale or when he can get the best price. Such a person never has to be concerned about debts. The disadvantage is that the cash buyer does not have a credit rating that may be needed at some time. For example, a family with six children was able to rent a home in Pennsylvania, but when the husband was transferred to Ohio, it was necessary to buy a home, since it was impossible to find a landlord who would rent to a family with six children. The husband had great difficulty in securing a loan for a mortgage as he had no credit rating in Pennsylvania. The Fooshees (1980, 31) claim that paying cash does not prevent one from buying a home. Several savings-and-loan executives said "they are interested in the prospective buyer's bank account, income, and certainly their debt obligations." Apparently, some bankers will make loans without a credit rating for borrowers. Since it is easy to establish a credit rating without incurring debt, it seems a good policy to have a credit record in case it should be needed.

If a couple prefers to follow a cash-only buying policy, they should establish credit by taking a passbook loan at their local bank, or by buying some items on a "ninety-days-same-as-cash" basis (Fooshee and Fooshee 1980, 30). Each community has a credit bureau, and when a person moves to a new community the credit bureau in that town can get a reference from the office in the place of previous residence.

Many major items in the budget, such as an auto or furniture, are purchased on the installment plan. A down payment may be made, with monthly payments following until the principal plus interest is paid. This form of credit has helped to create the high standard of living Americans enjoy, for it enables many people to own products whose acquisition would otherwise be delayed. We could only wonder how many new cars would be sold if the buyers had to pay cash.

Easy credit has been a disadvantage for many families with low sales resistance. They tend to purchase too many items on the installment plan so that payments consume too much of their income. They are unable to meet their payments or to save some money for emergencies, such as the illness of the breadwinner or temporary unemployment. Instead of enjoying life, they struggle to make ends meet. The Fooshees (1980, 38) offer this interesting quote: "It is not the high cost of living that is our problem, but it is the cost of living high that is our problem."

One suggestion to avoid such financial straits is to buy only one major item on the installment plan at a time. A person paying for a car on a monthly basis should avoid buying a new color television set until the car is paid off. If the present set needs repairs, it could be fixed. This type of financial plan requires discipline and the ability to delay gratification for success, but this is true for success in any area of life. God is not pleased with Christians who are unable to meet their financial obligations, or with those who are so hard pressed financially they cannot give generously for his work.

Each family must face the question of using credit cards either from department stores or from banks. Credit cards are easy to use and bank cards can present a record of all transactions during the month, an aid to budget keeping. Bank cards also have the advantage that if one is lost or stolen, there is only one company to notify, whereas if a person were to lose his wallet with several company cards, each company would have to be notified. However, these cards also make it easy for individuals to buy things they don't need or can't afford. Impulsive buyers certainly should avoid the use of credit cards.

Burkett has excellent guidelines for families that use credit cards. The family must have a budget and never buy anything not in the budget for the month. Second, credit-card balances need to be paid off every month so that no interest costs are paid. Third, *"the first month you find yourself unable to pay the total charges, destroy the cards."* He concludes, "the problem is not the use of credit. It is the misuse of credit" (Burkett 1989, 154–55).

"A major disadvantage of using credit cards is that the family spends approximately 33 percent more than if they used cash for purchases." Blue, a certified public accountant (1986, 124), heard this statement and decided to disprove it. He and his wife went on a cash-only basis for a year, and to his surprise discovered their spending was 33 percent less than the previous year's "barebones" budget. The reason is that individuals give more thought when they spend cash than they do when they use credit cards. They will not buy as often nor as much when using cash. He suggests that everyone try this for a year to develop a budget based on cash spending habits rather than on credit.

> *Individuals give more thought when they spend cash than they do when they use credit cards.*

Whenever it is necessary to borrow money, the individual should shop for the lowest net interest cost. The Truth in Lending Act requires the lender to state the true annual rate and the total interest cost for any loan made. If a family has a savings account in a bank or in a savings and loan institution, it is possible to take out a passbook loan. The bank loans the money with the individual's savings as security and the passbook to the account is kept by the bank. There are two advantages to this type of loan. The savings are not spent and continue to earn interest. This results in the second advantage of a low net interest cost. If a person borrows one thousand dollars at 6 percent for one year, the interest cost is sixty dollars. His savings earn 5 percent interest or fifty dollars. Thus, the net cost for borrowing one thousand dollars is ten dollars or 1 percent interest. The loan is usually limited to 90 percent of the account and may be paid back in one lump sum or in monthly installments.

> ## *The critical factor is that most home-equity loans are demand notes, so the lender can call for full payment at any time.*

If an individual does not have a savings account on which to borrow, he might have cash value in a life-insurance policy on which a loan can be made. These loans usually carry a lower annual interest rate, but they do not have to be repaid since the loan can be taken out of the policy proceeds on the death of the policy holder. An individual may pay interest on a loan for years and years, a practice that is not good money management.

Another good source of credit is a credit union. The interest rate may be lower, but it should be compared with other sources of credit. It is always unwise to borrow from a small loan company. These companies cater primarily to people with poor credit ratings. Consequently, states that charter these companies permits them to charge higher interest rates than those charged by other lending institutions. A typical rate is 1.5 percent per month on the unpaid balance or approximately 18 percent per year. In some states where the amount of the loan is less than six hundred dollars, the finance companies may charge up to 40 percent per year (Burkett 1989, 157). Any unpaid interest on a missed monthly installment is added to the amount, and interest must be paid on the interest also the following month. If a person cannot secure a loan from any other source, it is a good sign he should not borrow the money.

The home equity loan is highly advertised as one of the few ways to borrow and still deduct the interest on the federal income tax form. Burkett (1989, 157) indicates that such loans are dangerous to the family's finances for three reasons. They encourage a person to add debt to his home when he should be repaying the present mortgage. The interest rates are not fixed, so the borrower does not know what his future costs are. The most critical factor is that most home-equity loans are demand notes, so the lender can call for full payment at any time. If the borrower is unable to pay in full, the home can be sold to pay the loan. Very serious thought should be given before taking a loan that jeopardizes the future of the family home.

Occasionally it is possible to borrow from relatives and friends. This may result in a lower interest cost, but may cause hard feelings if payments are missed. There are times, such as borrowing for a down payment on a home, when an individual may lack sufficient collateral for a loan and the only source may be a relative or a friend. However, as a general rule, it is best for personal relationships to avoid borrowing from friends and relatives unless it is absolutely necessary.

Buying on credit is a part of American family life, but credit must be used intelligently. Bowman (1974, 51) says, "Uncontrolled credit buying is the best proof I know to support the statement that dollars and *sense* do not always go together. Credit buying can be a blessing or a curse. It becomes a curse when we fail to control it." And he warns, "Never agree to pay a monthly payment that will eat into your savings, hurt your family's standard of living, or send you into heavy debt. Surely one does not need very much intelligence to realize that to make such sacrifices in order to buy on credit is wrong" (Bowman 1974, 53). A proper understanding of Christian stewardship should enable the young couple to limit the use of credit and avoid stress in their marriage caused by financial problems.

The Steward and a Will

A will is an important item in Christian stewardship. Blue (1986, 206–7) defines a will as "a written, witnessed document that defines your final wishes and desires regarding many things, including property distribution." Many couples neglect to make a will, but one should be made immediately after marriage. As the financial worth of the family improves, it becomes even more important to have a will. If a person dies with a will, the state disposes of the property according to its laws. This may impose real restrictions and even hardship on the wife and children.

A will must be processed through a probate court on the death of the one who made it. The costs of probating a will consume a portion of the estate. Many Christians are using devices known as trusts to bypass the probate process and costs. Blue (1986, 193–215) has an excellent chapter on "Stewardship After Death" in which he indicates the need for estate planning. He describes the various items in such a plan, including the use of trusts. Most Christian organizations today have a stewardship department that will provide advice in estate planning. They will help formulate an estate plan to realize tax savings where possible and enable the family to exercise their stewardship toward Christian organizations. Blue concludes, "Estate planning is an integral part of financial planning. . . . Both . . . need to begin at an early age. They are dynamic in nature and to procrastinate in either is poor stewardship."

Whenever there are minor children, it is necessary for the parents to designate a person to serve as their guardian in case something happens to both parents (Klein 1987, 218–19). This may be made part of the will. Usually state law requires the guardian to be a resident of the state where the children live. If no guardian is designated, the court is at liberty to appoint one of its choosing, and this may not be in the best interest of the Christian family. Certainly children of Christian parents should be reared in a Christian atmosphere, so it is incumbent upon parents to see that a Christian guardian is designated for their children.

> ## It is incumbent upon parents to see that a Christian guardian is designated for their children.

In the parable of the unjust steward, Jesus said, "the children of this world are in their generation wiser than the children of light" (Luke 16:8). It is disappointing to see Christians who do not manage the money God entrusts to them. Christians should discipline themselves in their spending habits and hold to a savings and investment plan that enables them to give more to God. In view of the "pay day" at the judgment seat of Christ (2 Cor. 5:10 *Williams*), it is important that money received each pay day here be used wisely for the glory of God.

Study Questions

1. List several reasons why a couple may have conflict over money.
2. Give several examples illustrating that the Bible has much to say about money and possessions.
3. Do you agree with the statement, "The husband should always handle the money"?
4. Discuss the relationship of tithing and Christian stewardship.
5. What should be the attitude of the steward toward the accumulation of wealth?

6. Discuss the steps involved in developing a financial plan for the family.
7. List and discuss three ways to accumulate a surplus in the family's finances.
8. Design a monthly budget for a husband and wife with two preschool children. You may choose the income level.
9. List the advantages and disadvantages of the use of credit by a family.
10. Why is a will important to the Christian family?

Personality Inventory

What Are Your Values Concerning Money?

1. What is your view of Christian stewardship?
2. Have you established the habit of systematically giving a portion of your income to the Lord?
3. Discuss George M. Bowman's "10-70-20" plan: after tithes and taxes a family saves 10 percent, lives on 70 percent, and uses 20 percent for debts or savings.
4. Who do you feel should manage the family income? Why?
5. If you received a legacy of one thousand dollars, how would you use it?
6. If a wife works either full- or part-time, how much control over her income should she have?
7. If you had a choice of buying a so-called new car and not saving any money, or of buying a slightly used car and saving fifty dollars per month, which car would you buy?
8. Which type of budget plan do you think the young family should follow? Why?
9. In what ways would you handle your income differently from the ways your parents did?
10. In what ways do you feel you need to "keep up with the Jones family"?

Suggested Readings

Baldwin, S. C., and M. MacGregor. 1984. *Your money matters.* Minneapolis: Bethany Fellowship. Written by a certified public accountant who gives valuable insight into practical money management. Suggestions are given on how to shop wisely and how to stay out of debt. There is a helpful section discussing why credit cards should not be used.

Blue, R. 1986. *Master your money.* Nashville: Nelson. Blue is a certified public accountant who manages his own Christian financial-planning service. In this book he lays out steps to financial freedom. Every young couple should have this book to guide them as they do their financial planning.

Burkett, L. 1987. *Answers to your family's financial questions.* Ponoma, Calif.: Focus on the Family Publishing. Another helpful volume by America's premier Christian financial counselor. As the title indicates, it is written in question-and-answer format and treats thirteen subjects, including budgeting.

———. 1989. *Debt-free living.* Chicago: Moody. More than 40 percent of American families are in debt in any given year. This volume was written to help these people understand what debt is, how they became debtors, and what they can do to get out of debt and to stay free of debt.

Crosson, R. 1989. *Money and your marriage.* Dallas: Word. This book has three excellent chapters—"The Myth of the Working Mother," "The Dilemma of the Male Checkbook," and "A Woman Looks at Finances and the Woman's Role." Highly recommended for every family's library.

Davis, L. E. 1984. *In charge: Managing money for Christian living.* Nashville: Broadman. This volume treats the usual subjects in relation to personal finances. It has two excellent chapters on what constitutes a biblical lifestyle. It has a good indictment of the secular lifestyle.

Fooshee, G., and M. Fooshee. 1980. *You can beat the money squeeze.* Old Tappan, N.J.: Revell. The authors approach personal finances by contending that all couples are caught in a money squeeze. They give suggestions for unsqueezing the various items facing the ordinary family. A good chapter on "Avoiding the Newlywed Squeeze."

Goldsmith, W. B., Jr. 1981. *Basic programs for home financial management.* Englewood

Cliffs, N.J.: Prentice-Hall. This book contains computer programs that constitute a complete personal financial-management system. It covers four areas: money management, credit control, major asset management, and investment factors.

Moster, M. B. 1980. *When Mom goes to work: Managing motherhood and a job.* Chicago: Moody. Moster shares her experiences in combining motherhood and work. Concrete examples are given to help mothers adjust to playing two roles.

Patterson, R. 1991. *The money makeover.* San Bernardino, Calif.: Here's Life. Written by an attorney specializing in bankruptcy cases, the book gives specific instructions on how to avoid debt and how to get out of debt. Patterson strongly feels that people should live debt-free, but debt should never exceed 20 percent of spendable income.

Rushford, P. H. 1984. *From money mess to money management.* Old Tappan, N.J.: Revell. Most financial books are written by men, but Rushford has written one specifically for women. It is filled with practical suggestions to help women understand the elements of money management.

14

Major Purchases and Investments

By humility and the fear of the Lord are riches . . .

—Proverbs 22:4a

The United States is rapidly becoming a part of a global economy. Christian stewards must be alert to these changes. Every generation has its prophets of doom and the present generation is no exception. It must be admitted that the staggering national debt and the incredible amount of consumer debt are two factors that previous generations did not have to contend with. However, Blue (1986, 15–16) points out that Christians recognize the sovereignty of God and must make all their financial plans with the realization that he is in control. He writes, "I believe God is more interested in each of us individually than he is in any failure or success of our economic system." The believer proceeds day by day "recognizing His omnipotence, wisdom, purposes and plans."

The Steward and Savings Accounts

Every family has certain major purchases to make that consume a large share of the family income. The ability to buy these items wisely largely determines how much of the disposable family income is left for savings and investments. Lowe (1990, 40–52) suggests that a family should have three types of savings accounts—short-term, such as taxes and insurance premiums; middle-term for automobile purchase or educational needs; long-term for children's college education, weddings, and retirement.

The amount saved varies with the family life cycle. A single person should save 15 to 20 percent of his or her income. A family with children may set a goal of 10 percent. A retired couple might consider 5 percent. The best way to save is to "pay yourself first" (Lowe 1990, 50). A principle of budgeting is that the family always lives on the amount available. If the income is one thousand dollars per month or ten thousand dollars, the family will consume on that level. If income increases, the spending will increase accordingly. A family who wishes to save 10 percent must take that out of the paycheck after the taxes and tithes are paid.

A family may say they cannot live on that amount. If the wage earner received a 10 percent cut in pay (as often happens in times of recession), the family would live on it. So to save 10 percent the family takes that out first and live on what is left. Failure to do this explains why a person can earn hundreds of thousands of dollars and end up at retirement with very little saved. Money to be saved must be taken out before any debts are paid; you are your number one creditor. Payroll deductions for tax-sheltered pension plans, direct deposit of part of a paycheck into a bank savings account, a money-market account or a mutual fund, and the purchase of United States savings bonds are all techniques to help you pay yourself first. The Christian steward must put a high priority on saving a portion of the income if financial security is to be achieved.

> *Money to be saved must be taken from a paycheck before any debts are paid; you are your number one creditor.*

The Steward and Home Ownership

Most young families start married life in a rented apartment or home. An increasing number are discovering that a mobile home provides good housing at a reasonable cost, particularly if the couple buys a used one that has depreciated in value. A new mobile home decreases about 25 percent the first year and continues to depreciate annually in following years (Burkett 1987, 166). It is not good stewardship to buy a new mobile home due to the depreciation loss, but one that is two or three years old may be a wise purchase if it meets the needs of the couple (Rosefsky 1983, 205).

There are times, however, when it is better for a family to rent rather than to buy a home. If a family intends to be in an area for only two or three years, the costs associated with buying and selling a home may make it economically undesirable to buy a home. Many retired families or individuals find the upkeep and maintenance of a home too great, and prefer to sell the home and rent an apartment or buy a condominium where a fee is paid for maintenance. Many such retired individuals are also discovering that mobile-home living has many advantages, particularly in parks that cater to adults only, especially in warm climates such as Florida and California.

Whenever a family intends to be settled in an area for a long period of time, it is best from a financial viewpoint to buy a home. The person who pays rent does not build up equity or value in a home. For the person who buys a home, a part of each mortgage payment is credited to the principal of the loan, and month by month the homeowner's equity is increased. For the past two decades inflation has also contributed about 3 percent per year to the value of real estate so that the homeowner has gained added value. Both interest costs and real estate taxes are deductible from the federal income tax. However, Rosefsky (1983, 268) suggests that due to the rise in the standard deduction "to such a high percentage of income that careful arithmetic is necessary before final decisions are made" in reference to buying or renting.

During the inflation of the seventies and eighties, the price of homes increased dramatically in most areas of the country. It was nearly always better to buy than to rent. However, prices decreased just as dramatically in New England, Texas, and California, and many homeowners were left with mortgages larger than the value of their homes. Values have dropped in other parts of the country. So "the question of whether to buy or rent is not easily answered" (Havemann and Lehtinen 1990,

315). However, over the period of years a home has been the best investment and greatest asset for the average family. Case (1985, 65) agrees that "our house should be our primary investment." The equity will increase as the mortgage is paid off. When the owner retires the house can be sold and the cash received will make the senior years less stressful.

A couple should always rent until they have a sufficient down payment to buy a house they can afford. Burkett (1989, 71) states, "Buying a home too quickly and one that is too expensive is the number one reason most young couples end up in financial trouble. And since about fifty percent end up in divorce, the home will eventually be sold anyway." It is better for a young couple to save enough to pay 20 or 30 percent down on a smaller home than to go deeply in debt for a larger home.

If the decision is to buy a home, the couple must decide whether to buy a new home or a used one. Whether new or used, the three most important factors are "location, location, location." If a home is bought in a neighborhood that is beginning to decline, then the house will decline in value. If a home is bought in an area where prices are advancing, one can usually expect the price of the home to appreciate.

The advantages of the new versus the used home are discussed by Burkett (1987, 164–65). A new home can be located where the couple desires, it can be designed to fit their needs, financing is usually easier to get, and the builder may give a repair warranty. On the other hand, a new home usually costs more than a family expects to pay, and the oversight of the construction of a new home takes much time and effort. The used home has a set price so the family knows what the cost will be, and extras such as curtain rods, towel racks, and landscaping come with the house. The disadvantages are that financing is more difficult to secure, the buyer must accept the location of the house, and the house is bought "as is," which indicates some wear and tear. In an older home, the heating, air conditioner, roof, and hot water heater should be checked by competent service people.

When a family has decided to buy or build their own home, they must decide how to finance it. Rosefsky (1983, 206) suggests the couple visit one or two financial institutions in the area to determine what the family can afford. It is generally agreed the monthly payment should not be more than 25 percent of the family's income after deducting tithes and taxes. There are other expenses such as insurance, taxes, utilities, and maintenance that must be considered. Burkett (1989, 142) figures these will bring the total to 35 or 36 percent. Rosefsky (1983, 206) believes 40 percent or more of the income will be needed to finance a home and its maintenance. Burkett (1989, 142) warns that "the purchase of a home for a young couple should *never* be determined on the basis of their combined incomes." If one income should fail because of unemployment or pregnancy, the "entire purchase will be in jeopardy." Pregnancy always entails additional expense which will compound the problem.

> *Forty percent or more of one's income will be needed to finance a home and its maintenance.*

A large part of the American dream is having a home with a yard for the children. This is a legitimate desire for young couples, but case histories detailed in the writings of financial advisors as Burkett, Blue, Crosson, and others indicate that overbuying a home is a major problem for young families. Crosson (1989, 114) elaborates: "I have seen innumerable couples with tremendous stress in their marriages because they stretched to get their 'dream house.' The dream has turned into a nightmare. The husband works long hours; the wife puts the children into daycare so she can work long hours too—all for the mortgage." Ironically, they are not home to enjoy the house because they are so busy working. The children are neglected so they can live in a big house.

He continues, "The children couldn't care less. All they want is mom and dad around to love them. Stop and think about it. Do you really think your five year old (or fourteen year old . . .) really cares how big the house is?" During the engagement period, couples should discuss their feelings of status concerning housing and determine what priority it will have in their marriage. This will help avoid problems caused by too big a house for the income.

After the amount the family can afford to pay has been decided upon, they usually need to secure a mortgage to help buy or build a house. There are two major types of mortgages—the conventional loan or a government-insured loan such as Veterans Administration (V.A.) or Farm Home Administration (F.H.A.). A conventional loan may be either a fixed rate or an adjustable rate mortgage (ARM). A young family usually pays 10 percent down on a conventional mortgage. To purchase an eighty thousand dollar home requires a down payment of eight thousand dollars in order to secure a seventy-two thousand dollar conventional mortgage. A similar home can be purchased with an F.H.A. or V.A. loan which would require less down payment and smaller monthly payments.

Since the 1980s there has developed what is called "creative financing." It usually involves the buyer, seller, real estate agent, and a lending institution. This type of financing is ordinarily resorted to when the buyer does not have enough down payment. The persons involved work out some way for the buyer to purchase the property. It may involve the seller taking a second mortgage for part of the down payment, or the seller may sell it on a land contract, which permits the buyer to make payments to the seller for a number of years until the buyer secures a conventional loan. Sometimes a builder will pay part of the interest for the first two or three years in order to sell the house. Some financial institutions will absorb a certain percentage of the interest cost on the loan with an agreement that they will receive that percentage of the profits when the house is sold. Rosefsky (1983, 243) warns, "Creating financing can be very complex, and neither buyer nor seller should enter into such a plan without competent legal advice."

Interest rates may vary, and in most communities some financial institutions have better reputations than others, so it is important for the prospective homeowner to shop for the lowest interest rates. The best financial planning requires as large a down payment as possible and the lowest interest rate available. To illustrate, the interest cost of a $60,000 mortgage over thirty years at 10 percent is $129,648. The same mortgage over thirty years at 12 percent has an interest cost of $162,264 or an additional $32,616 for the same mortgage.

A similar savings in interest cost can be achieved by making the mortgage for as short a term as possible. Sixty thousand dollars at 12 percent paid off in twenty years with monthly payments of $661.20 has a total interest cost of $98,688. If the period is extended to thirty years with monthly payments of $617.40, the interest cost increases to $162,264. Even greater savings can be achieved with a fifteen year mortgage. On a $60,000 mortgage the monthly payment is $720.60 and the interest cost would be $69,708. This places greater pressure on the monthly budget, and in times of recession might cause a foreclosure on the home. A better way to save interest costs and to pay the loan off earlier is to take a thirty year loan, then make extra payments on the principal of the loan. Burkett (1987, 92) recommends this method with the warning to mark the check, "to be applied to principal payment only." This method works because the interest on a mortgage is figured on the principal due each month.

The importance of having a lawyer care for legal details for the buyer of real estate cannot be overemphasized. His costs are nominal in relationship to the total cost of a home. He can check to see that the title to the property is clear and free from all claims. He can advise concerning the signing of a contract to buy. It is also important to have the property surveyed if property lines are not clearly indicated by surveyor's pins. Stories abound of people buying a home and discovering half of their garage is on the neighbor's property. Again, the cost of surveying is small compared to the possible cost of moving a garage.

If a young family is willing to practice what the sociologists term deferred gratification in buying a new home and make their first real estate purchase an income-producing property, they can enjoy a better home later. The idea is to defer present gratification in order to enjoy greater pleasure in the future. If a couple buys a duplex or a small apartment building first, and live in one apartment until they have good equity, then they can use this equity and income from the apartments to afford a nicer home at a later date. This implies that they are willing to assume the obligations of a landlord in exchange for the added income. Burkett (1987, 147) observes that not everyone has the temperament to be a landlord. He writes, "There is nothing more irritating than getting a two A.M. call from a tenant who says the plumbing is stopped up." Those who have acquired rental property successfully have generated additional income to use for the work of the Lord.

Buying a mobile home may also be deferred gratification. When the couple are ready to buy a regular home, they rent the mobile home, which will give them a good return on their investment and increase the amount of income available for their needs and giving to the Lord's work. The "children of this world" (Luke 16:8) use every legitimate means to increase their assets and wealth for selfish gratification, and it is incumbent on Christian stewards to see that their assets are put to the best advantage for the glory of God.

After the home is purchased, the lender requires that it be insured. Most companies issue a homeowners policy that covers losses by wind, hail, fire, and vandalism. Most policies also provide personal liability coverage which protects homeowners from lawsuits arising from a person who injures himself on the property. Some also protect against losses from burglary. These policies are usually written for a three-year term, which saves paperwork for the company but also protects the owner against a rise in premium during that period, a good feature in a time of inflation. The homeowner must shop for the best buy in insurance coverage, as the price for identical coverage varies from company to company. If possible, the policy should have an "inflation clause" that automatically increases coverage to keep pace with inflation. These policies do not cover damage caused by floods or sinkholes, so a separate policy may be needed if one lives in an area where these may occur.

The Steward and Automobiles

The largest single purchase a family ever makes is that of a home, but they spend many more dollars over the life of a marriage for automobiles. The American economy is largely based on the production and sale of new autos. The credit business thrives on the financing of autos as most are bought on the installment plan. Autos have become so important as status symbols to so many Americans that it is not difficult for the industry to sell ten to twelve million new cars annually. Consequently, the money spent for payments, gas, oil, and maintenance consumes a good percentage of the average American family's budget. Social pressure motivates many people to buy new or expensive cars as status symbols even though they cannot afford them. Blue (1986, 115–16) states, "There may be more pride and ego involved in decisions about automobiles than any other financial decision. A recent quote in a newspaper points this out, 'Logic and automobile purchases do not go hand in hand.'"

Social pressure motivates many people to buy new or expensive cars as status symbols even though they cannot afford them.

Since Christians are influenced by these same cultural pressures, many of them have their values warped by society and join in the race to achieve social status. They forget that the major purpose of an auto is to provide transportation rather than to function as a status symbol. Consequently, they spend money for expensive autos—funds that should be used in the Lord's work or saved for their children's education, retirement, or some other financial goal of the family.

The Christian steward may let his money work for him at compound interest by buying a car for transportation rather than for status. Blue (1986, 34–39) has an amazing illustration of how much a family can save by investing one thousand dollars a year at 12.5 percent instead of using it for car payments. He points out that a person who "pays a lender $1000 a year for car payments for a working life (about forty years), and the lender in turn lends out your payment to another borrower at 12.5% interest, the lender will have accumulated $1,000,000 from your mere $40,000 of car payments. That works out to be an average annual return of 2,400%." This percentage is arrived at by dividing $960,000 interest earned by the forty years, which gives $24,000 as the average interest earned on the $1000 payment each year.

A Christian family must decide whether their auto is going to serve as transportation or as a status symbol. Since a new car depreciates roughly one-third in value for each of the first three years, it is impossible to justify the purchase of a new car for transportation. An ad for Volvo cars once showed a man putting a "for sale" sign in the window of his old car. The ad read, "You don't buy a new car. The bank buys a new car. By the time you buy your car back from the bank, it's old!" The only thing the buyer receives for the thousands of dollars in depreciation the first year is the status of owning a new car. Today new cars are usually financed on a forty-eight- to sixty-month basis while the trade-in cycle is from forty-two to forty-eight months. When a new car is purchased to replace the old one, the unpaid balance of the old loan is added to the new loan. Christian stewardship demands this money be more wisely used as savings, investments, or as a contribution to the Lord's work.

Some years ago people justified buying a new car by saying they were getting rid of problems or avoiding prospective problems. New cars were supposed to be, and usually were, relatively free from problems for many thousands of miles. However, in recent years the quality control exercised in the manufacture of new cars has been so poor that many of them arrive from the factory with mechanical or body defects.

Since the arrival of Japanese cars in large numbers, the American manufacturers have made great improvement in quality control. However, each year in the J. D. Powers ratings of customer satisfaction most of the top ten are foreign cars, with only one or two American cars achieving that distinction. A friend of the author's purchased one of these top-ranked American cars only to have so many troubles with the transmission he had to trade it in for another car.

If the couple wants a car for dependable transportation rather than a status symbol, the size of the family and the daily use of the car are the major factors in making this choice. If the car is to be used for long trips, consideration should be given to an intermediate or full-sized car. Many families find that a subcompact or compact model is adequate when most of the driving is for relatively short distances.

The buyer should read and become informed on how to buy a good used car. The December issue of *Buying Guide of Consumer Reports* and the April issue of each year feature excellent articles on the subject. The April issue is devoted to cars and lists the frequency of repair record of various makes. They recommend the models that make good used car buys and which models to avoid. Some models develop a reputation for certain mechanical troubles, particularly when a new model is introduced; it is wise not to buy one of them.

One should follow some basic principles in seeking to get the best used-car buy. One is that the mileage the car has been driven is more important than its age. As far as basic transportation is concerned, a three-year-old car with eighty thousand miles does not have as many miles of transportation left as a five-year-old car with thirty-five thousand miles. The latter is a much better bargain than the former, assuming of course that both have equally good bodies and interiors.

It is also wise to shop for a low-mileage car at the dealers of prestige cars such as Cadillac,

Oldsmobile, Lincoln, or Chrysler. Here the informed buyer can take advantage of social status, for many people who drive more expensive autos may drive lower priced cars as a second car. In order to keep up with their neighbors they need to trade their cars in even though they do not have many miles on them. Thus, the prospects of finding a Ford or a Chevrolet with low mileage is better at the prestige dealers. The individual who trades a Ford or a Chevrolet in to a dealer of that make is more likely to own only one car that will be driven by all members of the family and is likely to have high mileage.

It is also wise to buy only from a franchised dealer. Although there are exceptions, franchised dealers will sell their less desirable used cars to independent dealers either directly or through a dealer's auction. Ordinarily the best used cars are kept by the franchised dealers.

In some areas where there are factories owned by auto manufacturers, the executives are allowed to buy cars at reduced prices each year. The executives then sell them at the end of a model year. Many times it is possible to buy such a late-model car on which some depreciation has already taken place. Since a dealer allows only the wholesale price (usually one thousand dollars to fifteen hundred dollars less than retail price) to the person trading in a car, many individuals try to sell their cars privately and hope to realize more for their car than the dealer allows. This is a good way to buy a car, particularly where the seller bought the car new. Many times a service record may be available, and some cars carry a guarantee that is transferable. There is a charge connected with this transfer and the buyer must decide if the benefits promised are worth the one hundred dollars to two hundred dollars it costs to transfer the warranty.

Some rental-car companies have retail divisions to sell their cars when they are through renting them. These cars are usually replaced every six months. They are well maintained and serviced regularly. Since they have been used commercially, they are sold at a good discount. Even though they are purchased at a discount, these late models will continue to depreciate approximately 25 percent for the next two years.

If a person is knowledgeable about cars, or has a friend who is, then a good buy may be a repossessed car. When a person fails to make payments on a car, the finance company can repossess it and sell it for the balance due plus the expenses incurred in reselling it. Most large cities have auto auctions that sponsor the sale of repossessed autos. About one out of every one hundred cars financed are repossessed, so a large number are sold this way. The buyer or his knowledgeable friend must know how to evaluate a used car in order to buy in this manner. The cars available include nearly new cars with just a few thousand miles and range downward to clunkers. Since these cars are sold without a guarantee, they sell for much less than a dealer charges. If a person can judge used cars, one may be purchased reasonably at such an auction.

One should follow some basic principles in seeking to get the best used-car buy.

The question may be asked, "Why doesn't the person whose car is going to be repossessed sell it, pay off the loan, and save the credit rating?" Unfortunately, a car depreciates faster than it can be paid off, so the loan is nearly always more than the car is worth. The person losing the car is in financial trouble anyway and cannot afford to pay the amount owed the loan company after the car is sold. The only recourse is to allow the loan company to repossess it. The difference will still be owed, but as the old saying goes, "You can't get blood out of a turnip," so the finance company has to take a loss.

A disadvantage to buying a new car is that it depreciates rapidly. The insurance coverage is insufficient to replace a new car in the event it is totaled in an accident. The owner still owes the difference between the balance of the loan and what the insurance pays. This must be paid before another car can be financed. Some companies are now offering insurance to cover this difference. This is another reason to buy a two- or three-year-old car rather than a new one.

Almost any used car being bought to replace an older model will cost thousands of dollars more. In order to protect that investment, the car should be taken to a competent mechanic for an inspection. If minor difficulties are found, the dealer will usually make the repairs. If items requiring major repairs are discovered, then it is wise not to purchase the car. Rosefsky (1983, 150) concludes, "The cost of an inspection can be a very inexpensive way of finding out whether you're getting a good deal or a bad deal. The bad deal will end up costing you many times what the inspection will cost."

> **It is not necessary to get a loan through the dealer, and financing will probably be cheaper somewhere else.**

Some garages now have diagnostic machines that give a computerized read-out of the mechanical condition of the motor. It is worth paying fifty to one hundred dollars for such a diagnosis since thousands of hard-earned dollars are at stake. Due to the high cost of labor and parts, repairs that used to cost fifty to one hundred dollars can now run into hundreds of dollars, and major engine repairs may cost thousands of dollars. One person had a four-cylinder engine replaced in a Japanese car and the bill came to twenty-five hundred dollars! However, it is better to plan on an occasional repair bill on a good used car than to be

burdened with large monthly payments on a new car that does not match the monthly depreciation.

Most dealers now offer some kind of extended repair warranty. It is usually good for a certain number of miles or months. Since the warranty covers expensive repairs, the insurance itself becomes costly. The buyer must determine if the cost of potential repairs is worth the insurance. If one does buy the warranty, it must be from a reputable company (check with the Better Business Bureau) and one that is honored nationwide. It is discouraging to need coverage for a repair only to discover the insurance company is bankrupt. This has occurred.

Another principle in buying any used car is to plan to spend at least five hundred dollars for a tune-up and minor repairs. If tires are needed, this amount will need to be increased. Tires can be bought reasonably if the buyer looks for sales on factory-blemished tires, tires with discontinued tread designs, or new car take-offs. Some new car buyers like a particular brand of tire so much that when they buy a new car, they go to a tire dealer and buy a set of the brand they like. The tire dealer then sells the take-offs at a discount of up to 50 percent. These types of tires are not always available so it pays to begin shopping for them a month or two before the actual need.

If a person cannot pay cash for a car, one must secure a loan and must shop for credit to find the lowest net interest cost. The dealer often tries to influence the buyer to secure a loan from the auto manufacturer's loan company, but it is not necessary to get a loan through the dealer, and financing will probably be cheaper somewhere else. The usual sources of credit such as a credit union or bank should be explored, and the loan secured from the institution with the lowest net interest cost. Burkett (1992, 140) suggests buying a car that can be paid off in "two years or less and shop for a simple-interest loan. Stay away from add-on interest loans because they carry a front-end interest penalty if you want to accelerate the payments."

Large dealerships employ full-time people to sell financing and insurance. They use the same hard-sell tactics of the car salesmen. One of the most profitable items they sell is credit life insurance, a policy that pays off the balance of the loan if the borrower dies. They charge a high premium for this insurance. It is a simple decreasing term insurance policy (payoff decreases with each payment made by the borrower). This same type of policy can be bought from a regular life insurance company for a fraction of the amount charged by the dealership. Never buy credit life—go to an insurance agent and purchase a term policy to cover the loan.

When the car is purchased, it must be insured. Most states require the auto owner to carry personal liability and property damage liability. This will usually be a minimum figure but higher coverage such as fifty to one hundred thousand dollars costs only a few dollars more per year and is recommended. The lending institution will require the auto purchaser to carry protection against collision. This is usually a deductible policy whereby the owner pays the first one hundred to five hundred dollars and the insurance company the remainder of the damage bill. A higher deductible is recommended. When a car gets old and its value decreases, collision insurance can be dropped. The lending institution also requires comprehensive coverage, which takes care of loss by fire, theft, or vandalism. This is not expensive and should be continued after the loan is paid off.

Optional coverages include medical payments, which are inexpensive and worthwhile in view of the high cost of medical services. Some states that do not require all auto owners to have insurance give the buyer of insurance the option to take out coverage for the uninsured motorist. If the policyholder has a claim against an uninsured motorist for personal injury, the policyholder's own insurance company reimburses him for his loss. When the coverages needed have been determined, the buyer must shop to get the best rate, as rates may vary as much as several hundred dollars between different companies for the same coverage. A car dealer may try to sell the buyer insurance, or the company making the loan may also sell insurance, but the buyer is under no obligation to buy either. He should contact various companies and get the best price for the coverage he needs. *Consumer Reports* rates auto insurance companies occasionally, so it is worthwhile to check their ratings.

No-fault auto insurance, whereby each motorist involved in an accident would be paid by his own insurance company for any loss up to a specified amount, is becoming more common. Each state that has enacted no-fault auto insurance legislation has its own peculiar regulations, so you should become familiar with the provisions in your state.

Just as a person seeks out a good doctor and lawyer when he moves into a community, he should also look for a good, honest mechanic. These people are discovered by asking friends and associates who they use to perform these services for them. Once a good mechanic who can be trusted is discovered, he or she should be given your business whenever possible, for such individuals need to be encouraged. A dependable mechanic is fairly accurate in diagnosing problems and stands behind any work done. However, do not expect perfection, for an auto is a complicated piece of equipment, and at times it is difficult for even the best mechanic to pinpoint the source of some problems.

An ordinary person formerly could do much of the routine maintenance on an auto. However, due to the high technology involved in the modern auto, there is little that can be done. It is still possible to change the oil and filter on most cars, and to wash and wax the exterior, but everything else should be done by a trained mechanic with the equipment required to work on today's autos. Since little can be saved by do-it-yourself maintenance, it is all the more important to save on depreciation, which is the highest cost item in owning a car.

Leading financial counselors advocate buying used cars rather than new ones. Rosefsky (1983, 149–50), author of the most widely used textbook in personal finance, admonishes that you should "clearly distinguish between your automotive needs and your automotive desires. The difference between the two can cost you thousands of dollars with little to show for that money but some chrome, vinyl, and extra things that can go wrong with the car." He observes that Americans have been conditioned to consider the auto a status symbol that reflects "an individual's power, prestige, sex appeal and success." He emphasizes, "A used car in *good mechanical condition* [italics added] can provide you with decent transportation for many years and many thousands of miles at a much lower cost than a similar new model."

Leading financial counselors advocate buying used cars instead of new ones.

Two of the leading Christian counselors and writers in the area of finances are Ron Blue and Larry Burkett. Both advocate purchasing used cars for transportation rather than status. Burkett (1987, 43) expresses the view that "new cars are very expensive. As soon as you drive it off the lot, you have a *used car* with a *new car* mortgage on it. I recommend to the majority of couples I counsel that they purchase a good used car (between two and three years old)."

Blue (1986, 116–17) a certified public accountant, relates that he had an Oldsmobile with 150,000 miles on it. He considered buying a new car but decided to see just what car was the most economical to buy and maintain. He spent many hours considering all the factors involved in owning a car. He decided to keep the Oldsmobile. He concludes, "Even though the cost of repairs was substantial, and the gas mileage incredibly low, they did not offset the much higher costs related to a new car. . . . The cheapest car anyone can ever own is always the car *they presently own,* unless it is sold and the proceeds reinvested in a lower priced car; and the longer a car is driven, the cheaper it becomes to operate." For those who are satisfied with good, safe, dependable transportation rather than a status symbol, a used car is not a burden but a blessing, allowing the family to have more surplus to invest and to give more to God's work.

The Steward and Insurance

Insurance for the home and auto have been discussed in the preceding pages, but there are other types of insurance the family should have. Most families in the United States today are covered by Social Security. This government program provides for benefits in case the covered worker is totally disabled for twelve months or longer, for benefits to the widow and children on the death of the worker, income and Medicare benefits for the worker and spouse upon retirement, and a small sum to aid with burial expenses. The benefits depend on the length of time the worker has been covered and the amount of taxes paid into the Social Security fund. Taxes and benefits are relatively small and are designed to be supplemented by the worker with additional insurance or income. Any Social Security office has pamphlets available explaining the various coverages.

Two areas the family must provide for are hospital and physician fees, for sickness or a disabling accident. Many companies provide group plans for hospitalization and physician fees. This can be supplemented by a major medical policy that usually has a deductible amount and pays for charges not covered by a hospitalization or physicians' plan. Hospitalization plans are expensive and the family may be tempted not to carry a policy, but with the rapid increase in the cost of medical care, it would be most unwise not to be covered.

Some companies have employee coverage that pays benefits when a person is disabled by accident or sickness, but most people are not covered. The coverage is not expensive and can be bought from private insurance companies. The policy usually has a waiting period of seven or fourteen days before benefits begin, and then pays so much per day until the person is able to return to work. The breadwinner should not be without sickness and accident coverage.

The family should also be protected by life insurance on the breadwinner, with enough on the wife and children to pay for burial expenses. If the wife is employed, then her income should also be protected by insurance. There are four basic types of life insurance policies, with many variations of each type. The first is term life insurance, which is pure protection. A policy is bought for a specific number of years or term and expires when the time limit of the policy is reached. Auto and home insurance policies are term insurance. A variation of this is decreasing term or reducing term whereby a policy is taken out for a term of several years but the coverage decreases each year, although the premium remains the same. This form is commonly used to insure a mortgage. Term life insurance is the cheapest form since the policyholder is buying only protection and not using his life insurance as a vehicle for savings.

The second major form is called ordinary or whole life insurance, which is a combination of decreasing term insurance and a savings plan. As the value of the life insurance decreases each year, the insurance company uses the policyholder's savings to make up the difference between the term insurance and the face amount of the policy. For example, John Doe has a $10,000 policy with a cash value of $3,780 after paying the policy for twenty years. If John Doe were to die, his widow would not receive the face amount plus the cash value or $13,780. She would receive $10,000, which would be his savings of $3,780 plus the term insurance of $6,220. The longer John Doe lives the less insurance he has and the more savings he has. If he lived to be one hundred years old. the cash value would probably equal the amount of the policy. This is the type of policy most frequently sold because the salesman gets more commission for selling this kind.

The growth of term insurance with the premium savings over whole life invested in mutual funds, forced the life insurance companies to develop new policies. Blue (1986, 97) comments, "none of these products are truly investments; they are merely forced savings plans with front-end costs." One new policy, universal life, combines term insurance with investment opportunities for the savings feature. Universal life now includes many different forms, including variable life, but it provides a stated amount of protection with various forms of investments. It has other fea-

tures such as permitting the client to raise or lower the amount of protection. It also allows the policyholder to increase savings contributions, which are tax sheltered. One of the best features is that the insurance company gives the beneficiary the savings accumulated in the policy rather than taking it from the widows and orphans as occurs under simple whole life policies. Now a beneficiary of a $10,000 variable life policy with a cash value or savings of $3,780 will receive a total of $13,780 rather than the $6,220 received from a whole life policy. However, the universal life policy is still too expensive for a young family because the emphasis is on savings rather than pure protection.

> *The universal life policy is still too expensive for a young family because the emphasis is on savings rather than pure protection.*

Endowment policies place the emphasis on savings rather than protection and are therefore more costly than term or ordinary life. They are usually written for a given number of years, such as twenty or thirty. This type was once widely sold to help provide money for college expenses. When a child was born, the salesman would sell a policy on the child's life. The difficulty here was that if the breadwinner died there was no one to pay the premium for the child. Any insurance for such a purpose must be on the breadwinner!

A fourth type of policy sold today is the annuity. It is designed to provide income to a person over an agreed-upon amount of time.

The policy may be paid for over a period of years or it may be purchased with one lump sum. This type of policy is often used to supplement retirement income. A straight-life annuity pays each month until the purchaser dies. If he dies within one month, that is all the insurance company pays. An annuity with installments provides payments for a specific time period, such as ten or twenty years. If the purchaser dies before the period expires, a beneficiary receives the remaining payments.

Many Christian organizations offer annuities to their constituents. The principal of the gift provides income for the person while living, and on death it becomes a gift to the institution. Some of the old, well established Christian organizations can boast of having never missed a monthly annuity payment, which is most commendable.

Writers in the field of family-life education have for years recommended that young families buy life insurance for protection only, and to invest their savings in other areas that provide for a good return and also serve as a hedge against inflation. Savings in a whole life insurance policy do not have such a hedge and are eroded by inflation.

> *Writers in the field of family-life education have for years recommended that young families buy life insurance for protection only, and to invest their savings.*

Consumer Reports periodically carries special articles on life insurance designed primarily for those who buy insurance for the first time or for those who need to acquire additional coverage. These articles discuss such subjects as "estimating how much coverage you need," how to "decide what type of insurance you want," how to "shop for the best price." They also list and rate major term and cash value policies and give illustrations of the cost at different ages by various companies.

Most workers today are covered by Social Security insurance whose benefits are a major factor to be considered in determining the life insurance needs of a young family. A family can receive up to two hundred thousand dollars in benefits from Social Security. It provides for disability payments for total disability. Survivor benefits are paid to the widow and children until the youngest child reaches age eighteen. The widow may begin receiving benefits at age sixty if she chooses. The benefits are calculated on the basis of the number of years worked and the amount of taxes paid.

An important question for the young family is, "How much insurance is needed to provide for the family, for college education for the children, for the widow during the 'black-out' period (she receives no Social Security funds after the youngest child is eighteen until she is sixty years old), and for supplemental retirement income?" Different answers are given by different financial advisors. Blue (1986, 96–97) recommends a young family needs coverage equalling ten times the annual income. If the income is thirty thousand dollars per year, then three hundred thousand dollars would be needed. Lowe (1990, 210) indicates the traditional rule of thumb has been five times the annual income. She realizes this will be insufficient today. Since the family will need 60 percent to 75 percent of the husband's salary to maintain the standard of living, she suggests that the income and expenses of the survivors be tabulated and sufficient insurance be secured to cover the decrease in income. Social Security benefits will make up part of the income.

Term insurance is reasonable for young people to buy. Two hundred thousand dollars can be purchased by a thirty-year-old male for as little as $220 annually. If the purchaser of such a policy dies, the money received invested at 10 percent will yield $20,000 income per year with no loss of principal. A young family could never afford this kind of coverage with a whole or universal life policy. The argument is made that term insurance becomes more costly as the policyholder ages. This is true, but as a person ages the need for protection decreases as assets increase and family needs decrease. Policies should be purchased in $50,000 units, be renewable *without medical examination,* and be convertible to whole life policies. Five- or ten-year renewable policies make a flexible plan as units may be dropped when the need for coverage decreases. If a person buys a $200,000 policy, he cannot drop just part of it—the entire policy must be given up.

One area of Christian stewardship that has not been fully utilized is the naming of a Christian institution as beneficiary of a life insurance policy. Under many circumstances, premiums for such a policy are deductible from federal income tax. If a term policy were used, a sizeable amount of insurance could be purchased for a modest premium, and the Christian steward will be a real benefactor to the chosen institution.

There are hundreds of insurance companies and hundreds of different policies. These are confusing to the young family so becoming an informed insurance consumer is most important. Diligent research in the library will provide a wealth of information. In case of the breadwinner's death, adequate protection for all the needs of the family can be bought reasonably if renewable term is purchased. Insurance salesmen can present many reasons for buying other types of policies containing a savings feature, but these should never be bought until provision is made for the needs of the family.

It is wise for the family to keep their protection and savings separate. An insurance company is a savings bank. However, it is *radically different* from an ordinary savings bank. The insurance bank takes *all your deposits* or premiums paid for the first two years (to pay the agent's commission). They charge you *each time you make a deposit*—your annual premium (agents continue to get a commission on the policy). The insurance company keeps the earnings on your savings. If you want to use your savings, you must take a loan, for which they *will charge you interest.* If you withdraw your savings (take out the cash value), the company *will cancel your protection* (your policy) for which you have paid a number of years. When the policyholder dies, the company *will keep the savings,* as it is part of the death benefit of the policy and is not an addition to the face amount (Van Caspel 1975, 206). *No one* would save money in an ordinary bank under similar terms, but the insurance companies have convinced millions of whole life policyholders that their bank is the best place to save money. In 1987 "ordinary life insurance totaled $3.3 billion representing fifty-four percent of all life insurance" (Rukeyser 1988, 334). When these policyholders die, most of these billions of dollars will go to the insurance companies rather than to the beneficiaries.

> *Insurance policies should be purchased in $50,000 units, be renewable without medical examination, and be convertible to whole life policies.*

The insurance "banks" lack the federal insurance that guarantees the savings in ordinary banks up to one hundred thousand dollars. Until the 1980s, the large insurance companies were considered the strongest financial institutions. However, to compete in the financial world of that period, some made questionable investments in junk bonds or in commercial loans. Both of these markets collapsed at the end of the decade. "From 1988 to 1991, fifty-two insurance companies failed leaving millions in unpaid claims." Most of these were smaller companies but the eighteenth largest,

Mutual Benefit of New Jersey, also failed (Burkett 1991, 133). Consequently, before buying a policy, the issuing company should be thoroughly investigated. Several firms such as A. M. Best, Duff and Phelps, Inc., Moody's Investors Service, Inc., and Standard and Poor's Corporation rate insurance companies (Burkett 1992, 253). *Consumer Reports* also rates them periodically.

The young family must buy term insurance and invest the difference where it will earn the greatest interest. Burkett (1992, 138) points out that a young couple "in their twenties can save an average of $15,000 in premiums before the age of forty by buying term rather than cash value (whole life) insurance. That money, if invested wisely, will grow to nearly $200,000 by age 65." If the Christian family follows a well-defined financial plan as outlined in books by Larry Burkett and Ron Blue, the time will come when savings and assets will be sufficient to protect the family and insurance may not be needed.

> *The young family must buy term insurance and invest the difference where it will earn the greatest interest.*

The Steward and Investments

The Lord Jesus taught that God expects an increase whether it is in the spiritual realm (parable of the sower, Matt. 13:1–23), or in the material realm (parable of the talents, Matt. 25:14–30). He asks the question in the parable of the unjust steward, "And if ye have not been faithful in that which is another man's, who shall give you that which is your own?" (Luke 16:12). The Christian steward is under divine obligation and has a divine purpose in saving money and investing it, that is, he wants to see it increase in order to bring glory to God.

As indicated earlier, at least 10 percent of the family's disposable income should be saved. A savings account is basic to financial security. The money should be put in a bank, credit union, or savings and loan association where it will earn the most interest and be readily available if needed. The financial institution should be covered by a federal insurance program so that the saver's account is insured up to $100,000. The savings account provides a fund for emergencies, for children's education, special family goals, and a supplement to retirement income. Few people realize how money doubles at compound interest, and the higher the interest rate, the sooner it doubles. At 4 percent it doubles in eighteen years; at 5 percent in fourteen years; at 6 percent in twelve years; at 7 percent it doubles in ten years. In like manner it is amazing how quickly a sum saved regularly each month grows to a sizeable sum. If a family were to save in a savings and loan association 10 percent of $500 income or $50 per month at 5 percent compounded quarterly, it would amount to $3,412.65 in only five years. In ten years it would amount to $7,787.80; in twenty years it would total $20,507.97.

If a couple accepts the suggestion given previously and saves the wife's entire income for two or three years, they will have a fund that can undergird their complete marriage cycle. Ten thousand dollars in ten years will grow to $16,436.19 and to $27,014.85 in twenty years at 5 percent interest compounded quarterly. With such a nest egg and a regular savings plan the family will be able to give more to the Lord.

After the savings account reaches an amount that equals at least six times the family's total monthly income, they should begin to invest their savings in a manner that brings a higher return. Before investing any funds, the Christian steward needs to be informed. *Investing for the Future* by Larry Burkett or *The Super Saver* by Janet Lowe are a good introduction to the field of investments. The library will have books on different forms of investing.

Many Christian institutions offer bonds that pay higher interest rates than a bank pays on savings accounts. If money is invested in such bonds, it will provide a good profit and also aid the cause of Christ. In reference to this type of bonds, Burkett (1992, 196) believes *"that loans made to Christians (and Christian organizations such as a church) should be made without interest."* As prooftexts he lists Leviticus 25:35–37, Deuteronomy 23:19–20, Nehemiah 5:7–10, and Psalm 15:5. He also indicates that church bonds are risky, and should be bought only with funds a person can afford to lose. Some government and high-grade corporate bonds also pay a high rate of interest. Bonds are usually a safe investment, but they do not have any hedge against inflation.

Some individuals may wish to purchase stocks on the American or New York exchanges. Any library has numerous books explaining techniques of buying and selling stocks. For a small sum one may buy a paperback, *How to Buy Stocks* by Louis Engel. A cardinal rule of stock investing is that the family have a good savings account before investing in stocks. Money cannot be lost on the stock market unless a company goes bankrupt (which seldom happens to blue-chip companies), for if a stock is down in price, it also will probably go up. People lose money only when they are forced by some financial emergency to sell while the market is down. If a family has a fund for emergencies, it will never have to sell its stock at a loss, and it cannot lose if it holds *good stock*. Home computers can now be linked to on-line brokers. Software is available that allows the individual to place orders after business hours. It also is possible to do bookkeeping for the transactions (Klein 1987, 342–43).

A fairly recent development that can greatly affect the finances of a family is the availability of individual retirement accounts (IRAs). An employed husband and wife can invest up to $4000 in IRAs ($2250 if the wife is not working), and under certain conditions they do not have to pay federal income tax on this amount. The money can be deposited anytime between January 1 and the April 15 tax-filing deadline in the next year. The earlier the funds are deposited, the more interest will be earned over a period of years. These funds compound tax free until they are withdrawn, preferably at retirement. Merely saving $9.60 per week amounts to $500 a year, which compounded for thirty years will make a nest egg for retirement. If funds are withdrawn before 59 1/2 years of age, there is a 10 percent penalty for early withdrawal. An IRA can be opened at any bank, savings and loan, mutual fund, insurance company, or brokerage house. There is usually a small start-up fee and also an annual maintenance fee. A person may have several accounts to diversify his investments, but the fees will hinder the growth of the accounts. Since an IRA is a long-term investment, a mutual fund is an excellent avenue to achieve growth.

> *A fairly recent development that can greatly affect the finances of a family is the availability of individual retirement accounts (IRAs).*

Investing surplus savings funds in a good mutual fund has several advantages. The fund is diversified in its holdings, which gives it opportunity to share the gains of different stocks. The fund has professional management, who has greater know-how than the average small investor does. Most mutual funds have done well over a period of years. It must be remembered that a mutual-fund investment is a long-term investment—for at least five years and preferably ten years or longer. The fund also enables the small investor to share in the splits and dividend distributions of more stocks than he could invest in alone. There is less paperwork and record keeping in owning mutual fund shares than in stock ownership. "Mutual fund shares are owned by about one in every four U.S. households" (*Forbes*, 31 August 1992).

Most mutual funds have done well over a period of years.

There are more than three thousand funds, some of which have specific objectives, such as growth funds, income funds, and balanced funds (growth and income). Some charge commissions to sell the buyer shares (load funds), others do not (no-load funds). The investor must read and be informed about mutual funds. Public libraries and brokers' offices have books that list the past performance of all mutual funds. Two of the best known are *Johnson's Investment Company Charts* and Arthur Wisenberger's *Investment Companies.* The past performance is a good indicator of the value of a fund but it is not infallible! After doing research and deciding the family's objectives, consult a broker in a brokerage firm for additional information. Only then should one invest in a fund. However, a good fund can be a good investment. Some of the top funds have impressive records. Twentieth Century Select Fund is up 2,113 percent over fifteen years; $10,000 invested in this fund would have grown to $220,434. The Linden Fund is up 1,617 percent, and $10,000 in fifteen years would have amounted to $161,956 (*Mutual Fund Investor,* November 1991, 2). Past performance is no guarantee of future results, but these funds, and many others, have performed very well over a long period.

The Christian family can be as wise as "the children of this world" and use and increase their money for the cause of Christ. It takes dedication, information, and self-discipline, but Christians can manage money well and increase the number of faithful stewards able and willing to help the cause of Christ at home and abroad. Pierson (Petersen 1971, 347) wrote, "what I thus surrender for the sake of others comes back to me in larger blessing. It is like the moisture which the spring gives out in streams and evaporation, returning in showers to supply the very channels which filled the spring itself. 'It is more blessed to give than to receive.'"

Study Questions

1. What are the advantages and liabilities of buying a mobile home?
2. When is it advantageous to rent rather than to buy a home?
3. Larry Burkett believes the best investment a family can make is to buy a home. Why is it such a good investment?
4. Define the term *deferred gratification.* How can this be practiced in relation to home ownership?
5. List the advantages and disadvantages of buying a new home; of buying a used home.
6. Why should a young family buy a used car? What factors should be considered in purchasing one?
7. Explain the different types of insurance coverage needed by the average family.
8. How does the insurance "bank" differ from a regular bank? Why do people save with insurance companies?
9. If you were an insurance agent, what type of life insurance policy, and in what amount, would you recommend for a husband, wife, and two preteen children? The family income is thirty thousand dollars annually.
10. Why are mutual funds a popular form of investments? How long should money be kept in a mutual fund?

Suggested Readings

Burkett, L. 1992. *Investing for the future.* Wheaton: Victor. Investing according to the principles contained in the Bible is the thesis of this volume. Burkett explains the best and worst investments and gives instruction on how to evaluate investments.

Jones, C. P. 1991. *Investments, analysis and management.* 3d ed. New York: Wiley. Designed as a textbook on investments, the book goes into detail about most aspects of investing. Very helpful for those not familiar with investments.

Klein, R., ed. 1987. *The money book of money: Your personal financial planner.* Boston: Little, Brown. A comprehensive volume covering nearly every item in a family financial plan. It has excellent suggestions in the areas of buying homes, cars, and insurance. It also contains "the first and last word on investing."

Lowe, J. 1990. *The super saver: Fundamental strategies for building wealth.* Chicago: Longman Financial Services. Saving money used to be a virtue of American people, but the author claims that this is no longer a fact. Her purpose in writing is to encourage the habit of saving money and to cite some of the financial vehicles available for saving money.

Rosefsky, R. S. 1983. *Personal finance.* 2d ed. New York: Wiley. This volume was written as a textbook for a course in personal finance. It covers the areas most important and has excellent advice on autos, homes, insurance, and investments. A valuable book for young families.

Tucker, J. F. 1988. *Managing your own money: A financial guide for the average wage earner.* New York: Dembner. The author covers the main areas of financial concern for the average person. He has a good explanation of stocks, bonds, and government securities.

Weiss, M. D. 1989. *How to survive the money panic: Risk-free investing in a high-risk environment.* Westport, Conn.: T. J. Holt and Co.. The author is among those who feel the huge burden of debt in America will lead to a collapse of the financial markets. He believes the safest investment is in Treasury bills. The interest earned is the only money used for other investments. Read with caution.

Williams, G. 1981. *Financial survival in the age of new money.* New York: Simon and Schuster. An interesting treatise on the history and use of money. It explains the function of government in the maintenance and expansion of the money supply. Explanations and warnings are given concerning different types of investments.

Wollack, R. G. 1985. *The financial desk book.* Emeryville, Calif.: Consolidated Capital Communications Group. A reference book designed as a tool to be used by investors and financial planners. A wealth of information on a wide variety of financial subjects. It includes charts and graphs. The articles concerning taxes are outdated.

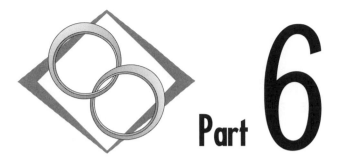

Part 6

Fragmented Families

The Single Life

But every man hath his proper gift of God . . .

—1 Corinthians 7:7

The Single Life and the Will of God

A large number of young people today are delaying marriage until their late twenties or early thirties. This is a departure from a few decades ago when people were in their early twenties on their first marriage. This is due partly to a change in the attitude of society toward early marriage. In years past, there was extreme pressure put on young people to get married. Havemann and Lehtinen (1990, 294) observe that "almost everybody got married, usually as quickly as possible. . . . The pressure to marry was especially strong on women." It is now more acceptable to remain single. The authors estimate that "about thirteen percent of women will never marry compared to about four percent in the past. For men the figure is ten percent, up from about three percent in the past."

The high divorce rate also accounts for a large segment of the single population. Sincere Christians who do not believe in divorce are often forced into this situation by mates who no longer love them. A small number are single because they have lost a mate through death. There are always some young people who, for various reasons, decide not to get married. Unfortunately, there are also a large number of single people who decide to live together without marriage (cohabitation).

The term *singles* includes at least four categories: the never married, the widowed, the divorced, and separated individuals (Anthony and Koons 1991, 166). In this chapter, the term will apply primarily to the never married, although some references will be made to the widowed or divorced.

Singles compose a large group of the population. Many features of the single lifestyle are contrary to Christian principles and are not shared by believers. However, Christian singles are now recognized by churches as a distinct group, and churches are attempting to effectively minister to their needs.

> *Christian singles are now recognized by churches as a distinct group, and churches are attempting to effectively minister to their needs.*

God said, "It is not good that the man should be alone: I will make a help meet [fit] for him" (Gen. 2:18). Man's loneliness resulted in the creation of Eve as a companion for Adam and in the institution of marriage. Consequently, it is ordinarily the will of God that young people should marry and establish Christian homes and families. However, there are cases when it is not the will of God for some to marry.

When our Lord commented on the beginning of marriage in Genesis (Matt. 19), his disciples were amazed that he would take such a firm stand against divorce, and they said to him, "If the case of the man be so with his wife, it is not good to marry." The Lord Jesus replied, "All men cannot receive this saying, save they to whom it is given. For there are some eunuchs [born incapable of marriage] which were so born from their mother's womb; and there are some eunuchs, which were made eunuchs by men; and there be eunuchs which make themselves eunuchs for the kingdom of heaven's sake. He that is able to receive it, let him receive it" (Matt. 19:10–12). The Lord teaches here that some people, in order to do the will of God, choose not to marry. Taylor (1984, 18) emphasizes, "I sincerely believe that there is a place for the unmarried in the perfect will of God, a calling to the single life, and that God has cho-

sen men and women to fill it." The will of God for their lives should be the major concern of every Christian young person. They have been redeemed by the blood of Christ for this one purpose. The decision to marry is one of the most important decisions that a person ever makes, so this decision must be made according to the will of God.

If it is God's will for the person to remain unmarried, and if this is accepted as the will of God, the individual experiences far more blessing and happiness than is possible in a marriage contrary to his will. Many young people rebelled against God's will and married unsaved individuals just to be married. They have broken God's command, "Be not unequally yoked together with unbelievers. . . ." The happiness they expected was short-lived, and they regretted their rebellion a thousand times. They wish they had never married, but are now bound by marriage vows and children, and must remain in an unpleasant union.

Anthony and Koons (1991, 87) make the point that "being married is no more an insurance policy for happiness than singleness is a guarantee of frustration and unhappiness. Many married adults wish they could trade their marital status for the freedom of independent living." Jeremiah (1991, 35) reminds the reader that "there is something far worse than single loneliness and that is marital misery." Marriage is a wonderful and blessed experience but only in the will of God. He promises an abundant life (John 10:10) and a life of joy (John 15:11), but these are experienced only as a believer walks in obedience.

An increasing number of young people also face the single life due to a larger number of divorces among Christians. Many a Christian young person has married another Christian in the will of God, but the marriage has been dissolved when the spouse sued for divorce. If the innocent party accepts that marriage is for life and remarriage is forbidden by the Scriptures while the divorced spouse is living, then a single life is forced upon the individual by providential circumstances beyond his or her control. It is necessary to remember that the situation of these people is no different from that of the single person who, in the will of God, never marries.

Deaths due to illness or accidents also leave many young widows to face life alone. Their situation is different from the divorced person, for scripturally they are free to remarry. However, with the shortage of Christian men available as potential husbands, many young widows also face the problem of rearing children without a father.

Reasons Why Some People Do Not Marry

There are some practical explanations why it is the will of God for some not to marry. There are still some areas of Christian service to which an individual may feel called where it would be difficult to take a wife and children. Long (Coleman 1985, 108) reflects, "A single person can devote himself or herself entirely to the ministry without the concerns of family relationships; a married person has responsibility to spouse and children." For some mission fields, the person may think it best to meet the challenge alone and take the gospel to some remote and primitive area. Life in those fields is difficult, and the person may be able to do more and take more risks to reach people than if he had a wife and children. However, in most mission fields the wife and children are assets, for they provide the model of a Christian home for new converts.

Some persons remain unmarried because they become overly dependent upon parents or siblings and become too emotionally attached to break the home ties. They may date during their young adult years but rarely become seriously involved. If they do, they find a rationalization for breaking the relationship as the marriage date approaches.

Some parents expect a son or a daughter to care for them and make every effort to prevent the (adult) child from marrying. This is abnormal behavior, for usually parents encourage their children to begin families of their own. One couple in Portugal was engaged for thirty-five years until the man's mother died. As long as she lived, marriage was out of the question, for she would not give up her son and he knew it would not be wise to bring a wife in to live with his mother! Where there are unmarried siblings, it is quite customary for them to maintain the family household after the death of the parents.

> *An increasing number of young people face the single life due to a larger number of divorces among Christians.*

Some people do not marry because of poor personality development. They may be too shy to interact with the opposite sex. Some men can never get up the courage to ask a woman for a date, and if they do, they cannot carry on a conversation. Some young women are so shy and afraid of the opposite sex that they would not accept a date even if they were asked. This should not happen, for Christians have a divine obligation to develop socially so they can be witnesses and testify for their Savior. Occasionally a bashful person will ask or be asked for a date and rise to the situation. In such cases the persons ask for and receive from the Lord the ability to interact, and many times develop lovely, warm personalities even though they would not qualify to teach a Dale Carnegie course.

Marriage demands that individuals give much of themselves to satisfy the needs of the partner. The attitude of those unable to share themselves has been caught in the title of a book by Nancy Peterson (1981), *Our Lives for Ourselves*. When those who are too self-centered to meet the needs of others marry, they are unable to fulfill these personality needs and the marriage may fail because they cannot respond sufficiently to bring happiness and enjoyment to the union. They like to receive love but cannot give it. It is best for such persons not to marry, for they can be happy if they have only themselves to think of and care for.

They become the model for the stereotypes of the old maid and old bachelor who are set in their ways and who must have everything done their way.

It is unfair to intimate that all unmarried persons are misfits, for the majority are well-adjusted and reasonably happy in their single life. There are exceptions such as the sixty-year-old lady who is still anxiously seeking a husband. Most single men are single by choice, and most single women have had opportunities to marry but for various reasons chose to remain unmarried. Many have sweet, likeable personalities, are attractive physically, and are devoted Christians. They are unselfish and concerned for the needs of others, and are just the opposite of the stereotype of the old maid or old bachelor. They enjoy good interpersonal relationships in their employment and in their church. Their Christian testimony is evident wherever they go. They must not be judged as having inadequate personalities simply because they have chosen to remain single in the will of God.

> *It is unfair to intimate that all unmarried persons are misfits, for the majority are well-adjusted and reasonably happy in their single life.*

Some persons fear the responsibilities that accompany marriage. For a young man, it means he must assume the responsibility of caring for and providing for a wife and possibly children. In American culture, he may be expected to take on these added duties while he is still trying to complete his education. If he waits until he completes years of professional training, the best prospective mates near his age may have already been chosen.

For a woman, marriage means caring for a home and bearing and rearing children. Some women have heard old wives' tales about the dangers and difficulties of childbirth, and are so frightened by the prospect of having children that they avoid marriage altogether. If these kinds of people are not able or willing to take the responsibilities of marriage, it is better for them to remain single. One of the disadvantages of teenage marriages is that many of those involved are not old enough or mature enough to carry the responsibilities they so often are eager to assume, and the marriage fails.

The dysfunctional home life that some young people are reared in turns them against marriage. The parents are unhappy with each other and make life miserable for themselves and the children. The son or daughter resolves never to get married for fear of having the same disagreeable experience. It never occurs to them to examine their parents' relationship to find out what went wrong and produced such unhappiness. Was it poor mate choice? Does either parent have personality defects that would make it impossible for any mate to live with them? Is it a mixed marriage with built-in conflict? What happened to their Christian experience? Are they backslidden or hypocritical in their testimony? There are many reasons for such unhappiness and young people can avoid these problems if they are wise. They do not need to avoid marriage itself, but with a wise choice of partner and real effort to make a marriage work, they can expect to have the happiness that they see in well-adjusted married couples around them.

Many young women choose a career rather than marriage, for they do not feel adequate to combine the two. The women's liberation movement has influenced some young women to realize there are many more areas of employment open to them. Formerly, nursing, secretarial, teaching, and library work were the main occupations open to women. Today, young women are able to enter any field they choose, with higher education available to prepare them. Anthony and Koons (1991, 97) quote a survey by Bequarent in which he asked single women what their most important wish was. Interestingly, 45 percent wished for a good man to marry, but another 45 percent wanted a satisfying career. Although there still is a glass ceiling above which women do not rise, some women have achieved executive positions in many corporations. These, and the achievers in other occupations, are role models for young women.

It takes years of time and much money to prepare for a career, and many young women feel they must receive some benefit from all the effort spent in preparation. Since they are strongly motivated toward a career, they will turn down a proposal for marriage. This is particularly true when the career is a call to full-time Christian service, such as that in a foreign mission field. Many a young woman has rejected the opportunity to marry and has chosen to remain in the mission field in obedience to the call of God.

Many young people do not marry because they are in a geographic area where there is little opportunity to meet compatible mates. This is particularly true of Christian women who attend small churches where there are not enough Christian men. A young woman in such a church who desires to be obedient to the Lord, and who is not willing to date unbelievers will face the possibility of living a single life. The situation can be just as difficult in a large church where there are many young men and women to date. Females usually outnumber males, which makes the competition for husbands very stiff, so some young women will be unsuccessful.

Since propinquity (nearness) is one of the greatest factors in mate selection, young people need to be where the opposite sex is available. They might plan to attend a Christian college. Adams (1972, 63) writes, "'What? Go to college to find a husband? Isn't that an unworthy motive?' This motive should be high on the list of reasons for a woman to attend a Christian college." Christian camps and Bible conferences are excellent places to meet other Christian young people. Employment in Christian organizations where there are opportunities to meet people has brought many couples together. Denominational conferences and youth rallies also provide possibilities of meeting persons of the same faith. The important thing for young people to remember is to be where other young people are if they desire to find a life partner.

> *Many young women choose a career rather than marriage, for they do not feel adequate to combine the two.*

Adams (1972, 63) also has several suggestions for young women who desire a Christian husband. Several things can be done discreetly to help find one. He suggests the following: ask for the pastor's help, for in such a position he may know of men looking for a wife; ask Christian families for their help—they can invite an eligible man to their home to meet a young woman; ask married women who married later in life how they met their husbands.

A fairly recent development is the rise of Christian "lonely hearts" clubs, advertised in Christian periodicals, that attempt to match up potential mates through correspondence (Jeremiah 1991, 29). There is a great risk involved in such a proceeding, and consequently this avenue is not recommended. Newspapers in large cities now carry "personal ads" by which individuals attempt to locate a mate. These are not recommended either for they can also be dangerous. It may be true that some good marriages have resulted from such attempts, but the risks outweigh the advantages.

Some widowed persons are eligible to remarry but choose not to do so. Sometimes the marriage was so happy that the individuals cannot think of marrying someone else. They live with the memories of the years spent together and do not wish for anyone to intrude into them. Others have children and are afraid there may be difficulties between the children and the new spouse, so they remain unmarried.

Some widowed persons have had such an unhappy marriage that they resolve never to marry again. They do not desire to run the risk of repeating the unpleasant experience. They fail to see the many happy Christian marriages around them and to realize there were reasons for the unhappiness in their marriage that could have been avoided. Many widowed persons do remarry and are able to use the knowledge and experience of the previous marriage to help make the second more successful than the first.

Advantages of the Single Life

There are some advantages to being single, even though the adult culture largely revolves around married couples and families. Single persons are free to do the will of God as they see fit. They are not hampered in their desire nor decision making by the necessity of considering the wishes of a spouse and children. Paul said, "He that is unmarried careth for the things that belong to the Lord, how he may please the Lord: but he that is married careth for the things that are of the world, how he may please his wife" (1 Cor. 7:32–33). Single persons can move and change their place of service if they feel this is the will of God. The single person has more time to cultivate a life of devotion to the Lord. As Paul indicates, the unmarried are not burdened with the care of a spouse or children. Consequently, if they utilize their time well, there should be more time for prayer and Bible study. They do not have the problem of trying to find a quiet place in which to study and pray. Some singles may disagree, stating they not only spend time in a career, but also must do all the household duties. This may be true if compared with a childless couple, but when children are factored in, the single person will have more time.

The unmarried person also has more free time to serve the Lord than the married person. Many churches have been blessed by some faithful single women who were active in church life and could be depended upon to do jobs that married women were "too busy" to do. The tasks such people perform are too numerous to be detailed, but the fact that these persons are single and therefore without the demands of a family gives them time to serve the Lord in these capacities.

Often single persons are able to do things for friends and neighbors that others do not have time for. They perform acts of kindness that enhance the testimony of Christ and the local church, such as carrying in meals to sick persons or shut-ins. They stay with small children when a neighbor becomes ill and is taken to a hospital in a distant city. They have opportunities to serve others and to glorify Christ *because* they are single.

Although they are not as numerous in the local churches as single women, single men also have free time to make a real contribution to the Lord's work. They are able to do manual work around the church that women cannot do. They can be involved in ministries for children and youth. If they have musical talent, this can be shared with the body of believers. They can also have an effective ministry in a singles group within the church.

Another advantage single people enjoy is that they have free time for recreation and travel. Sometimes several unmarried individuals can travel together and share expenses: they may be able to see things the average family cannot.

Some mission boards are using short-term missionaries, and many single persons who are not called to full-time missionary service are able to fill critical needs in the areas of teaching and nursing. They are able to relocate more easily than a family, and the expenses of travel and maintenance are much less. Sometimes they are able to combine a return trip with an extensive sightseeing tour.

The single individual can enjoy a greater measure of financial security than married persons can. With the advent of equal pay for equal work, single persons can earn as much as a married person with a family. The extra money which would otherwise be spent on a spouse and children can be saved and invested. However, DeVault and Strong (1989, 155) indicate that if both spouses work, a couple or family earns more than does a single person.

The single person may achieve financial independence earlier, and provision can be made for an adequate income during retirement years.

The same principles of money management as discussed in chapters 13 and 14 should be followed by the single person except in the area of life insurance. If the person has no dependents, it is necessary only to carry enough insurance for burial expenses. The exception to this would be the desire to make a church or other Christian institution the beneficiary of a sizable policy (see chap. 14). Since single persons have no one responsible for them in times of illness and incapacity, it is necessary to have sufficient sickness and accident insurance to care for such contingencies. It is also important that single persons make a will as soon as they are of legal age. With good management, they may be able to do more for Christ in the area of Christian stewardship than the married couple can if only one spouse works.

Disadvantages of the Single Life

One of the great disadvantages of the single life is loneliness. There is a difference between being alone and loneliness according to McGinnis (L. Swindoll 1985, 27). To be alone is physical, that is, the person is in a situation where no one else is nearby. Loneliness is psychological. A person can have other people near by but still be lonely. McGinnis quotes Park as saying, "Loneliness is when you are forced to be alone against your will." He concludes, "Aloneness is positive. Loneliness is negative." For example, there are times when we need to be alone for a quiet time with the Lord or just to get away from people to enjoy solitude after a time interacting with people. Loneliness is not usually a problem if a young person continues to live at home with his parents. If a person lives alone, loneliness may be experienced.

Some people are happiest when they are by themselves. Most individuals are sociable, and although they may enjoy times of solitude, they are not happy to spend the majority of their free hours alone. The problem is compounded

if the single person moves to another state and must establish a new group of friends. Christians have an advantage, for they can locate a good local church and make friends and enjoy Christian fellowship. The church cannot take the place of loved ones, and excruciating loneliness may be experienced especially on holidays such as Thanksgiving and Christmas when the family is gathered back home.

This problem can be helped by singles gathering together to share a meal and fellowship on holidays. Witte (1982, 74–76) tells of one experience when she wanted very much to be with her family at Christmas but could not get a plane ticket. She had formerly worked for a Christian radio station in town, so she asked the station to announce that any singles who could not be with family to come to her home for the day. She prepared gifts for each one, plus a traditional meal. More than twenty people came and enjoyed the day. Some she knew, but others became newly found friends. Admittedly, this took courage, but it was rewarding for her and those who attended.

> *There is a difference between being alone and loneliness.*

One solution for loneliness is for two or more unwed persons of the same sex to establish a joint household. If these persons are compatible, a relationship can be formed on the basis of friendship, common interests, and love for the Lord Jesus, providing companionship and preventing loneliness. There is also an economic advantage, for the cost of maintaining the household is shared. If property is bought with joint ownership, the individuals need to have wills made that clearly define and protect the interests of all concerned. A clear agreement should be established as to the sharing of costs for maintenance. Such an arrangement can be beneficial financially over the years, but it can also be the means by which good friendships are broken if misunderstandings develop.

Psychologists teach that all persons have a need to belong. Singles can help to overcome loneliness by belonging to support groups. The singles class or group in church is a prime example. Opportunities for fellowship and service are provided by such groups. Athletic groups such as bowling or softball teams also provide times to be with others.

> ## Singles can help to overcome loneliness by belonging to support groups.

However, just being with a group does not necessarily alleviate loneliness. At times everyone suffers loneliness, but there are those whose lives are filled with loneliness and depression. Sroka (1981, 32–33) believes this problem is caused by low self-esteem—such persons do not love themselves and cannot accept love from others. It is important for such people to recognize God's love for them. This is easier said than done, for such individuals have difficulty accepting God's love. Sroka suggests the lonely person must take the initiative to solve the problem. The person must risk rejection by reaching out to others. She uses the illustration of the Lord Jesus who was rejected in his darkest hour by his closest friends. She concludes, "What it comes down to is: me and/or them? If it's *me or them,* then life will be filled with loneliness. If it's *me and them,* then life will be filled with risks, high stakes and great gains."

Five principles to help singles overcome loneliness are given by Jeremiah (1991, 32). He advises the lonely person: "acknowledge your singleness, accept singleness as God's gift, allow yourself to grow, activate your singleness, and affirm your singleness with gratitude."

The sexual revolution perhaps has affected the lives of singles more than those of any other group. In the society at large it has given rise to a whole new industry catering to the need for singles to meet other singles, often for sexual purposes, at bars, clubs, apartments, and health clubs. Adherents to the new morality have created an entirely new lifestyle called cohabitation in which a single man and woman live together without being legally married. Two million young people are now living in this arrangement. Some will eventually marry but most of these are short-term relationships. Such behavior is clearly immoral and un-Christian.

The loose moral attitude of the unsaved poses real problems for Christian singles. How much sexual expression is permitted between a believing man and woman? Is virginity still a virtue to be treasured? With the well-known standards of chastity taught in the Bible, one could assume that these questions are easily answered and obeyed. But when one reads of church singles groups having a problem with "body snatchers" who wander from one group to another seeking "to satisfy their own sexual needs and experience another conquest," it is apparent not all singles are committed to biblical morality (L. Swindoll 1985, 110).

Those subscribing to the new morality can find many reasons to engage in sex outside of marriage. Even when these are rejected, there remain some difficult questions. Can a person live a lifetime without engaging in sex? Can a person who has known a satisfying sexual relationship with a spouse be denied this gratification after the mate dies? Is it all right to have sex if you have a "meaningful relationship"? The Bible's answer to this question is a resounding no! Paul writes in 1 Corinthians 6:18, "Flee fornication." In 1 Timothy 2:22 he warns Timothy to "flee also youthful lusts." First Peter 1:16 exhorts the believer in the words of God, "Be ye holy for I am holy." First Corinthians 10:31 is very plain, "Whether therefore ye eat or drink . . . do all to the glory of God." Sex is a gift from God, but given to be shared within marriage (L. Swindoll 1985, 112).

The distinction between sex (as a physical relationship) and sexuality (the expression of masculinity and femininity) needs emphasis. "Our male or female sexuality is part of God's good plan" (Coleman 1985, 20). Sexuality, according to Smoke, "includes intimacy, love, feelings, consideration, kindness, caring, support and trust. . . . It is involvement with another person that is total and complete . . ." (L. Swindoll 1985, 108). Many singles expect to build a relationship with the opposite sex and this involves the expression of their sexuality. Holding hands, kissing, and other forms of physical affection are necessary and healthy. Couples must talk about their emotions and how they feel about various levels of physical affection. What kissing means to one, for example, may mean something entirely different to the other person. Communication enables a couple to draw guidelines "early enough so as not to get so involved sexually that they reach as point where it's difficult, if not impossible to stop. . . ." With guidelines in place, "they are not in battle with each other" (Coleman 1985, 20, 56). Once this ground is established, couples are free to test their compatibility in other areas of their relationship.

The specter of AIDS (Acquired Immune Deficiency Syndrome) is causing even unsaved singles to reevaluate their sexual relationships. This disease is a viral infection caused by the human immunodeficient virus (HIV). McIlhaney (1990, 143) indicates that "AIDS is spread by the exchange of HIV-infected body fluids: blood and blood products and semen (and possibly saliva and even tears). Most individuals acquire the virus through sexual contact which includes "oral-genital contact, anal intercourse, and even 'French kissing.'" Drug users who utilize needles contaminated with HIV virus can also become infected.

HIV may not show up in a blood test for years, but the person is capable of passing the disease to others during this time. McIlhaney (1990, 147) makes the sad statement, "there is no known cure for AIDS, and HIV-infected individuals will probably develop AIDS and eventually die from its effects. . . . AIDS is essentially a death sentence." He further points out that there is no such thing as safe sex when one person has AIDS. In a study where one person had AIDS and the couples were being very careful, 17 percent of those using condoms became infected. There is *no safe sex!*

Christian young people must practice abstinence until marriage. After citing the experience of William, a man who had infected several unsuspecting individuals with HIV, McIlhaney (1990, 142) warns, "Whenever two people who are *not virgins* have sex, there is the chance that one (or both) of these people already have AIDS, and/or is capable of transmitting it." If there are "body snatchers" going from one singles group to another practicing promiscuous sex (L. Swindoll 1985, 110), it gives added emphasis for every single person to obey the scriptural commands for *virginity.* AIDS is no respecter of religion! "It is imperative that all singles and the ministries that serve them acknowledge the physical and emotional dangers of unmarried sexual activity beyond the moral issues involved" (Anthony and Koons 1991, 211).

> *The distinction between sex (as a physical relationship) and sexuality (the expression of masculinity and femininity) needs emphasis.*

Unmarried persons also have the disadvantage of a higher income tax rate. The present system rewards those who have children and penalizes those who do not marry or have children. Demographers who are concerned about the population explosion are campaigning to have this situation reversed. It is unlikely that their views will be accepted by Congress, and single persons can expect to keep paying a higher tax rate. Unmarried Christians should be careful in their Christian stewardship to give sufficiently to Christian organizations in order to get the maximum benefit that the income-tax laws allow.

Persons who choose not to marry also face the discomfort of having to cope with friends who desire to see them married. Usually such friends find it difficult to understand that their single friends are happy. One young woman described the difficulty her co-workers had in understanding why she wasn't married: "When I told them I was happy, and that I neither wanted to marry nor to be a mother, they looked upset. . . . They couldn't understand my position and I think they didn't believe me" (Havemann and Lehtinen 1990, 296). A 1982 survey indicated that 55 percent of single women and 50 percent of single men said their lifestyle was either "wonderful" or "basically" fine (Havemann and Lehtinen 1990, 299). The desire to see single adults enter marriage is part of the cultural pressure that results from the high esteem given to the state of matrimony.

> ## *The desire to see single adults enter marriage is part of the cultural pressure that results from the high esteem given to the state of matrimony.*

No one can deny that there are tremendous blessings enjoyed by a happily married Christian couple, blessings that an unwed person can never know. It is only natural that such a couple would desire their single friends to marry and enjoy such blessings also. Consequently, if a happily married couple see the prospect of helping a single man and woman get to know each other, they cannot resist the temptation to play Cupid. Sometimes their efforts may be appreciated, and many happy marriages have eventuated from such efforts. However, in many cases they result in embarrassment to both the couple and single persons.

If a couple feels led to introduce a man and woman to each other, or to help along an already established friendship, it should be done only with the knowledge and consent of the individuals concerned. The happily married couple should recognize that some people do not wish to be married and realize that some people do not need marriage in order to find happiness in the will of God. Unhappily married couples will not attempt such matchmaking, for they usually wish they were single again and are not likely to encourage others to marry.

Self-Fulfillment and the Single Life

Single adults must face the possibility, when they pass the age when most of their friends are married and they are not, that it may be the will of God for them to remain single. Many young people find it difficult to reconcile themselves to this possibility, and they resist the will of God. The result is a continual spiritual battle that saps the person of spiritual vitality. The way to victory in this battle, as in any other, is a complete surrender to the will of God. The sooner a young person makes this decision, the sooner he or she will know peace, joy, and strength in life. God wants each person to mature in the Christian life. "God so desires to ingrain his image in the wood of your character, not so much to prepare you for a partner, as to prepare you for *life*. Your ultimate good and His glory are His primary concerns" (Rinehart and Rinehart 1983, 129).

This submission to the will of God does not mean the young adult entirely gives up the idea of marriage and makes no effort to change his status. It does mean, however, that the will of God becomes the goal. "If God has a mate for you, He knows how to bring the two of you together. Don't take things into your own hands" (Jeremiah 1991, 35). Young adults should be as pleasant and attractive as possible, but should not be continually frustrated by their single status. Taylor (1984, 19–20) emphasizes the gift of singleness: "singleness is a gift from God; his perfect will for you. Can you believe this? If you can, you're on your way to achieving that confidence and sense of self-worth which will stand you in good stead whether you are married or single." She proceeds to point out to those who question the single state of another by asking, "Why challenge God's choice for my life? Is your plan for me better than his?" This submission to the will of God is basic to a full and rich experience as a single person. This truth applies to both single men and women.

In order to have a full life, a young single adult should be active in some form of Christian service in the local church. If a church is so family oriented that there is little opportunity for the single person to get involved, individuals must seek out a church where their services are needed and welcomed. Teaching a Bible class, leading a children's group or youth group, helping in church programs, or church visitation are some of the activities that can enrich the life of the participant.

Towns (1967, 112–18) lists other types of service that young adults can perform in the local church. He suggests the formation of a group for young single people who could help maintain church property; write a church paper, keep Sunday-school records or aid in the church office; plan and direct recreational activities; use technical skills to assist the pastor with architectural or construction work; and volunteer in "serving through 'helping' jobs," such as ushering, singing, or directing traffic in the church parking lot. He concludes, "As the young single adult 'gives' his life in service to God he usually finds 'abundant life.' This life is characterized by good personal and social adjustment, once again giving truth to the statement, 'it is more blessed to give than to receive.'"

The creative use of leisure time is a necessity if a single person is to have a well-rounded life. The short workweek and longer vacation periods give the average person a lot of free time. Some of this can be used in Christian service, but there is time for other activities. For some, additional education can be acquired to better prepare the person for a vocation. Every individual ought to have one or more hobbies from which to receive personal enjoyment. Such activities as stamp or coin collecting, photography, music, art, restoring antique or classic autos, travel, and sports activities are illustrative of the types of hobbies engaged in by young single adults. Clubs formed by hobbyists provide opportunities to meet new friends, and occasionally a single person finds a mate through such propinquity.

> ## *Submission to the will of God is basic to a full and rich experience as a single person.*

Of course, no life is complete without friends. The person with interesting employment, who is active in Christian service and enjoys a hobby probably will not lack friends. Each of these provide opportunities for cultivation of friendships on the basis of common interests. The Bible says, "A man that hath friends must shew himself friendly . . ." (Prov. 18:24). A person cannot expect others to be friendly if he himself does not act friendly.

Single persons can have rich, full, victorious lives if they accept the will of God and proceed to live for his glory. Taylor (1984, 68) comments, "the state of singleness as a calling from God may not be very well understood by people around us. . . . [but] if we can find happiness and fulfillment in the single state, we can be a living testimony to the grace and enablement of God in a very special calling." Diligently seeking to do the will of God will result in an abundant life.

The Single Missionary

A difficulty faced by many mission boards is that of single missionaries, especially the single woman. Single men usually do not remain single long. On almost every mission field there is an abundance of eligible young women. A young man needs to take extra precautions to avoid any situation that might compromise his testimony and hinder his ministry for Christ. Mission boards would rather have a male candidate come to them with a wife. A young man who feels the call of God to missionary service should make a diligent effort to seek a compatible mate among the many young women who share a similar calling.

> *A person's perception of the will of God changes from time to time as God leads and directs by his Spirit.*

The situation is different for a single woman who is called to the mission field. Since there are so many more young women than men who are obedient to the Great Commission, there are not enough young men to go around. This means that a large number of women will necessarily face life on the field alone. No one knows why men do not volunteer for service on the foreign field as women do. Perhaps it is because of the attitude many young men have that a call to Christian service is an automatic call to the pastorate, and consequently they never honestly confront the needs of the world and the call of Christ to foreign fields. This attitude is reinforced by many sincere Christians who think a boy is destined to be a pastor and a girl a missionary. When one young couple had a baby girl, a Christian woman said, "Now you have a little missionary."

Regardless of the cause, many more young women than men respond to the call for missionary service. Sometimes a woman with such

a call is led by the providence of God to a courtship with a young man who is not called overseas, or perhaps to a different field. She then has to make a decision whether to break the relationship and remain single or to continue the relationship and marry. In such cases it is helpful for a young person to realize that a Christian's *understanding* of the will of God changes from time to time. Many a missionary has gone to the field with the firm expectation that it was the will of God for a lifetime, only to be stricken with illness and the need to return to a ministry in the homeland. Many a man has started out in his first pastorate believing the church ministry was to be his life work only to discover in a few years that God was leading him into a ministry of Christian publications, radio, or education. Other illustrations could be given how a person's perception of the will of God changes from time to time as God leads and directs by his Spirit.

Consider the case of a young woman and the decision she must make. In both cases she is responding to the will of God. She heard a call to the foreign field and volunteered. Now, God in his providence brings into her life a young man with whom she is compatible and to whom she is drawn by cords of love. It would seem perfectly natural for her to say to her Lord whom she desires to obey, "Lord, when you spoke to my heart about the mission field, I was willing to go to the ends of the earth. Now you have brought this man into my life and I accept this as a further leading in my life. He does not feel called to the field (or to the same field), but since you have led us together, and as your Word teaches, the wife is to be submissive to the husband, I accept your call to him as your leading in my life. May we serve thee acceptably."

This may sound strange, but a little reflection will show this is precisely the way a wife is led after she is married. Suppose Jane is called to Liberia and meets Tom, who is providentially called to the same field, and they are married. After three years on the field, Tom has to return home with a heart condition and the physician states he can never serve abroad again. Does Jane say to him, "Tom, I'm sorry you are ill and can't return to Liberia. However, you know God called me to Liberia so I must return without you. Please write at least once a week and send the letters airmail!" No, she accepts the will of God for her husband as his will for her life and will seek to be a helpmate here in the homeland.

In the same way, the wife of a pastor accepts the call to a new church as the will of God for her life as well as for her husband. It may be that God will call the young man to the field and this would be wonderful. On the other hand, God does not bring two dedicated young persons together only to have them separate because the man does not accept the call of the woman as God's will for their lives.

The illustration may be reversed; a young man called to a mission field meets and learns to love a woman who is not called to missionary service. Should they break the relationship or does the woman accept the call of the young man as her call to service?

If these two young people are sincerely seeking to do the will of God, then the young woman could say a similar prayer: "Lord, you have brought this man into my life and I accept this as your will for my life. He feels called to a mission field, and I do not, but I know you have led us together. Your Word teaches that the wife is to be submissive to the husband so I accept your call to him as your leading in my life. May we serve thee acceptably." With such a yielded attitude, the Lord will give this young woman a burden for the field and when she is examined by a mission board, other things being in order, she will be considered a good prospect.

Many areas of the world are evangelized today because young women were willing to go and do the work God called them to do. They have established churches, schools, hospitals, and dispensaries because there was no one else to do the task. The question of whether a single woman should go to the field would be unnecessary to ask if enough young men answered the call of God to foreign mission fields. Until enough men are willing to accept the responsibility of world evangelism, God continues to use women to spread the gospel to the ends of the earth.

The Church and Its Responsibility to Single People

The average church is unaware of the needs of single young adults in its congregation. It has a Sunday-school class for senior-high youth, young marrieds, and adults. This leaves young single adults the choice of either staying home or else sitting in a class with young marrieds. The same is true of Sunday evening youth groups. They usually stop at the senior-high level with no provision for young adults. With the large increase in the number of single young people, a church is not meeting its responsibility unless it has some program to help young adults.

One reason churches do not do more for singles is that the church is organized around married couples. Singles comprise a small (sometimes *very* small) minority and are often overlooked by the church in its organization and planning (Sroka 1981, 31–32). She concludes, "What a sad testimony that bars, TM, religious sects, sleep, and sitting in front of the 'boob tube' meet more of the needs of the single adult population than does the church." It is hoped that churches will become more aware of the need to minister to singles.

The Barna Research Group in 1987 made a study of adult singles in America. The survey included singles of all regions of the United States, ages eighteen to over sixty-five, from four different races, all levels of education, and various levels of income. Sixty percent of the respondents were female and 40 percent male. They used the broad definition of singles (never married, divorced, separated, and widowed). Their objective was to see how singles could be incorporated into the church and how the church could more effectively minister to them.

Among their findings (Barna 1987, 3–4) were the following: Fifty-three percent of the singles believed religion to be very important in their lives. (The sample included Christians and non-Christians.) Eighty percent believed that Jesus is the Son of God. Singles said that "friendly" and "concerned with all people" described the churches today. The most common reasons why *unchurched* singles did not attend church services were that they worked on Sunday, or that was their day off, or they preferred to do other things on Sunday. *Churched* singles mentioned the desire for "personal growth," spiritual growth, worship, or "reasons dealing with their beliefs."

When asked what they thought were the two most important characteristics of a church, the reply was "making visitors feel welcome" and "providing a strong youth program." Researchers point out that in surveying this question, "seventy-three percent of all singles said 'preaching based on the Bible' was very important, and even sixty-three percent of the non-Christians also listed it as very important."

The most common activity engaged in in the last six months was "praying to God (82%)." Of the singles surveyed, 79 percent of the Christians listed "investing time and effort in close friendships" as a top priority, and 78 percent listed "having a growing relationship with Jesus Christ" as their top priority. Seventy-eight percent of the Christians had discussed religious beliefs during the last month. Only 30 percent of the singles surveyed were considered to be "born-again Christians."

Many singles leave the church in their late teens and early twenties.

These statistics *seem* to indicate that churches are succeeding in reaching the singles minority. However, the editors concluded that churches are not really reaching singles (Barna 1987, 75–79). For example, singles say churches are friendly, but the survey discovered that singles do not feel "welcome into the fellowship." They believe the churches' emphasis on the traditional family gives singles the feeling they are not accepted as "full-fledged, whole human beings," that they are "second-class citizens." "Many single adults are interested in a spiritual asylum, not a hostile challenge to their very existence."

It is apparent that churches need to do some self-analysis to determine if they have the proper attitude toward singles, and to check with singles to see if that attitude is being properly perceived.

Many singles leave the church in their late teens and early twenties. Some churches attempt to remedy this situation by establishing a college-and-career class to meet the needs of the post-high-school group. Some question whether the two age groups should be combined since their interests are different. Other churches have started a youth group for young unmarried adults that meets either before or after the evening service. These groups can help meet the social needs by means of parties, rallies, and retreats. They provide additional opportunities to teach the Word, and also for young people to meet each other.

Churches desiring to minister to singles must recognize their need for independence, identity, and intimacy (Peterson 1984, 60–80). They must also be treated as adults. Any form of condescension will turn singles away. For example, if singles are planning a retreat, it would be improper to ask, "Who are the chaperones?" Stubblefield (1986, 101–2) emphasizes that "the church should always treat single adults as adults because they are adults." Consequently, the planning and programming for any activity must be entirely done by the singles themselves. Many are leaders in areas outside the church and are capable of leadership in the church. This does not mean that churches may not lay down certain ground rules and guidelines for a singles ministry. Once this is done the ministry should be turned over to the singles themselves.

Society provides few places outside of restaurants and bars where single people can find a social outlet. This gives church single groups opportunities not only for biblical teaching, but also for providing a place where young people can gather to enjoy activities and fellowship unavailable in the world at large. They want a group that can give more than just a good time or a few laughs. They want a group that has substance to it, a group that can minister to "their inner needs and desires seriously while not asking them to be other than single. . . . The social and recreational events should be qualitatively different from those of non-church groups" (Johnson 1982, 55–56).

Since developing intimacy is one task of the young adult years, there will necessarily be dating between members of the group. This is natural and normal. Some groups have discouraged this practice in an attempt to keep the focus on the ministry aspect of the group. The idea is to reinforce the belief that singleness is a gift of God and that the purpose of the group is to afford "opportunities to develop caring and supportive relationships among *singles*" (Johnson 1982, 54). Since marriage is not an option for many Christian single women due to the smaller number of available Christian men, this emphasis on ministry rather than on "marriage bureau" may prevent some of the pressures some groups place on women.

The entire program of the church should be open to the ministry of singles. Those qualified scripturally for office should be given the opportunity to serve. Singles will welcome the opportunity to minister in vacation Bible school, music programs, children and youth activities, and any capacity where their abilities can be utilized.

Church families also need to be conscious of the social needs of singles. Many are separated from their families and would enjoy being with another family occasionally. Families need to consider the feelings of singles when there are church social functions and make an effort to include them. Witte (1982, 44–45) relates the story of a church picnic that she and another single woman attended. They waited and arrived after lunch because they had no family to sit with. As she drove home, she prayed, "Oh, God, if I am so blessed someday to have a family, help me always look for the person that might need one. Thank you for giving me days like this because they will help me never to forget just how much a family including me today would have meant. And Lord, please help the families in our church to be sensitive to our needs, as singles, without it becoming a burden for them. I love them so much."

Conclusion

Singles as a group have increased dramatically over the last two decades and will continue to do so. Reaching singles for Christ poses a challenge to the church. Winning, discipling,

and engaging them in Christian ministry gives rewards here and hereafter.

The challenge for singles is to accept their singleness as a gift from God (1 Cor. 7:7). It matters little whether a young person remains single by choice or by circumstances as long as he is in the center of God's will. If a marriage partner is not available in the will of God, then the sooner a person accepts that fact and adjusts to the idea of remaining single, the sooner the frustration is replaced by a life filled with his peace and joy. God's will is the place of blessing and here the greatest happiness is found. After all, God's only Son was single, and he accomplished God's will for his life through obedience to that will.

> *The challenge for singles is to accept their singleness as a gift from God.*

Study Questions

1. Explain the terms *singles* and *singleness*.
2. Discuss this phrase: "Singleness is a gift of God." Is there a scriptural basis for the phrase?
3. Why do some Christian young people fail to marry?
4. List some advantages and disadvantages of the single life.
5. Distinguish between aloneness and loneliness.
6. List and discuss several reasons why a young person should remain a virgin until married.
7. What is the difference between "sex" and "sexuality"?
8. Discuss HIV, AIDS, safe sex, and virginity.
9. What is meant by the statement, "An individual's understanding of the will of God for his or her life will change from time to time"?

10. What factors should a church consider before beginning a ministry to singles?

Suggested Readings

Barna Research Group. 1987. *Single adults in America.* Glendale, Calif.: Barna Research Group. The purpose of the study was "to give a broad overview of the singles population, toward a better understanding of how to more effectively incorporate them into the church, and how the church can more effectively minister to their needs." Singles are such a diverse group that the data do not give a good picture of any one of the four segments (never married, divorced, separated, widowed).

Coleman, B., ed. 1985. *Sex and the single Christian.* Ventura, Calif.: Regal. The results of a roundtable discussion on the subject of *Sex and the Single Christian* by some of America's leading authorities on Christian sexuality such as Ed Wheat and Tim and Beverly LaHaye. One chapter concerns "Celibacy, the Gift of Singleness."

Hedges, C., and T. Timmons. 1988. *Call it love or call it quits: The singles guide to meaningful relationships.* Fort Worth, Tex.: Worthy. An interesting book that outlines the stages through which a relationship progresses. It includes a chapter on commitment, which is helpful because commitment is a problem for many singles. The authors counsel couples that a time comes in a relationship when they either must "call it love or call it quits."

Jeremiah, D. 1991. *Overcoming loneliness.* Nashville: Nelson. Jeremiah treats loneliness as a "disease of our times." He then proceeds to prescribe a remedy for various groups such as saints, singles, spouses. An interesting chapter is "The Lonely Savior."

Johnson, D. W. 1982. *The challenge of single adult ministry.* Valley Forge, Penn.: Judson. A "how to" book. It goes through all the steps necessary to create an effective ministry to single adults. Johnson has an important discussion on group size and how it affects the ministry. He states, "The average attendance of a ministry is like the blood pressure of an individual."

Karssen, G. 1983. *Getting the most out of being single: The gift of single womanhood.* Colorado Springs, Colo.: Navpress. It is interesting that this book, written by a Dutch woman, treats many of the same subjects as American writers do. This may indicate that the problems single women face are similar in the Western world. Her purpose, like that of American writers, is to help "many women learn how to enjoy the fullness of their lives." The answer is the same: acceptance of the will of God.

Sroka, B. 1981. *One is a whole number.* Wheaton: Victor. A volume in the Victor Books Family Concern Series, it is written with thirteen chapters to be used in Sunday school or group study. The author writes from her experience as a single woman. She has an excellent treatment of the difference between aloneness and loneliness.

Swindoll, L, ed. 1985. *Soloing: Experiencing God's best as a single woman.* Old Tappan, N.J.: Power. In this book, a collection of articles on singleness by well-known authors such as Gary Collins and Joyce Landorf, Swindoll relates the delightful experience she had with her vocal music teacher while in college.She uses words of advice from Miss Bergendahl as section headings for the book.

Taylor, R. 1984. *Single and whole.* Downer's Grove, Ill.: InterVarsity. Written by a woman who spent twenty years in Africa as a missionary. She enlivens her story by tales from the mission field. Her willingness to open her heart gives real insight into the peace one can have accepting singleness as a gift from God.

Witte, K. 1982. *Great leaps in a single bound.* Minneapolis: Bethany House. Karen Witte has been a radio and television personality in her hometown of Minneapolis. She found contentment as a single woman in the will of God. She relates experiences that helped her come to the place of surrender and happiness.

16

The Single-Parent Family

When my father and my mother forsake me,
then the Lord will take me up.

—Psalm 27:10

The Single-Parent Phenomenon

Webster defines "phenomenon" as "anything that is extremely unusual, extraordinary experience." The rise in the number of single-parent families in American culture has been extremely unusual. The norm for families has always been a two-parent family—a mother and father jointly supporting and socializing their children. However, within the last three decades there has been a tremendous increase in the number of single-parent families. "It is the fastest growing family form" (DeVault and Strong 1989, 26).

Historically, single-parent families constituted about 10 percent of all families. These families were headed by widows or widowers, or divorced, separated, or unmarried parents. In the past, the death of spouses from disease was the main cause of most single-parent families. However, the large increase in the number of divorces and the number of children born to unmarried women since 1970 have almost tripled the percentage of these families. The number of two-parent families has decreased drastically. The fact that a single parent may divorce and remarry more than once creates a situation whereby it is estimated "that 37 percent of all women and 60 percent of all children can expect sooner or later to live in a single-parent household" (Cargan 1991, 235).

Who Are the Single Parents?

Although divorce is a major contributor to the increase in single-parent families, the greatest change has been caused by the increased number of families headed by unmarried women. According to DeVault and

Strong (1989, 490), "Between 1970 and 1983, single-parent families headed by divorced women increased 178 percent but such families headed by unmarried women increased by 377 percent; by contrast there was a 15 percent decrease in families headed by widows." There is no indication of a decrease in the number of unmarried women having children, so the number of single-parent families will continue to increase.

Many of these unmarried women are teenage girls, and more than a million of these girls get pregnant each year. The new morality with its emphasis on promiscuous sex has exacerbated the problem. Young people are continually confronted with sexual stimuli. Virginity and abstinence are frowned upon. High schools are passing out condoms, a practice that can only encourage premarital sex. Peer pressure—"everybody is doing it"—helps to break down natural inhibitions. Then high schools have to provide classrooms for teenage mothers and their babies to encourage these teenage mothers to finish their high-school education.

> ## Within the last three decades there has been a tremendous increase in the number of single-parent families.

Christian teenagers are not immune to these societal pressures. Many Christian parents have had to face this situation. Abortion is never an option for the Christian girl. Unbelievers take the lives of unborn children, but the child of God knows that this is murder and should never consider it. The spiritual and psychological consequences suffered by Christian women who have had abortions have been ably documented. The majority of teenage marriages do not last so

marriage is usually not a good option. Many times the baby is given up for adoption, and most denominations have organizations to help in this process. Some girls do choose to become single mothers and accept the responsibilities. The church can provide role models for their young people by encouraging them to pursue goals of chastity and abstinence. When a girl does become pregnant, the love of Christ can be demonstrated in concern and help when needed (Smith 1983, 30–35).

At the other extreme are older single women who do not wish to marry, yet still have children. Through various means, such as artificial insemination, they conceive and bear children and join the ranks of single parents. Single men and women are now allowed to adopt children. Due to the scarcity of adoptable babies, they may have to parent a handicapped child, and many choose to do this.

Sincere Christian men and women sometimes find themselves as single parents because of divorce. Even for believers, there is always an element of risk involved in marriage. Spouses change and some backslide and leave a mother or a father with the children. Formerly it was fathers who left, but Christian women are now leaving their children with the father. Some of these cases may be influenced by feminism. When a marriage flounders, it is easier to leave. Mary was involved in her church work but because of an affair with the pastor, she left her husband and children in spite of all her husband's attempts to keep her love and save their marriage.

Many single parents are placed in that role because of fatal accidents to their spouses. Mary Jane Worden (1989, 21), mother of three children tells of the telephone call in the middle of the night informing her that her husband of sixteen years had been killed. A drunken driver had crashed head-on into the car in which her husband had been a passenger. In one quick moment she became a single parent. This scene is repeated over and over each day. Deaths due to fatal illnesses also leave many spouses as single parents. There is hardly a family in America that has not been touched by cancer. Smith (1983, 38–39) relates how her husband died after a lengthy illness, leaving her with four children. She shares the joys and difficulties she encountered as a single parent. She and Worden were dedicated Christians who sought help from their heavenly Father to aid them in their tasks as single parents.

There is an attempt by social scientists to recognize the single-parent family as a normal family type since it is fulfilling its functions (DeVault and Strong 1989, 484–85). It may be possible for academicians to consider such a family normal, but anyone who has parented alone or who has been reared with only one parent knows that it is impossible to describe such a family as normal. The difficulties of single parenting and the emotional and psychological stress endured by children preclude such a description. When a two-parent family has been wracked by violence, cruelty, or psychological or physical abuse, the departure of the offending parent may result in a more normal situation, but it is far from the normal family where two parents share their love and parenting responsibilities.

The Single Parent and Children

The loss or absence of a parent affects each form of the single-parent family differently. Smith had five years of her husband's illness to prepare her children for his death. (He was a classmate of this writer at Moody Bible Institute.) The task was complicated because the doctors first indicated he would live only two years but instead he lived for five. Nevertheless, the separation was difficult for the children, who ranged in age from five to seventeen. It affected the children differently but their mother had the task of helping them work through their grief.

Worden's husband died without any warning. The shock to her and the children (ages five, ten, and twelve) was greater in its impact, but the loss had to be explained in terms the children could understand. She, like all widows and widowers, had to work through her own grief while trying to help the children with theirs. As believers, both of these families had the encouragement of family, friends, and their churches.

The parent facing divorce or separation also has a difficult task. It may be a little easier—no, it's never easy—in that there is usually time to prepare children for the break in the relationship. Many children feel they are the cause of the separation so they must be assured that their behavior has nothing to do with it. This is easier said than done, and some children will require professional help to restore their emotional health.

The unmarried mother also has a burden in having to face the inevitable question, "Where is my daddy?" Honesty is the best policy. However, just as in sex education of children, enough information should be given to fit the age and maturity of the questioner.

Discipline of children by single parents may be more difficult than it is in a two-parent family. In the latter, the parents develop rules and back each other up in enforcing them. Some single parents believe that being the sole maker and enforcer of rules is an advantage. However, in most cases the single parent, and especially the mother, becomes closer to her children. This places children in a "more egalitarian situation" whereby they are able to negotiate the rules (DeVault and Strong 1989, 402). They can argue, cry, or whine until they get their way. As a result, "children acquire considerable decision-making power . . . the single parent finds it too difficult to argue with them all the time" (DeVault and Strong 1989, 492). Brenda Hunter, reared by a widowed mother who worked at a full-time job, relates how she was disciplined. Her mother was usually tired from her job and homemaking, so Brenda "knew that if I pressed my tired mother long enough, she would usually capitulate." There were occasions when she went too far and then her mother came "running after [her] with a hairbrush. . . . Her attempts at discipline were abortive, and I . . . grew up with little respect for authority" (Hunter 1982, 27–28).

Miller (1990, 107–19) lists several stumbling blocks that single parents face in disciplining. There are overly permissive parents who feel guilty because of a separation. They do not enforce rules and cannot punish unacceptable behavior. He gives the example of a well-to-do father who had custody of his daughter. When she approached her sixteenth birthday, she threatened to get pregnant if he did not buy her a Mustang for her birthday. He had never enforced rules before, so the girl received the

Mustang. The father feared she would carry out her threat.

The overly strict single parent refuses to allow children to do things other children do, such as going to bed at a certain hour when other children that age are allowed to stay up. When teenagers "*seriously* rebel" over what "the parent considers a minor issue," the parent may become overly strict. Miller states this overly strict attitude is a reflection of the parent's lack of security. "Strict single parents make their children feel safe and secure. . . ." The ideal is to reach the middle ground between overly permissive and overly strict.

Neglectful single parents are those who give up. The pressures of earning a living and the burdens of everyday living leave little time for parenting, including discipline. Wallerstein (DeVault and Strong 1989, 480) quotes Chuck as saying, "She does not pay any attention to me. I want her to be a mom with an interest in what I am doing with my life, not just a machine that shells out money." Children get into trouble, become truants, and become involved in premarital sex and drug usage. These children are difficult to reach because of a disorganized home life.

> # Children in a single-parent home may become more self-reliant and responsible.

The opposite extreme is the enmeshed single parent. These parents become overly involved in the lives of their children in order to meet unfulfilled needs in their own lives. They must attend every school function engaged in by the child. They want him to relate details of all activities including dates. These parents attempt to live vicariously through their children. If the children marry the parent cannot let go and becomes an in-law problem. Parents recognizing this type of behavior in themselves need to correct it for the good of the children and themselves. Miller (1990, 115) reflects, "Christian parents who are enmeshed need to be reminded that we are *loaned* these children to raise for God, and we are never to have *our* needs met by our children."

Children in a single-parent home may become more self-reliant and responsible. Anthony and Koons (1991, 121) observe that "this may be true because practical concerns in a single-family household often make it expedient for these children to acquire a sense of personal accountability and family cooperation at a younger age than children with the ongoing presence of two parents." When a single parent is also employed, the children usually are required to do tasks around the home. They realize the mother or father has to work outside the home so they try to help out in the home. Girls, more than boys, try to fill the void when the parent is absent. Mowday (1990, 70) comments that the young women she interviewed "had learned to do domestic chores very soon after their father was gone." When they saw their mothers needed help, they had a desire to help. A danger is giving an older sibling too much responsibility in the care of younger siblings and the home.

The care of children while the single parent works is a major problem. Some are fortunate enough to have relatives or friends who will care for them. Where these are not available, then children are usually placed in day-care centers. Many churches are establishing these as a form of ministry and evangelism. The center is open to all and unchurched families are contacted.

Commercial centers are available in most communities, but these need to be thoroughly investigated before a parent entrusts a child to their care. The nation has been rocked by highly publicized cases of child abuse in some care centers. The United States Government Printing Office in Washington, D.C., publishes a pamphlet, "A Parent's Guide to Day Care," which gives instructions on finding an adequate day care center. Bustanoby (1992, 115–30) has an excellent chapter on child care.

He also gives suggestions to help meet the needs of latchkey children.

The goal of the Christian single parent is to rear children with a good self-image who will love God sincerely and desire to do his will. It is more difficult to do this alone, but God has a special concern for widows, orphans, and the fatherless (or motherless). Exodus 22:22–23 reads, "Ye shall not afflict any widow or fatherless child. If thou afflict them in any wise, and they cry unto me, I will surely hear their cry." In the New Testament, James 1:27 defines pure religion: "to visit the fatherless and widows in their affliction. . . ." Without a father in the home, the children can be reminded of the promise in Psalm 27:10, "When my father and my mother forsake me, then the Lord will take me up." Since children derive their concept of God as Father from their earthly father, the mother without a father present in the home will have to be the role model for this concept. A loving, kind, gracious mother will present a God who is likewise loving, kind, and gracious. The responsibility to be a good role model can be fulfilled by either parent alone. A friend offered Worden this advice: "Don't try to be both father and mother to your kids. Just be the very best mom [father] you can be" (Worden 1989, 178).

Although most single parenting is done by mothers, about 3 percent of minor children "are living with their fathers only" (Eshleman 1991, 215). It is generally thought that single fathers cannot do as good a job as single mothers. Eshleman (1991, 216) presents conclusions from two research studies concerning single fathers as parents. The first found that single fathers "feel comfortable and competent" in their role. The second study discovered that there were no "significant differences" in children reared by single fathers and single mothers. He concludes "clearly successful mothering is not exclusively a female skill. Men *can* 'mother.'" They have some advantages over single mothers. They usually have more education and are more likely to be employed, and thus experience fewer economic difficulties.

About 3 percent of minor children live with their fathers only.

The single father does suffer some disadvantages. Few men are prepared to care for children, cook, and do laundry and housework. These are all skills they have to learn. Bill Rose, with three children to care for, had "seven basic meals." When the children began to visit their friends at mealtime, he knew it was time to prepare some new foods. At first, he thought if he could clean the house in three hours it would stay clean, but it didn't (Dayton *Daily News*, 21 June 1992, p. 1).

Adjusting to grief and loneliness is also more difficult for men than for women. In American culture men are not supposed to cry. They are to be strong and unemotiona. Feelings are not to be expressed. They do not feel as free to show grief by crying as women do. Thus, it is more difficult for single fathers to adjust to the loss of a wife or child through death or the loss of both wife and children by divorce (Smith 1983, 116). It is also harder for men to conquer anger and resentment caused by divorce.

Men not only have trouble with their own emotions, but also have difficulty understanding the emotions of their children. A psychoanalyst says, "They [single fathers] often have an appalling ignorance about the emotional needs of children" (Bustanoby 1992, 14). A single father faced with this problem needs a mother, grandmother, or aunt to help interpret the emotions of his children. He must also read books that describe the emotions of children and how to help them. He may need professional therapy to clarify his own feelings.

A single father with a daughter may find educating her about sexuality a difficult task. The explanation of the menstrual cycle may be especially difficult. He may want to delegate this task to her mother or grandmother. If not, a female friend can be asked to share this information. A school nurse or the family physician can also be resource people.

Bustanoby (1992, 36) points out that "the father is responsible both to reinforce the incest taboo and to affirm his daughter's sexuality." He does this by informing her when she is not dressed properly and by "letting her know that she's no longer a little girl but is becoming an attractive woman." The aim is to reinforce the incest taboo and at the same time help the daughter to "grow up to be a confident, morally prudent woman."

A single father with custody of the children will have increased financial problems. If he has lost a wife through death, there may be some insurance funds to supplement the income, but unfortunately, few families have sufficient coverage. It may be necessary for him to work extra hours to make ends meet (Smith 1983, 117).

> *"Divorced women experience a seventy-three percent decline in income the first year after a divorce, while a divorced man's income increases by forty-two percent."*

Single parents can do a good job of parenting, even though it is difficult. Anthony and Koons (1991, 121) describe a study to compare the emotional and social growth of third- and fourth-grade children being reared by single parents and two parents. They discovered dysfunctional children in both types of homes. "They found no significant differences be-

tween the two groups. . . . The conclusion was that the level of a child's adjustment is related to the *quality* of parenting, rather than whether there was one parent or two."

The Single Parent and Finances

Most single parents face severe economic problems after a divorce or separation. Unmarried mothers usually face them from the time of pregnancy with the expenses of childbirth.

Some widows are well provided for by their husbands through good financial planning. Every husband with children needs several hundred thousand dollars in *term insurance.* This will provide for all the needs of his family. It is so relatively cheap that no young family need be without it. Worden's husband had provided sufficient funds so she could stay home and rear her children. She in turn wisely took out term insurance on her life so the children would be provided for in case of her death (Worden, 1989, 62). Studies show that 75 percent of life insurance proceeds are gone within two years (Case 1985, 79). This may indicate the funds were wasted or more likely that there was little insurance money available to spend. However, where there are large sums available, the widow must seek expert help (Case 1985, 37). There are so many ways to invest money that a financial planner with a good record of returns should be employed to help safeguard the family's financial future.

The problems are different for divorced and unmarried mothers. The divorced woman suffers an immediate drop in family income. Anthony and Koons (1991, 123) report a study that indicated that "divorced women experience a seventy-three percent decline in income the first year after a divorce, while a divorced man's income increases by forty-two percent" (*Newsweek,* 15 July 1985). Cargan (1991, 239) comments, "single parenthood for women appears to be a major factor in what has been called the 'feminization of poverty.' Over half of all single mothers live below the poverty line. . . ."

The mother usually has a court order for the father to pay child support. However, few fathers are faithful to that obligation. Garfinkel and McLanahan (1986, 24–25) relate that about "forty percent of absent white fathers and nineteen percent of absent black fathers pay child support." These payments amount to "about ten percent of the income of single white mothers and for about 3.5 percent of the income of single black mothers." The remainder of their income is derived from employment or from welfare benefits such as Aid for Families with Dependent Children (AFDC), food stamps, subsidized housing, and Medicaid health care. When women do work, they receive about 35 percent less than men. Consequently, a majority of single-parent families live in poverty. "Economic stress is their only financial constant" (DeVault and Strong 1989, 490).

Case (1985, 92–99) gives several suggestions on "how to spend wisely." The first is "Ask the Lord first." The principle here is to find out if God *really* wants us to buy the item in question. God is our Father and is interested in our needs and our wants, but he wants us to trust him for his provision.

Develop sales resistance is the second principle. Advertising is a strong motivation to get people to buy. The displays in shopping malls also create a desire for things that are not necessary. Credit cards make it easy to buy them, but it may not be easy to pay for them. It is better to wait and shop for a specific item when money is available.

The third suggestion is to get the best buy. One must learn to comparison shop—to go from store to store when seeking a particular item and then compare prices. The *Consumer Reports Buying Guide* should be consulted if it is a product tested by their laboratories. Always look for quality rather than price.

The fourth idea is to pay promptly. Pay monthly bills when they are due so that interest charges are avoided. It is better to get on a cash-only basis. Save the funds needed before purchasing larger items. Single parents can rest upon the promise of Philippians 4:19, "But my God shall supply all your need according to His riches in glory by Christ Jesus." He does not promise to supply all a person wants but he does promise to supply the needs.

The Single Parent and Dating

To date or not to date is a major problem for the single parent. Those who have been widowed may find it difficult to date because doing so may cause them to feel guilty and disloyal to the deceased spouse (Anthony and Koons 1991, 129). The sexual frustration of one who has been deserted by a wife or a husband can only be imagined. The desires remain but there is no legitimate manner to satisfy them without violating one's Christian principles. The unsaved single parent has no problem, for there are enough singles desiring sexual partners. These individuals may or may not be interested in establishing an intimate relationship. They have a biological need, and its gratification is their primary motivation.

> ## *Dating for single parents is very different from dating for adolescents.*

Dating for single parents is very different from dating for adolescents. One who has been out of the dating scene for ten or twenty years and who has children realizes that things have changed. Some of the emotions may be the same, but the norms are different. Children have to be considered. If they are old enough, they may still have real emotional ties to the noncustodial parent and may resent the possibility of the custodial parent developing a relationship that would displace the absent mother or father. Very often children will attempt to prevent the development of a dating relationship by negative behavior. The opposite is also true. If a parent has a long-term relationship with a date, then a child may get attached to that person. Bustanoby (1992, 165) writes of a single mother who dated the same man for three years, during which time she and the children came to love him. Then he left her and they were all hurt. To prevent this happening again she seldom has the man pick her up, "and if he does it's just an introduction. . . . I don't get the men involved in any family stuff." If possible, it is best if single parents keep their dating separate from their family life.

Single parenting is a transition stage for many. Bustanoby (1992, 11) gives the results of a survey that asked single parents if they wished to remain unmarried. Two-thirds indicated they desired to remarry. Unmarried mothers hope to find a first-time husband. The other single parents expect to remarry and the majority do. Worden (1989, 50), less than three weeks after her husband's death, describes with frankness her desire for another husband. He needed to be a "special kind of man," for her first husband was very special. She relates her fear of long-term singleness, but also her "confidence" that the right man would eventually come. At various times in her journal of her first year as a single parent, she describes her discussions with the children about another mate.

Single parenting is a transition stage for many.

It is during this time that single parents are vulnerable to sexual temptation. Christian single parents face these same situations. If all held to the biblical norm of abstinence except in marriage, there would be no problem, but many have rejected these norms.

The Millers (1981, 238–41) discuss the problem of sex with a preface stating that the New Testament teaches "sexual intercourse is to take place within marriage." They counsel two people who are attracted to each other to discuss the limits of their physical involvement before they start to make out. Physical feelings are difficult to control once touching begins between two people who are in love. The lim-

its must be set before the evening begins, "since the sex drive is so strong that it may be impossible . . . to set limits after you begin touching in a potentially loaded sexual situation."

Someone may ask, "Is it possible for a single parent to live a chaste life in a society preoccupied with sex?" The majority of Americans have accepted sexual exploitation in American culture. However, the believer has the promise of 1 John 4:4b, "Greater is he that is in you than he that is in the world," and James 4:7, "Submit yourselves, therefore, to God. Resist the devil, and he will flee from you." Hunter (1982, 67–77) became a single parent with two small daughters when her husband left her for another woman. She was single for five years, during which time her commitment to Christ in her adolescence was renewed. She gives several reasons why she remained chaste during this period. She admits it was difficult and that during the first year she almost had an affair with a married man. Her Christian convictions and the counsel of a good friend saved her from that experience. She tells how she asked herself, "What kind of a person would I become if I slept with every man who asked me?" Her answer was that these episodes would leave "invisible marks on the soul" and change her life forever. It is true that God forgives sexual sins, but the individual often continues to bear a feeling of guilt that is not easily eliminated. Having two beautiful daughters, she realized she could never teach them to be chaste if she herself was not. She was able to spend two years at L'Abri Fellowship in England, an experience that deepened her spiritual life. When she returned, she knew she had the help of the Holy Spirit to enable her to resist sexual temptations. She also met women who were having affairs and saw the pain and hurt that such behavior entailed. She had the help of "strong, supportive Christians who openly encouraged [her] to live by the Biblical ethic." She concludes, "it is possible to come to terms with one's self as a warm, loving woman without hopping into bed with the available men."

Eventually Hunter married a husband who had been looking for a committed Christian who shared his values of chastity. She emphasizes that "nothing is lost in terms of sexual feeling during periods of celibacy. If anything, sexual feelings become more intense." It is evident that it is possible for single parents to resist the cultural pressures and to live chaste lives. There must be a strong commitment to live a life pleasing to God, and a recognition that this is possible only with the help of the indwelling Holy Spirit. A daily yielding of the body to be his temple will help keep it pure. The help of caring friends is an invaluable aid. The fellowship Hunter found at L'Abri should be available also in the local church.

Although single parenting is a transition period for most, some single parents enjoy their status and do not wish to remarry. For those who come out of unhappy marriages, the fear of another experience motivates them to remain single. They do not desire to go through the pain and rejection again. Some have no interest in entering into another sexual relationship. Others may be loners and do not experience the agonizing loneliness which is often a major disadvantage of singleness. They immerse themselves in their work and the care of their children. Bustanoby (1992, 153) gives Cindi as an example of a satisfied-to-be-single parent. He quotes her: "I would like to see an organization that isn't pushing single parents to get married. Some single parents, like myself, are happy to be single. It seems to the world that this idea is hard to deal with." Cindi later comments that she gets lonely but overcomes it by working on her problems and by "keeping active with her children." For such people, companionship isn't necessary, and they function well as single parents.

Dating can be an experience in which an individual can grow emotionally and spiritually. The single parent often has feelings of guilt, rejection, and loss of self esteem. There are questions of what went wrong in the marriage and a desire to determine the cause of failure. Very often dating partners have had similar experiences and the sharing of these can help the healing process. This type of sharing cannot take place until a relationship has been established. If it is attempted too early, it will probably break the relationship. Persons need to make whatever changes are needed in themselves in order to be better persons and thus better dating partners.

The Single Parent and the Extended Family

For many single parents, the help they receive comes from the extended family. When a spouse dies, the family is the first to offer comfort and help. When most of the friends have gone after the funeral, the family is still there and will be there whenever needed. Support is more difficult, of course, when the single-parent family is separated by distance from the extended family. Though they may not be physically present after the funeral, phone calls and letters from Mom and Dad to the grieving child are still a comfort.

> *For many single parents, the help they receive comes from the extended family.*

The situation is different when a divorce or separation is involved. These separations are usually not amicable. Both sets of grandparents may experience anger, and blame for the breakup will be projected on to the child of the other family, although both spouses usually are equally at fault. Rarely will a family admit their child is the offending spouse and worthy of blame. DeVault and Strong (1989, 468) quote one study that indicated that 70 percent of in-laws disapproved of the former spouse.

Grandparents are greatly affected because of their love for their grandchildren. Grandparents often help grandchildren cope with the divorce. Often the custodial parents will move great distances that make it impossible for not only the noncustodial parent but also the grandparents to visit. The grandparents often provide economic assistance to the custodial parents. Some custodial parents have denied visitation rights to grandparents. Certain states have enacted laws providing for visitation rights for grandparents.

The extended family often can furnish role models for children of single parents. A single mother trying to rear sons needs male models to enable them to develop as normal boys. An uncle or a grandfather often can fill that role by teaching a son about male things such as athletics and autos. Likewise, a single father without a wife may have daughters who need role models. A grandmother or an aunt can teach daughters the roles of young women. Although feminists have attempted to eliminate the differences between male and female roles, they have not made much progress. It is still important for boys and girls to learn their appropriate roles.

The Church and the Single Parent

It is likely that the number of single-parent families will continue to increase, due to liberalized divorce laws and the number of children born to unwed mothers. The single-parent family faces greater difficulties than a two-parent family. The Christian parent has the help of the Savior, the Bible, and the Holy Spirit. These offer "extensive information and guidelines to help single parents understand God's will so they may live to His higher standards" (Smith 1983, 99). They should have the help of the local church, but many churches have not responded to their needs, often because they fail to realize that the needs of single parents are different from the needs of other singles. There are some things that most any church of any size can do for them. The formation of support groups is one method of helping single parents. Concerns and problems of parents could be discussed and solutions proposed. Seminars on such subjects as parenting and finances could be led by informed leaders. Many churches are sponsoring child-care centers which are a boon to single parents. A strong program of family-life education may help prevent some marriage breakups that result in single-parent families.

Every church could have a Christian big brothers and big sisters program modeled after the secular organization (Bustanoby 1992, 224–26). This group can enlist men and women to become role models for children of single parents. These individuals are screened to make sure they are born-again Christians, have high moral values, and can be successful role models for children. Children in the program generally range from six to fourteen years of age. (It seems a higher limit of sixteen or eighteen might be advisable.) The volunteers "must be eighteen years old or older, willing to make at least a six-month commitment, and willing to spend three to six hours a week with the child." Bustanoby proceeds to give guidelines for establishing such a program in the local church.

Christian colleges can also offer a similar service to local churches in their area. College students are busy people, but being a Christian big brother or sister can be a part of their practical Christian work assignments. Children look up to college students so they have a built-in advantage as role models.

The story of Abraham having to send Hagar and her son away from his home is a touching one (Gen. 21:9–21). Hagar became a single parent that day, but God did not forsake her. The angel of God called to her from heaven and said, "Hagar, fear not . . ." (v. 17) and verse 20 reads, "and God was with the lad. . . ." Christian single parents have the resources of the God of Abraham, the faithful God, to enable them to perform the required roles in a manner pleasing to him. He knows those who are single parents and the enormous tasks they face in rearing children for his glory. He will not fail them, so they need not fear failure. He is the same yesterday, today, and forever.

Study Questions

1. What factors account for the increase in the number of single-parent families?
2. Discuss the discipline of children by single parents.
3. List the advantages and disadvantages of being a single father when compared to being a single mother.
4. What percentage of life-insurance proceeds are spent within two years? What kind and how much life insurance should a father of young children have? How much should the mother have?
5. Why do a majority of single-parent families live in poverty?

6. List several suggestions to help the single-parent family spend their income wisely.
7. Why is single parenting called a "transition period"?
8. How does the dating experience of a single parent differ from the dating experience of an adolescent?
9. Why is the extended family so important to the single-parent family?
10. What kind of programs can a local church sponsor to help single parents?

Suggested Readings

Anthony, M. J., and C. A. Koons. 1991. *Single adult passages: Uncharted territories.* Grand Rapids: Baker. The authors surveyed fourteen hundred single adults (including single parents). They have an excellent chapter on "The Storms of Single Parenting" and give suggestions on how to help the children of divorce.

Bustanoby, A. 1992. *Single parenting.* Grand Rapids: Zondervan. Written by a marriage and family therapist who covers the subject thoroughly. Especially helpful are the chapters on child development. Several appendices list where valuable resources may be found. The best book on this subject.

Case, R., R. Meier, and F. Minirth. 1985. *The money diet.* Grand Rapids: Baker. A financial counselor shares his views on financial planning, which can be of value to any single-parent family. At the end of each chapter are brief psychological comments by the operators of the Minirth-Meier Clinic in Dallas.

Garfinkel, I., and S. S. McLanahan. 1986. *Single mothers and their children: An American dilemma.* Washington, D.C.: The Urban Institute Press. The Urban Institute studies social problems and makes the information available to governmental authorities, along with recommended solutions. Poverty and inadequate child support were two problems addressed in this study.

Hunter, B. 1982. *Where have all the mothers gone?* Grand Rapids: Zondervan. A former feminist tells of her change to traditional values. She spent five years as a single parent and refers to those years in offering encouragement to mothers. Her story of remaining chaste while a single parent is an encouragement to those facing sexual temptation.

Keshet, H. F., and K. M. Rosenthal. 1981. *Fathers without partners.* Totowa, N.J.: Rowman and Littlefield. The writers, one a father without a partner, became interested in divorced fathers and how they handled the problems of single parenthood. The book is the result of a survey of fathers who had full or partial custody of their children.

Miller, D. R. 1990. *Single moms, single dads.* Denver: Accent. A valuable volume on the problems faced by single parents. Miller describes the needs of the eleven- to fourteen-year-old children in a chapter entitled "The 'Tween-Ager.'"

Mowday, L. 1990. *Daughters without dads.* Nashville: Nelson. As a widowed mother of two daughters, the author became concerned about the large number of girls without fathers. Her aim is to help these mothers and daughters to adjust to this status. The chapter on the abundant life challenges them to seek it in spite of the absent father and husband.

Smith, V. W. 1983. *The single parent.* Old Tappan, N.J.: Revell. A comprehensive guide to help the single parent do the job of parenting written by a widow who reared three children. She has a good chapter on "Living Creatively with Children."

Worden, M. J. 1989. *Early widow: A journal of the first year.* Downer's Grove, Ill.: InterVarsity. A young widow kept a journal of her first year as a single parent. She opens it so the reader can enter into her sorrows and joys as a single parent. She relates how she dealt with her own grief and that of her children.

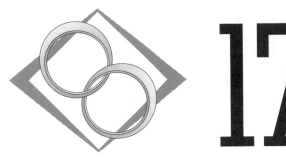

The Blended Family

> My grace is sufficient for thee: for my strength
> is made perfect in weakness.
>
> —2 Corinthians 12:9

Introduction

"Today was the blackout of my life. I became a dissolvement statistic in the judge's chambers. How could this happen to me? I had written *Little Things That Keep the Family Together.* . . . I'd dreamed of a . . . glorious geriatric bash on our Golden Wedding Day. . . . But this will never be! There are no more dreams to dream. Only the pain of today." These are the words of a Christian woman on the day her marriage of twenty-seven years to a Christian man was "dissolved" (Thrash 1991, 17–18).

These words illustrate the suffering of those going through a divorce—suffering formerly known by only a few Christians. Today there is an epidemic of divorce among Christians. Hardly a family has not been touched either directly or indirectly by divorce. It is an emotional subject. Wallerstein (1989, xxi) emphasizes that "divorce has ripple effects that touch not just the family involved but our entire society. . . . When one family divorces, that divorce affects relatives, friends, neighbors, employers, teachers, clergy, and scores of strangers." All the pain and problems that inevitably accompany the break-up of a home are encountered in the churches. Consequently, it is necessary to write about divorce and remarriage even though the church discourages both. It is a fact of life that confronts believers everyday.

Because of the negative connotation attached to "stepfamily," different terms have been used to describe the family that is formed when two formerly married people are united. It has been called a "reconstituted" or "restructured" family, but the most widely used adjective is "blended." The task is to blend the two families into one harmonious unit. It is not always easy, and sometimes it becomes what Art Buchwald calls a "tangled" family (DeVault and Strong 1989, 497). Since two families are involved, it is also referred to as a "binuclear family" (Bustanoby 1992, 10).

The blended family will be treated from a sociological viewpoint first, and then from a biblical viewpoint in the latter part of the chapter. Young people today face many temptations and problems that their parents never encountered. It is a real world controlled by Satan, and to be forewarned is to be forearmed. The description of the trauma of divorce and the unhappy consequences for all involved should encourage a couple to adopt an attitude that divorce is *never* an option and force them to diligently work at enriching their marriage.

> *In 1969, California passed the first no-fault law, whereby couples who agreed to separate could file for a dissolution of their marriage with little expense.*

The Prevalence of Divorce

Divorce is a legal term describing the dissolution of a marriage by a court of law. In the eighteenth century and the early part of the nineteenth century, divorce was frowned upon by society. However, the effects of industrialization, urbanization, and secularization created more tolerance to divorce and resulted in more liberal divorce laws (Phillips 1988, 582–84).

Prior to 1969, a person who wanted a divorce had to prove that the spouse was "at fault." This often made the process of obtaining a divorce a long, bitter, and expensive procedure. In 1969, California passed the first no-fault law,

whereby couples who agreed to separate could file for a dissolution of their marriage with little expense. The immediate effect of the new law was that dissolutions increased 46 percent from 1969 to 1970. Most states now have no-fault dissolutions if the parties are in agreement, but they also permit divorces for contested cases.

California has also pioneered an even simpler method to dissolve marriages. It has been called the "no-lawyers, no-courts, no-legal-hassles divorce." This law permits a childless couple married less than two years and owning little property to get a divorce by mail. Courts and lawyers are not involved. The couple pays the state a fee of fifty dollars, fills out a form, and in six months they receive their divorce. In effect, it is a do-it-yourself divorce and is as simple as getting a marriage license (Korman and Leslie 1985, 505).

The women's movement became active in the 1960s and encouraged women to acquire education and enter the marketplace. The economic problems of the 1970s brought large numbers of women into the "paid labor market, and many women became self-supporting for the first time. . . . The economic institutions interacted with family institutions to 'pull' women into economic independence and to 'push' them out of unsatisfactory marriages" (Steinmetz and Sussman, 1987, 597).

Other factors such as the increase in individualism, wars, and the reduction of the social stigma attached to divorce resulted in an alarming increase in the number of divorces in the United States. In 1970 there were 708,000 divorces; in 1981 there were 1,219,000. By 1990 the number had decreased to 1,175,000. In that year there were 2,448,000 marriages, which gives a divorce rate (4.7 per 1000 people) nearly one-half that the marriage rate (9.8 per 1000 people) (*1992 Information Please Almanac*, 806). Havemann and Lehtinen (1990, 263) observe, "If you are reading this chapter on a working day, you can be sure that several divorces were granted . . . just while you were reading this sentence. By the end of the day, nearly 5000 will have taken place."

Such statistics are often cited as evidence that monogamous marriage as an institution is failing in society and will be replaced by some alternate form of family structure. However, the statistics used to compare the marriages of one year to the divorces of people who married in previous years are misleading.

The figures also fail to account for the people who marry and divorce several times. This makes possible serial polygamy—a person may have a number of spouses in a lifetime, even a dozen or more! This factor skews the marriage and divorce rates in that "25 percent of divorced brides and grooms remarried within four to five months after divorce" (Kephart 1981, 486). This being true, then 25 percent of those divorcing in any given year are also included in the number of marriages in that same year. These divorced people remarrying within the same year increase the marriage number by 25 percent, so much of the marrying and divorcing is done by the same persons. Thus, while it may be said that in a given year 50 percent of the marriages will end in divorce, "it is not accurate to say that of all marriages one-half will end in divorce" (Eshleman 1991, 579). Since the divorce rate is heavily influenced by the matrimonial activity of only a small percentage of men and women, the majority of couples have never been divorced.

Mediation is a new legal process that attempts to resolve differences when a couple seeks a divorce. "A mediated settlement lays the groundwork for an amicable and therefore more personally productive separation. This in turn reduces the turbulence surrounding the divorce itself and shortens the period of adjustment experienced by all divorcing couples" (Haynes 1981, 3). It is a practice borrowed from the labor movement. When an impasse occurs between labor and management, an impartial mediator is brought in to settle the differences. In a similar manner, a professional therapist is used to mediate the differences between a couple and to prepare a settlement for a lawyer to present to the court. The aim is to reduce some of the hostility and frustration that often accompany divorce proceedings, and thus to make re-entry into life after divorce less burdensome. California now requires mediation in all cases where there is disagreement over child custody. A study there showed that 76 percent of the men and 62 percent of the women stated that mediation "helped them to become more reasonable in their dealings" with each other (Skolnick 1992, 320).

The Causes of Divorce

It is suggested by Kephart (1981, 498–99) that there are societal causes and personal causes for divorce. He lists six societal causes:

1. Changing family functions. Many things the family used to do, such as education and recreation, have been taken over by outside agencies.
2. Casual marriages. The cultural emphasis on romantic love leads to hasty marriages and quick divorces.
3. Jobs for women. Women are no longer dependent on men for their livelihood and feel more free to leave when difficulties arise in the marriage.
4. Decline in moral and religious sanctions. The Roman Catholic Church still opposes divorce but most others have taken a liberal view toward it. Less social stigma is attached to divorce.
5. The philosophy of happiness. The main goals of marriage are personal satisfaction and happiness. When these goals are not met, the marriage is dissolved and new mates are sought.
6. More permissive divorce laws. With nearly all states having some form of no-fault divorce law, divorce on demand is now readily available with relatively little expense. Divorce has become so common that couples do not seek to heal or to restore their broken relationships. They take the easy way out. Some brides refuse to have their linens monogrammed. It is reported there are places in Reno where wedding rings can be rented!

A seventh cause can be added in reference to the church. Someone has suggested "that there would not be so many divorces in the church if it were not so easy to remarry." Churches need to decide what their beliefs are concerning divorce and remarriage, and take

285

a stand upon those principles as they understand God's Word.

Researchers usually list several reasons for divorce. Raschke (Steinmetz and Sussman 1987, 603–7) lists low socioeconomic status, early age at marriage, premarital pregnancy, religion, and intergenerational transmission (divorce runs in families); Kephart (1981, 500) adds prior divorce and certain kinds of cross-class marriages.

Several personal causes that are particular to certain couples are put forward by Peterson (1984, 276):

1. Negative behavior. This includes personal abuse, nagging, drinking, power struggles, and the improper use of sex.
2. Boredom or satiation. Couples get into a routine and take each other for granted. Then one will blame the other for the loss of romance and personal satisfaction. Instead of trying to revive the relationship, they decide to separate.
3. Acquiescence. If one partner wants a divorce, the other gives in. More than 40 percent of divorces include spouses who really don't want a divorce.

Another cause is financial problems. Couples who divorce often list this as one of the main causes. Continual friction over the use or misuse of money is damaging to any relationship, and kills many of them. Counseling for money problems is readily available, and many of these marriages could be saved.

Infidelity is a much more serious problem and most difficult to solve. Men and women today are often placed in close interpersonal relationships at work, at play, and in the church. When a couple experiences unhappiness in their relationship, there is often a person of the opposite sex ready to lend a listening and sympathetic ear. Gradually, the new relationship develops into an affair. Jenkins (1989, 7–14) cites the example of John and Sue, professing Christians with families. While they were working together they developed an intimate relationship that destroyed both marriages. These situations should not occur, but Christians are susceptible to temptations.

(Jenkins defines "hedges" that should surround every marriage.)

Albrecht and Kunz (Cargan 1985, 297–308) made an extensive study of 500 divorced people. The majority (168) listed "infidelity" as the major cause of divorce. It is commonly perceived that men are the transgressors, but in this study seventy-four men listed their wives as transgressors as compared to ninety-four women who had been betrayed by their husbands. This statistic may reflect the increased participation of women in the workforce.

However, Hunter (1978, 136–39), whose husband left her for another woman, takes an opposite view. He had been reared in a Christian home, had graduated from a prestigious Christian college, and had lived a professing Christian life. When Hunter confronted him and asked why he had become involved in the affair, he answered, "It was quite simple. I decided to have an affair. It was an act of the will." Because of her experience she writes, "Affairs do not just happen: they are willed into existence. Prior to the affair, there is a deliberate turning away from the spouse and a willful search for another person." Whether it is an act of the will before passion is aroused or the passion comes first, it is always a painful and damaging emotional experience for the offended person.

God instituted marriage to be monogamous and gave man a clear admonition to cleave unto his wife. The seventh and tenth commandments of God's law prohibited adultery (Exod. 20:14–17). The Book of Proverbs is filled with warnings against adultery. "Can a man take fire in his bosom, and his clothes not be burned? Can one go upon hot coals, and his feet not be burned? So he that goeth in to his neighbor's wife: whosoever toucheth her shall not be innocent. . . . But whoso committeth adultery with a woman lacketh understanding; he that doeth it destroyeth his own soul" (Prov. 6:27–29, 32). "Let not thine heart decline to her ways, go not astray in her paths. . . . Her house is the way to hell, going down to the chambers of death" (Prov. 7:25, 27). When a Christian becomes involved in an affair, it is not because of ignorance or lack of warnings of the dangers. God knew that the greatest happiness of man and woman exists where there is faithfulness in marriage, and his divine will for Israel and the church is that children be reared according to his Word in stable homes.

Knowing the weakness of human nature, the Holy Spirit inspired Paul in 1 Corinthians 7:2–5 to urge believing spouses to satisfy each other's sexual needs in order to avoid any temptation to infidelity. Nevertheless, Christians may still yield to temptation, and the couple must face the problem and consider the consequences of the decisions they make.

A general principle can be set forth: whenever possible the chief concern should be the maintenance of the home. This principle should be practiced when children are involved. The offended party is always filled with pain and feelings of rejection. Hunter (1978, 137) indicates that "we have no Richter scale for measuring human pain, and so we cannot evaluate at the outset how much injury the affair will cause. . . . The pain of rejection . . . is like no other. It conjures up enormous rage." However, the relationship should be restored so that the needs of the children can be met.

If the erring mate repents, confesses his sin to God, and receives forgiveness from him, God gives grace to the offended mate to forgive and receive the offender back into the home. True forgiveness includes forgetting the offense, for God says, "Their sins and their iniquities will I remember no more (Heb. 8:12), and "As far as the east is from the west, so far hath he removed our transgressions from us" (Ps. 103:12). It is difficult to forget the transgressions of a spouse, but if the person is sincere in forgiving the spouse, God gives the grace to erase, as far as possible, the sin from the mind of the forgiver. Extra grace will be needed to reenter into the sexual relationship with one who has been unfaithful, but God has promised that his grace is sufficient for every need (2 Cor. 12:9), and that promise includes such a need.

Where a breach in the marriage has occurred and restoration is attempted, the couple should seek to discover the cause of the waywardness. All behavior has a cause. The possible causes are numerous, but if the marriage is to succeed the second time, the source of the problem that ruptured the relationship must be discovered and changed. Sometimes the cause will be obvious to the couple—poor sexual adjustment or problems over money management—and they themselves can take the necessary steps to remedy the problem. In other cases, the cause may not be readily ascertained, or the obvious cause may be only a symptom of a deeper problem. These couples need to seek professional counseling.

> *God instituted marriage to be monogamous and gave man a clear admonition to cleave unto his wife.*

The possibility for renewed happiness exists if the couple will exert the effort to make their marriage a success. God forgives the sinner a whole lifetime of sin on the basis of the blood of Christ, and a mate ought to be willing and able to forgive on the same basis the erring spouse who repents. "Be ye kind one to another, tenderhearted, forgiving one another, even as God for Christ's sake hath forgiven you" (Eph. 4:32). God forgives the sinner not on the basis of how good he is, or how worthy he is, but he does it in grace for Christ's sake. In like manner, Christians are to forgive one another for Christ's sake, that his name might be exalted and glorified in their lives.

There is no Christian marriage threatened with destruction by infidelity that cannot be restored if the couple sincerely makes an attempt to reunite and asks God to help them make the adjustments necessary for success in their relationship. Wheat and Perkins (1980, 40–42) cite the case of Dean and Carol, one of whom had an extramarital affair, as an illustration of a marriage saved and strengthened through counseling in which both individuals experienced spiritual and emotional growth.

Limited Divorce

The question arises regarding what course of action to take if a partner refuses a reconciliation. The answer is found in 1 Corinthians 7:10–11, where Paul writes, "An unto the married I command, yet not I, but the Lord, Let not the wife depart from her husband: But and if she depart, let her remain unmarried, or be reconciled to her husband: and let not the husband put away his wife." Stowell (n.d., 22) writes that "this might be thought to cover cases where, as a last resort after everything has been tried, a separation could be instituted." If there is a separation, the wife or the husband is to seek a reconciliation. If this is not possible, they are to remain in that state in order to be free for a reunion in the future. If the spouse is infatuated with a third party, the situation may look discouraging. However, there are many cases where a person has recovered from the infatuation and returned to his family, so such a situation is not hopeless.

> # Most states have some kind of "separate maintenance" or "limited divorce" law.

If it is the husband who is unfaithful, the wife and family may be in need of support if he refuses to care for the family. Most states have some kind of "separate maintenance" or "limited divorce" law whereby the husband can be forced to support his family even though he is separated from them. If the wife has to take such a drastic step, it may widen the rift between them. If the husband wants a divorce and the wife does not believe in it, the situa-

tion is even more difficult. Even in these circumstances the wife and family have a right to support. However, the erring partner may sue for divorce against the wife's desire.

Desertion is also a problem that often leads to a separate maintenance order by the court. The number of spouses who desert the family is unknown. The Census Bureau (*Current Population Reports* 433, 3) lists 6.2 million persons as having a spouse absent. Some of these are separated because of service in the armed forces. Others are separated because of employment. However, a large number are men who for varied reasons have left home either temporarily or permanently. For many it is a pattern of leaving and returning, a pattern that creates great emotional instability in the family.

Some public policies, such as denying public assistance to a family if the father is present, encourage fathers to leave for the financial benefit of the family. However, the majority of "deserting husbands are inadequate or depressed males who characteristically handle problems by withdrawal" (Kephart 1981, 496). Their families are sometimes supported by taxpayers through various forms of public welfare.

The Effects of Divorce on Parents

There are times when, even for the Christian, divorce is inevitable. Usually a marriage goes through some difficult times before a divorce, and there may be a momentary feeling of relief from the unhappiness of the situation. The spouse who wants to end the marriage usually feels guilt for breaking up the family. The one who is offended often has feelings of rejection, abandonment, pain, outrage, and frustration. A wife usually suffers a loss of self-esteem. She may experience a real sense of failure for not being able to hold the marriage together. A husband whose wife leaves him for another man has doubts about his manliness and virility. On the Holmes-Masuda Stress Scale, the death of a spouse is rated most stressful, but a divorce ranks second (Smith 1983, 71–73).

Dealing with the emotions of divorce is often compared to the grief suffered in the death of a loved one. Malcolm (1987, 22) points out how the plague devastated Europe and Asia in the fourteenth century. Often only one or two members of a family were left to weep. She writes, "When families disintegrate, our society falls apart. That's why we call divorce the new Black Death that stalks the land and leaves the wounded and dying to fend for themselves, often alienated and alone in the world." There are differences that make divorce a more difficult experience than death. In death, the spouse is gone, but in divorce there is the former spouse with a hostile attitude who must be faced from time to time. In death, there is the support of society, but divorce is still looked upon as personal failure. In death, the spouse left behind is expected to mourn, and family and friends rally around to comfort and help. In divorce, friends and relatives may be embarrassed and "hardly know whether to offer congratulations or condolences" (Havemann and Lehtinen 1990, 285). In the death of a spouse, the children can eventually be reconciled to the absence of the parent. In divorce they may become pawns in a custody battle, or at best be shuttled from one home to another.

In both cases a time of grief and mourning is necessary for the healing of emotional scars. For some it takes a long while. Thrash (1991, 23) shared some of her feelings while grieving: "Grief has no fixed seasons. I've been carrying these heart scalds about too long. . . . I hurt all over, as if someone had taken a sledge hammer and bludgeoned my insides. Talking is not easy; I can't verbalize this grief, this loss. In vain I try to keep my pain from showing." She eventually recovered with God's help and is now conducting divorce-recovery seminars. Another person writes (Marshall 1988, 119), "divorce feels like being chopped into pieces. We were one whole—one unit. Now we are two bleeding, scarred half-pieces. . . . The wound . . . is a gape here and a deep stab mark there, and a mass of bruises. . . . They are all bleeding and hurting at the same time. . . . We pray to die, but death won't come." Divorce may be popular, and it may be glamorized by the media, but in reality it causes much pain and grief to those experiencing it.

The goal of the divorced man or woman is to regain emotional health. There is a period of time when they will be conscious of their status. Rosenstock and Weiner (1988, 1–106) state that recovering divorced persons go through five stages: denial, depression, anger, resolution, and recovery. Adjusting to the new status will consume considerable energy. The time will come when they "will give up this role and start thinking of themselves as 'single' rather than 'divorced.' . . . They discover new productive ways of surviving, they discover strengths they were sure they never had, and they lead fuller lives" (Marshall 1988, 106).

> "We call divorce the new Black Death that stalks the land and leaves the wounded and dying to fend for themselves, often alienated and alone in the world."

DeVault and Strong (1989, 465) indicate that the divorced person goes through two periods during recovery from the trauma of divorce. There is a "transitional period" lasting about a year in which the person grieves but also begins to function in the new role as custodial or noncustodial parent. They "have begun to date. Their new loves are taking shape." The "recovery period usually lasts from one to three years." During this time the intense feelings toward the former spouse dissipate, and emotions come into balance. By the end of the period many people are ready for remarriage.

The financial consequences of divorce are different for men and women. Under the new no-fault divorce laws men are entitled to one-half of the family assets. Very often this requires the sale of the family home so the husband can receive his half of the proceeds. This often creates great difficulty for the wife and mother. Weitzman (1985, 80–81) uses the illustration of a young mother with a school-age child. The judge gave her three months in the middle of a school semester to vacate the home. She could not get a loan to buy it because her only income was child support she was receiving, and the bank knew this was not a reliable source of income. (Most child-support payments are not made after two years.) Her only recourse was to move into rental housing. Massachusetts probate Judge Edward Ginsburg prefers to keep children in the home but "he reluctantly allows homes to be sold out from under children in a third of divorce cases he handles. 'It has really become terrible' he laments" (U.S. *News and World Report,* 19 October 1992, 59).

Under the new no-fault divorce laws men are entitled to one-half of the family assets.

Weitzman (1985, 80–81) gives another example of a fifty-four-year-old woman who had been married for twenty-six years. When the time to vacate arrived, she still had no place to go. Landlords would not rent to her because of her "unstable" income (seven hundred dollars per month spousal support). The husband's lawyer finally had her brought back before the judge for contempt of court. He gave her ten days to leave. Older women are especially hard hit by no-fault divorce because many of them have been out of the job market so long their skills have eroded. Others have always been homemakers and never were in the job market. A custodial spouse sometimes can trade off other assets such as pension

rights or second homes for equity in the home, but few families have such assets to divide. It is hoped that this inequity of taking the home from the mother and children will be changed. However, the fact remains that giving the husband one-half of the equity in the home places him in a much more favorable financial position than the wife and children.

The husband often has more education and higher earning power than the wife. A California study showed that divorced men in the first year after a divorce "experience a forty-two percent rise in their standard of living" (Eshleman 1991, 597). This is possible because a man does not share his income equally with the family or adequately support the children. In another California study husbands were allowed to keep two-thirds of their income and wives and children only received one-third for their support (Weitzman 1985, 34). The situation will change when he remarries, for he will have a new family to support plus child support payments (if he continues them).

Wives suffer financially after divorce. The courts ignore the lower earning power of most women and burden the wife with supporting the children. "The wife must find a new place to live and a new school for the children. . . . They have become the new poor" (Havemann and Lehtinen 1990, 274). Under the old divorce laws a wife could refuse a divorce until there was an adequate provision made for her and the children. The new no-fault laws stress "equality," which works against the wife and mother. Instead of an ample single income or a dual income if she worked, the wife is reduced to living on her own income, child-support payments, help from her family, and welfare payments. "The most damaging unintended consequence of the no-fault divorce laws is that they systematically impoverish divorced women and their children" (DeVault and Strong 1989, 475). On the average, the standard of living for divorced women and their children suffer a 73 percent decline in the first year after divorce (Weitzman 1985, 362). Since so many children (more than 60 percent) will live in single-parent homes sometime in their childhood, "through no-fault divorce rules we are sentencing a significant proportion of the next generation of American children to periods of financial hardship" (DeVault and Strong 1987, 475). According to Weitzman (1985, xi) divorced women "now face a divorce law that treats them 'equally' and expects them to be equally capable of supporting themselves after a divorce."

Mothers with custody of children usually are awarded child support by the courts. However, the overburdened courts are lax in enforcing the orders for child support. About 50 percent of fathers never fully comply with the court orders and approximately 30 percent never make a single payment (Weitzman 1985, 284). The burden of collection is on the wife, and she has little recourse if he refuses to pay. She can have his wages attached but judges are reluctant to order it. The result is the wife and children are forced onto welfare rolls.

Michigan has the best rate of collection of all the states. "The fathers make their payments to the court. If the father fails to make a payment, a Friend of the Court begins a series of actions to get his compliance. If these fail, the father is put in jail and Michigan jails one out of every seven men ordered to pay child support. Consequently, Michigan collects more child support per case than any other state in the country" (Weitzman 1987, 299).

Weitzman calls the failure of our child support system a "national disgrace." She writes, "Child support awards that go unpaid and unenforced make a mockery of the judicial system and the value of court orders. They also leave millions of children without the basic necessities of life" (Weitzman 1985, 262). Congress passed an act in 1984 that mandated the withholding of federal and state tax refunds to those in arrears in child support payments (Weitzman 1985, 262). This has done little to alleviate the situation. One million divorces each year involve children, so each year more women and their children will join the ranks of the poor. These unfortunate ones are overlooked by those who tout the advantages of divorce in freeing persons from bad marriages and giving them a new beginning. For the vast majority of women it is a new start on the road to poverty.

Most men and women usually recover from the effects of divorce. Blakeslee and Wallerstein (1989, xii), whose clinic has dealt with more than two thousand divorced families, found that "it takes women an average of three to three and one-half years and men two to two and one-half years to reestablish a sense of external order after the separation." Some men and women never recover. The trauma of the divorce leaves them so embittered that they turn the children against the noncustodial parent. Their lives are consumed with hate and rage.

The Effects of Divorce on Children

One of the great concerns of most parents is the psychological effects of divorce on their children. It is generally recognized that children of divorce make better adjustment to life than children reared in homes filled with conflict between parents (Steinmetz and Sussman 1987, 616). Such homes are often places where parents physically abuse one another and the children. Children reared in a violent atmosphere will often be aggressive and violent in their behavior. Children in such homes are at a greater disadvantage than children of divorce.

> *"If [child support payments] fail, the father is put in jail and Michigan jails one out of every seven men ordered to pay child support."*

Blakeslee and Wallerstein (1989, 283–308) made a unique ten-year study of sixty families in order to learn the long-term effects of divorce. The families chosen were normal families with no history of psychological or deviant behavior. The results are not encouraging: divorce has long-lasting effects on children.

The effects do not always show up the first year after divorce since some children are able to repress their feelings. Preschoolers react strongly to the separation. They do not want to let the custodial parent out of their sight for fear they will be abandoned—if one parent has gone the other might also leave. They have trouble sleeping, become sad and withdrawn, and may feel their misbehavior caused the divorce. They may wet the bed and seek a security blanket or object.

> # *In the five-year follow-up, about one-third of the children were worse off than before.*

Children of five to eight suffer "feelings of loss, rejection, guilt and loyalty conflicts." They fear the permanent loss of the absent parent and fantasize about the parent's return. School work suffers. "Many little boys show an intense longing for their fathers that seems physically painful." The loyalty conflicts are intense.

Intense anger is felt by children nine to twelve toward their parents for getting divorced. "They also suffer grief, anxiety, an acute sense of loneliness, and a sense of powerlessness." They may complain of "somatic symptoms such as stomachaches and headaches. Delinquent behavior may appear such as lying, petty theft, and early sexual misbehavior. They worry about their parents and try to help them to cope."

Adolescents react most strongly. This is surprising to many, but they are at a stage when they need a stable family structure to help them deal with awakening sexual and aggressive impulses. "Teenagers may also grow acutely anxious as they see the vulnerability of their parents." They are fearful they will repeat the failures of their parents. They will spend much time away from home since they feel abandoned by their parents. Many adolescents become delinquent because they lack the control and guidance to overcome the extreme peer pressure they feel. Some will respond differently and will assume responsibility in the home and help with chores.

The disturbing factor is that in the five-year follow-up, about one-third of the children were worse off than before. They were still intensely angry with their parents for divorcing, and a majority still hoped for a reconciliation even though the noncustodial parent had remarried. "Children's fundamental attitudes about society and themselves can be forever changed by divorce, and by events experienced in the years afterward. These changes can be incorporated permanently into their developing characters and personalities. . . . People may get their lives back on track, but . . . the track runs a wholly different course than the one they were on before the divorce" (Blakeslee and Wallerstein 1989, xii). Children are profoundly and permanently changed by divorce.

Social scientists have been criticized for "generalizing their findings to all children of divorce" (Steinmetz and Sussman 1967, 616), but when one sees these results in children from normal homes, what must the results be on children from homes with histories of psychological and deviant behavior"?

Blakeslee and Wallerstein (1989, 175) discovered that very young children adjusted best in the long run. At the end of ten years 68 percent were doing well compared to 40 percent of the older children. The most critical factor in how well children adjusted was the mother-child relationship (Blakeslee and Wallerstein 1989, 187). If the mother was psychologically stable and able to "restore a nurturing, maternal relationship," the children developed normally.

When there are children involved in a divorce, the question of custody is most important. In 90 percent of the cases, the wife is awarded custody, fathers get custody in 6 percent of all cases, and joint custody is awarded in the remaining 4 percent (Steinmetz and Sussman 1987, 619). The ability of parents to handle custodial responsibilities also affect the development of the children. However, even when children receive proper care, it is difficult for many to be shuttled back and forth from one home to another under joint custody. Yorkey (1990, 65) relates that often they are called ping-pong kids. One seven-year-old girl who grew weary of being shifted back and forth between her parents said, "I wish I could split myself in two." Often there are stepparents and stepsiblings in the noncustodial home with whom the child has to interact.

Unfortunately, many noncustodial parents lose interest after a few years and "estimates suggest that half of all divorced fathers have no regularly scheduled contact with their children, and about three out of four see their children less than once a week" (Pocs 1989–90, 168). Yet it is known that one of the strongest determinants of a child's healthy adjustments to divorce is the extent of the father's continued participation as a parent.

Fathers are important to a growing boy for he is the role model for his male behavior. The son's identification with the father will determine his ability to deal with other males. Even though the father is noncustodial he will still influence the son's behavior toward females by his treatment of the mother. Much of the boy's self-esteem will be derived by the treatment received from the father.

The father's continued relationship with the daughter is also important. A girl learns how to relate to males from the interaction with her father. She learns that male personalities, their way of thinking and reacting, and their likes and dislikes differ from those of females. Girls also develop much of their self-concept from the manner in which the father interacts with the mother. Especially important is the love a girl receives from her father. If she feels rejected by her father, she may seek male affection from her male peers. "This is the reason girls from father-absent homes are so much more at risk for teenage pregnancy" (Miller 1990, 170–71).

Divorce and Sexuality

A real consequence of divorce is the cessation of a regular sex life. For the 25 percent who remarry within a few months, or for those already involved in an affair before the divorce, this is a not a problem. But for the woman who waits an average of three and one-half years or the man who waits two and one-half years before remarriage, these can be difficult periods. Anthony and Koons (1991, 142) quote Gagnon *(Human Sexualities)* as estimating "that 90 percent of those who were once married have had sexual intercourse since their divorce or widowhood." Koons also quotes Hunt *(The Divorce Experience)* as stating "only one in twenty men who have been single for one year, and only one in fourteen women are celibate."

Celibacy and abstinence are Christian virtues, but according to surveys that have been made, many Christian singles have abandoned these standards. Koons and her associates made the first large-scale survey of Christian singles. In regard to sexual practices, they discovered that only 18.4 percent of the divorced had not engaged in intercourse. Twenty-five percent had two to three sexual partners, but an alarming 9.5 percent had more than twenty partners. However, when asked the frequency of intercourse in the previous six months, 72.6 percent indicated they had not engaged in intercourse during the period. Ten percent indicated an activity of once or twice a week. This illustrates the negative influence of the new morality on Christian morals.

> *Celibacy and abstinence are Christian virtues, but many Christian singles have abandoned these standards.*

The specter of AIDS should deter sexual activity outside of marriage. But for the Christian there is the higher goal of chastity for God's glory. Malcolm (1987, 34) has a valuable comment: "'But what do I do with my sex drive?' a

293

single woman asked. What people through the ages have done. Single men and women have loved God and challenged the god of sex to run their lives. Whether married or single, our sex drives are under the control of God who made us sexual beings. Both alternatives demand chastity—the married person has sex with only one, and the unmarried with none!"

The divorced person has the choice of seeking a new mate through dating. DeVault and Strong (1989, 469) comment that dating is important to widowed and divorced people for several reasons. It lets society know the person is available for marriage again. It enhances the person's self-esteem. It marks an entrance into the singles' subculture to learn new roles. For the Christian it means engaging in heterosexual conduct once again and yet remaining celibate.

Smith (1983, 105–6) gives several suggestions that are helpful in maintaining purity. One is to "commit your life (sex included) to God"—"Likewise reckon ye also yourselves to be dead indeed unto sin, but alive unto God" (Rom. 6:1). Next, "control your thoughts." She quotes John Stott (*Your Mind Matters*) who contends that the "battle is nearly always won in the mind." "Be ye transformed by the renewing of your mind . . ." (Rom. 12:2). Then "count on God to help you." "For it is God that worketh within you, both to will and to do his good pleasure" (Phil. 2:13). Get involved with "an empathetic church and understanding Christians" to help provide spiritual food and fellowship to facilitate growth in grace. "But grow in grace and in knowledge of the Lord Jesus Christ" (2 Pet. 3:18). She writes, "Love is life's greatest experience. . . . Love must be viewed . . . from a different perspective from the world's. . . . God's love . . . should motivate us to greater creativity throughout life—single or married, and with or without sexual intimacy." It is possible, though admittedly difficult, for the divorced and widowed to live pure lives with God's help as long as they remain single.

Establishing the Blended Family

The purpose of divorce, according to Wallerstein (1989, xi), is twofold—to get out of a bad marriage and to build a new life. Consequently, three-fourths of divorced women and five-sixths of divorced men remarry. There are more than eleven million blended families including at least fifteen million children (Olson 1990, 59).

The stress on remarried families is much greater than on a first marriage. The result is a high divorce rate in these marriages also. Houmes and Meier (Olson 1990, 60) note "that the divorce rate is thirty to forty percent for first marriages, sixty percent for second marriages, eighty percent for third marriages, and ninety percent for fourth marriages." Another sad statistic is "that forty percent of all second marriages end in divorce within four years. Persons in remarriages face a most difficult task, and particularly so in the early years of that remarriage" (Olson 1990, 60).

What makes these remarriages so difficult? Olson (1990, 60–61) points out that first marriages have well-defined roles with appropriate terms assigned to them. Everyone knows who a father is and what role he plays. The same holds true for a mother. In the blended family these statuses and roles are not well understood. A father becomes a stepfather, but his role in the blended family will be determined by the age of the stepchildren. If they are young he may function as a father, but if they are teenagers he may be accepted only as a friend or he may be rejected entirely. At the same time he is still a father to his natural children, and the roles of father and stepfather may conflict at times.

Another problem in the blended family concerns the couple themselves. In the first marriage they were able to learn their roles as husbands and wives in the passing of time. In a second marriage, they bring the habits and patterns of behavior from the first marriage into the relationship immediately, so not only must personalities but also behavior patterns have to be harmonized. These patterns come from two marriages, since divorced people tend to marry divorced people (Miller 1990, 137).

This problem of established behavior patterns also concerns the children. Both parents have established beliefs and habits in relationships with their children. Who is going to discipline the children? What role will the stepparent play? Will physical punishment be used? What authority will the stepfather exercise? Since he is usually considered an outsider, there can be problems with the children, and this often leads to difficulties with their mother (Miller 1990, 139). Even though an agreement is made on discipline before marriage, the reality of daily living may undermine it. Failure to resolve conflict over discipline may be one reason so many second marriages fail.

Finances can also be a stressful point for the blended family. Many women with children are at the poverty level. When a woman remarries, her condition should improve since the husband brings an additional income to the family. However, if he is burdened with court-ordered support of his own children, his income may not help that much. It also may become a source of conflict since the new wife may resent his having to support his children. Sometimes she may insist he terminate his payments; if she handles the checkbook, she may fail to send the payments.

Couples contemplating remarriage need to have a prenuptial agreement that details the financial responsibilities of each party. Many individuals reject this idea because it seems to indicate a lack of trust in each other, and some even refuse to take part in such an agreement and break off the relationship. Nevertheless, a prenuptial agreement is both a practical and wise arrangement because it protects the children of both spouses. They are assured of receiving the estates of their biological parents. Some people neglect to make an agreement because they have few assets, but over the years wealth can be accumulated or inherited. The agreement should also spell out the responsibilities of each spouse regarding cost of child care, share of household expenses, car expenses, and payment of college education (Hunter 1991, 148–52).

It is apparent that the blended family faces many obstacles on the way to happiness. Consequently, it is easy to see why such a large percentage fail to reach the goal. Those families that succeed seem to be as happy and well-adjusted as first marriages. Miller (1990, 156) calls attention to research that demonstrates that "82% of all second marriages involving children are seen as either good [18%] or excellent [64%] by the children and teenagers in those step families." The spouses have learned lessons in human relationships from the first marriage that they are able to apply in the second marriage (Havemann and Lehtinen 1990, 285).

The success of these families indicates that spouses have been more selective in choosing compatible mates the second time around. First-time spouses are often chosen on the basis of physical rather than psychological compatibility. Having failed the first time, the divorced person is often more careful the second time. These people are not under the intense biological pressures that often accompanied the choice of a first spouse. They must also consider the ability of the prospective mate to effectively parent their children, and so they tend to make wiser selections the second time. Being older, they are able to choose on a realistic basis rather than on a romantic basis only.

The Church, Divorce, and Remarriage

The prevalence of divorce and remarriage among Christians raises serious questions for which there are no easy answers. The Scriptures do not give clear, easy-to-follow guidelines where divorce and remarriage are concerned. Few verses refer directly to these subjects. Eminent Bible scholars have given various interpretations down through the centuries, and the debate continues today. Consequently, several different views are found within evangelical churches.

> *The Scriptures do not give clear, easy-to-follow guidelines where divorce and remarriage are concerned.*

Nearly all conservative Bible scholars teach that marriage was instituted by God and the marriage bond can only be broken by death. Sell (1981, 59) comments, "Ideally, marriage is to be dissolved only be death. . . . Confronted by the Pharisees with a question concerning divorce, Jesus appealed to God's standard 'at the beginning.' This clearly indicates that marriage is an exclusive and lasting relationship." In commenting on Genesis 2:24, Jones (1989, 19) writes, "We can see from this verse also that God planned in the beginning for marriage to last for life. . . . This oneness is to last as long as they live. This is confirmed in the New Testament by Jesus (Matt. 19:3–6) and Paul (Rom. 7:2; 1 Cor. 7:39). Joseph Stowell, Jr., president of Moody Bible Institute (*Moody Monthly*, November 1991, 15) asserts that "churches need to emphasize that not only is marriage an indissoluble contract between two people, it is also a sacred commitment sanctioned by God and sealed by vows spoken in His Name." These statements clearly indicate the consensus that marriage between two people is to last a lifetime, is indissoluble, and can be broken only by death.

> # Much of the disagreement about divorce and remarriage centers around the interpretation of Matthew 19:3–9.

There is another area where Bible teachers are mostly in agreement. Although they acknowledge the marriage union is permanent, most of them agree that it can be broken. This seems illogical by Western patterns of thought. According to Webster, "permanent" means "lasting or intended to last indefinitely, without change . . . abiding . . . opposed to 'temporary.' Synonyms are 'unchangeable, constant, changeless.'" How can a marriage union that is to last "indefinitely, without change" be broken? This is confusing until one discovers that the dictionary gives a second definition of "permanent." In this sense, "permanent" means "lasting a relatively long time, as a 'permanent wave,'" that is "a hair wave made to last for several months, produced by the use of chemicals or heat." So to logically understand Bible teachers who speak of the marriage tie as "permanent" and then admit it can be broken, one must use the second definition. Incidentally, many marriages do not last as long as a permanent wave—they end in divorce within three or four months.

Much of the disagreement about divorce and remarriage centers around the interpretation of Matthew 19:3–9:

> The Pharisees also came unto him, tempting him, and saying unto him, Is it lawful for a man to put away his wife for every cause?
>
> And he answered and said unto them, Have ye not read, that he which made them at the beginning made them male and female,
>
> And said, For this cause shall a man leave father and mother, and shall cleave to his wife: and they twain shall be one flesh?
>
> Wherefore they are no more twain, but one flesh. What therefore God hath joined together, let not man put asunder.
>
> They say unto him, Why did Moses then command to give a writing of divorcement, and to put her away?
>
> He said unto them, Moses because of the hardness of your hearts suffered you to put away your wives: but from the beginning it was not so.
>
> And I say unto you, Whosoever shall put away his wife, except it be for fornication, and shall marry another, committeth adultery: and whoso marrieth her which is put away doth commit adultery.

Particular difficulty is found in trying to determine the meaning of the exception clause of verse 9, "except it be for fornication." Some Bible scholars believe these verses permit divorce but do not give the divorced persons a right to remarry. Others maintain that the exception clause permits remarriage of the innocent party.

Another view is presented by William J. Hopewell in a scholarly booklet, *Marriage and Divorce*. He cites eight passages (Gen. 2:24; Mal. 2:14–16; Rom. 7:2–4; 1 Cor. 7:10, 39; Matt. 19:3–8; Mark 10:1–12; Luke 16:18) and states, "This aggregate of eight passages gives overwhelming and indisputable evidence for the permanency of God's institution of marriage . . ." (1976, 9).

Hopewell gives a logical explanation of the exception clause of Matthew 19:9, "Whosoever shall put away his wife, except it be for fornication . . ." as referring to putting away a wife during the second stage or betrothal period of the Jewish marriage custom. The first stage was the promise to marry and the third the actual consummation. The betrothal period usually lasted a year to prove that the bride was not pregnant, and if she was, she could be put away by a bill of divorcement. The decision of Joseph to "put away Mary" (Matt. 1:19) is the only biblical example of the exception clause. A consummated marriage, the third state, could never be broken. Such an interpretation of this clause agrees with Jesus' teaching in the passage on the permanency of marriage in verses 4–6, and with the passages in Mark 10:1–12 and Luke 16:18 where the exception clause does not appear (Hopewell 1976, 12). In this viewpoint, since there is no possibility of divorce, there can be no remarriage. According to this view marriage is permanent in the sense of the first definition, that is, it is "intended to last indefinitely, without change."

Others take a broader view and insist that in the age of grace, divorce and remarriage should be treated like any other failure or sin. Divorce and remarriage are then permissible for any reason. These scholars teach that permanence is God's ideal, but today it is difficult to realize God's ideal. Whenever one falls short of the ideal, then confession and forgiveness prepare the divorced person for a new beginning. "Jesus' statement about divorce is not unlike other declarations of His, such as 'Be perfect, therefore, as your Heavenly Father is perfect' (Matt. 5:48). The indissolubility of the marriage bond is a standard of perfection, just as holiness is . . ." (Sell 1981, 64). The proponents of this view use the gracious treatment by Christ of the woman at the well (John 4:10) and the woman taken in adultery (John 8:11) as indications that grace should be the principle to follow in questions of divorce and remarriage. "The answer is not to be found in analyzing an exception clause; it is to be realized in God's indisputable words about grace. Marriage is part of the created order; divorce is part of the redemptive order" (Sell 1981, 65). Small (1986, 184) summarizes this position: "But all alike are invited to come in penitence, to confess whatever sin may have been involved, and to apply to God's unlimited grace in Christ Jesus. All is renewable in God's grace. . . . Remarriage is a question of grace, and of nothing more."

> *Others insist that in the age of grace, divorce and remarriage should be treated like any other failure or sin.*

In view of so many different interpretations of what the Bible teaches about divorce and remarriage, it is easy to understand the confusion among pastors and churches. Some major denominations have set standards for their churches, but other groups have left it up to individual churches and pastors to decide what their practice will be. In this situation, problems arise when a pastor and his church disagree on what the practice should be. However, most churches now agree that those individuals and families who have been hurt by divorce need all the love and compassion the churches can give. Stowell (*Moody Monthly*, November 1991, 15) makes a strong plea for the church to teach and uphold the ideal "that marriage should last forever, and that divorce is not an option." While holding to this truth, the church must also exercise the "touch of grace." God's grace is remedial, supportive, understanding, and caring. "Grace is the heart of the truth. It is the tender arms and tear-stained cheeks of truth applied" (Stowell, *Moody Monthly*, November 1991, 14–15). As the "black death of divorce" increases, churches will have the opportunity to display the love and compassion of Christ in new and different ways. Stevens (1991, 16) suggests that "although the church as an entity may not approve of casual divorce, it still must recognize the divorced individual's needs, the reality of pain and hurt. The church must minister, as many are doing, to the person who is single once more."

> **Most churches now agree that those individuals and families who have been hurt by divorce need all the love and compassion the churches can give.**

Prevention of Divorce

What can be done to reduce the rate of divorce? It seems logical to begin with the home, since divorce runs in families. Existing marriages need to be strengthened by marriage-enrichment programs. Husbands and wives need to place hedges (Jenkins 1989, 21) around their relationships. Parents need to be consistent role models for their children and demonstrate a proper respect for each other and a genuine display of affection. This will help children learn how to give and receive affection.

Good communication skills are a characteristic of a strong home. Children need to be trained in these skills and in socially accepted means of settling conflicts. Young people must

be taught that one of the primary purposes of dating is to test the *psychological* compatibility of prospective mates. This should help them to be selective in choosing a mate. The emphasis on romantic love, especially the physical relationship, is responsible for many mismatches in personalities that end in divorce. Christian high schools, colleges, and seminaries need to require a course in marriage and family living. Students who have taken such a course rate their marriages happier, and have lower divorce rates than those who haven't taken such a course.

Financial problems lead to divorce in many situations, so it is incumbent upon parents to teach their children to be responsible in handling money.

There may be times when families will need to either homeschool or place their children in Christian day schools. The influence of secular humanism rampant in many public schools is difficult to overcome. However, no amount of Christian education can overcome the inconsistencies of Christian parents who fail to live up to what they profess.

Many churches now have family life education programs. These need to emphasize the indissolubility of marriage. Sermons, Bible-school lessons, and youth study materials should be aimed at strengthening the family structure. Peterson (1984, 286–87) suggests that a church needs "a mechanism for detecting problems and providing encouragement and counsel where needed." Mature couples can be trained especially for this ministry. They can reach out to troubled couples and attempt to aid them in solving their problems.

There are social scientists who believe that divorced people, single parents, and blended families should be accepted as normal forms of family life. Raschke (Steinmetz and Sussman 1987, 620) proposes that divorce should be recognized "as one of the normal consequences of marriage" and should be removed "from the socially created, and socially defined deviance milieu of our society." In doing this "concerned professionals will be taking a step out of the 'dark ages of such deviance' into the 'sunlight of healthy normalcy.'" The true beneficiaries of such a change will be those already divorced and those who will be divorced.

This attitude can be contrasted with that of Blakeslee and Wallerstein (1989, xx). After concluding a ten-year study of the effects of divorce on families, Wallerstein wrote, "Having worked with more than two thousand families since 1980, I have to say that things are not getting better and divorce is not getting easier. If anything, it is getting worse." It is difficult to believe that these two thousand families would consider their divorces as bringing them into "the sunlight of healthy normalcy." It may be easy for someone seated in an academic ivory tower to say divorce is normal, but those who experience the pain of divorce and those who work daily with families affected by divorce realize that it can never be normal. Men and women are made for the intimate relationship of marriage, and the rupture of this relationship will always bring heartache and grief. It never can become normal.

The church must do all it can to stem the tide of divorce. God has instituted marriage for the good of mankind, as well as for the blessing of his people. Peterson (1984, 238–39) aptly expresses this truth: "The coming together of a man and a woman is ordained of God, with the intentions of human joy, love, and fidelity, intimacy, and the conception, birth, and nurture of offspring. . . . We modern lovers of God through His Son Jesus Christ, tossed about on the waves of *social change* [italics added], do well to keep our eyes on that pole star of marriage and family presented in God's Word, for it is so evidently God's will for His offspring."

Study Questions

1. Discuss the term *blended family.*
2. Define "no-fault divorce," "divorce mediation," and "do-it-yourself" divorce.
3. List and discuss several reasons there are so many divorces today.
4. Why is an affair so damaging to a relationship? What steps should be taken to restore a broken relationship?
5. Compare the grief suffered in divorce to that suffered in the death of a spouse.
6. Why have the no-fault divorce laws led to the "impoverishment of of divorced women"?
7. Discuss the effects of divorce on children of various ages.
8. List several reasons the divorce rate is higher for second marriages than for first marriages.
9. Summarize three views concerning divorce and remarriage prevalent in evangelical churches.
10. What can churches do to help stem the tide of divorce among Christians?

Suggested Readings

Blakeslee, S., and J. S. Wallerstein. 1989. *Second chances: Men, women and children a decade after divorce.* New York: Ticknor and Fields. The authors studied sixty middle-class families over a period of ten years, and some for fifteen years, to see what the consequences of divorce were for the families involved. They wanted to see if the popular belief that time heals all wounds was true. It is not. They found many of the participants suffered long-lasting effects from divorce, both psychological and social.

Brissett, M., and B. Burns. 1991. *The adult child of divorce: A recovery handbook.* Nashville: Nelson. This book is designed to help adults whose parents divorced to recognize the attitudes that carry over from one generation to another. It has worksheets to help the individual in sorting through these attitudes.

Hunter, H. 1991. *Remarriage in midlife: Plan it first, make it last.* Grand Rapids: Baker. Written by a woman who had remarried in midlife, the book covers problems faced by those who marry in midlife. She gives helpful advice about remarriage and stresses the necessity that both individuals be committed Christians.

Jones, K. E. 1989. *Divorce and remarriage in the Bible.* Anderson, Ind.: Warner. Although the author takes the position that marriage is permanent, he maintains that the marriage bond can be broken by sexual infidelity. There is a discussion on divorced and remarried pastors that suggests it would be best for churches if such men left the pastorate.

Phillips, R. 1988. *Putting asunder: A history of divorce in western society.* Cambridge: Cambridge Univ. Press. A scholarly treatment of divorce, mainly from the Reformation to the present. The discussion of the changes in attitudes toward divorce helps to explain the increase in divorces.

Small, D. H. 1986. *Remarriage and God's renewing grace.* Grand Rapids: Baker. The author was one of the early writers in the field of marriage and the family with the publication of the excellent volume *Design for Christian Marriage.* In the present volume he argues that divorce is a sin, and like any sin, the grace of God can forgive it. This prepares for and gives the individual the right to remarry.

Stevens, H. 1991. *Hope for the divorced.* Nashville: Convention Press. Designed as a unit in a church study course, this book provides insight into the causes and consequences of divorce. It has a chapter on how to conduct a divorce-recovery workshop. The final chapter is an introduction to small-group dynamics and how to conduct a support group for divorced people.

Thrash, S. A. 1991. *Dear God, I'm divorced.* Grand Rapids: Baker. A sad story of a woman who had been married for twenty-seven years when her husband left her for another woman. However, Thrash openly shares her sorrows and feelings after the divorce and also her joys as she recovered from the experience. Her reaction to the call from the "other" woman after Thrash's former husband left his new marriage is most interesting.

Weitzman, L. J. 1985. *The divorce revolution.* New York: Free Press. No-fault divorce laws were designed to bring equality to divorce settlements. The author's research shows that these laws do not provide an equal settlement to both parties. On the contrary, they favor the husband, and this has led to the "impoverishment of divorced women and their children." Divorced men in California experienced a "42 percent rise" in their standard of living while the women experienced a "73 percent decline."

18

Counseling for Family Problems

Where no counsel is, the people fall: but in the multitude of counselors there is safety.

—Proverbs 11:15

The Importance of Counseling

"I can't understand why he would leave me and the family. It's true we had occasional arguments about disciplining the children. I repeatedly had to remind him he was spending too much time and money on the golf course when he should be doing things with the boys. Between his work and his golf game the boys saw him only on Sunday. Of course most of that day was spent in church." Mary is unburdening her heart to her pastor because John had just left her for another woman. Pastor Jones will attempt to get the couple to resolve their differences and reestablish their relationship.

It is evident that both individuals will have to make changes if the marriage is to be saved. A well-trained counselor will help each one to see the necessity for change. Many times the counseling is successful and marriages are saved.

Changing attitudes toward marriage exert a strong pressure on families today. The rapid increase in sexual promiscuity among single and married individuals threatens marriages more than it did in the past. Society, particularly through the media, glorifies and encourages adultery and no longer considers sexual fidelity as a norm for marriage. Economic pressures and the dual-income family create stresses unknown a generation ago. The emphasis on personal gratification and the rise of individualism have also increased stress in marriages. When there is no commitment to a lasting relationship, problems arise when perceived needs are not met. Consequently, it is estimated by Meier (1991) that "half of those coming for counseling come primarily because of marital conflicts and another quarter come because of marital-related conflicts."

The rapid increase in sexual promiscuity among single and married individuals threatens marriages more than it did in the past.

There has been a large increase in the number of professionals trained in the area of marriage and family counseling (Gladding 1988, 356–60). Couples can solve many of the problems and conflicts of marriage if they seek the help of these professionals. They can avoid the unhappiness and oftentimes the heartbreak such conflicts generate. This generation has seen such a proliferation of Christian counselors and literature that most couples should be able to find a Christian professional therapist to help in a time of need.

Why Counseling Services Are Not Utilized

Counseling as a profession is relatively new but has received enough publicity that most people know counselors are available (Gladding 1988, 9–18). Collins (1986, 7) states, "We currently are living in the midst of a 'counseling boom.' Surely there has never been a time in history when so many people are aware of psychological issues . . . and willing to talk about their insecurities, inadequacies, and intimate concerns." However, it takes initiative to seek out a counselor, and most couples are reluctant to take the time and energy to find one. When a spouse is sick, medical help is sought immediately. The public has *not* been educated to call for help at the first sign a marriage is ailing. Until this concept is accepted and

practiced, many marriages that could be preserved will end up in divorce. Seeking the help of a counselor when a marriage encounters problems should become as common as calling a plumber when there is a plumbing problem.

Even when couples are familiar with counseling, they may hesitate to visit a counselor because of the fear such an appointment engenders. "Many people think that beyond the waiting room door lurks a fiendish manipulator of human behavior who has X-ray vision and can plumb the depths of the human soul, recklessly uprooting cherished beliefs and relationships" (Roe 1982, 37). With such attitudes toward counselors it is easy to see why many fear to visit one. It must be recognized that this is a distorted picture. Counselors are dedicated people who refuse to manipulate clients. College students have an advantage over the general public since they are exposed to counseling services of various kinds on college campuses. They should not be afraid to seek counseling if a problem arises in their marriage.

The reluctance to seek help for personal problems may also stem from the fact that in American culture much emphasis is placed on being independent and self-reliant. People do not like to depend on others. Many times they "view their marriage as nobody's business but their own" (Coleman 1988, 359). When they encounter a problem in their marriage they feel able to solve it. Some are able to do so but many others fail and marriages dissolve when they could have been rescued with some outside help.

Christian subculture also emphasizes dependence upon the Lord for the solution of all Christians' problems. The cliche is, "Christ is the answer to all of life's problems." Young people are taught to pray and seek God's help with every problem. Collins (1988, 41) observes, "Christians sometimes feel that they shouldn't have overwhelming problems so the need for counseling is seen as an indication of personal and spiritual failure." As Roe (1982, 31–36) reflects, "nice Christians are not supposed to have problems." When "nice Christians" do have a problem in their marriage they are afraid to let others know. It does not occur to such persons that a Christian counselor might be part of God's way of helping them find his solution to their problem.

Others fail to seek counseling because it is relatively expensive. However, when one considers not only the high monetary cost of a divorce but also the human suffering involved, it makes good economic sense to pay whatever is necessary to try and preserve a marriage. A couple will spend hundreds of dollars for a wedding and thousands of dollars for a car, but will not spend money for help when the marriage is in trouble. For those who can't really afford it, most communities have agencies that will provide counseling on an "ability to pay" scale. The counselee pays only what he can afford according to the family income. Many times expense and time are involved in traveling to a counselor's office.

Why Couples Fail to Seek Counseling

The failure to seek counsel when needed may be due to the fact that people are unaware of their need for help from someone not involved in the situation. As a rule, a person or couple can use, and should use, the services of a counselor if they cannot resolve a problem after giving it careful attention and prayerful consideration. When a couple is constantly bickering or fighting, they need help. If a spouse is frequently finding fault with his or her mate, the marriage is in trouble. When some personality trait antagonizes a mate so that chronic unhappiness results, it is time to seek outside help. Cases of EMS (extramarital sex) are a danger signal and many times can be helped with counseling. When a spouse is constantly discouraged and depressed, a counselor can help. Failure to resolve financial problems indicates the need for a counselor. These are just a few of the many types of cases seen by marriage counselors. Unfortunately, many couples with these danger signals do not recognize them. They either endure unhappy marriages or eventually divorce.

In marital difficulties, there are emotional overtones to most problems. Intelligent people may not be able to solve a problem because emotions hinder the reasoning process. The principle restated is that couples need coun-

seling when they have made an honest effort to resolve their problem but cannot find a solution. When this fact is recognized, the services of an uninvolved, well-trained, objective third party can often provide answers that the emotionally involved couple has overlooked.

> *Intelligent people may not be able to solve a problem because emotions hinder the reasoning process.*

Counseling is also needed when communication is broken between two spouses. Miller (1985, 4) recognizes that "the lack of communication between the husband and wife is the most often listed cause for seeking counsel." Collins (1988, 410) believes "that occasional miscommunication between spouses is inevitable. When miscommunication is more common than clear communication, however, the marriage begins to have serious problems. Poor communication tends to breed more of the same. . . . Communication is a learned behavior . . . people can learn to make it better." Grunlan and Lambrides (1984, 169) quote Bustanoby, a Christian counselor, as saying that "almost without exception the couple with a troubled marriage is having a communication problem." Before communication breaks down entirely, it is imperative that a counselor become involved.

When a couple fails to communicate, it is most often the wife who seeks counseling. However, some therapists feel that it is necessary to see both spouses from the beginning (Gladding 1988, 365). He will meet separately with each spouse, listen to both sides of the story, and enable both spouses to express hostility without hurting the absent person. This process enables the counselor "to build rapport and trust with both spouses" (Friesen and

Friesen 1989, 9). As progress is made, the counselor will bring the couple together, and if all goes well, communication can be reestablished, problems can be solved, and the marriage relationship resumed. If the counselor is able to help them resolve areas that have frequently caused conflict, the marriage may be reestablished on a firmer basis that it previously enjoyed.

However, if the relationship has been broken by one spouse leaving home, it becomes difficult for the therapy given to one partner to influence the absent one. Many times the mental condition of the one seeking help may be such that therapy is necessary even if it cannot influence the absent partner. Many counselors have discarded saving the marriage as the goal of marriage counseling. The new theory is to help individuals cope with the difficulties they are facing in the marriage or will face in case of divorce.

> # *Many counselors have discarded saving the marriage as the goal of marriage counseling.*

Occasionally there is such disharmony and conflict in a marriage that it disintegrates beyond repair. It is difficult to maintain spiritual fellowship with God under such a situation, and often the couple is in no condition spiritually to seek the Lord's help for their troubles. Little by little conflict generates hostility in the relationship, and the love they once knew gradually becomes hatred. Just as love grows on pleasant emotional responses, so the opposite emotion (hate) develops because of unpleasant responses (Gottman 1993).

Adams (1972, 33) cites the interesting case of a woman in a counseling session who produced a "manuscript that was at least one inch

thick, on 8" x 11" size paper, single-spaced, typewritten on both sides. . . . It turned out to be a thirteen-year record of wrongs that her husband had done to her. They were all listed and catalogued." This is an extreme illustration, for most people never keep a list of unpleasant emotional responses, but the effect of destroying the relationship is the same.

Whenever a couple senses that disharmony or conflict is damaging their relationship, they should seek help from a counselor. Since all behavior has a cause, a counselor with good training and experience, can pinpoint the cause of the difficulties and make suggestions how they may be eliminated. Couples should not wait until irreparable harm has been done before seeking professional help. It is much easier to restore a relationship before a couple has begun to hate each other. Capps (1981, 200) points out that "in contrast to premarital and grief counseling, where the pastor is able to give counseling at the 'proper time,' marriage counseling is often frustrating because it seems to come too late to do much good." The fact that Christian couples do get divorces indicates that this process of love turning to hate can operate in Christian marriages as well as non-Christian marriages, but when God's love dominates a relationship between two of his dear children, love can never turn to hatred.

A couple with good overall marital adjustment may still be able to use the services of a professional in some particular area of the marriage where there is maladjustment, such as sex or finances. "Marriage counseling is not just for marriages in trouble, but a resource that can help relationships" (Lamanna and Riedmann 1988, 501).

Sometimes children may need professional help. Much attention is being paid at the present time to neurologically impaired children. No one knows the difficulties that parents have encountered in the past in trying to rear such children when neither physicians nor psychiatrists were able to pinpoint their problems. Now there is diagnosis and treatment for these children that solves many of the mysteries and difficulties other families have faced.

A limited amount of parent/teenager conflict may be normal as young people attempt to reach adult independence, but severe conflicts may be eased if a professional counselor can give insight to both parties involved.

Dysfunctional Families

Much attention today is being given to the needs of dysfunctional families. Brissett and Burns (1991, 4) defines such a family as one "not able to function in a healthy manner." He suggests that all families are dysfunctional in some areas and that families can be charted on a continuum:

Functional   Dysfunctional
100%————————————100%

A functional home is one in which family members feel safe and protected. In a dysfunctional home people are fearful and often are abused physically, sexually, and psychologically.

Most often a dysfunctional family is characterized by abuse, alcoholism, and drug use. Some Christian families fall into one or more of these categories. Certainly such families need the help of counselors. Oftentimes the offending spouse may refuse to cooperate, such as a case of an alcoholic or abusing spouse. If counseling fails, then a legal separation would be a viable solution to the problem.

Children reared in dysfunctional families often require counseling in their adult years because of the damage to their personalities. Books have been written to help them, and there are therapists who specialize in helping such adults. Problems in a marriage often can be traced to the harmful effects of a dysfunctional family.

The Church and Counseling

Many churches have responded to the need for counseling by adding full-time counselors to the church staff. These individuals consider counseling as a ministry. Some are pastors who have prepared as counselors by taking seminary training in this specialty. Most of the large seminaries have recognized the need for individuals trained in counseling and have established graduate programs in pastoral psychology and counseling. Others have graduate degrees in psychology and have been certified to counsel. They are committed Christians and desire to serve God by helping individuals find solutions to their personal problems.

However, most churches are not large enough to afford full-time counselors, so the pastor usually does the counseling. Wynn (1982, 18) makes the point that most pastors have no choice when family counseling is concerned. He writes, "that they will become involved with marriage conflicts and dysfunctional families is inevitable; there is no escape. Parishioners and townspeople alike bring to the clergy their squabbles, their misunderstandings, their desperation with one another." When Christians are in trouble, most turn to their pastor. One study quoted by Rekers (1988, 12) indicated that "77 percent of people in a community preferred clergy counseling for family problems compared to 14 percent who preferred non-religious family counseling." However, a limited survey by *Christianity Today* (14 December 1992) indicated that 61 percent of the respondents sought help from a Christian therapist versus 41 percent from a pastor.

> ## A good counselor is always aware of his limitations and is able to recognize behavior problems that are beyond his ability to treat.

People know the pastor is there to help them in any way he can, which accounts for their willingness to turn to him in times of stress and strain. An open ear, an empathetic heart, and kindly words of wisdom and counsel from the Scriptures in one counseling session may be all that are required to help the couple find the answer to their need. At other times, it may require many sessions and extensive probing and analyzing to find the source of the difficulty.

A good counselor is always aware of his limitations and is able to recognize behavior problems that are beyond his ability to treat. He is also informed as to the resources of the community designed to deal with various problems people have in today's society. There are those difficult cases where a pastor recognizes the couple's need for help from a person with more education and experience than he has. He then refers the couple to a counselor whom he thinks is capable of helping them in their distress. Today there are Christian counselors available within driving distance in most parts of the country.

> *One of the fundamental rules of counseling is that the privacy of the client must be protected.*

Some pastors are not equipped either by education or by personality to be good counselors. Rekers (1988, 20) found in one survey that one-half of the pastors had never attended a workshop or a seminar on marriage counseling. They either lack an understanding of the basic elements of human behavior or the ability to relate to individuals on a face-to-face basis. These pastors do well in the pulpit, but they cannot share the burdens of individuals.

Other pastors who faithfully preach the sufficiency of the grace of God to save sinners seem to forget that the same grace operates to restore sinning saints. When a member transgresses by being unfaithful to his spouse, there is often pressure to immediately dismiss the person rather than a supportive attempt to reestablish a Christian home. This is not to say

that church discipline is not to be invoked, but it should be a last resort rather than an immediate reaction to the erring brother's (or sister's) conduct. The statement of Paul in Galatians 6:1, "Brethren, if a man be overtaken in a fault, ye which are spiritual, restore such a one in the spirit of meekness, considering thyself, lest thou also be tempted," puts a divine obligation on the pastor and spiritual leaders to diligently try to mend the home broken by the waywardness of a spouse.

One of the fundamental rules of counseling is that the privacy of the client must be protected. The code of ethics of the Christian Association for Psychological Studies requires the counselor to advise the client of the limits of confidentiality, to protect the identity of the client and the problem, and to handle all records of the case in a manner that will protect them from disclosure (Collins 1991, 183). Some pastors cannot or do not keep the confidence that is placed in them when a parishioner comes for help. Either they or their wives spread private information to other church members, to the embarrassment of the person concerned. Needless to say, not many individuals will seek help from a pastor who behaves in this fashion.

Many pastors do share with their wives the burdens of their people so that they can pray for them together. However, if a man has a wife who cannot be trusted with confidential information, he must not share it with her. The privacy of the client must be protected if the pastor is to have a successful counseling ministry.

Counseling requires building a trusting, accepting relationship between the therapist and the counselee (Grunwald 1985, 34). This poses a danger to which many pastors have succumbed. In building the trust needed to help people with problems in their marriages, it is possible for the counselor to become "emotionally overinvolved instead of remaining objective. . . . This is especially true when a counselee is deeply disturbed, confused, or facing a problem that is similar to the counselor's own struggles" (Collins 1988, 27). This has occasionally led to a pastor getting involved sexually with a client.

According to McBurney (1986, 15–18), this happened to Henry. Without knowing it Henry had been called to a church that had a problem between some of the members. Henry was unable to solve the problem, which frustrated his wife. She became angry with the church members because of their disharmony and with Henry because of his inability to solve the problem. After a couple of years Henry's marriage was deteriorating because of his wife's attitude toward him. At this time he was counseling a young, attractive woman with a problem marriage. After one of his wife's tirades against him, Henry went in to counsel the young woman. He broke down, she put her arms around him and comforted him, and this was the beginning of physical intimacy that eventually led to sexual involvement. In this case Henry and his wife ended up in McBurney's retreat for troubled Christian workers. Unfortunately, many times these situations result in broken marriages.

Some pastors who have seen their colleagues fall because of such experiences have decided against a ministry of counseling. Persons who come to them are guided to professional Christian counselors in the area. These men rely on their pulpit ministry to encourage individuals to appropriate the power of the Holy Spirit to enable them to live a life of victory in Christ. Clinebell (1984, 40) comments that "growthful preaching offers a regular opportunity to communicate the Christian message (the gospel of good news) in a life-affirming, esteem-strengthening, growth-nurturing, and challenging way. It can 'speak the truth [that frees] in love' Eph. 4:15." Many people do not have the courage to admit they have a problem. Collins (1986, 36) writes that "when these people attend church, they can find encouragement and guidance in the pastor's message. There is no need for these listeners to admit to others that 'the speaker is talking about my problem'. . . . For such people, public help [from the pulpit] is the only counseling they may ever get."

One pastor preached a series of messages on "Valley People," illustrating how God is faithful to help those going through difficult times as well as those with mountain-top experiences. It helped people realize that whether their emotions were high or low, God was faithful to see them through. For two years after-

ward more members referred to "Valley People" than to any other sermons, indicating they had been helped by the series. "By teaching biblical standards with biblical illustrations or illustrations from life, people beginning to go through those kinds of experiences often appropriate those principles. They experience the remedial effect of preventive counseling" (Shelley 1986, 64–67).

On the other hand, pastors must be careful to preach the gospel rather than psychology, as a number of well-known television preachers are doing. These preachers could be included among those who have "replaced their theological uniqueness with 'a mess of psychological pottage'" (Collins 1986, 29). The church must always use psychology as a people-helping tool and not make it the core of its message.

> *Counseling requires building a trusting, accepting relationship between the therapist and the counselee.*

Pastors who rely on their pulpit ministry to teach their congregations also stress the enrichment of marriage and family life through educational programs of the church. The aim is to help families realize the joys and blessings that come from dedication to Jesus Christ. When this ideal is not reached and families do have problems, then they are directed to professional counselors.

As the number of Christian counselors increase, the day may come when they will replace pastors as the choice of those needing help with their problems. Until that time arrives, young men preparing for the pastorate need to get all the training in counseling they can afford. Undergraduate majors in psychology, sociology, and social work provide an excellent background for a future ministry of working with individuals. The postgraduate seminary can equip them for their public ministry.

Most churches today provide liability insurance for their pastors to protect them from lawsuits arising in counseling situations. This need became apparent when a prominent pastor in California was sued by the family of a young man who committed suicide. The church had provided counseling for the young man so the family filed a malpractice suit. The pastor won the case. Since that time churches have been careful to carry insurance.

If a church institutes a counseling center, it must be careful to follow all legal requirements. Collins (1988, 48) indicates that "laws in your area may determine who is legally competent to counsel, what titles the counselor may use, which counselors are exempt from revealing details about counseling in a court of law. . . ." There are also laws as to the amount of education required to be a counselor and the fees that may be charged. These vary from state to state so the church and counselor need to be informed of and conform to all that the law demands. The counselor is liable for civil and criminal malpractice (Gladding 1988, 247–48). The church must carry adequate liability insurance to protect itself and the counselors.

> *If a church institutes a counseling center, it must be careful to follow all legal requirements.*

The church's main goal is to evangelize and disciple converts to Jesus Christ. The Christian family is the main source from which most converts come. It is often stated that "the church is only one generation from extinction." In this time when so many influences are trying to destroy the home, it is incumbent upon the church to do all in its power to help stabilize Christian families. Godly Christian counseling should be a major weapon in the battle to preserve Christian homes.

Christian Psychologists and Psychiatrists as Counselors

Another source of counseling is the psychologist or the psychiatrist. These terms are not always understood. According to Belkin (1984, 40–41), a psychologist is "a person who holds an advanced degree in psychology from an approved institution of higher education, and has passed a State licensing examination." There are specialists within the field such as social psychology and clinical psychology. The psychiatrist is a "medical doctor who had advanced training (a residency [usually three to five years beyond the M.D. level]) in the specialty of psychiatry." Psychiatrists can prescribe medication for their counselees.

Most believers prefer a Christian counselor because unsaved professionals have a value system that often conflicts with a Christian's value system. They generally do not use Scripture and prayer in the healing process. They may even be antagonistic towards the Christian faith. Miller (1985, 6) records the case history of a believer who was bluntly told to "get off that Bible kick."

Benner (1987, 16) lists several advantages of Christian psychotherapy. The Christian therapist can use the power of faith in God to help the person make needed changes. This includes prayer, worship, and biblical assurances. Second, the therapist can use Jesus Christ as the model for change and as a basis for values. Third, he can use biblical concepts such as forgiveness, confession, repentance, grace, and the new birth for those not born again. Also a Christian can usually establish rapport more quickly with a Christian therapist since the "framework is biblical" and the "values are familiar."

The work of Clyde Narramore, who founded Rosemead Graduate School of Psychology, has resulted in the establishment by others of several graduate schools of psychology in various parts of the United States. As a result, there are a large number of well-trained psychologists across America. Every city of any size has at least one or more Christian counseling centers.

There has also been a large increase in the number of Christian psychiatrists. The rapid growth of Christian psychiatric hospitals was described in *Christianity Today* (18 May 1992, 22–26). Although there are individual hospitals, the trend is for Christian psychiatrists to take over operation of a psychiatric ward in a community hospital. They are allowed to exercise their Christian commitment as long as they "make money, show effectiveness, and don't get sued." Christians who would never enter a secular psychiatric ward feel safe to enter when it is operated by Christian therapists.

Individuals living near a Christian college or Bible institute may find qualified counselors available who serve on the faculties of those institutions. Many Christian colleges offer courses in psychology, and many Bible institutes have courses in pastoral counseling. These courses are usually taught by professors who have had considerable education and training in the field. Although they may not have a professional practice of counseling services, yet they are men of God. If they are called upon in a time of great need, they would attempt to help an individual.

Christian Social Workers as Counselors

Professionally trained social workers with master's degrees have been called poor man's psychiatrists. They are educated in the dynamics of human behavior and are able to help solve many kinds of problems. Christians in this field have started their own organization, The National Association of Christians in Social Work. They hold an annual meeting for fellowship and discussion of problems concerning the Christian and social work. A directory of members is published biannually and members holding a master's degree in social work are so indicated. Again, if Christian psychologists or psychiatrists are not available, people can contact one of these dedicated Christian

social workers and find help or be referred to someone who can help.

> ## *Professionally trained social workers with master's degrees have been called poor man's psychiatrists.*

There is a trend in the field of social work for social workers to enter private practice, and the supply of Christian counselors has increased as Christian social workers offer their services on a fee basis. Many in social work do not approve of this trend toward private practice, but it must be recognized such a practice makes it possible for many to receive help who can afford this service but not the services of a psychiatrist.

Secular Counselors

If the person with a problem cannot find a source of competent Christian counseling, then he must turn to the secular realm. Roe (1982, 44) writes, "The Christian counselor takes the position that all truth is from God and that non-Christians have access to this same truth through observing, researching, and practicing counseling. This is comparable to any other scientific process of discovery." In every community of any size there is a private, nonprofit, community-supported family service agency. These agencies exist to help families with problems. If the difficulty is mainly financial, they will refer the individual to the proper agency where such aid is available. A family service agency is mainly concerned with nonfinancial problems, and the social workers usually are well trained and can provide excellent help, although they may not have the

Christian perspective. Most couples with marital problems *that are not essentially spiritual in nature* could benefit greatly from the services offered by a family service agency. Since it is supported by the community, its fees are usually correlated with the ability of the individual to pay, and no one is refused service because of inability to pay. Social workers in such an agency can deal with problems that people usually face and are taught to recognize deep-seated psychological problems that require the services of a psychiatrist.

> ## *Social workers are usually well trained and can provide excellent help, although they may not have the Christian perspective.*

The national government is concerned about the availability of mental health services to the American people. Consequently, it is channeling large sums of tax money back to the states to help them establish comprehensive mental health centers that include counseling services on an outpatient basis. It is the plan for every area to have such facilities available to help meet the needs of people with problems. At the present time there is a shortage of qualified people to staff many of these centers, especially in the area of psychiatry.

These centers are primarily concerned with emotional and psychological problems, but many times these may be related to a marital problem. The treatment includes dealing with environmental factors, such as marriage problems. Where such mental health centers have been established, there are qualified counselors to help. However, the ability to aid a person who has a spiritual problem may be limited because the unsaved therapist does not understand spiritual concepts.

Families with children who have problems may find help at a child guidance center or at a similar clinic. The federal government has also been active in helping such clinics, for it realizes today's problem children often become tomorrow's problem adults. Many children can be helped if problems are treated before they become too deep-seated. If a qualified Christian counselor is not available, a Christian parent should not hesitate to take a child with a problem to such a center, for counselors are dedicated to serving children and are able to effect some remarkable changes in behavior. Usually the center requires the cooperation of the parents in the treatment process. It is impossible to help the child unless environmental factors contributing to his problem also are changed.

Private Marriage Counselors

There is a growing number of well-educated individuals who engage professionally in a full-time practice of marriage counseling. They are usually located in larger cities where there is sufficient demand for their services. They charge a fee and many middle-class people prefer to seek help from a private counselor rather than from an agency supported by the United Fund. Many individuals who engage in full-time marriage counseling belong to the American Association of Marriage and Family Therapists. This group was organized in 1942 and has provided leadership to establish the standards for a profession of marriage counselors.

The association also has been active in the movement for state licensing of marriage counselors. This has become a necessity since any person who wishes to call himself a marriage counselor may do so in many states. Unscrupulous individuals with no specialized education in counseling have set themselves up in business, harmed many marriages, and brought disrepute on the whole area of marriage counseling. This has led to the desire to have state laws governing who may enter the practice of marriage counseling. Many states now have laws regulating the practice.

Persons who seek help from a marriage counselor in private practice should investigate the qualifications of the counselor before visiting him, since quacks will be in business until all states have laws regulating the profession. A person needing medical help does not refuse the help of a physician even though there are quacks and incompetents in the medical profession. In like manner, a person needing counseling should not refuse to seek out a qualified counselor even though there are unscrupulous persons calling themselves counselors.

Necessity of Seeking Help Early

The important thing for a family to remember is to seek help when it is needed. Counselors are unanimous in their opinion that the earlier help is sought for a problem, the easier it is to find a solution. Pride is one factor that prevents people from seeking counseling early (Roe 1982, 113). Roe points out that counseling is a "humbling experience." He suggests "there is a considerable amount of wisdom in 'swallowing your pride' to seek help *early* [italics added] rather than publicly 'losing face' when a correctable problem has gone too far." The counselee must have a sincere desire to change and cooperate with the counselor even when a problem has an early diagnosis. The changing of the situation must be done by the counselee, but it is important to remember that divine help is also available.

If a couple waits until all communication lines are down between them, or waits until a child is emotionally disturbed before seeking aid, the task of restoration becomes far greater. The Christian, of course, has resources that the average person does not possess, so that he does not have to solve the problem alone. However, it is still true he must cooperate with the counselor while seeking divine help and comfort.

Conclusion

It is hoped that the young person who reads this book will be able to choose a life partner realistically and strive continually to improve the marital relationship. A successful Christian

marriage does not "happen"; it is created with God's help by selecting the right mate, and then the two partners work to build the best relationship possible.

> *A successful Christian marriage does not "happen"; it is created with God's help.*

Modern marriage makes many demands upon those who choose to enter into the bonds of matrimony, but none of these demands are too great for those who seek the help of the "God of all grace." He is able to enrich and to bless the lives of those who put their trust in him.

The task of achieving such a successful marriage will be easier if the mates are well chosen, but even where incompatibilities exist, there are no problems that cannot be solved between a Christian husband and wife who honestly seek his help.

The great number of happy Christian families indicates that the miracle of marriage is still possible. The fine, dedicated Christian young people that are products of these homes are evidence that biblical principles of child rearing are still effective when conscientiously and consistently followed.

Study Questions

1. Why is there a greater need for marital counseling today than there was in previous generations?
2. Why are individuals reluctant to seek counseling when there is a problem in the marriage?
3. What are some danger signals in a marriage that should alert a couple to the need for counseling?

4. List several areas where a couple with a good overall adjustment could benefit from marriage counseling.
5. Discuss the issue of seeing one spouse first versus seeing both spouses together in the first counseling session.
6. Why do some people turn to a pastor when they need counseling?
7. What are some guidelines a church should follow in establishing a counseling center?
8. Why do some counselors become sexually involved with their clients?
9. How can preaching be used as an avenue for counseling?
10. List several sources of counseling in the secular field.

Suggested Readings

Aden, L., and J. H. Ellens. 1984. *The church and pastoral care.* Grand Rapids: Baker. Second volume in the Psychology and Christianity Series published by Baker in cooperation with the Christian Association for Psychological Studies (CAPS). It is a collection of articles that covers topics in the field of pastoral care.

Carter, L. 1991. *Broken vows: How to put the pieces of a marriage back together again.* Nashville: Nelson. Carter uses cases from his marriage counseling practice to show the causes of infidelity and how such relationships can be restored. His commitment to biblical principles is evident throughout the book.

Collins, G. 1988. *Christian counseling: A comprehensive guide.* Rev. ed. Dallas: Word. A revision of a popular textbook in Christian counseling. It is scriptural, thorough, and scholarly. It should be in the library of everyone interested in Christian counseling.

Friesen, D., and R. Friesen. 1989. *Counseling and marriage.* Dallas: Word. A volume in the Resources for Christian Counseling Series. A how-to book for those involved in marital counseling. It covers the usual topics faced by a marriage counselor and suggests ideas to help solve these problems.

Gladding, S. T. 1988. *Counseling: A comprehensive profession.* Columbus: Merrill. A textbook overview of the counseling profession. It covers the history, theories, and major types of counseling. It emphasizes the importance of the counselor in the therapist-client relationship. A good introduction to the profession.

Rassieur, C. L. 1988. *Pastor, our marriage is in trouble: A guide to short-term marriage counseling.* Philadelphia: Westminster. The author wrote this volume to help pastors who have limited education in marriage counseling. He warns pastors to be aware of their "personal, cultural and theological biases." A helpful questionnaire for marriage counseling is included for pastors to use.

Rekers, G. A. 1988. *Counseling families.* Waco: Word. Another valuable volume in the Resources for Christian Counseling Series. Edited by Gary Collins, this series is designed to be an encyclopedia of Christian counseling. This volume, as all the others, is edited by a dedicated Christian and experienced family therapist.

Roe, J. 1982. *A consumer's guide to Christian counseling.* Nashville: Abingdon. Roe has written a volume that many who are not acquainted with counseling will find most helpful. He discusses when counseling is needed, where to find competent counselors, what questions to ask them, and how much one can expect to pay various types of counselors.

Shelley, M. 1986. *Helping those who don't want help.* Waco: Word. An interesting book that focuses on techniques one can use to help those who don't want help. The chapter on "When to Intervene" stresses the necessity of having the right motivations before deciding to help.

Welch, E. T. 1991. *Counselor's guide to the brain and its disorders.* Grand Rapids: Zondervan. A valuable book that describes the brain and diseases associated with it. Then specific suggestions for counseling are given for each disease. Every counselor needs the information in this volume.

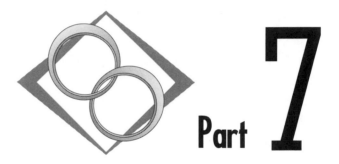

Part 7

The Future of the Family

19

International Living

Now then we are ambassadors for Christ . . .

—2 Corinthians 5:20

Our Global Society

The world is rapidly becoming a smaller place. During the twentieth century, as countries linked up for world trade, global exchange became commonplace. This change came about through aggressive marketing by multinational corporations, increased air travel, and expanded telecommunications systems. In many urban centers, an international youth culture has emerged sharing similar values and preferences regarding food, music, fashion, and material possessions. This culture is consumer-driven and companies see the world as a single market. English has become the universal language, and global television networks have linked countries together through its use. All these changes take place at a breathtaking pace (Naisbitt and Aburdene 1990).

Traditionally, four careers have taken people overseas. Government services, including military and foreign diplomatic service, have posted their personnel in almost every country. Second, businessmen are assigned overseas to expand their company's business. Third, humanitarian workers bring relief, medicine, and social development to needy countries. Last but not least, religious workers, such as missionaries, take the gospel to all corners of the earth. As the world shrinks and the Lord's return draws near, more and more workers from these four occupational groups will find their way to a life overseas.

International living is an exciting opportunity full of adventure and challenge. Many countries have strong family values, even stronger than American, and make great places to rear a family.. At the same time, family life overseas involves a major transition. Just as going away to college, getting married, and becoming a parent are major life transitions, living overseas is also a transition. Family members must adjust to the new roles of foreigner, outsider, and minority. The key to any transition in life is adjustment—bringing yourself into alignment with new roles, relationships, and living conditions. Adjustment requires learning and preparation, both crucial to having a positive cross-cultural experience. Good preparation leads to good performance.

> ## Adjustment requires learning and preparation, both crucial to having a positive cross-cultural experience.

The Cross-Cultural Experience

When a family moves overseas, it confronts a different mind-set on how life should be perceived and organized. This value clash is especially difficult for adults. For children, adapting to a different mind-set is much easier, as they are natural imitators and learn to accept the mores and folkways around them as normal (Torbiorn 1982). It is typical for young children growing up overseas to take on the new culture without realizing it. They learn to switch languages according to what is spoken to them and do this without consciously understanding that they are doing so. Children also pick up behavior that reflects the cultural values of the host country. This may or may not be good. Some cultures spoil little children while others almost seem to disregard them. Parents have to understand what is taking place in their children's lives as they seek to cope with a different culture's value system.

Successful cross-cultural living requires a basic knowledge of cultural anthropology. Although space will not allow an in-depth study of this discipline, a simple definition of culture is in order. The word *culture,* used in an anthropological sense, refers to the total way of life of a group of people who share an integrated system of learned behavior patterns. Each member learns and accepts what the culture deems important, right, and proper. This total way of life includes everything the people of a culture think, say, do, and make. In other words, a culture is comprehensive, encompassing its customs, language, material artifacts, and shared systems of values, attitudes, and feelings. Culture is passed on to each new generation, who are taught these shared patterns of belief (Kohls 1984).

Children reared in a certain country take on that culture as their basic identity. For example, an adopted Korean or Vietnamese infant brought up in America is considered American. Although they are ethnically Asian, they grow up learning to think, feel, and identify with America. They speak English, think like an American, and view themselves as Americans. They prefer hamburgers to rice. This is a result of having been enculturated into the American way of life, its norms, its mind-set. They are Americans because they have been reared in the American culture, even though their biological parents are Asian.

Adjusting to Culture Shock

When families move into a cross-cultural environment, they usually suffer from what is known as culture shock. Culture shock results when one encounters ways of doing, perceiving, organizing, and valuing things that are different from their own enculturation. Gone are the familiar cues, the ways of interpreting the subtle nuances of interpersonal communication (Kohls 1984). Culture shock occurs when a person can no longer interpret the cues, signals, and signs necessary for social interaction. Also gone are the familiar support systems of family, friends, and familiar institutions. The resultant state is one of loss, uncertainty, helplessness, and anxiety (Furnham and Bochner 1986; Torbiorn 1982).

When people enter new cultures, they are surprised how different life can be. In a Third-World country, there are beggars and bribes, unfamiliar food, and an unfamiliar language. But culture shock is more than being shocked by the landscape, smells, and different artifacts used in the host country, as these become familiar over time. When people are stripped of being able to interpret how and why others communicate and behave, they feel increasingly confused and frustrated and in a state of disequilibrium. This feeling comes from living in an ambiguous, uncertain environment where a person's own values are questioned. In effect, his psychological rug has been pulled out from under him. Not understanding the host culture's ground rules quickly leads to anger, frustration, and homesickness. The result is emotional anxiety, disorientation, discomfort, and an overwhelming sense of incompetence. It is easy to become paranoid, asking, "Why are they doing that? What's that funny noise? Is it safe to do that?" Culture shock usually sets in within the first six months to a year of residing in a new culture (Torbiorn 1982). Some of the worst cases of culture shock occur in cultures similar to but still different than one's native country, such as would occur when Americans go to live in Britain or Australia. Because Americans know the British speak the same language and perhaps share a common ancestry, they expect the British to be like themselves. They are surprised to find that Britain has a distinct culture, quite diffcrent from America.

Adjusting to culture shock is a growing experience. People experiencing it soon learn quite a bit about themselves and sometimes discover emotions they did not know they had. It is important to get over culture shock as best as possible. Doing that requires constant learning, discovering the logic behind different behavior patterns, and having a friend from the culture explain things to you. Most of all, the person suffering from culture shock must refrain from sliding into a cultural shell, feeling superior (ethnocentrism) and disengaging mentally from the cross-cultural environment (Ward 1985). It is easy to project one's frustrations onto the members of the host culture and fall into the trap of being negative and critical. As people slide into ethnocentric views, they become hostile, bitter, and ineffective in their work. The newcomer may psychologically

"check out" before even having a chance to get settled in. The overseas environment is littered with casualties—those who chose not to cope, retreating instead into the security of their own cultural mind-set.

> *The overseas environment is littered with casualties—those who chose not to cope, retreating instead into the security of their own cultural mind-set.*

How parents cope with culture shock affects the children. If parents recoil in horror when they are touched by a beggar or react in anger to a misunderstanding, the child will quickly learn to look down upon the culture. A child will interpret the new culture by how the parents react to different cultural experiences. If parents view everything about a culture as being horrible or uncivilized, then their children will pick up the same prejudices. At the same time, if parents see each confusing experience as a learning experience, children will be positive and accept the new culture (Sharp 1988).

There is a difference between culture shock and culture stress. After newcomers pass through culture shock, they come to the realization that no matter how hard they try, they will never be accepted by the new culture as an insider, nor can they change to accept everything about it. This presents an ongoing tension between values and customs of the host culture with the enculturated ones. Living daily with values different from one's own produces continual stress, known as cultural stress, and one must learn to cope to live effectively in such an environment. For example, most American women never get used to living in a filthy house or being treated as less than human.

What are some of the coping mechanisms that can help to lessen culture shock and culture stress? Learning about the culture is a good way to rationally accept a new environment. Another is to learn its language. Personnel living in a different culture for the long haul, such as missionaries, have to learn the language. Language learning is a window into the culture and lets a person focus on its thought patterns. Learning a new culture is an enormous task, requiring an open mind and a positive outlook. Learning a language and culture can be a humbling experience for adults—they learn to imitate basic phrases and cultural cues, just as they did when they learned their own language and culture when they were toddlers.

> ## It is easy to lose perspective when one is going through culture shock.

A second way of coping is to copy or imitate the behavior patterns of the host culture. These may range from nonverbal cues, such as the way a person nods his head to mean agreement, to verbal ones, such as using acceptable phrases to politely decline on a matter. In fact, it is best to copy as much as possible up to the point that the host culture's values conflict with your own. For example, one time a missionary tried his best to get the meter reader to accurately read the electric meter without resorting to bribery, which the meter reader expected. When the missionary talked with a national friend who happened to be the district attorney, the friend said, "Well, just beat him . . . he'll do what you want." When the missionary said

he couldn't do that, the lawyer laughed, even though he himself had been trained at an Ivy League law school and knew Americans do not believe in solving problems in that way.

A third way of coping is to find a foreign friend who understands the frustration and upheaval taking place. It is emotionally helpful to share and discuss what is happening with a person who cares. As a fourth coping mechanism, it is often helpful to make a list of all the host culture's good characteristics to be reminded that not all is bad. It is easy to lose perspective when one is going through culture shock. A final method, and an important one, is to pray. When one talks to God about discouragements and cultural mistakes, the Holy Spirit can minister in ways only God can. Sometimes, true cultural adjustment comes through the spiritual realm as God gives grace to cope with seemingly unbearable stresses and concerns (Heb. 4:15–16). It is good to have family prayer and to let your family understand what is happening.

Setting Up a Household

Living standards differ around the world. In Europe, living standards may be higher than in North America. Countries of the Third World usually have a lower standard of living. Even within a developing nation, there are two worlds—a modern urban one and a traditional rural one. In the rural world, living conditions range from living among the peasantry to living among Stone-Age peoples.

Once a family arrives in the host country, they usually have to find a place to live. Until they find a place to rent or buy, they must live in a temporary place. This is the first adjustment as the family learns to live together, perhaps one or two months, until they locate their own place. Missionaries sometimes live in one room in a guesthouse for several weeks unless the mission has already found them a place.

Once a permanent place is rented, the family may have to adjust to differing amounts of space. In some Asian cities, a family may only afford a six-hundred-square-foot flat, whereas in some towns in the developing world they may easily afford a house with three to four thousand square feet. Maintaining a house in the tropics has its own troubles as the family battles continual dirt, dust, and insects. (The best remedy for cockroaches is to enter a dark room and close your eyes for several seconds after you have turned on the light; by then all the roaches will have disappeared!) To help children adjust to a new home, it is wise to pack a suitcase of each child's favorite things (e.g., toys, blankets, mobile, perhaps even curtains) for each child's room. In a matter of minutes, the new room can have the flavor of the child's room back home, making it seem warm and familiar.

In the developing world, the family will have to make some additional adjustments in the area of household conveniences. Many places in the world still do not have disposable diapers, canned goods, fast food, and baby food. The tropics are especially hard on clothes. Because of the high temperatures, clothing must be changed sometimes two or three times a day. With a family, that quickly adds up to a lot of dirty clothes. The hot tropical sun bleaches out colors and the rainy season keeps them from drying. All of this can try the patience and energy of the best housewife.

A usual practice in developing countries is to hire household help. Although having servants may sound rather elitist, in some parts of the world it is almost a necessity. There are several reasons for having servants, and an important one is security. Because of high crime rates, having a person in the house all the time is a must. In some parts of the world, to leave a house unattended is to encourage thieves. Often thieves carry out their work with the approval and assistance of the local police. In addition, it may be necessary to hire a guard for outside the house as well. Second, having servants provides employment to needy people. For the little it costs, employing servants may put food on the table for many people. Third, people living overseas often entertain a great deal, and without automatic dishwashers and grocery stores there is a lot of preparatory work and washing. Fourth, servants are often good with children and can help the family by babysitting. This can free up the husband and wife for ministry or career responsibilities.

Additionally, some cultures expect you to have servants, and in fact, most homes come with servant quarters. The local people may perceive you as stingy if you do not give a local a job. Even the servants may have servants of their own taking care of their families. A final reason is that in some cultures, particularly in Muslim countries, it is not safe or morally appropriate for the wife to go into the bazaar or the marketplace. This means that either the husband or servant must do the family shopping. Servants can save enormous amounts of time by standing in line (sometimes for hours); paying utility bills; washing the car; shopping for groceries; washing, drying, folding, and ironing clothes; babysitting; and watching the house. For the little cost to employ them, it gives them a livelihood and frees up parents to spend more time with family, career, and ministry.

However, living with servants can sometimes be the greatest adjustment Americans may face in living overseas (Kinney 1983). A woman who enjoys being a housewife discovers she is the household manager rather than a housewife. Westerners value their privacy a great deal and having servants seems to violate their privacy as every action and attitude is watched. Moreover, having servants can sometimes grate on a Western person's middle-class values of equality. In a culture where servants expect to be beaten for stepping out of line, treating servants as equals lowers their view of the employers. Treating servants as equals may encourage disobedience or theft, and cause employees to view employers as weak and as being out of control of the household.

In the developing world, the family will have to make some additional adjustments in the area of household conveniences.

A further concern is that servants often spoil children by giving them everything they want and by letting them talk back and boss them. In Muslim countries, boys are often encouraged to have a low view of girls and women, and young boys can quickly become sexist. Another disadvantage is that not all servants are trustworthy. The family may have to dismiss a servant because of theft or deceit, making a difficult situation for both the family and servant. If the servant is a Christian and attends the same church as the family, it becomes an embarrassment to the church. In an effort to save face, the servant may make up a story that hurts the reputation of the foreigner. Some foreigners have a policy of not employing members of their church for this reason.

Although having servants is not easy, it is most difficult to live without them. The family will have to decide whether they want servants, how many they need, and who will manage the household. Once they decide to have them, it is not uncommon for Americans to go through a set or two until they learn how to deal with them according to their culture.

A final adjustment in setting up a new household is getting into a new routine. Business hours vary from country to country. In Asia, office hours can begin at ten in the morning, break for lunch from two to three, and close between eight and ten at night. This may affect mealtimes and the rest of the daily schedule. Compounding this is the children's school schedule, which also differs according to the country. In large cities, the school bus may arrive at six in the morning to beat rush-hour traffic. In contrast, on a remote mission compound school may not start until nine o'clock. Regardless of the schedule, it is important for the children's adjustment to start a routine right away.

Rearing Children Overseas

Americans have their own value system about raising children, and it all revolves around the main theme of independence. They want their children to be self-sufficient, self-confident, and self-respecting. Americans accomplish this by treating each child as an individual who has his own identity in the family. Even from birth a newborn may often have his own crib in his own room, separate from other members of the family (Fantini and Cardenas 1980). The way Americans rear their children is in marked contrast to many other places in the world. Many cultures value making children totally dependent upon the family and would see putting an infant alone in a room as being cold, indifferent, and cruel. It is a surprise to many Asians that American parents do not know about their adult children's finances, and the adult children do not know the financial situation of their parents or their brothers and sisters. In cultures where belonging and supporting the extended family is a supreme value, Americans appear to lack care for the family. However, Americans are shocked to find a husband from an Asian culture leaving his wife and family for years at a time, merely because of employment opportunities. The point is that both Americans and cultures that foster family dependency are both family-oriented. The difference lies in whether children are reared to be independent or dependent members of the family.

As American children grow up overseas, they are influenced by American culture in the home and also by the host culture. The resulting effect is that they are neither totally American, nor totally a member of the host culture. Their two cultures combine to produce a third culture. They become adept at switching between cultures and are usually not aware of it. Some children growing up in a foreign environment may learn several languages and cultures simultaneously, with no ill effect. For example, a six-year-old missionary child on the way home from Europe asked a Swiss lady for a glass of water. He asked for it in all five of the languages he knew, but unfortunately none of them was French!

Actually, these unique children are competent and comfortable in functioning in such a cross-cultural milieu. The younger the children entering the host culture, the more easily they assimilate it, assuming they have an opportunity to play and interact with members of the host culture. It is possible for a child to learn up to ten different languages at the same time without getting confused or overloaded. It is a wonderful opportunity for children to grow up in a foreign environment. From an educational standpoint, it is the ultimate field trip, as every day children are exposed to a rich and varied environment. They can observe other religious customs first-hand and see New Testament Christianity at work, especially when national believers are persecuted for their faith.

Children adjust to seeing poverty, disease, disfigured bodies, death, and insanity, as many developing countries do not have resources to hide such social problems from the public eye. Consequently, they learn compassion and tolerance early. They learn to take military-coup attempts and riots in stride, and if parents do not show their fear, they actually get excited about bizarre instances. Once, while a coup attempt was taking place at a cantonment less than a mile away, missionary parents were surprised to see their boys in the backyard playing G.I. Joe, complete with sound effects of the actual fighting taking place close by! Unless they are told otherwise, children adapt to the local environment and assume such events to be normal. The parents' reaction to difficult times overseas will directly affect the outlook of children.

There are some disadvantages to growing up overseas for which parents must compensate. Often there are not many outside opportunities for children to get experience, particularly teens who never get the chance to work at a job. Parents may have to think up innovative ways to teach children outside responsibilities. Usually the peer group is small among Americans and a third-cultural child does not have opportunities to develop social skills in large group settings, particularly if the child is brought up in a sheltered jungle mission compound. Not having a strong local church with good programs in English may stunt a child's spiritual growth. Parents may have to supplement their child's Bible knowledge at home if a good Sunday-school program is not available. Even large, international English speaking churches found in capital cities often do not have spiritual instruction for children that parents are used to in America. Another disadvantage is that children do not have their extended family nearby and may grow up not even knowing who their relatives are or have

the intimacy of an extended family, other than their adopted missionary family.

> *It is a wonderful opportunity for children to grow up in a foreign environment. From an educational standpoint, it is the ultimate field trip, as every day children are exposed to a rich and varied environment.*

A major challenge parents face in bringing up children overseas is providing a good education. There are seven options and all seven have advantages and disadvantages (Buffam 1985). First, a parent or short-term teacher or tutor may teach children in the home using a correspondence-course curriculum. This may be the only alternative in remote situations where parents do not want to send children to a boarding school. A second option is to enroll them in a boarding school in the host country. Third, American parents living close together may start their own small school and share teaching responsibilities or incorporate a school as a satellite of a larger boarding school. Fourth, in some large cities, there may be good parochial schools. Fifth, in capital cities of many countries, the U.S. government may sponsor an international American school, although this may be an expensive option. Sixth, some areas such as Europe, South America, and Japan may have native-speaking national urban schools, but with a standard of instruction Americans desire. Seventh, parents may opt to leave their children with friends or relatives in America to attend school. This option may be more appropriate for older high-school and college students.

> *Research repeatedly demonstrates that children attending school overseas do better in school than their counterparts back home.*

All of these options have their advantages and disadvantages. Regardless which option parents choose, research repeatedly demonstrates that children attending school overseas do better in school than their counterparts back home (Sharp 1988). But how do parents decide which schooling option is best for their children? They can decide which is best for each of their children on the basis of the following five criteria: First, they must find out what schooling is available for each child in the host country or countries nearby. It is important to visit each school with each child before making a final decision. Before choosing, both parent and child should be comfortable with the school. Second, they need to determine which of the available options they can afford. Some schools may be too expensive. Third, parents need to find the best option that will also prepare their children for reentry in America's school system and job market (Hill 1988). Fourth, they need to determine the educational needs of each child. For example, if a child has a learning disability, some options may not be sufficient. Fifth, each child's social

maturity should be taken into account. Some organizations may view boarding school as a logical choice, but the child may be too immature to live in a boarding situation or it may violate family values.

Parents have to decide which options for schooling agree with their own values about the family. Some parents are categorically opposed to sending their children to boarding school. Other parents would consider it unthinkable to leave them behind in America. Some parents are strong believers in home schooling. The crucial point is all children are different; they are in different grades, have different needs, and are at different levels of maturity for their age. It is not unusual to have several children from the same family in different schools. For example, a young child may be taught at home by the mother, while another in later elementary may be attending a national or missionary school in town. At the same time, a high-school student may be in a boarding school while a college student is studying in America.

A wise thing to do is get advice from expatriates and their children who are familiar with the options in the host country. Be ready to be flexible, and if a particular plan does not work, be willing to adjust for the sake of the child. Above all, view the options with the child's best interest in mind. God has given parents the sole responsibility for rearing children, and no one knows the child better than the parents.

Coping with Stress

The first two years of living overseas can be the most stressful years of one's life. Adjustments to a new lifestyle, culture, language, and job can be difficult. A missionary who had served as a pastor for nine years at a large church before going to an overseas mission field believes that ministering overseas was at least three times more difficult than pastoring in the States. Except for death and divorce, living cross-culturally is the ultimate stress, taxing the resources of the most well-adjusted people. Learning to cope becomes a basic survival skill.

What makes living overseas so stressful? First, it may be physically difficult, particularly if one lives in a tropical climate. Tropical heat saps energy, and when one is tired it is easy to get stressed out. In developing countries, just to survive is sometimes a daily battle. Often electricity is off several hours a day, and in the dry season a household can run out of water. Living in the tropics can expose people to tropical diseases, which, fortunately, are no longer as life-threatening as they once were, since the development of excellent prophylactic and curative medicines.

Second, it is emotionally difficult to interact with a culture that has different values. Schedules are quickly sabotaged by people who are event-oriented rather than time-oriented. In some cultures, you are not considered late unless it is an hour beyond the agreed time. Public transportation is often delayed, interrupted, or canceled, particularly in the Third World. Another frustration is coping with lower expectations about quality. It is difficult for Americans to accept imprecision, incompetence, and lack of planning. Having to cope with corruption, deception, and constant cheating is also a strain.

Another emotional stress involves the family. Being separated from children in boarding school, in college, or at home can make parents feel helpless and guilty because they cannot provide in person needed encouragement, advice, and assistance. Not being able to care for elderly parents can produce feelings of guilt as well.

Third, it may be spiritually difficult to cope in some lands. Religions mixed with the occult can produce a spiritual depression as an inordinate amount of demon activity affects Christians endeavoring to live the daily Christian life. In some Islamic countries, there is a lack of religious freedom; Christians, including missionaries, may be ridiculed and harassed for their faith. For instance, it is against the law in Saudi Arabia to carry an uncovered Bible in public, and open evangelism is punishable by death.

Finally, living cross-culturally can be challenging to a marriage. Some American women have a difficult time in cultures where women are to be seen and not heard, or maybe not seen either! In scores of countries, women are looked down upon and men dominate the culture. Getting settled or living in a harsh overseas environment can affect a couple's sex life, as they are often so physically and emotionally exhausted that they do not have anything left for each other (Foyle 1988). Husbands are often required to travel regularly for extended periods of time to check on businesses or ministries, and this separation can also affect a couple's sex life. Regular travel may interfere with parents' spending sufficient time with the children. While the husband is gone, the wife may suffer anxiety, particularly in areas where security is a problem.

Success in Living Overseas

In spite of all the stresses associated with cross-cultural living, it is still wonderful, challenging, and exciting. The key to success is twofold. First, a couple and their family should be well-adjusted before they go overseas. Otherwise, the stresses of cross-cultural living can tear apart a weak marriage as well as a weak family. If a couple has marital problems or their children have emotional problems, living overseas will only intensify the problems. Second, the family has to learn to cope and adjust to new roles, relationships, and living conditions.

> *In spite of all the stresses associated with cross-cultural living, it is still wonderful, challenging, and exciting.*

Research has shown there are four interrelated elements to serving overseas effectively (Ward 1985). First, the family must adjust and cope with day-to-day life. Parents have to provide access to good schooling, recreational opportunities, and medical care for their children. Second, good intercultural interaction is necessary to function effectively in a cross-cultural environment. Success depends on knowledge of the host country, learning the language and the nonverbal communication system, and establishing meaningful working relationships with nationals. Third, successful overseas living involves fulfilling the daily responsibilities demanded by the job. The overseas worker must be able to function on a daily basis. Fourth, the person is able to adequately transfer skills and procedures into the host culture's context. One is able to perform by adapting skills to meet the needs of the new environment. In other words, a person is able to do the same things differently by adapting to local norms and practices. A missionary would probably plant a church differently in Bangladesh than he would in Boston. Successful overseas workers are able to transfer what they know by contextualizing their knowledge and skills to the local situation.

> *The ideal candidate for cross-cultural living has a sense of humor. Humor is the ultimate weapon against despair, for there is so much to make a person sad, angry, annoyed, embarrassed, and discouraged.*

What is the profile of an ideal candidate for cross-cultural living? Research has examined many factors, but three tend to rise to the top

(Kohls 1984). First, the ideal candidate has a sense of humor (Prov. 17:2). Humor is the ultimate weapon against despair, for there is so much to make a person sad, angry, annoyed, embarrassed, and discouraged. If people cannot laugh at themselves, they are in trouble. Second, the ideal candidate has a realistic goal orientation (Prov. 16:9). Goals may be too ambitious and must be adjusted to fit the local situation. Having unrealistic expectations that are simply not attainable can only bring frustration and despair. The successful person knows how to relax and go with the flow. Those that do, tend to enjoy overseas experiences more and are ultimately more effective. Third, successful workers are able to tolerate failure. Some Americans have never experienced failure in their personal or professional lives. Learning through failure is important, for people mature when they fall on their faces and discover they are not invincible (Ps. 51:17).

On the contrary, some personality characteristics are not conducive to proper cross-cultural adjustment. A person who is insecure or takes himself or herself too seriously and has no sense of humor will struggle in a foreign environment. The dogmatic, rigid, and inflexible person will discover these traits work against normal acculturation. The proud, ethnocentric person will incur the disdain and ire of the local populace. People who have poor interpersonal skills and poor communication skills will only be worse in a foreign context. Furthermore, if a person is a perfectionist, is unable to set realistic goals, and gets easily frustrated, the overseas experience can turn out to be an unhappy one. This does not mean people who have any or all of these traits cannot adjust to overseas living. It simply means that coping and adjusting will be much more difficult and will require extra effort.

Having these traits is compounded when the family is also having problems. The overseas experience will only exacerbate any problems the family might have. The insecure, the negative, the inflexible, and the conceited are ill-prepared for cross-cultural living, and those who have adolescent children going through puberty, shaky marriages, or personal crises will also have great difficulty. The only hope for such a family is the sustaining grace of God.

Organizations who send people overseas must be very discriminating. The stronger the worker's self-image, marriage, and family are, the easier it will be to adjust to a foreign environment.

The Foreign-Living Cycle

Personnel living overseas go through a three-stage cycle. The first stage is the preparation stage, when a family finds out it is going overseas and begins preparing. This stage is marked with excitement, anticipation, and exhaustion. During this time, the family learns about the new country, begins packing, and finalizes affairs in the States. It is an incredibly hectic time. The way to survive this stage is to plan well and use plenty of checklists. It is a time of busy work as parents get pictures, passports, visas, work permits, medical records, school records, wills, trusts, and insurance documents in order. A power of attorney must be arranged to handle any necessary affairs. The house has to be sold or rented and a manager found to oversee the tenants. Finances must be put in order by paying off debts, cancelling unused charge cards, and changing addresses so that mail can be forwarded. Travelers' checks should be purchased, shots taken, and a home found for the family pet. By the time the family embarks on the plane, they are usually exhausted and emotionally wrung out, especially since they just said goodbye to their friends and family, who are convinced they will never see them again!

The second stage, the foreign living stage, begins when the family arrives in a new country. It is characterized by jet lag, exhilaration, uncertainty, culture shock, and adjustment. The American community can play a big role in helping to get settled, so it is important to make friends with Americans who have already gone through the adjustment. The American embassy will help with emergency health problems, if you are robbed, or if you lose your passports. They will want to register your family to be able to notify you of civil unrest and advise you on travel restrictions. Some American embassies in developing countries have an American club for their personnel, and memberships may be open to other Americans living in the country. It is worth the membership fee to be able to retreat into a little American enclave when culture shock gets overwhelming.

After the family has lived for two to four years in a foreign country, they usually are entitled to return to America for furlough or extended leave. Upon returning to America, the family encounters the final stage of the cycle—reentry. It is not uncommon for a family to go through a reverse culture shock, known as reentry shock, as they cope with changes that have occurred while they were gone. Parents will discover that life in America is boring and unchallenging after an exciting, stimulating, exotic life overseas. Their friends have a short attention span and really do not care to hear all their bizarre stories. Children are now third-cultural and find it hard to identify with America and its strange value system. They have to adjust to a new home, a new school, and new friends.

> *Upon returning to America, the family encounters the final stage of the cycle—reentry.*

Some third-cultural children are terrified of life in America because it is unknown and overwhelming. One missionary child who spent his years on a remote African jungle station became paralyzed when confronted with thirty-three flavors of ice cream to choose from. He was used to only one. It is not surprising for the whole family to want to pack up and go overseas again, because the family is not the same anymore. They are different, unusual, and unique. They have experienced life on the outside, where the rest of the world lives, and they itch to get back.

Living and working overseas is a tremendous opportunity to present the gospel and serve the Lord, whether in full-time ministry or in a secular career. It is a unique and challenging life, full of rewards and surprises. Rearing a family overseas is a great privilege as children learn to experience a fascinating environment rich with cultural variety. They are mature for their age and capable of traveling the world. These three stages to the foreign living cycle are in reality growth stages, whereby family members encounter a life of self-discovery, self-renewal, and self-sufficiency. The international career is the most difficult and most rewarding work one can encounter. It leaves one with a new sense of self, strong family ties, and a realization that no member of the family will ever be the same.

> *The international career is the most difficult and most rewarding work one can encounter. It leaves one with a new sense of self, strong family ties, and a realization that no member of the family will ever be the same.*

Study Questions

1. Discuss the major careers that have taken people overseas.
2. Define "culture." List five cultural behavior patterns that you might encounter that would differ from your own culture.
3. Why is it important to understand the symptoms of culture shock when entering a different culture?
4. Discuss several mechanisms that can be used to help cope with cultural stress.
5. List some of the problems one may encounter when setting up a household in a third-world country.
6. How do American childrearing patterns differ from those found in some Asian countries?
7. What are some of the advantages and disadvantages of rearing children in another culture?
8. Discuss the education of children living overseas.
9. Why is living abroad so stressful?
10. How would you describe the ideal candidate for cross-cultural living?

Suggested Readings

Kinney, B. J. 1983. *The missionary family.* Pasadena, Calif.: William Carey Library. A comprehensive treatment of the process of rearing children in a foreign culture. Succinctly explains how children develop as third-cultural persons.

Kohls, L. R. 1984. *Survival kit for overseas living.* 2d ed. Yarmouth, Maine: Intercultural Press. A handy manual containing excellent summaries of what a person needs to know about going overseas.

O'Donnell, K. S., and M. L. O'Donnell, eds. 1988. *Helping missionaries grow: Readings in mental health and missions.* Pasadena, Calif.: William Carey Library. A practical and insightful guide to helping missionaries adjust to overseas living.

Ward, T. 1985. *Living overseas: A book of preparations.* New York: Free Press. An indispensable book for anyone anticipating a career overseas. Excellent treatment of readiness factors crucial to cross-cultural success.

Trends in the American Family

Take heed unto thyself, and unto the doctrine, continue in them.

—1 Timothy 4:16

A New Definition of the Family?

A furor erupted in New York City when parents learned that two books on homosexual lifestyles were included in the first-grade teacher's guide. *Heather Has Two Mommies* tells the story of a lesbian couple having a baby through artificial insemination. *Daddy's Roommate* concerned a child with two male parents who was taught that "being gay is just one more kind of love." Parents objected that the books approved homosexuality as a normal way of life and rejected the moral values of the community (*U.S. News and World Report*, 17 August 1992, 16). Such controversies illustrate the changes in attitude toward the traditional family.

Homosexuals are not the only ones trying to redefine the family. Social scientists are stating that what used to be called alternative lifestyles are just different forms of the family. They insist that these illustrate the strength and ability of the family to adjust to the changing needs of society.

Social scientists also claim the traditional family is an anachronism and cite statistics that indicate that only 26 percent of families today consist of two parents and children. They forget to include millions of newly married couples who do not yet have children but intend to do so. Nor do they include the tens of millions of parents whose children have grown and left the nest (*Forbes*, 20 January 1992, 86). Even though many traditional marriages do end in divorce, it may be said that the nuclear family is alive and well, and is well suited to meet the needs of parents and children.

Efforts to redefine the family will continue, but Christian families should demonstrate to the world why God chose the traditional family to illustrate the relationship of the believer to his Son Jesus Christ.

Technology and the Family

The family, as one of the basic institutions of society, has experienced many changes in the last two centuries. The change from an agricultural to an industrial society resulted in a movement from a rural to an urban culture (see chap. 1). American society is now in a postindustrial stage characterized by the widespread use of high technology and a service-oriented economy. Bernard (1972, 313), writing on the future of the family a generation ago, stated, "The great technological innovations that created the first Industrial Revolution had to do with production; increasingly, the great technological innovations that will influence, if not determine, the future of marriage, will have to do with consumption." She proceeds to relate how many technologies will affect the family, such as "fertility control, genetic engineering, surrogate or artificial gestation devices, sperm banks, and preventative geriatrics." Others have labeled ours "the information society" and "the service society" (Skolnick 1992, 433). The computer is the symbol of this new age (Skolnick 1987, 408). Settles (Sussman and Lewis 1986, 165) indicates that "Toffler's extremely popular book, *The Third Wave* (1980) has emphasized how computer wizardry, video display, telephone interface, and automation could create opportunities for flexibility in the workplace and the return to the home of many tasks now carried on outside." This may be still in the future, but the transformation has resulted in the closing of great industrial plants resulting in massive unemployment.

> *Families with children now constitute a large proportion of the homeless in our cities.*

Millions of families lost their means of livelihood and face a bleak future. Some younger workers may be retrained. Few men and women in their forties to sixties will be able to take advantage of such training. Young people who choose not to acquire higher education will be destined to low-paying service jobs. Families will have to migrate to areas where employment is available. Stress will increase, and so will family friction and violence. Many have lost their homes, and families with children now constitute a large proportion of the homeless in our cities (Skolnick 1992, 446). Most families will adapt to this technological change, but many will disintegrate from the stresses created by the upheaval.

The family is also affected by advances in medical technology. Many of these new discoveries involve ethical decisions. Is it right for a woman to have an abortion when ultrasound indicates the fetus has no brain? Should the fetus be carried to term and its organs used to save the lives of other infants? (*Christianity Today*, 18 May 1992, 40). Should a fetus be aborted when genetic testing indicates it will be a Down's syndrome child? If a family desires a boy and genetic testing indicates a girl, should the fetus be aborted? When is it morally permissible to pull the plug on a terminally ill loved one? Some states have already had initiatives on the ballot to legalize euthanasia, although these have been defeated. The question of doctor-assisted suicide was defeated by California voters in the 1992 election. As more technological advances are made, similar questions will arise and have to be answered by the family. For Christian believers the answers to these questions are obvious; they have an infallible guideline in the Bible. For non-Christians the answers will be more difficult, for they no longer have moral absolutes to guide them.

Dual-Income Families

The economic pressure on the family will result in more women entering the work force. The numbers of mothers in the labor force with children under age one grew from 24 percent in 1970 to 50 percent in 1987 (*Newsweek*, 27 November 1989, 87). As the number of mothers in the work force grows, the demand for federal regulation and subsidization of day-care centers will increase. The sharing of household duties in the home will slowly become more equal. Cargan (1991, 391) suggests that "androgynous behavior will become more common as both females and males adopt similar sexual attitudes and behavior. That is, there will be increasing symmetry in sex roles." The downsizing of corporations may provide stress for dual-career couples when one must move to another city to retain their position. More than one million couples are now sharing this type of "commuter marriage."

Adult Children at Home

Another trend affected by the economy is the number of young adults who either fail to leave home or who return home when their economic situation deteriorates. Living at home is much cheaper than living in an apartment. Some parents are selling their homes and buying small condominiums or renting small apartments as one way of discouraging their young adults from returning home to live (Cargan 1985, 284). Settles (Sussman and Lewis 1986, 160) points out that "adults today complain not of the empty nest, but of the returning 'adult' child with his or her children." These children of baby boomers who return home have been facetiously called "boom-rangs." This illustrates the truth in a "Robert Frost (1946) poem [which] suggested, 'Home is the place where, when you have to go there, they have to take you in'" (Sussman and Lewis 1986, 159). The census figures in 1990 indicated that 65 percent of never-married persons ages eighteen to twenty-four were still living at home and 32 percent of the men and 20 percent of the women aged twenty-five to thirty-four were also living with their parents (*World Almanac and Book of Facts* 1992, 943).

Often it is divorced young mothers or fathers with children who are forced to return home. Child support is often inadequate, so the only way to survive is to move in with parents. Many times the grandmother serves as a baby-sitter so the son or daughter can find employment. No-fault divorce often forces women into poverty, and until these inequities are rectified,

the numbers of adult children living with their parents will certainly increase.

> # *Often it is divorced young mothers or fathers with children who are forced to return home.*

Age at Marriage

The median age at first marriage reached a low for both men and women in 1950. Men married at 22.8 years and women at 20.3 years. This increased, reaching a high of 25.9 years for males in 1988 and 23.9 years for women in 1990 (*Information Please Almanac* 1992, 808). Woodward (*Newsweek,* 27 November 1989, 55) writes, "Physically, today's youth are maturing earlier than previous generations, but emotionally they are taking much longer to develop. . . . They are marrying later than their parents did—partly for economic reasons—and many college graduates are postponing marriage beyond age 30." Two other factors influencing these statistics are the large number of unwed mothers and the widespread practice of cohabitation, whereby millions of young people postpone marriage for a few years.

The Women's Movement

The changes brought about by the women's movement will continue. More women are choosing to remain single in order to pursue careers. Others will combine both career and marriage and fill the "supermom" role. More women will enter traditionally male vocational areas. The glass ceiling that prevents women from rising to the highest levels of corporate management will eventually be broken. However, there is little likelihood that the gap between what men earn and women earn will narrow. At the present, women only earn two-thirds what a man earns in a comparable job. Women are seeking and winning political offices in large numbers. They recognize that male politicians do not always serve the best interests of women and the family. Skolnick (1987, 406) observes, "Many problems stem from the fact . . . women have achieved equality in principle, but not in economic or social reality. . . . [This] is responsible for a great deal of strain now felt by women . . . it is likely that these strains will make the family become an even more central issue on the public agenda."

Biblical feminists will continue their battle against traditional family roles. Scanzoni and Hardesty have issued a third edition of *All We're Meant to Be,* a book that ignited the Christian women's liberation movement (*Christianity Today,* 14 December 1992, 43). The struggle for the ordination of women will continue. Many denominations are struggling with the issue. Some liberal groups have agreed to ordain women, but ordination is strongly resisted by the more conservative ones. The Christian Reformed Church, a conservative Reformed church, considered the issue of ordaining women at its 1992 synod. A compromise encouraged churches to "use the gifts of women to the fullest extent possible" and to let "women expound the Word of God." Two hundred women demonstrated against the vote. A leading biblical feminist, Mary Stewart Van Leeuwen (a professor at Calvin College [the denominational college] and author of *Gender and Grace*), stated, "We're saying we're not going to go away" and indicated that the compromise was "patronizing." This issue, plus those of creation and evolution, are dividing the fellowship. A number of churches have left the group and formed the Alliance of Reformed Churches (*Christianity Today,* 20 July 1992, 51). The issue is "not going to go away" and will eventually divide many local churches and denominations.

Women will continue to face the issue of career versus homemaking. Some will continue to attempt to fulfill both desires. It is interesting that there is a trend for some women who have chosen both to give up their employment in order to spend all their time with their families. Society still frowns upon such a choice but more and more women, Christian and non-Christian, are deciding it is more satisfying to be a wife and mother. They are willing to sacrifice luxuries the wife's salary provided and economize in order to enjoy a more fulfilling family life.

Dobson, in a "Focus on the Family" radio broadcast (17 November 1992), interviewed four women from different areas of the country who had left careers in order to be full-time homemakers. One was a physician who stated that people criticized her for not using her education. Her reply was that she uses it to informally teach her children. The consensus of the panel was that it took a real commitment on the part of the husband, but the so-called sacrifices were worth the gains in terms of satisfying family life.

Choosing Not to Marry

An interesting trend is the increasing number of men and women who elect not to marry. A noticeable change has taken place since 1970. In that year 35.8 percent of women and 54.7 percent of men twenty to twenty-four were never married. In 1990 the number for this group increased to 62.8 percent of women and 79.3 percent of men. The figures for the next age group (25–29 years) are also astounding. In 1970 only 10.5 percent of women and 19.1 of the men were single. However, by 1990, 31.1 percent of the women and 45.2 percent of the men were unmarried. The number tripled for the women and more than doubled for the men (*World Almanac and Book of Facts* 1992, 943).

An explanation for part of the increase may be the larger number of years of education required to prepare for employment. The large number of men and women who are delaying marriage are included in these groups. The large number of young adults cohabiting also is a factor. The women's movement and its emphasis on the ability of women to find fulfillment in careers rather than in marriage accounts for a high percentage of women. However, the emphasis on finding sexual satisfaction outside of marriage, coupled with a desire for personal fulfillment without the responsibilities of a family, explains why many people are avoiding marriage. Since many homosexuals have "come out of the closet," they also are included in these statistics on the unmarried. There is intense pressure on the part of the gay community for legalization of so-called marriages between gays, but they have not yet achieved this goal.

The "Birth Dearth"

Many baby-boomer couples have decided not to have children. The availability and reliability of modern contraceptive devices help make it possible for them to remain childless. Careers take priority over children for many women. They do not feel they can meet the demands of both motherhood and a career so they choose the latter. Others recognize the problems many families face during their teenage children's rebellious years and decide the struggle is not worth the effort. The instability of marriage and the threat of becoming a single parent may cause some people to decide against having children. For others, children would interfere with their hedonistic lifestyle. On the other hand, there are those genuinely concerned about overpopulating planet Earth who decide against having children of their own.

There are at least two serious implications of this "birth dearth." Many couples will encounter the illnesses of old age without anyone to care for them. It also will affect the Social Security system. This pay-as-you-go plan depends on the taxes of the present workers to support those who are retired. It appears that when large numbers of baby boomers retire, there will not be sufficient numbers of workers to support them. "By the year 2000 there will be only 3.2 workers for every retiree. In 1960 there were 14 workers for every retiree" (Burkett 1991, 138). This could well cause the failure of the Social Security system.

Changing Economic Patterns

It is estimated that one out of every five families moves each year. It may be around the corner or clear across the country. (The Census Bureau gathers these statistics from commer-cial moving companies.) There has been a movement of manufacturing plants from the rust belt of the northern states to the sun belt of southern states. This has resulted in a lower standard of living for working-class families in the north and an increase for those in the south. The flow of manufacturing jobs to foreign countries ultimately will result in a lowering of the standard of living for many Americans. A service-oriented economy cannot provide the jobs or wages needed to maintain the present level. Many wage earners will find it difficult to support their families and also save for a college education of their children and for their own retirement years. Many are being forced to move to other areas to find employment because of failure of their local economy.

> *The flow of manufacturing jobs to foreign countries ultimately will result in a lowering of the standard of living for many Americans.*

Richard and Vicki Huffman faced unemployment with two children to provide for. They went through severe financial problems before a move from Alabama to Tennessee and a new job. Vicki gives this testimony to God's faithfulness and its effects upon the children (*Moody Monthly*, September 1991, 29): "No matter what you preach to them [the children] all these years . . . if they see you go through a crisis and you don't crumble and fall apart, they know they can trust what you have told them."

331

One of America's great companies, IBM, had a reputation of guaranteeing employment for its workers. However, recession has forced it to lay off thousands of employees. Many of these were able to retire but others were faced with the necessity of moving if they expected to secure a job. This type of experience will be repeated. People will have to leave friends and relatives who help to strengthen families. Moving to a new area requires finding a new church and new friends. Young (1973, 10) reflects that "mobility, with its necessary disruption of continuing relationships, ends by starving them into superficiality, and . . . experiences shared with a succession of unconnected people become more impressions than lasting parts of a life pattern." The families of the future will encounter these new economic challenges, and must adapt to new situations.

The Christian family has divine resources to aid them in overcoming these obstacles to family unity and strength. Charlotte and Steve Marcus have lived in several different states. She comments (*Moody Monthly*, September 1991, 30), "My way would have been to stay in one place . . . but God has allowed us to grow spiritually through our frequent moves. By trusting Him when we didn't live close to family and friends, He really became our dwelling place."

> # In each city the family sought out a Bible-believing church where they found friends and received spiritual motivation.

One family faced a similar situation as the father worked for a construction company that built large electric generating plants. It took three or four years to complete one, which meant the family moved that often. Because this required moves from one region to another they resided in Michigan, Illinois, Washington, Texas, and four other states. However, in each city the family sought out a Bible-believing church where they found friends and received spiritual motivation. In spite of mobility, their family life remained strong. The two daughters attended a Christian college where they found Christian husbands. One is a pastor and the other a Christian businessman. This family used the divine resources and God rewarded them accordingly. On the other hand, examples could be given of Christian families who had to move, neglected to find a good church, and became spiritual casualties of geographic mobility.

Social Mobility

Upward mobility has been part of American culture since the beginning of the Industrial Revolution. Parents of each generation encouraged their children to seek a higher social status. They aided them in this quest in every possible manner. Immigrants from Europe sacrificed their own comforts so that their children could get an education and become professional people. The pattern is being repeated today by the immigrants from Asian countries. They have a vision of the American dream and make education the highest family value. For those fortunate enough to achieve higher education and professional status, the American dream may still be a reality. For those less fortunate, it will be much more difficult, if not impossible, to achieve a social status higher than their parents'.

The continual downsizing of American corporations, the movement of manufacturing jobs abroad, and the tax burden on businesses caused by welfare spending and the national debt all contribute to a decline in opportunities for economic advancement in pursuit of the American dream (*U.S. News and World Report*, 6 April 1992, 8).

Owning a small business has been the second major avenue to advance up the social ladder (higher education is first). To be one's own boss, to set one's own working hours, and to make a profit has been part of the American dream. This aspect of the dream is still very much alive. In 1989, family businesses generated 60 percent of the gross national product and employed forty million people (*Newsweek* special report, winter-spring 1990, 83). These figures include some large corporations that are still family-controlled, such as J. M. Smucker Company and Wang Laboratories. The article states that "family values are in. Entrepreneurship is in. *Ergo* family business is in."

To capitalize on this trend will require the family to take advantage of all the many available resources. The Small Business Administration offers seminars on how to start an individual enterprise and under certain conditions will make loans. Books and magazines devoted to the entrepreneur are available. Most college and universities have courses to teach the fundamentals relating to small businesses.

However, the failure rate is staggering. Most new companies fail for a lack of working capital. An attempt to start a business should be done only after much prayer and education, and with sufficient working capital. Otherwise it will become one of the statistics and the owners may experience downward mobility rather than a move up the social ladder.

Christian families who subscribe to placing their children higher on the social ladder will need to concentrate on providing higher education for their children. However, in view of the need for full-time Christian workers, the question could be raised if this should be the ambition of Christian parents for their children. The answer is found in the truth that all of God's children are to be full-time workers for Christ and his church. Whether children become physicians or factory workers, the aim of parents is to prepare them for a life of testimony for Jesus Christ. D. L. Moody, while working as a shoe clerk, was quoted as saying, "My business is serving the Lord and I'm selling shoes to pay expenses." In a family where such an attitude is encouraged, God will call some children to serve in Christian work and others to serve in so-called secular work. Keeping up with or getting ahead of the Joneses will not really be that important.

> ## *All of God's children are to be full-time workers for Christ and his church.*

Divorce and Remarriage

The divorce rate reached a high of 5.3 per thousand in 1981 with 1,219,000 divorces, and has been slightly decreasing with a rate of 4.7 per thousand in 1990. At the same time the marriage rate has fallen from a high of 10.8 in 1982 to 9.8 in 1990 with a total of 2,448,000 marriages in that year. It is hoped this decrease in divorces will continue (*1992 Information Please Almanac*, 806).

The manner in which one views the divorce rate depends on the frame of reference used in approaching it (Cargan 1991, 386). Whyte (1990, 258) relates that to some social scientists, "the undeniable increase in the divorce rate appears to be a sign of an often successful effort to find more satisfying marital partners, rather than reflecting casualness toward, or alienation from, marriage as an institution." DeVault and Strong (1989, 458) write, "Scholars suggest that divorce does not represent a devaluation of marriage but oddly enough, an idealization of it. We would not divorce if we did not have so much hope in marriage fulfilling our various needs (Furstenberg and Spanier 1987). . . . Social scientists, however, are increasingly describing divorce as one path in the normal family life cycle." According to this frame of reference, divorce may be seen as a device to enable dissatisfied individuals to leave one marriage in order to look for another relationship that fulfills their needs.

The traditional and Christian frame of reference makes divorce a deviant act—not a normal one. It stresses the failure of a legalized relationship with enormous consequences for the couple, their children, and society. Divorce causes great emotional pain for all concerned, including the extended family. The effects on children are well-documented and are not just the result of "the new social environment—most notably poverty and parental stress—into which the children are thrust" (DeVault and Strong 1989, 458). After all, it is the divorce that thrusts the children into poverty and parental stress. Leo writes (*U.S. News and World Report,* 30 November 1992, 22), "an accumulating body of evidence shows that family breakup devastates children in great numbers, often opening up psychological wounds that never heal, and that threaten the children's ability to form their own families as adults."

> ## The traditional and Christian frame of reference makes divorce a deviant act—not a normal one.

Single-parent families and stepfamilies will continue to increase. Most divorced people remarry. More than one million children will enter stepfamilies each year. According to DeVault and Strong (1989, 459), "the number of [divorced] families with children has significantly increased. With the current divorce rate, there is a fifty percent probability that a person will be a member of a blended family as a child, parent, or stepparent. . . ."

The Stepfamily Association of America has been formed to serve the needs of these blended families. For example, in most cases, a stepparent has no legal rights. If a stepchild needs consent to enter a hospital, the stepparent cannot sign the admission papers. A biological parent or a legal guardian must sign. The association would like to see this and other discriminatory rules and regulations changed (*Newsweek,* 27 November 1989, 27).

There is a movement to combat easy divorce and its results. In an article entitled "Wedding Bands Made of Steel," Schrof details some of the attempts to resist divorce (*U.S. News and World Report,* 6 April 1992, 63). She indicates there is a "loose antidivorce coalition encompassing an array of lawmakers, therapists, clerics and scholars, all bound together by the belief that divorce is the greatest disaster in American history." She comments that they are united in their efforts to overturn the no-fault divorce laws. They have joined in a case before the U.S. Supreme Court against no-fault laws. Their argument is that these laws permit one party to break a contract, a practice that has always been against the law in other situations. Therapists in the coalition believe divorces are unnecessary and "coach troubled couples to stay together." Some legal scholars "promote the idea of simply outlawing divorce for parents of minor children." The sale of the family home has been one serious unintended consequence of no-fault laws. Pro-family groups favor a change that would make it almost impossible to sell the family home. "To pro-family groups, the traditional family is the *irreplaceable bedrock* [italics added] of society."

The efforts of James Dobson and his "Focus on the Family" organizations are to be commended. Dobson, who has written numerous books on the family, also produces materials to strengthen the family and wages a continual battle against the forces that are trying to undermine and weaken the traditional Christian family. His work on the commission to investigate pornography received national attention. The organization maintains the Family Research Council in Washington, D.C., to lobby Congress on behalf of pro-family policies. As a part of a religious group, the FRC was limited in its lobbying efforts. In 1992 it was released by Focus on the Family and the FRC became an independent organization free from the restraints placed on religious organizations (*Focus on the Family Newsletter,* November 1992, 6).

Another large pro-family group is Concerned Women for America. It was founded in 1979 by Beverly LaHaye "as the first major alternative women's voice to feminist activities. Its motto is: 'Protecting the rights of the family through prayer and action.'" This group has enlisted more than six hundred thousand women who take a conservative position on the family and political issues. They publish a magazine, *Concerned Women for America,* which encourages women to support their agenda against abortion on demand, secular humanism, euthanasia, and other antifamily issues (*Christianity Today,* 9 November 1992, 23).

An extended list could be made of smaller groups scattered across the country that support the pro-family movement by holding seminars and publishing literature. Christian publishing companies have produced large numbers of publications covering many facets of family living. These have been a blessing to those willing to take advantage of them.

These parachurch organizations seem to be doing the most to combat antifamily sentiment. The evangelical denominations appear to have adopted a policy of avoiding the discussion of divorce and remarriage. Occasionally one of the groups will pass a resolution affirming the permanence of marriage as an ideal and soliciting support for those who fail to reach it.

The Elderly

One of the results of modern medicine has been the increase in average life expectancy. It has gone up by twenty-eight years since 1900. Not only has the average age crept up, but the actual number of persons over sixty-five has greatly multiplied. In 1920 there were 4,900,000 people in that category, whereas in 1990 there were more than 30,000,000 (Dychtwald and Flower 1989, 6).

Gerontologists use the age of sixty-five years as the passage point between middle and old age because it was chosen by Congress as the point one could claim full Social Security retirement benefits. Now that so many people are living longer, it has been suggested that the aged population be divided into two groups— the "young-old" (65–74) and the "old-old" (75 plus). "Those who in 1900 might have been considered old may now appear to be 'young-old' because at the turn of this century few people lived to be over eighty. Currently, there are

over 2.3 million persons in the United States who are over eighty-five, and the number is growing" (Lasswell and Lasswell 1987, 480). Barring any great catastrophe, it is estimated that by 2030 there will be seventy-seven million senior citizens, or one-third of the present population (*Newsweek,* 27 November 1989, 62).

These figures are of extreme importance to the family. Already there are four- and five-generation families. This means there are parents who must be concerned not only with their parents but also their grandparents. Skolnick (1992, 442) quotes Hagestad as labeling this the "generation crunch." "Today's senior citizens" have been described as "new pioneers who are shaping roles for themselves and carrying out patterns for survival, all without the benefit of well-traveled paths to follow" (Lasswell and Lasswell 1987, 508). It has also been called the sandwich generation because these people are caught between "the needs of their children on the one hand and of their aging parents on the other" (Dychtwald and Flower 1989, 238). Studies indicate that 95 percent of the elderly still live in their communities. Whenever necessary, they are helped by their families and friends. This still leaves 5 percent or 1,450,000 in some form of institution and half of those in nursing homes have no living children. Those with children have probably been placed there only after great personal and economic stress, for families do have children to educate and need to prepare for their own retirement (Skolnick 1992, 443).

There is a shortage of nursing homes. "Researchers estimate that 220 new nursing home beds must be added *every day* between now and the year 2000 just to meet the demands of the next decade—long before the baby boomers arrive in their wheelchairs." The government is not interested in building more nursing homes, as 65 percent of the residents are supported through Medicaid (*Newsweek,* 27 November 1989, 66). Consequently, more families will be forced to care for their elderly loved ones at home. Since women live longer than men, they will find themselves in the role of care givers as the health of their husbands decline. "Family care for the elderly often translates to 'spouse care,' which most often means 'wife's care' of her husband" (Lasswell and

Lasswell 1987, 509). The large number of DINK couples (DINK—double income, no kids) and single persons will encounter problems unless they can find relatives to help provide for their care. However, having earned larger incomes, many will have ample resources to purchase care. This is not the case presently because "half the women over 65 are single and live in poverty, with the bulk of their income coming from Social Security or Old Age assistance [public welfare]" (Lasswell and Lasswell 1987, 481).

One factor creating the need for nursing-home care is that modern medicine has been able to extend life, but it has not been able to slow the debilitating diseases that afflict the elderly. Arthritis, strokes, senile dementia, and Alzheimer's disease afflict many of the patients now in nursing homes. More than 2.5 million people are afflicted with Alzheimer's disease today, but 7 million could have the disease by 2040 if no cure is found (*Newsweek*, 27 November 1989, 66).

> # Many grandparents have to play a different role—that of full-time parent to their grandchildren. They are known as second-time-around parents.

One pleasant feature of aging is the role as grandparents. Most acquire this role in their forties and fifties, while they are still young enough to actively enjoy the role. The difficulty is that such grandparents are still working and cannot play the role as often or as much as they would like. Consequently, it is possible for

great-grandparents to get involved. In single-parent families where a father is absent the grandparent often serves as a role model. They can also be a source of knowledge and lend a sense of history to younger families (Lasswell and Lasswell 1987, 489).

Unfortunately, many grandparents have to play a different role—that of being a full-time parent to their grandchildren. They are known as second-time-around parents. More than 3.2 million children live with their grandparents, and often it is a grandmother alone who has the responsibility. These children come from homes devastated by drugs and violence or are simply given to their grandparents by their irresponsible divorced parents. Sometimes these persons marry or remarry but refuse to take their children into the new family. Grandparents are often in poverty themselves. When they do receive help for the grandchildren, it is only one-third what the state pays foster parents to care for children. With the increase of drugs, violence, and irresponsibility, the situation can only worsen (*U.S. News and World Report*, 16 December 1991, 80–89).

Education for Marriage

Living together as a married couple requires abilities and skills that few possess on the wedding day. American culture has never recognized the need to teach young people what they must know in order to live together successfully. Studies have shown that formal courses in marriage and family living result in more stable marriages and happier families. Before one is granted a driver's license, many states now require applicants to complete a driver's education course. The interaction of two different personalities in marriage is much more complex than driving an automobile, but no education is required before one receives a marriage license.

Most colleges and universities offer courses in marriage and family living, usually within the home economics division. Other courses may be taught in the departments of psychology and sociology to fulfill requirements for a major or minor area of concentration. Since most college students marry, it would seem logical that such a course should be one of the general education requirements. If general education courses are necessary to prepare students for living rather than to make a living, it would seem reasonable to require a course to prepare them for living in a family. In determining general education requirements, the difficulty would seem to be in determining which subjects to include and which to omit.

Stinett (Cargan 1985, 172), who did pioneering studies to determine what contributes to strong family life, writes, "We have considerable evidence that the quality of family life is extremely important to our emotional well being, our happiness, and our mental health as individuals. . . . Obviously, it is to our benefit to do what we can to strengthen family life and strengthening family life should be one of our nation's top priorities." In view of this statement, a course to prepare students for family life should have a high priority on every list of general education requirements. Many young people do not enter college, so a required course at the high-school level would be helpful.

The government of Australia has a strong program of educating young people for marriage. It subsidizes more than twenty different programs. The course contains materials on "communication skills, expectations, sexuality and contraception, decision making, finances and budgeting, housing and legal matters" (Cargan 1985, 152). It also sponsors postmarital programs that are similar to the American weekend retreats of Marriage Enrichment and Marriage Encounter.

Christian couples must understand that the best, and sometimes only, course in marriage and family living their children will take is the one they receive in their home (Wheat and Wheat 1981, 33). The manner in which a husband and wife behave toward each other will largely determine how their adult children will treat their spouses. A son who observes his father expressing love, caring, and affection to his mother will learn to act toward his spouse in a similar manner. A daughter who is loved and respected by her father, and who sees her mother revere and love her father, will likewise respond to a loving husband. "The only person who knows how to love is the person who has been loved, who has seen love, who has expe-

rienced love. The Christian home is a laboratory in which the love of God is demonstrated" (Wheat and Wheat 1981, 33).

If young people have not experienced such a home life, then it is necessary to resolve that their homes will be thoroughly Christian homes where children will receive a proper course in Christian family living. The cycle of unhappy and unloving homes can be broken with commitment and the aid of the Holy Spirit. The Christian family will encounter many problems in the future, but God's promises of help and victory are secure.

> *The government of Australia has a strong program of educating young people for marriage. It subsidizes more than twenty different programs.*

Social Policies and the Family

Family values are a dominant theme in much of American politics. Liberals and conservatives have taken opposing positions on many issues confronting the family.

Abortion is the most volatile issue. Conservatives are encouraging the Supreme Court to overturn *Roe v. Wade*, the case that legalized abortion. They achieved some success in 1989 in a case that allows states to impose some restrictions on abortions. However, the pro-life forces suffered a setback in November 1992 as the court reaffirmed *Roe v. Wade*. The issue will be a main consideration in the appointment of justices to the Supreme Court. President Clinton has promised to appoint justices who favor abortion on demand. As one of his first official acts, he "signed five executive orders lifting restrictions on access to abortion" (*USA Today*, 25 January 1993, 3A). However, Christians will continue to fight for elimination of abortion.

There will be continued tension between meeting the needs of the elderly and of children. Is it more important to provide day care and nursing care for Alzheimer's patients, or should the government dollars be spent to expand prenatal care and day-care facilities for children? As the elderly become a greater proportion of the population, and those who work a smaller group, will the latter be willing to pay the Social Security taxes needed to sustain the former?

> # The future of America depends on the quality of its citizens. The family is the place where citizens are socialized.

Is it reasonable to require companies to pay benefits for maternity leaves? How much time must family members be given from their jobs to care for ill family members? Should companies be forced to provide flexible hours or shared-time jobs for mothers with small children? Is it fitting for the government to encourage teenage girls to become mothers by providing welfare benefits? If a young girl has an illegitimate child, the government defines her as an adult and provides "sufficient income to set up an independent household" (Caplow et al. 1982, 334). How can welfare as a way of life be changed? Is it possible or desirable to place a limit on how long a person can stay on welfare rolls? Should homosexual couples be allowed to legally marry and receive all the rights and privileges of heterosexual families?

These are all questions whose answers have much to do with the future of family life in America. Many of them concern the state of the economy, which will be influenced by the staggering annual deficits of government spending and the steadily increasing national debt.

The intrusion of government into the parent-child relationship is also an issue. Until recently parents were responsible for decisions made by their minor children. In two vital areas the courts have taken away parental rights. They decided that underage girls can have abortions without informing their parents or securing their consent. "This is the only operation that can be performed on a child without the parent's consent" (*Forbes*, 20 January 1992, 86). In a similar manner minor children can be given condoms without the consent of the parents. Both of these actions undermine the authority of parents in the home.

Some Congressmen are seeking ratification of the United Nations' "Convention on the Rights of the Child." If it is ratified, the convention will have the same legal status as the Constitution. It would seriously curtail the rights of parents in relationship to their children. The pro-family forces continue to oppose the acceptance of this convention (*Focus on the Family Newsletter*, November 1992, 4–5).

One of the major concerns of the future is the matter of health care for the family. Many feel that the government must institute some form of socialized medicine. Others believe that private insurance with some revisions can provide the best care. The increasing number of AIDS patients with the high cost of care complicate the situation. The demands for better care of children and elderly will not be easy to meet. As a result, governmental authorities need the wisdom of Solomon to solve these problems.

Conservatives generally support social policies that encourage the traditional family. Many present policies fail to do this. "Former vice-president Walter Mondale has noted that we have housing policies that destroy family life, welfare regulations that force families apart, and tax policies that penalize the poor!" (Wynn 1982, 11). The use of tax money has its limitations. "The government will never be able to mandate loving commitments. The relationship between a welfare official and an unwed mother is a poor substitute for a bond between husband and wife. Nor will the tie between a day-care worker and her 'client' ever properly replace maternal devotion" (Christensen 1990, 118).

The future of America depends on the quality of its citizens. The family is the place where citizens are socialized. National policies must be those that will strengthen the nuclear family and encourage the rearing of law-abiding, caring citizens.

The Church and the Family

A special report on the family in *Moody Monthly* (September 1991, 10) begins with the statement, "There's good news for the Christian family. Despite rumors, we're not extinct—or even on the endangered list. But because believers do not live in a vacuum, we face serious challenges." As one reads the special report, it could be argued that the family is on "the endangered list." If it is to endure, the evangelical church must do more than it is doing. The epidemic of divorce, the moral failure of leaders, the increase in abuse, the number of young people involved in sexual promiscuity, and the use of drugs and alcohol all indicate that the Christian family is in deep trouble.

The church must somehow help individuals bridge the gap between the profession of faith and a possession of faith that changes a person's lifestyle. Almost fifty million Americans claim to have had a born-again experience, but they have little influence on American culture (Gallup 1984, 67). This is particularly true in regard to the family. Instead of the Christian family providing inspiration to the secular family to embrace greater faithfulness and dedication to family values, it has fallen prey to the same problems.

The church must reaffirm its allegiance to the biblical pattern of the home and institute programs that will inculcate these truths into its members. The formation of the National Center for Fathering by Ken Canfield in Manhattan, Kansas, is most encouraging for the future of the family. The motto is "to turn the

hearts of the fathers to their children, and the hearts of the children to their fathers." The center surveyed more than five thousand fathers and developed a "Personal Fathering Profile Report" to help men understand their role as fathers. It conducts seminars in churches and trains pastors to conduct their own seminars on fathering. Brian Newman of the Minirth-Meier clinics recommends the center's seminars as "a wonderful vehicle for equipping the rest of us for the important task of being effective dads" (Pamphlet, National Center for Fathering, 2). There have been many and varied seminars to help women in their roles, but little has been done for men. If churches will avail themselves of the resources offered by the center, many families could be strengthened.

> ## *Almost fifty million Americans claim to have had a born-again experience, but they have little influence on American culture.*

"Promise Keepers" is a group founded in 1990 by Bill McCartney, head coach of the University of Colorado football team. The purpose statement is "to unite men to become Godly men—by making promises to Jesus Christ and to one another that last a lifetime." Twenty-two thousand men attended the second national conference at the University of Colorado in 1992. In addition to the national conference, the organization plans "regional conferences, pastors' conferences, one-day leadership training seminars, books, study guides, . . . and a newsletter (*Christianity Today,* 14 September 1992, 57). The aim of the organization is to help men "learn how to be better husbands and fathers and better men of God." This organization will become another major force in the pro-family movement.

Pastors and church leaders must model the family roles in such a manner that young people will desire to imitate them when they marry. In order to accomplish this goal, there must be a total commitment of individual lives to the lordship of Jesus Christ. Godly leadership and homes grow out of godly lives. All the instruction and programs on family living will fail unless there is total consecration to God through his Son Jesus Christ.

Godly leadership and homes grow out of godly lives.

The Christian family faced difficult times in the past and is still here today because previous generations were willing to face the issues and pay the price. Futurists may imagine that the family will be displaced by "loosely knit clans" but history proves otherwise (*Time,* Fall 1992, 42). This generation of Christian young people must rise to the challenge and present their homes to a secular world as "havens in a heartless world" (Lasch 1977).

Study Questions

1. Why is it important to resist efforts to redefine the family?
2. How do the changes in technology affect the family?
3. In what ways is the women's movement influencing the Christian family?
4. How can the Christian family prepare to meet the economic changes of the future?
5. Discuss the relationship between the Christian family and the quest for higher social standing.
6. List several activities of the pro-family movement that aim to strengthen family life.
7. What is meant by the term *sandwich generation?*
8. Why is the role of grandparents becoming increasingly important?
9. Discuss the statement, "A course in marriage and family living should be a general education requirement."
10. List and discuss several governmental policies concerning the family on which conservatives and liberals disagree.

Suggested Readings

Bernard, J. 1972. *The future of marriage.* New York: Bantam. The author, an ardent feminist, predicted that the future of marriage would be based on the patterns of upper-middle-class young people. However, it seems that lower-class patterns have become the model for many in this generation— "unsanctified liaisons, female-headed families, and out-of-wedlock births—regardless of race."

Burkett, L. 1991. *The coming economic earth-quake.* Chicago: Moody. A Christian best seller that warns the reader of the economic danger posed by the large federal annual deficits and the staggering total of the national debt. The author encourages Christians to get out of debt as the best preparation to meet what he feels is a coming economic disaster.

Dychtwald, K., and J. Flower. 1989. *Age wave: The challenge and opportunities of an aging America.* Los Angeles: Tarcher. The writers are concerned about the tremendous growth in the number of elderly in America. They believe the coming "age wave" is being produced by three factors: the senior boom, the birth dearth, and the aging of baby boomers. They postulate that significant intergenerational strife could take place in the future.

Ehrlich, A. H., and P. R. Ehrlich. 1990. *The population explosion.* New York: Simon and Schuster. Overpopulation is the world's number one ecological problem, according to these writers. This volume is a sequel to *The Population Bomb* (1968) that drew attention to this problem. They suggest that the government should institute policies to achieve zero population growth or less. They contend most of our ecological problems are due to overpopulation, and the future looks bleak unless population growth is curtailed.

Naisbitt, J., and P. Aburdene. 1990. *Megatrends 2000*. New York: Morrow. The authors, husband and wife, devote their research to trends in American and foreign cultures. Two interesting chapters concern the role of women and the increase in religion. They predict that the so-called glass ceiling will be broken, resulting in many women rising to top corporate management positions.

Stacey, J. 1990. *Brave new families: Stories of domestic upheaval in late twentieth century America*. New York: Basic. This volume was written by a feminist who has "learned to respect and understand some of the social appeals of widespread nostalgia for eroding family forms even though [she] oppose[s]

the conservative gender, class, and sexual politics of the pro-family movement." A study of two families who illustrate the complex extended kin relationships created by divorces. Very well written.

Toffler, A. 1990. *Power shift*. New York: Bantam. This is the final volume of a trilogy on change in American culture. The first was *Future Shock* (1970), followed by *The Third Wave* (1980). The first volume dealt with the process of change; the second with the directions of change, and the final volume deals with the control of changes in the future.

Zins, S. 1987. *Aging in America*. Albany, N.Y.: Delmar. The aging of the population is a problem facing American culture in the next few decades. The writer discusses the demographics and the sociological and psychological implications of aging.

Bibliography

Abraham, K. 1985. *Don't bite the apple until you check for worms.* Old Tappan, N.J.: Revell.

Achtenmeier, E. 1976. *The committed marriage.* Philadelphia: Westminster.

Adams, J. 1972. *Christian living in the home.* Nutley, N.J.: Presbyterian and Reformed.

Alberoni, F. 1983. *Falling in love.* Trans. L. Veniti. New York: Random House.

Alcorn, R. 1985. *Christians in the wake of the sexual revolution.* Portland, Ore.: Multnomah.

Alford, H. n.d. *The New Testament for English readers.* Chicago: Moody.

Anderson, R. S., and D. B. Guernsey. 1985. *On being family: A social theology of the family.* Grand Rapids: Eerdmans.

Anthony, M. J., and C. A. Koons. 1991. *Single adult passages: Uncharted territories.* Grand Rapids: Baker.

Baldwin, S., and M. MacGregor. 1984. *Your money matters.* Minneapolis: Bethany Fellowship.

Balswick, J., and J. Balswick. 1989. *The family, a Christian perspective on the contemporary home.* Grand Rapids: Baker.

Barna Research Group. 1987. *Single adults in America.* Glendale, Calif.: Barna Research Group.

Barnes, A. 1868. *Notes on the Gospels.* Vol. 2. New York: Harper.

Barnes, M. L., and R. J. Sternberg, eds. 1988. *The psychology of love.* New Haven: Yale Univ. Press.

Beck, M. 1989. "The geezer boom." *Newsweek* special report, 62.

Beck, R. 1992. "Washington's profamily activists." *Christianity Today,* 9 November, 21–26.

Beers, R., and J. Kessler. 1984. *Parents and teenagers.* Wheaton: Victor.

Belkin, G. 1984. *Introduction to counseling.* 2d ed. Dubuque, Iowa: Brown.

Benner, D., ed. 1987. *Christian counseling and psychotherapy.* Grand Rapids: Baker.

Benson, L. 1971. *The family bond.* New York: Random.

Berman, P., and F. Pedersen. 1987. *Men's transition to parenthood: Longitudinal studies of early family experience*. Hillsdale, N.J.: Lawrence Erlbaum.

Bernard, J. 1972. *The future of marriage*. New York: Bantam.

Besson, C. 1985. *Growing together: Growth coaching for couples*. Millford, Mich.: Mott Media.

Blakeslee, S., and J. S. Wallerstein. 1989. *Second chances: Men, women, children a decade after divorce*. New York: Ticknor and Fields.

Blood, R., and M. Blood. 1978. *Marriage*. New York: Free Press.

Blue, R. 1986. *Master your money*. Nashville: Nelson.

Bogarth, A. 1987. *Love's prism: Reflections from the heart of a woman*. Kansas City: Shedd and Ward.

Bowman, G. 1974. *Here's how to succeed with your money*. Rev. ed. Chicago: Moody.

Bradbeer, R., P. DeBono, and P. Laurie. 1982. *The beginner's guide to computers*. Reading, Mass.: Addison-Wesley.

Branden, N. 1992. *The power of self-esteem*. Deerfield Beach, Fla.: Health Communications.

Brandt, H., and H. Dowdy. 1960. *Building a Christian home*. Wheaton: Scripture Press.

Branon, D. 1991. "Waking up from the American dream." *Moody Monthly*, September, 29.

Bridges, J. 1983. *The practice of godliness*. Colorado Springs: Navpress.

Brissett, M., and B. Burns. 1991. *The adult child of divorce: A recovery handbook*. Nashville: Nelson.

Buffam, C. 1985. *The life and times of an MK*. Pasadena, Calif.: William Carey Library.

Burkett, L. 1975. *Your finances in changing times*. San Bernardino, Calif.: Campus Crusade for Christ.

———. [1979] 1982. *The financial planning workbook*. Chicago: Moody.

———. 1982. *How to manage your money*. Rev. ed. Chicago: Moody.

———. 1987. *Answers to your family's financial questions*. Ponoma, Calif.: Focus on the Family.

———. 1989. *Debt-free living*. Chicago: Moody.

———. 1991. *The coming economic earthquake*. Chicago: Moody.

———. 1992. *Investing for the future*. Wheaton: Victor.

Bustanoby, A. 1992. *Single parenting*. Grand Rapids: Zondervan.

Butler, E. W., and D. B. Gutknecht, eds. 1985. *Family, self, and society*. 2d ed. New York: Univ. Press of America.

Bynum, J., and W. E. Thompson. 1989. *Juvenile delinquency*. Boston: Allyn and Bacon.

Calonius, E. 1989. "Blood and money." *Newsweek* special report, 83.

Canfield, K. 1992. News release. National Center for Fathering, Manhattan, Kan.

Caplow, T., et al. 1982. *Middletown families: Fifty years of change and continuity*. Minneapolis: Univ. of Minnesota Press.

Capps, D. 1987. *Deadly sins and saving virtues*. Philadelphia: Fortress.

Cargan, L. 1991. *Marriages and families*. New York: Harper Collins.

———, ed. 1985. *Marriage and family: Coping with change*. Belmont, Calif.: Wadsworth.

Carmody, D., and J. Tulley. 1984. *Becoming one flesh: Growth in Christian marriage*. Nashville: The Upper Room.

Carter, W. 1991. *Kid think*. Dallas: Word.

Case, R., R. Meier, and F. Minirth. 1985. *The money diet*. Grand Rapids: Baker.

Chapian, M. 1986. *Growing closer: The intimacy of love and friendship*. Old Tappan, N.J.: Revell.

Chapman, A., and S. Chapman. 1989. *Married lovers, married friends*. Minneapolis: Bethany House.

Chapman, G. D. 1982. *Hope for the separated*. Chicago: Moody.

Christensen, J. 1983. *Before saying "I do."* Old Tappan, N.J.: Revell.

———. 1990. *Utopia against the family*. San Francisco: Ignatius.

Christensen, L., and N. Christensen. 1977. *The Christian couple*. Minneapolis: Bethany Fellowship.

Clinebell, C., and H. J. Clinebell. 1970. *The intimate marriage*. New York: Harper and Row.

Clinebell, H. J. 1984. *Basic types of pastoral care and counseling*. Rev. ed. Nashville: Abingdon.

Clinton, S. 1988. "Fathers and teenagers: Social facts and biblical values." In G. Regier, ed.,

Values and public policy. Washington, D.C.: Family Research Council.

Coleman, B. 1984. *Encyclopedia of Christian marriage.* Old Tappan, N.J.: Revell.

———. 1985. *Sex and the single Christian.* Ventura, Calif.: Regal.

Coleman, J. C. 1988. *Intimate relationships: Marriage and the family.* 2d ed. New York: Macmillan.

Coleman, M., B. Robinson, and B. Rowland. 1986. *Latchkey kids: Unlocking doors for children.* Lexington, Mass.: Lexington Books.

Coleman, W. L. 1990. *What makes a marriage last? Secrets for a lasting romance.* San Bernardino, Calif.: Here's Life.

Collins, G. 1982. *Beyond easy believism.* Waco: Word.

———. 1985. *Your magnificent mind.* Grand Rapids: Baker.

———. 1986. *Innovative approaches to counseling.* Waco: Word.

———. 1988. *Christian counseling: A comprehensive guide.* Rev. ed. Dallas: Word.

———. 1991. *Excellence and ethics in counseling.* Dallas: Word.

Consumer Reports Buying Guide. 1991. Consumers Union of the U.S. Mt. Vernon, N.Y.

Conway, J., and S. Conway. 1991. *Traits of a lasting marriage.* Rev. ed. Downer's Grove, Ill.: InterVarsity.

Crabb, L. 1982. *The marriage builder: A blueprint for couples and counselors.* Grand Rapids: Zondervan.

———. 1991. *Men and women: Enjoying the difference.* Grand Rapids: Zondervan.

Cretser, G., and J. Leon, eds. 1982. *Intermarriage in the U.S.* New York: Haworth.

Crosson, R. 1989. *Money and your marriage.* Dallas: Word.

Curran, D. 1983. *Traits of a healthy family.* Minneapolis: Winston.

Dale, R. W. n.d. *The Ten Commandments.* New York: Hodder and Stoughton.

Davis, L. E. 1984. *In charge: Managing money for Christian living.* Nashville: Broadman.

DeJong, P. 1979. *Husband and wife: The sexes in Scripture and society.* Grand Rapids: Zondervan.

Derlega, V. J. 1984. *Communication, intimacy, and close relationships.* Orlando, Fla.: Academic Press.

Dertouzos, M., and J. Moses. 1980. *The computer age: A twenty-year view.* Cambridge, Mass.: The MIT Press.

DeSanto, P., and T. Williams. 1988. *Putting love to work in your marriage.* Scottdale, Penn.: Herald.

DeVault, C., and B. Strong. 1989. *The marriage and family experience.* 4th ed. St. Paul: West.

Diehm, W. J. 1984. *Finding your life partner.* Valley Forge, Penn.: Judson.

———. 1986. *Staying in love.* Minneapolis: Augsburg.

Dobbins, R. 1985a. *Narrowing the risk in mate selection.* Akron: Emerge Ministries.

———. 1985b. *Venturing into a child's world.* Old Tappan, N.J.: Revell.

Dobson, J. 1974. *Hide or seek.* Old Tappan, N.J.: Revell.

———. 1975. *What wives wish their husbands knew about women.* Wheaton: Tyndale.

———. 1978. *The strong-willed child.* Wheaton: Tyndale.

———. 1980. *Emotions, can you trust them?* Ventura, Calif.: Regal.

———. 1987. *Love for a lifetime: Building a marriage that will go the distance.* Portland, Ore.: Multnomah.

———. 1992a. *The new dare to discipline.* Wheaton: Tyndale House.

———. 1992b. Radio broadcast, 17 November.

———. 1992c. "What effect will a Clinton administration have on the institution of the family and on the moral underpinnings of the nation?" *Focus on the Family Newsletter,* November, 2.

Dobson, J., and G. Bauer. 1990. *Children at risk.* Dallas: Word.

Duncan, R. 1979. *You're divorced, but your children aren't.* Englewood Cliffs, N.J.: Prentice-Hall.

Duvall, E., and B. Miller. 1985. *Marriage and family development.* 6th ed. New York: Harper-Collins.

Dychtwald, K., and J. Flower. 1989. *Age wave: The challenge and opportunities of an aging America.* Los Angeles: Tarcher.

Earles, B. D. 1984. *The dating maze.* Grand Rapids: Baker.

Edelman, M. W. 1987. *Families in peril: An agenda for social change.* Cambridge, Mass.: Harvard Univ. Press.

Elkin, D. 1988. *The hurried child: Growing up too fast too soon.* Reading, Mass.: Addison-Wesley.

Encyclopedia of Christian parenting. 1982. Old Tappan, N.J.: Revell.

Engel, L. 1982. *How to buy stocks.* 7th ed. Boston: Little, Brown.

Eshleman, J. 1991. *The family.* 6th ed. Boston: Allyn and Bacon.

Fantini, M., and R. Cardenas, eds. 1980. *Parenting in a multicultural society.* New York: Longman.

Field, D. 1986. *Marriage personalities.* Eugene, Ore.: Harvest House.

Finsterbusch, K., and G. McKenna. 1990. *Taking sides: Clashing views on controversial social issues.* 6th ed. Guilford, Conn.: Dushkin.

Fisher, M., and G. Nass. 1984. *Sexuality today.* Boston: Jones and Bartlett.

Fitzpatrick, M. A. 1988. *Between husbands and wives: Communication in marriage.* Newbury Park, Calif.: Sage.

Fooshee, G., and M. Fooshee. 1980. *You can beat the money squeeze.* Old Tappan, N.J.: Revell.

Foster, R. J. 1985. *Money, sex and power: The challenge of the disciplined life.* San Francisco: Harper and Row.

Foyle, M. 1988. "Stress factors in missionary marriages." In K. S. O'Donnell and M. O'Donnell, eds., *Helping missionaries grow: Readings in mental health and missions.* Pasadena, Calif.: William Carey Library.

Friesen, D., and R. Friesen. 1989. *Counseling and marriage.* Dallas: Word.

Fryling, A., and R. Fryling. 1977. *A handbook for engaged couples.* Downer's Grove, Ill.: InterVarsity.

Furnham, A., and S. Bochner. 1986. *Culture shock: Psychological reactions to unfamiliar environments.* New York: Methuen.

Gallup, G., Jr. 1984. *Religion in America.* Princeton, N.J.: Princeton Religious Research Center.

Gangel, K., and E. Gangel. 1987. *Building a Christian family.* Chicago: Moody.

Garfinkel, I., and S. S. McLanahan. 1986. *Single mothers and their children: An American dilemma.* Washington, D.C.: The Urban Institute Press.

Garland, D. E., and D. S. Garland. 1986. *Beyond companionship: Christians in marriage.* Philadelphia: Westminster.

Garrett, W. R. 1982. *Seasons of marriage and family life.* New York: Holt, Rinehart and Winston.

Gay, K. 1988. *Changing families: Meeting today's challenges.* Hillside, N.J.: Enslow.

Genevie, L., and E. Margolies. 1987. *The motherhood report: How women feel about being mothers.* New York: Macmillan.

Gladding, S. T. 1988. *Counseling: A comprehensive profession.* Columbus: Merrill.

Gordon, S., and J. Gordon. 1983. *Raising a child conservatively in a sexually permissive world.* New York: Simon and Schuster.

Graham, N. 1989. *The mind tool: Computers and their impact on society.* St. Paul: West.

Greeley, A. M. 1991. *Faithful attraction: Discovering intimacy, love, and fidelity in American marriage.* New York: Tom Doherty Associates.

Grulan, S. A., and D. H. Lambrides. 1984. *Healing relationships: A Christian manual for lay counseling.* Camp Hill, Penn.: Christian Publications.

Grunwald, B. B., and H. V. McAbee. 1985. *Guiding the family: Practical counseling techniques.* Muncie, Ind.: Accelerated Development.

Hagan, J. 1990. *Gender matters: Women's studies for the Christian community.* Grand Rapids: Academic.

Hales, D. R. 1988. *The family.* New York: Chelsea House.

Hardesty, N., and L. Scanzoni. 1974. *All we're meant to be: A biblical approach to women's liberation.* Waco: Word.

Hart, K. F., and T. W. Hart. 1983. *The first two years of marriage.* New York: Paulist.

Hauer, G. 1983. *Longing for tenderness: Responsible love before marriage.* Downer's Grove, Ill.: InterVarsity.

Hausner, L. 1990. *Children of paradise: Successful parenting for prosperous families.* Los Angeles: Tarcher.

Havemann, E., and M. Lehtinen. 1990. *Marriages and families.* 2d ed. Englewood Cliffs, N.J.: Prentice-Hall.

Havener, V. 1983. *Our endangered children: Growing up in a changing world.* Boston: Little, Brown.

Haynes, J. 1981. *Divorce mediation: A practical guide for therapists and counselors.* New York: Springer.

Hazelip, H. 1985. *Happiness in the home.* Grand Rapids: Baker.

Helms, D. B., and J. Turner. 1987. *Lifespan development.* 3d ed. New York: Holt, Rinehart and Winston.

Hendricks, H., and J. Neff. 1988. *Husbands and wives.* Wheaton: Victor.

Henslin, J., ed. 1985. *Marriage and family in a changing society.* 2d ed. New York: Free Press.

Hess, J., and R. Hess. 1989. *A full quiver.* Brentwood, Tenn.: Wolgemuth and Hyatt.

Hill, B. 1988. "The educational needs of expatriates." In Kelly O'Donnell and M. O'Donnell, eds., *Helping missionaries grow: Readings in mental health and missions.* Pasadena, Calif.: William Carey Library.

Hillerstrom, P. 1989. *Escaping the trap of sexual impurity.* Eugene, Ore.: Multnomah.

Hine, J. 1985. *The springtime of love and marriage: Guidance for the early years of marriage.* Valley Forge, Penn.: Judson.

Hirning, A. L., and J. Hirning. 1956. *Marriage adjustment.* New York: American Book Co.

Hitchcock, J. 1982. *What is secular humanism?* Ann Arbor: Servant.

Hoekema, A. A. 1986. *Created in God's image.* Grand Rapids: Eerdmans.

Hof, L. 1981. *Marriage enrichment: Philosophy, process and program.* Bowie, Md.: R. J. Brady.

Hoffman, M., ed. 1991. *World almanac and book of facts.* New York: Pharos.

Hopewell, W. J. 1976. *Marriage and divorce.* No publisher.

Hudson, R. L. 1981. *Now that our kids have children.* Waco: Word.

Huggett, J. 1981. *Two into one: Relating in Christian marriage.* Downer's Grove, Ill.: InterVarsity.

———. 1982. *Growing into love before you marry.* Downer's Grove, Ill.: InterVarsity.

———. 1985. *Dating, sex, and friendship.* Downer's Grove, Ill.: InterVarsity.

Hunter, B. 1978. *Beyond divorce: A personal journey.* Old Tappan, N.J.: Revell.

———. 1982. *Where have all the mothers gone?* Grand Rapids: Zondervan.

Hunter, H. 1991. *Remarriage in midlife: Plan it first, make it last.* Grand Rapids: Baker.

Hurley, J. 1981. *Man and woman in biblical perspective.* Grand Rapids: Zondervan.

Hybels, B. 1987. *Who you are when no one's looking.* Downer's Grove, Ill.: InterVarsity.

Janosik, E., and E. Green. 1992. *Family life process and practice.* Boston: Jones and Barlett.

Jauncey, J. 1966. *Magic in marriage.* Grand Rapids: Zondervan.

Jenkins, J. 1989. *Hedges: Loving your marriage enough to protect it.* Brentwood, Tenn.: Wolgemuth and Hyatt.

Jeremiah, D. 1991. *Overcoming loneliness.* Nashville: Nelson.

Jewett, P. 1975. *Man as male and female.* Grand Rapids: Eerdmans.

Johnson, D. W. 1982. *The challenge of single adult ministry.* Valley Forge, Penn.: Judson.

Johnson, O., ed. 1992. *Information please almanac.* Boston: Houghton-Mifflin.

Johnson, R. A. 1983. *We: Understanding the psychology of romantic love.* San Francisco: Harper and Row.

Jones, B., and B. St. Clair. 1987. *Sex: Desiring the best.* San Bernardino, Calif.: Here's Life.

Jones, K. 1989. *Divorce and remarriage in the Bible.* Anderson, Ind.: Warner.

Juroe, D. 1981. *Money: How to spend less and have more.* Old Tappan, N.J.: Revell.

Kageler, K. 1989. *Helping your teenager cope with peer pressure.* Loveland, Colo.: Family Tree Group.

Kahn, R. 1964. *The Ten Commandments for today.* Garden City, N.J.: Doubleday.

Kantrowitz, B., and P. Wingert. 1989. "Step by step." *Newsweek* special report, 27.

———. 1989. "The day care generation." *Newsweek* special report, 87.

Kaufman, B. 1992. "Promise keepers rallies men to commitment." *Christianity Today,* 14 September, 57.

Kelley, R. 1969. *Courtship, marriage and the family.* New York: Harcourt, Brace, and World.

Kephart, W. 1981. *The family, society, and the individual.* 5th ed. Boston: Houghton-Mifflin.

Kessler, J. 1984. *Family forum.* Wheaton: Victor.

Ketterman, G. H. 1984. *Before and after the wedding night.* Old Tappan, N.J.: Revell.

———. 1989. *Understanding your child's problems.* Old Tappan, N.J.: Revell.

Kinney, B. 1983. *The missionary family.* Pasadena, Calif.: William Carey Library.

Klein, R., ed. 1987. *The money book of money: Your personal financial planner.* Boston: Little, Brown.

Kohls, L. R. 1984. *Survival kit for overseas living.* 2d ed. Yarmouth, Maine: Intercultural Press.

Korman, S., and G. R. Leslie. 1985. *The family in social context.* New York: Oxford Univ. Press.

Krutza, W. J. 1974. *25 keys to a happy marriage.* Grand Rapids: Baker.

Kurtz, P. 1983. *In defense of secular humanism.* Buffalo, N.Y.: Prometheus.

LaHaye, B., and T. LaHaye. 1976. *The act of marriage: The beauty of sexual love.* Grand Rapids: Zondervan.

LaHaye, T. 1982. *The battle for the family.* Old Tappan, N.J.: Revell.

Lamanna, M. A., and A. Riedmann. 1988. *Marriages and families.* 3d ed. Belmont, Calif.: Wadsworth.

Lamb, M., ed. 1987. *The father's role: Cross-cultural perspectives.* Hillsdale, N.J.: Lawrence Erlbaum.

Landis, J. T., and M. G. Landis. 1968. *Building a successful marriage.* Englewood Cliffs, N.J.: Prentice-Hall.

LaRossa, R. 1977. *Conflict and power: Expecting the first child.* Beverly Hills, Calif.: Sage.

Lasch, C. 1977. *Haven in a heartless world.* New York: Basic.

Lasswell, M. E., and T. Lasswell. 1987. *Marriage and the family.* 2d ed. Belmont, Calif.: Wadsworth.

Lawton, K. 1992. "Curing or killing." *Christianity Today,* 18 May, 40.

Leman, K. 1981. *Sex begins in the kitchen.* Ventura, Calif.: Regal.

LeMasters, E. 1957. *Modern courtship and marriage.* New York: Macmillan.

Leo, J. 1992. "Heather has a message." *U.S. News and World Report,* 17 August, 16.

———. 1992. "A family plan for Uncle Sam." *U.S. News and World Report,* 30 November, 22.

Leonard, J., Jr., and R. P. Olson. 1990. *Ministry with families in flux: The church and changing patterns of life.* Louisville: Westminster/John Knox.

LePeau, A., and P. LePeau. 1981. *One plus one equals one.* Downer's Grove, Ill.: InterVarsity.

Lester, A. D. 1983. *Coping with your anger.* Philadelphia: Westminster.

Lewis, K. 1981. *Your Christian wedding.* Old Tappan, N.J.: Revell.

Lewis, P. 1985. *40 ways to teach your child values.* Wheaton: Tyndale House.

Lewis, P., and J. McDowell. 1988. *Givers, takers, and other kinds of lovers.* Wheaton: Tyndale House.

Liddell, E. 1985. *The disciplines of the Christian life.* Nashville: Abingdon.

Lord, L. 1992. "Jobs and dreams drip away." *U.S. News and World Report,* 6 April, 8.

Lowe, J. 1990. *The super saver: Fundamental Strategies for building wealth.* Chicago: Longman Financial Services.

MacArthur, J., Jr. 1982. *Your family.* Chicago: Moody.

Mace, D. 1966. *Youth considers marriage.* Camden, N.J.: Nelson.

———. 1982. *Love and anger in marriage.* Grand Rapids: Zondervan.

Mace, D., and V. Mace. 1985. *In the presence of God: Readings for Christian marriage.* Philadelphia: Westminster.

Mains, D. 1985. *The religion of Anti-Christ.* Grand Rapids: Zondervan.

Malcolm, K. T. 1987. *Building your family to last.* Downer's Grove, Ill.: InterVarsity.

Marshall, S. 1988. *Surviving separation and divorce.* Grand Rapids: Baker.

Martinson, F. 1970. *Family in society.* New York: Dodd, Mead.

Mason, M. 1985. *The mystery of marriage.* Portland, Ore.: Multnomah.

Mayhall, P., and K. Norgard. 1983. *Child abuse and neglect*. New York: Wiley.

McBurney, L. 1986. *Counseling Christian workers*. Waco: Word.

McDonald, C. 1977. *God's plan for family living*. Des Plaines, Ill.: Regular Baptist Press.

McDowell, J. 1985. *The secret of loving: How a lasting intimate relationship can be yours*. San Bernardino, Calif.: Here's Life.

McGinnis, A. L. 1982. *The romance factor*. San Francisco: Harper and Row.

———. 1987. *Confidence: How to succeed at being yourself*. Minneapolis: Augsburg.

McIlhaney, J., Jr. 1990. *Sexuality and sexually transmitted diseases*. Grand Rapids: Baker.

Meier, P. 1993. *Child-rearing and personality development*. Grand Rapids: Baker.

Meier, P., and R. Meier. 1981. *Family foundations: How to have a happy home*. Grand Rapids: Baker.

Meier, P., F. Minirth, and F. Wichern. 1991. *Introduction to psychology and counseling*. Grand Rapids: Baker.

Meier, R., et al. 1988. *Sex in the Christian marriage*. Grand Rapids: Baker.

Michaels, G., and W. Goldberg. 1988. *The transition to parenthood: Current theory and research*. New York: Cambridge Univ. Press.

Miles, H. 1963. *Sexual happiness in marriage*. Grand Rapids: Zondervan.

———. 1983. *Singles, sex and marriage*. Waco: Word.

Miller, A., and K. Miller. 1981. *The single experience*. Waco: Word.

Miller, D. R. 1990. *Single moms, single dads*. Denver: Accent.

Miller, V. C. 1985. *A Bible centered seminar as a valid social change instrument*. Ann Arbor: University Microfilms.

Mollenkott, V. R. 1977. *Women, men and the Bible*. Nashville: Abingdon.

Moore, J. F. 1987. *Sexuality and marriage: A Christian foundation for making responsible choices*. Minneapolis: Augsburg.

Morris, L. 1981. *Testaments of love*. Grand Rapids: Eerdmans.

Mowday, L. 1990. *Daughters without dads*. Nashville: Nelson.

Murphey, C., ed. 1984. *Encyclopedia of Christian marriage*. Old Tappan, N.J.: Revell.

Murstein, B. I. 1986. *Paths to marriage*. Beverly Hills, Calif.: Sage.

Naisbitt, J., and P. Aburdene. 1990. *Megatrends 2000*. New York: Morrow.

Narramore, B. 1979. *Parenting with love and limits*. Grand Rapids: Zondervan.

Narramore, C. M. 1963. *A woman's world*. Grand Rapids: Zondervan.

———. 1985. *Parents at their best*. Nashville: Nelson.

Noller, P. 1984. *Nonverbal communication and marital interaction*. New York: Pergamon.

Olson, D. 1990. *Two thousand one: Preparing families for it*. Minneapolis: National Council on Family Relations.

Osborne, C. G. 1970. *The art of understanding your mate*. Grand Rapids: Zondervan.

Palkovitz, R., and M. Sussman, eds. 1988. *Transitions to parenthood*. New York: Haworth.

Penner, C. 1986. *A gift for all ages*. Waco: Word.

Penner, C., and J. Penner. 1981. *The gift of sex*. Waco: Word.

Petersen, J. A. 1971. *The marriage affair*. Wheaton: Tyndale House.

———, ed. 1977. *For families only: The tough questions parents ask*. Wheaton: Tyndale House.

Peterson, G. A., ed. 1984. *The Christian education of adults*. Chicago: Moody.

Phillips, R. 1988. *Putting asunder: A history of divorce in western society*. New York: Cambridge Univ. Press.

Phipps, W. E. 1975. *Recovering biblical sensuousness*. Philadelphia: Westminster.

Pocs, O., ed. 1989. *Marriage and family, 15th ed. 89/90*. Guildford, Conn.: Dushkin.

Pope, E. 1977. *Song of songs*. New York: Doubleday.

Pope, K., et al. 1980. *On love and loving*. San Francisco: Jossey-Bass.

Quinn, P. E. 1986. *The well-adjusted child*. Nashville: Nelson.

Regier, G. P., ed. 1988. *Values and public policy*. Washington, D.C.: Family Research Council.

Reiss, H. M., and I. L. Reiss. 1990. *An end to shame: Shaping our next sexual revolution*. Buffalo, N.Y.: Prometheus.

Rekers, G. A. 1988. *Counseling families*. Waco: Word.

Rinehart, P., and S. Rinehart. 1983. *Choices: Finding God's way in dating, sex, and marriage.* Colorado Springs: Navpress.

Robinson, H. 1992. "Sex, marriage, and divorce." *Christianity Today,* 14 December, 29.

Roe, J. 1982. *A consumer's guide to Christian counseling.* Nashville: Abingdon.

Rosefsky, R. S. 1983. *Personal finances.* 2d ed. New York: Wiley.

Rosenstock, H. A., and J. D. Weiner. 1988. *Journey through divorce.* New York: Human Sciences Press.

Rukeyser, L., ed. 1988. *Business almanac.* New York: Simon and Schuster.

Rushford, P. H. 1984. *From money mess to money management.* Old Tappan, N.J.: Revell.

Santrock, J. W. 1990. *Adolescence.* Dubuque, Iowa: Brown.

Schaeffer, F. 1982. *The complete works of Francis Schaeffer: A Christian world view.* Westchester, Ill.: Crossway.

———. 1983. *Who is for peace?* Nashville: Nelson.

Schrof, J. 1992. "Wedding bands made of steel." *U.S. News and World Report,* 6 April, 62–63.

Scott, S., and G. Smalley. 1982. *For better or for worse.* Rev. ed. Grand Rapids: Zondervan.

Seamans, D. 1982. *Putting away childish things.* Wheaton: Victor.

Sears, W. 1991. *Christian parenting and childcare.* Rev. ed. Nashville: Nelson.

Self, C. S., and W. L. Self. 1989. *Before I thee wed: A guide to help engaged couples prepare for marriage.* Old Tappan, N.J.: Revell.

Sell, C. M. 1981. *Family ministry: The enrichment of family life through the church.* Grand Rapids: Zondervan.

———. 1982. *Achieving the impossible: Intimate marriage.* Portland, Ore.: Multnomah.

Sharp, L. 1988. "Toward a greater understanding of the real MK: A review of recent research." In K. O'Donnell and M. O'Donnell, eds., *Helping missionaries grow: Readings in mental health and missions.* Pasadena, Calif.: William Carey Library.

Shedd, C. 1965. *Letters to Karen.* New York: Avon.

Shedd, C., and M. Shedd. 1984. *Bible study together.* Grand Rapids: Zondervan.

Shelley, M. 1986. *Helping those who don't want help.* Waco: Word.

Sizemore, F. 1989. *When caring parents have problem kids.* Old Tappan, N.J.: Revell.

Skolnick, A. 1987. *The intimate environment: Exploring marriage and the family.* 4th ed. Boston: Little, Brown.

———. 1992. *The intimate environment.* 5th ed. New York: Harper-Collins.

Small, D. H. 1959. *Design for Christian marriage.* Westwood, N.J.: Revell.

———. 1968. *After you've said I do.* Old Tappan, N.J.: Revell.

———. 1986. *Remarriage and God's renewing grace.* Grand Rapids: Baker.

Smalley, G. 1988. *The joy of committed love.* Grand Rapids: Zondervan.

Smedes, L. 1989. *Commitment: Learning to live the love we promise.* San Francisco: Harper and Row.

Smith, A. 1982. *Preparing for Christian marriage: Pastor's manual.* Nashville: Abingdon.

Smith, V. W. 1983. *The single parent.* Old Tappan, N.J.: Revell.

Snyder, B., and C. Snyder. 1988. *Incompatibility: Grounds for a great marriage.* Phoenix: Questar.

Sowell, T. 1992. "The new conformity." *Forbes,* 20 January, 86–87.

Spencer, D. 1986. *Computers in action, how computers work.* 2d ed. Rochelle Park, N.J.: Hayden.

Sroka, B. 1981. *One is a whole number.* Wheaton: Victor.

Steinmetz, S., and M. B. Sussman. 1987. *Handbook of marriage and the family.* New York: Plenum.

Stevens, H. 1991. *Hope for the divorced.* Nashville: Convention.

Stinnett, N. 1985. *Secrets of strong families.* Boston: Little, Brown.

Stowell, J. M. n.d. *Marriage is for keeps.* Des Plaines, Ill.: Living Reality.

Strommen, M., and I. Strommen. 1985. *Five cries of parents.* San Francisco: Harper and Row.

Stubblefield, J., ed. 1986. *A church ministering to adults.* Nashville: Broadman.

Sussman, M., and R. Lewis. 1986. *Men's changing roles in the family.* New York: Haworth.

Swindoll, C. R. 1980. *Strike the original match.* Portland, Ore.: Multnomah.

———. 1981. *Improving your serve.* Waco: Word.

Swindoll, L., ed. 1985. *Soloing: Experiencing God's best as a single woman.* Old Tappan, N.J.: Power.

Taylor, R. 1984. *Single and whole.* Downer's Grove, Ill.: InterVarsity.

Thrash, S. 1991. *Dear God, I'm divorced.* Grand Rapids: Baker.

Torbiorn, I. 1982. *Living abroad: Personal adjustment and personnel policy in the overseas setting.* New York: Wiley.

Towns, E. 1967. *Ministering to the young single adult.* Grand Rapids: Baker.

Trobisch, W. 1982. *I married you.* San Francisco: Harper and Row.

———. 1987. *The complete works of Walter Trobisch.* Downer's Grove, Ill.: InterVarsity.

Van Caspel, C. 1975. *Life insurance—the great national consumer fraud?* Reston, Va.: Reston.

Van Leeuwen, M. 1990. *Gender and grace: Love, work, and parenting in a changing world.* Downer's Grove, Ill.: InterVarsity.

Van Pelt, N. 1989. *How to talk so your mate will listen, and listen so your mate will talk.* Old Tappan, N.J.: Revell.

Wallis, C. 1992. "The nuclear family goes boom!" *Time* special issue, Fall, 42–43.

Ward, T. 1985. *Living overseas: A book of preparations.* New York: Free Press.

———. 1989. *Values begin at home.* 2d ed. Wheaton: Victor.

Webber, R. 1982. *Secular humanism, threat and challenge.* Grand Rapids: Zondervan.

Weitzman, L. 1985. *The divorce revolution.* New York: Free Press.

Wheat, E. 1977. *Intended for pleasure.* Old Tappan, N.J.: Revell.

———. 1983. *Love life for every married couple.* Grand Rapids: Zondervan.

———. 1991. *Love life for every married couple.* New York: Harper-Collins.

Wheat, E., and G. Perkins. 1980. *Love life for every married couple.* Grand Rapids: Zondervan, 1980.

———. 1989. *Secret choices: Personal choices that affect your marriage.* Grand Rapids: Zondervan.

Wheat, E., and G. Wheat. 1981. *Intended for pleasure.* Rev. ed. Old Tappan, N.J.: Revell.

Whyte, M. K. 1990. *Dating, mating, and marriage.* New York: Aldine de Gruyter.

Wiersbe, W. 1967. *Creative Christian living.* Westwood, N.J.: Revell.

Wilkerson, R. 1983. *Teenagers: Parental guidance suggested.* Eugene, Ore.: Harvest House.

Williams, C. 1991. *Forever a father, always a son.* Wheaton: Victor.

Williams, J., P. Williams, and J. Jenkins. 1985. *Rekindled.* Old Tappan, N.J.: Revell.

Williamson, R. 1966. *Marriage and family relations.* New York: Wiley.

Willimon, W. 1979. *Saying yes to marriage.* Valley Forge, Penn.: Judson.

Witte, K. 1982. *Great leaps in a single bound.* Minneapolis: Bethany House.

Worden, M. 1989. *Early widow: A journal of the first year.* Downer's Grove, Ill.: InterVarsity.

Wright, H. N. 1974. *Communication, key to your marriage.* Ventura, Calif.: Regal.

———. 1979. *The pillars of marriage.* Ventura, Calif.: Regal.

———. 1986. *Energize your life through total communication.* Old Tappan, N.J.: Revell.

———. 1989. *Always Daddy's girl.* Ventura, Calif.: Regal.

———. 1991. *The power of a parent's words.* Ventura, Calif.: Regal.

Wynn, J. 1982. *Family therapy in pastoral ministry.* San Francisco: Harper and Row.

Yates, J. 1986. *For the life of the family.* Wilton, Conn.: Morehouse-Barlow.

Yorkey, M., ed. 1990. *Growing a healthy family.* Brentwood, Tenn.: Wolgemuth and Hyatt.

Young, L. 1973. *The fractured family.* New York: McGraw-Hill.

Zimbelman, E. 1985. *Human sexuality and evangelical Christians.* Boston: Univ. Press of America.

Index